SPECIFIERS

Minimalist Approaches

SPECIFIERS

Minimalist Approaches

Edited by

David Adger, Susan Pintzuk,
Bernadette Plunkett, and George Tsoulas

OXFORD
UNIVERSITY PRESS

OXFORD
UNIVERSITY PRESS

Great Clarendon Street, Oxford OX2 6DP

Oxford University Press is a department of the University of Oxford.
It furthers the University's objective of excellence in research, scholarship,
and education by publishing worldwide in

Oxford New York

Athens Auckland Bangkok Bogotá Buenos Aires Calcutta
Cape Town Chennai Dar es Salaam Delhi Florence Hong Kong Istanbul
Karachi Kuala Lumpur Madrid Melbourne Mexico City Mumbai
Nairobi Paris São Paulo Singapore Taipei Tokyo Toronto Warsaw

with associated companies in Berlin Ibadan

Oxford is a registered trade mark of Oxford University Press
in the UK and in certain other countries

Published in the United States
by Oxford University Press Inc., New York

British Library Cataloguing in Publication Data

Data available

Library of Congress Cataloging in Publication Data

Data available

ISBN 0–19–823813–4 (Hbk)
ISBN 0–19–823814–2 (Pbk)

1 3 5 7 9 10 8 6 4 2

Typeset in Times
by BookMan Services
Printed in Great Britain on acid-free paper by
Biddles Ltd., Guildford and King's Lynn

Preface

Syntactic theory, especially the fundamentals of phrase structure, has undergone a revolution in the past few years with the introduction of Chomsky's Minimalist Programme. This book takes one of the major issues in phrase structure—the notion of *specifier*—and examines what place this notion has in the new framework, drawing on empirical studies of cross-linguistic phenomena, conceptual and theoretical argumentation, and results from language acquisition. The chapters are based on papers originally presented at a conference held at the University of York, 21–3 March 1996. We would like to thank all who were there for their enthusiastic participation.

We are grateful to the Department of Language and Linguistic Science and to the Innovation and Pump Priming Research Fund at the University of York for financial support (IPPRF Grant no. 2920). We would also like to thank all the students who helped out at the conference and the staff at King's Manor for their assistance.

Every stage of the conference and the present volume was extensively refereed. We thank all the reviewers of abstracts for their time and effort; we would also like to thank the anonymous referees selected by OUP for their comments on each chapter of the book, as well as the collection as a whole. We would also like to thank Frances Morphy and John Davey of OUP for their enthusiasm for the project and their publishing expertise, and we would like to thank the contributors for their patience and commitment during the process of refereeing and editing.

The editors would like to dedicate this book to the memory of Teun Hoekstra.

David Adger, Susan Pintzuk,
Bernadette Plunkett, and George Tsoulas

Contents

Figures

Tables

Contributors

DAVID ADGER, Department of Language and Linguistic Science, University of York, Heslington, York YO1 5DD, United Kingdom. E-mail: da4@york.ac.uk

ARTEMIS ALEXIADOU, ZAS, Jaegerstr. 10/11, 10117 Berlin, Germany. E-mail: artemis@zas.gwz-berlin.de

ELENA ANAGNOSTOPOULOU, University of Crete, School of Philosophy, Linguistics, 74100 Rethymno, Crete.

MISHA BECKER, Department of Linguistics, University of California at Los Angeles, 405 Hilgard Avenue, Los Angeles, CA 90025, USA. E-mail: mbecker@ucla.edu

ELABBAS BENMAMOUN, Department of Linguistics, 4088 FLB, University of Illinois, Urbana, IL 61801, USA. E-mail: benmamou@cogsci.uiuc.edu

RONNIE CANN, Department of Linguistics, University of Edinburgh, 40 George Square, Edinburgh EH8 9LL, United Kingdom. E-mail: ronnie@ling.ed.ac.uk

ANNABEL CORMACK, Department of Phonetics and Linguistics, University College London, Gower Street, London WC1E 6BT, United Kingdom. E-mail: annabel@ling.ucl.ac.uk

EDIT DORON, The Institute for Advanced Studies, The Hebrew University of Jerusalem, Givat Ram, 91904 Jerusalem, Israel. E-mail: edit@vms.huji.ac.il

NIGEL DUFFIELD, McGill University, Department of Linguistics, 1001 Sherbrooke Street West, Montreal H2X 3B5, Canada. E-mail: duffield@leacock.lan.mcgill.ca

GÜNTHER GREWENDORF, Institut für Deutsche Sprache und Literatur II, Universität Frankfurt/Main, Gräfstraße 76, D-60054 Frankfurt/Main, Germany. E-mail: grewendorf@lingua.uni-frankfurt.de

CAROLINE HEYCOCK, Department of Linguistics, University of Edinburgh, 40 George Square, Edinburgh EH8 9LL, United Kingdom. E-mail: heycock@ling.ed.ac.uk

TEUN HOEKSTRA, Department of Linguistics, Leiden University/HIL, P.O. Box 9515, 2300 RA Leiden, The Netherlands.

NINA HYAMS, Department of Linguistics, University of California at Los Angeles, 405 Hilgard Avenue, Los Angeles, CA 90024, USA. E-mail: hyams@humnet.ucla.edu

M. RITA MANZINI, Dipartimento di Linguistica, Università di Firenze, Piazza Brunelleschi, 50121 Firenze, Italy. E-mail: rmanzini@cesit1.unifi.it And Department of Linguistics, University College London, Gower Street, London WC1E 6BT, United Kingdom. E-mail: rita@ling.ucl.ac.uk

LYNN NICHOLS, Department of Linguistics, Harvard University, Cambridge, MA 02138, USA. E-mail: nichols@fas.harvard.edu

SUSAN PINTZUK, Department of Language and Linguistic Science, University of York, Heslington, York YO1 5DD, United Kingdom. E-mail: sp20@york.ac.uk

BERNADETTE PLUNKETT, Department of Language and Linguistic Science, University of York, Heslington, York YO1 5DD, United Kingdom. E-mail: bp4@york.ac.uk

LYNN SANTELMANN, Department of Applied Linguistics, Portland State University, 451-F Neuberger Hall, 724 SW Harrison Avenue, Portland, OR 97225, USA. E-mail: santelmann@pdx.edu

BONNIE D. SCHWARTZ, Department of Linguistics and English Language, University of Durham, Elvet Riverside II, New Elvet, Durham DH1 3JT, United Kingdom. E-mail: B.D.Schwartz@durham.ac.uk

ANDREW SIMPSON, Institut für Deutsche Sprache und Literatur II, Universität Frankfurt/Main, Gräfstraße 76, D-60054 Frankfurt/Main, Germany. E-mail: as4@soas.ac.uk

GEORGE TSOULAS, Department of Language and Linguistic Science, University of York, Heslington, York YO1 5DD, United Kingdom. E-mail: gt3@york.ac.uk

I

Specifiers in Generative Grammar

DAVID ADGER, BERNADETTE PLUNKETT, GEORGE TSOULAS, and SUSAN PINTZUK

I. BRIEF HISTORICAL OUTLINE

Chomsky (1970), in developing X-bar theory, introduces the term *specifier* to refer to an element (or a number of elements) that combines with a bar-level projection of a particular category in the base component of the grammar: [Spec, N'] is then the determiner, [Spec, V'] is the auxiliary, and [Spec, A'] is the set of degree modifiers. Jackendoff (1977) made Chomsky's proposal more explicit and paved the way for what became the standard view of specifier as an abbreviation over structural positions. This extended Chomsky's insight that possessives in nominals and subjects in clauses had similar structural positions to specifiers, with the precise nature of the element in the specifier position determined by the lexical properties of the head element.

As the theory of functional categories developed during the 1970s and 1980s, more and more elements that Jackendoff had analysed as specifiers came to be seen as functional heads that were associated with a particular lexical head that they locally c-commanded. Determiners were analysed as heads following Abney (1987); Pollock (1989) showed the utility of analysing auxiliaries as occupying functional head positions above the VP (see also Gazdar *et al.* 1982); Bresnan's proposal that complementizers were essentially higher-level specifiers of sentences (Bresnan 1972) was also reinterpreted within the same theoretical wave and they soon came to be analysed as heads (Chomsky 1986a). Curiously, however, the notion of specifier survived this wholesale massacre, partly through the development of the theory of movement, and partly because the position of the subject as the specifier of the sentence seemed unassailable.

The notion of head took on a fundamental importance as the theory of movement developed during the 1980s. Lexical heads were assumed to assign semantic roles to their complements in the base, but these complements could then move to some higher position where a functional head would license them (the core cases being *wh*-movement and passivization). The crucial distinction between theta-role assignment and surface licensing took shape in the notion of the chain (see especially Chomsky 1986b), and the symmetry was made complete with the adoption of the VP-Internal Subject Hypothesis (Koopman and Sportiche 1990, among many others). This stated that all theta-role assignment takes place within the projection of a lexical head, and that the surface subject position arises because of the raising nature of an inflectional head. Apart from subjects of lexical heads, specifiers were now almost entirely a position to which elements moved.

Because of these developments, by the early 1990s the notion of specifier was becoming very close to the notion of an adjoined position, except that specifiers hosted moved elements only (again, apart from the subject of a lexical head). The question of whether specifiers were actually any different from adjuncts was then thrown into sharp relief (although it had been anticipated somewhat by Stuurman 1985; see also Hoekstra 1991). Recently, two influential proposals have essentially answered this question in the negative: Kayne (1994) develops a system whereby the elements usually analysed as specifiers have the properties of adjuncts, while Chomsky (1995: ch. 4) outlines a system where some adjuncts are analysed as specifiers. Both theories are driven by a search for explanatory adequacy where the theoretical imperative insists that only the most elementary elements play a role in syntax. Specifiers as a structurally unique category are a casualty of this imperative (see Duffield's chapter in this volume for a critique of this approach at an empirical level).

Given the current state of play, it seems opportune to ask whether the notion of specifier really has any role to play in current syntactic theory and the areas it most directly impinges upon (e.g. the acquisition of syntactic structures by first- and second-language learners). The chapters in this book represent a range of views on the answer to this question.

All the chapters in the book are couched within the broad and developing framework of Chomsky's Minimalist Programme. The remainder of this introduction outlines the basic properties of this theory and assesses to what extent the chapters in the volume contribute to it.

2. THE MINIMALIST PROGRAMME

2.1. *An intuitive introduction*

The work which developed from Chomsky (1981), Chomsky (1986b), attempting to widen the empirical coverage of the theory, gradually introduced a whole range of concepts whose motivation was essentially theory-internal— for example, levels of structure, indices, bar-levels, government relations. Certain aspects of the theory had a desirable conceptual simplicity, especially aspects of the theory of movement and its interaction with the properties of heads, as discussed above; but the technology was becoming more and more baroque. In an attempt to evaluate which aspects of the theory were really necessary, Chomsky proposed in a series of papers (Chomsky 1989, 1993, and 1995: ch. 4) that all parts of the theory which were not strictly necessary should be subjected to a rigorous examination. The driving force of this examination is *virtual conceptual necessity*, which entails only that there be some computational system which combines properties of lexical items, and that this computational system feed the conceptual– intentional and articulatory–acoustic systems of the brain. Chomsky (1995) also motivates certain further aspects of the nature of the computational system: that it is derivational; that it involves a displacement operation; that the derivational nature of the system is constrained by 'least-effort' principles; and that principles of locality are 'built in' to the definition of the derivational operations.

Such a system is essentially constructive in nature: that is, it takes lexical items and operates on them, producing an output determined by the nature of those lexical items and the definitions of the operations. The output of derivations is not filtered at any point in the syntax. This contrasts with the previous model (the 'Government and Binding' model), which generates representations from its inputs and filters out some subset of those representations depending on their properties.

Let us take an example to show how the two models contrast. Under the Government and Binding approach, an ECM construction in English arises because there is a condition on the distribution of overt DPs (i.e. the Case Filter) at a level of representation that feeds more or less directly into word order (S-structure):

(1)   Anson expected Julie to dance

Assume, following the VP-Internal Subject Hypothesis, that the DP *Julie* is generated as the specifier of *dance*. In English, there is a set of configurations where Case is said to be assigned. The two most important are through government by a Case-assigning lexical head (V or P) and in a specifier–head agreement relationship with finite inflection. Movement is assumed to be optional. If the option to move *Julie* is not taken, given the base representation already described, then the resulting representation is one where *Julie* is not assigned Case. This representation is then filtered out by the Case Filter. If the option to move is taken, then movement will shift *Julie* to the specifier of the non-finite inflection of the embedded clause. In this position the matrix V governs *Julie* (via a special dispensation in the definition of government whereby IP does not block government, although all other maximal projections do) and *Julie* can be assigned accusative case. The resulting representation will not be filtered out by the Case Filter, and the sentence is grammatical.

This type of explanation of the grammaticality of (1) crucially allows the generation of more than one representation for the sentence, but all but the grammatical representations are filtered out. The theory is essentially one where representations are generated and then tested for well-formedness.

The constructive system that Chomsky proposes in *The Minimalist Program* (1995) assumes no such filter on representations. The displacement operation (Move, or Attract—see below) is defined in such a way as to eliminate immediately certain features that are specified on heads (these are termed *strong* features), and a further operation (Spellout) applies when all strong features are eliminated and delivers the resulting representation to the phonetic component. There are also other features which are eliminated post-Spellout; these are features which are not interpretable by the semantic component on the relevant head (more on this below). A verb like *expect* has an accusative case feature which is not interpretable on the verb itself and so must be eliminated. However, nothing requires that this feature is eliminated pre-Spellout in English. All inflectional heads in English do, however, contain a strong feature D, which must therefore be eliminated immediately. *Julie* thus raises pre-Spellout to eliminate the D-feature on *to*, giving the surface word order. *Julie* then raises post-Spellout to eliminate the uninterpretable case feature on *expect*. The PF representation is then one where *Julie* is in the specifier of *to* without any appeal to a filter at that level of structure—in fact without appeal to any particular level of structure at all.

A further crucial difference in the way the two systems work is that the Government and Binding model allows movement to apply freely whereas movement on the Minimalist system applies only when driven by the need to check a feature. This is one way in which the system is economical, since movement takes place only when forced.

The challenge of Minimalism is to investigate whether this type of explanation can be extended to cover all the empirical data garnered during work in the Government and Binding paradigm, without the introduction of further technical devices. The present volume examines the notion of specifier in this light.

2.2. *Some specifics of the theory*

This section is a brief introduction to the basic technical assumptions of Minimalism that lie behind the chapters in the volume, and may be skipped by those familiar with the theory.

The theory outlined in Chomsky (1995) is an attempt to define the basic elements of the computational system within a highly restrictive framework of assumptions. A particular language is simply a setting of the property of *strength* on features of lexical items, where a strong feature, as mentioned above, is one that must be immediately eliminated in the derivation. The computational system itself is uniform across languages, and no appeal is made to different structural configurations for different languages. Chomsky defines the computational system roughly as follows.

Assume that one can select a collection of items from the lexicon. Then the input to the computational system is a set of pairs consisting of a lexical item and an index i, where i represents the number of times the lexical item is selected. This set of pairs is the numeration N. The computational system then maps N to a pair of representations (π, λ), where π is a representation at the level of phonetic interpretation (PF) and λ is a representation at the level of semantic interpretation (LF). These levels interface with the articulatory–acoustic and conceptual–intentional systems of the brain.

The computational system consists of a few trivial operations: Select, Merge, and Attract (also termed Move). Select applies to elements of N, reducing the index of the element it applies to by 1 until all indices of all elements are reduced to 0. The elements of N are lexical items which are seen as simply bundles of features: phonological features determining aspects of phonetic interpretation; semantic features including conceptual information such as argument structure, s-selectional information, etc.; and syntactic features which are assumed to be either inherent on the lexical item or added as part of the Select operation. Syntactic features include case, tense, phi-features, and categorial features such as D, V, N. Syntactic features have a particular property depending on the head (or phrase) on which they are instantiated, the property of *interpretability* on that head (or phrase). Case features are never interpretable by the LF component. Categorial features are interpretable on the correct category: D is interpretable on DP, but not on T, for example. Likewise, number and gender features are interpretable on nouns but not on inflection. The precise nature of interpretability is rather murky in Chomsky's system, but the intuition is that the interface components are incapable of interpreting displaced features (see the discussion of Attract, below).

One important difference between two versions of Minimalism is reflected in some of the chapters in this volume: the first version of Minimalism (Chomsky 1989, 1993) assumes that agreement features project as a separate functional head, allowing the unification of argument case licensing in a specifier–head configuration; the second version (Chomsky 1995: ch. 4) dispenses with agreement projections and assumes that the only important functional projections in the clause are TP and CP (TP is occasionally written as IP; see e.g. Alexiadou and Anagnostopoulou in this volume). In the latter system, the elimination of uninterpretable features takes place via a system of multiple specifiers (discussed extensively below).

The operation Merge operates on pairs of elements chosen by Select and maps them from a pair into a single element with a more complex structure. Merge is an expression of the irreducible fact that expressions of human languages are (if not atomic) constructed out of smaller expressions. Merge is assumed to be unable to apply to the internal structure of a previously constructed expression; it always applies to the root nodes of two structures. Chomsky shows how these structures, usually considered to be tree structures topologically, can be thought of instead as set-theoretic entities, where the constituents of the structure are sets of sets within the structure. For example, imagine we have two lexical items, x and y. Then Merge will apply to x and y to give a set $\{x, y\}$ which may then be a further input to Merge.[1] Using sets in this way means that no appeal can be made to the notions of X-bar or XP as generalizations over structure: they can only be thought of as derived concepts stemming from relationships in particular structures. The more commonly used tree structures may still be used as a matter of ease and familiarity of notation, but they contain by their very nature extra information which is actually in-accessible to the computational system.

A proposal which is related to Chomsky's view of phrase structure, but pre-dates it slightly, is Kayne's Antisymmetry Theory (Kayne 1994). Kayne also argues that much of X-bar theory is derivable from a constraint on the proper linearization of hierarchical structure (the *Linear Correspondence Axiom* (LCA)). Kayne predicts that specifiers are always generated to the left of their heads while complements are always generated to the right, giving a universal base order of SVO. This means that leftmost complements of heads must be viewed as derived structures where a rightmost complement has moved into a specifier position (see especially the contributions by Hoekstra and Schwartz in this volume). Kayne's system, unlike Chomsky's, restricts specifiers to one per head.

Another operation, Attract (also termed Move), applies to a single element of a complex structure and displaces it to another part of the structure, leaving a copy. Attract is defined so that it applies only to eliminate a feature on the moved-to position (the attracting head). As mentioned above, this feature elimination occurs in certain configurations which are the outputs of Attract (these are termed *checking relationships*, so Attract always applies to establish a checking relationship; this property is sometimes termed *Last Resort*). Checking relationships are simply local non-complement structures (but see Simpson's chapter in this volume for an argument that checking relationships can be non-local), so head-adjoined structures and structures with specifiers and adjuncts are all checking relationships. Attract is also defined so as to obey the two requirements (i) that the moved-to position c-commands the moved-from position, and (ii) that the closest checkable feature is attracted (the *Minimal Link Condition* (MLC)). This last requirement is the implementation in this system of intervention effects such as the ban on superraising, the Head Movement Constraint, and the *Wh*-Island Constraint.[2] Attract crucially ap-plies to eliminate a feature rather than a category, so the moved element is mini-

---

[1] The actual result also includes the label of the merged constituents: see Section 3.1.

[2] Another operation is Delete, which deletes elements whenever possible. 'Whenever possible' here means simply that information that must be maintained at an interface level cannot be deleted.

mally a feature itself. If movement takes place pre-Spellout, then the feature will pied-pipe a certain amount of morphological material (a category or a projection of a category) in order to satisfy interpretability requirements at PF: specifically PF cannot interpret morphological features if they are scattered in the structure. When Attract applies post-Spellout, however, only the feature moves.

Derivations are simply applications of these various operations to lexical items, such that Attract applies to immediately eliminate a strong feature, and the operations apply until all uninterpretable features are in a checking relationship, where they are eliminated. The application of operations is strictly governed by a set of economy principles. The thrust of these principles is that an operation applies only if that operation will bring the derivation closer to a successful completion (*convergence*). However, the economy principles Chomsky proposes are specific instantiations of this idea with empirical effect. For example, the definition of Attract is specified so that Attract will apply only to eliminate an uninterpretable feature (this is Last Resort, mentioned above). When a feature is strong, then Attract applies immediately to eliminate it. Features which are not strong (sometimes termed *weak*) need not be immediately eliminated, and in general will not then be eliminated before Spellout unless they come to be in a checking configuration accidentally. This property of the system, whereby features will be eliminated after Spellout unless they are strong, is termed *Procrastinate*. This kind of economy is built into the definition of Attract. Another type of economy principle favours application of Merge over Attract, but this principle governs the choice of operation, rather than the specifics of its application.

Given any numeration, there are a number of possible derivations defined by application of the transformational operations discussed above. The set of possible derivations from a numeration is termed the reference set. Economy principles, such as the one which specifies that Merge applies in preference to Attract (let us term this Favour Merge), select the optimal derivation from the reference set. One can think of this as though the derivations are constructed in parallel, with derivations that fail to satisfy Favour Merge or the conditions on Attract, being immediately discarded. A broader conception would be that economy principles examine the whole reference set and select the optimal derivation.

Let us consider an example: assume that the relevant collection of items chosen from the lexicon is {a, pig, T, killed, mouse}, where *pig* has nominative case, *mouse* has accusative, T is specified as finite and thus has a nominative case feature (and a strong D-feature as a general property of English-type languages), and the verb, by virtue of its lexical specification, is past tense and has an accusative case feature. A numeration will then be a set of pairs where *a* has the index 2 and the other elements have index 1 (other numerations are possible but do not lead to convergent derivations). Select then applies to our set of lexical items, reducing the indices of all items to 0.[3] One can think of the output as a collection of lexical items on a desktop. We then begin to construct the reference set of derivations. Certain derivations such as one where we merge *pig* and T will immediately be discarded, since no further operation can check the strong D-feature of T. Other derivations, such as merging *a* and *pig* and then the result with *killed*, will simply not converge because the correct checking configurations cannot be constructed owing to a mismatch of Case features. In the case we are considering here, the nominative case feature on *pig* will never be close enough to T to be attracted and will survive to the LF interface, leading to a non-convergent (or *crashing*) derivation.

A convergent derivation for this numeration will look as follows:

(i)   Merge *a* and *mouse* giving a structural representation for *a mouse*.
(ii)   Merge this with *killed*.
(iii) Merge *a* and *pig*.

Two possibilities are now open: merge *a pig* with *killed a mouse* or attract *a mouse* to the root of *killed a mouse* to check the accusative case feature of the verb and DP. Favour Merge rules out the later derivation.

(iv)   Merge T with *a pig killed a mouse* to give T *a pig killed a mouse*.
(v)   Attract *a pig* to check the strong D-feature of T. Nominative case is now in a checking relation and hence eliminated as a 'free rider'.
(vi)   Spell out, since all strong features are eliminated.
(vii) Attract the case feature of *a mouse* into a checking configuration with V, eliminating accusative case. All uninterpretable features are eliminated. Derivation converges and terminates.[4]

In a language where the D-feature of T is weak, no subject raising takes place; in a language where the accusative feature of V is strong, the object will raise (violating Favour Merge). Linguistic variation in this model arises purely from a specification of the strength of features.

3. CONTRIBUTIONS OF THE CHAPTERS IN THIS VOLUME

3.1. *Merge*

Chomsky's definition of Merge takes two set-theoretic structures and combines them into a single one:

---

[3] It appears that the reason for this rather unintuitive system is simply to ensure that we are appealing to very basic entities like sets. Of course we could assume that the numeration was a multiset or some other more mathematically complex item, but Chomsky's concern is to maintain as simple a system as possible.

[4] We have ignored the tense feature on V here. The obvious account is to say that T contains V features which are uninterpretable on T forcing the V to raise post-Spellout. Tense features on V are then checked as free riders. See Ch. 5 by Alexiadou and Anagnostopoulou for discussion.

(2)   Merge (α, β) = γ, where γ is a set consisting of a *label* and a set consisting of the sets α and β. α and β are said to be the *terms* of γ.

The label of γ is derived by simply copying either α or β, or the label of either α or β. The element which donates its label is the *head*—much as in standard X-bar theory—because it projects. So, taking again our example where the lexical items are x and y, Merge forms the set $\{x, \{x, y\}\}$; x here is both a term of the new structure and the label of the new structure. Chomsky shows how this system can be used to derive some of the standard properties of X-bar theory, and argues that, where this theory makes different predictions, it is to be preferred.

One such case is that the new system allows *multiple-specifier structures*. Given the definition of Merge above, it is impossible to rule out cases where a term with its own internal structure is merged with another term with internal structure. One of these terms donates its label, and we have a specifier-type structure:

(3)   Merge $(\{x, \{x, y\}\}, \{w, \{w, z\}\}) = \{w, \{\{x, \{x, y\}\}, \{w, \{w, z\}\}\}\}$

Here w has been chosen as the label of the derived structure. But note that we may apply this operation again:

(4)   Merge $(\{v, \{v, u\}\}, \{w, \{\{x, \{x, y\}\}, \{w, \{w, z\}\}\}\})$
       $= \{w, \{\{v, \{v, u\}\}, \{w, \{\{x, \{x, y\}\}, \{w, \{w, z\}\}\}\}\}\}$

We now have a configuration where w has two specifiers, one labelled x (the inner specifier) and one labelled v (the outer specifier). We shall see that multiple specifiers arise after application of Attract too. As a tree structure (4) is:

(5)

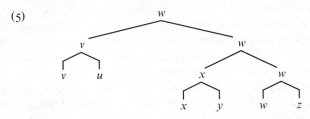

In principle there may of course be a series of specifiers, where specifiers are simply defined as non-projecting (i.e. they do not donate their label) terms merged with a projecting complex term. Complements are defined as terms merged with a projecting simplex (i.e. word-level) term. The system rules out multiple complements because trivially any term with a complement is not a simplex term.

This theme is taken up by two of the chapters in the current volume. The system outlined above allows the possibility of multiple subjects, where each subject is in an A-position. Doron and Heycock (Chapter 4) argue on the basis of evidence from ECM, control, coordination, and position that the external DPs in the so-called multiple-subject constructions found in Japanese and some Semitic languages are not cases of topic elements adjoined to IP, but are rather the outer specifier of TP, and that these DPs are merged into this position. This data shows that these subjects behave as though they are in an A-position, a possibility not open within the Government and Binding model. Doron and Heycock term these DPs *broad subjects*. The inner (or *narrow*) subject, however, is presumed to have moved into its SpecTP position to check a D-feature of T before Spellout. It falls out from this approach that only the narrow subject will trigger agreement, and that broad subjects take wide scope over any VP quantifier (since they are merged at [Spec, TP], the quantifier cannot scope over any VP-internal trace for which they serve as antecedent). Doron and Heycock argue that a TP with only a narrow subject may undergo a kind of lambda-abstraction over some clause-internal pronoun, or a David-sonian event variable. This is then interpreted as a one-place predicate over the broad subject, giving the correct interpretation. This analysis combines the ideas of Merge and multiple specifiers to provide an elegant account of these otherwise problematic constructions.

Grewendorf (Chapter 8) also argues that multiple specifiers occur in Japanese, and uses this idea to explain a curious effect that obtains in Japanese *wh*-questions: in this language an adjunct *wh*-word preceding an object *wh*-word leads to ungrammaticality. However, when the object is scrambled over the adjunct, or there is a preceding subject, the sentence is well formed. Grewendorf proposes that in certain languages a *wh*-word can check the features of another *wh*-word, giving rise to the clustering effect seen in Bulgarian and other languages which move all *wh*-words (see also Chapter 11 by Nichols for an extension of this phenomenon in Zuni). This checking may only take place, however, when the checker is in an A-specifier. This means that an adjunct preceding an object cannot check the *wh*-features of that object because the adjunct is, by definition, in an A'-position. When the object is scrambled over the adjunct, it moves into the outer specifier of an agreement head—that is, an A-specifier. The adjunct may then raise and check its *wh*-features against the *wh*-features of the object. A similar explanation is offered for the subject cases.

Another consequence of Chomsky's system is that the distinction between specifiers and adjuncts becomes somewhat otiose. The definition of Merge given above provides no way of distinguishing between an element that attaches to a phrasal projection and an element that attaches to a non-phrasal projection precisely because the notion of phrasal in this system is not a primitive. Chomsky does introduce a distinction between adjunction and substitution operations, which parallels the specifier/adjunct split, but his motivation here is purely empirical. He adopts a system whereby Merge applying to a projected category may construct an output with a simplex label or a complex label. The former corresponds to the specifier case and the latter to adjuncts. An adjunction structure formed as in (3) above will have the following specification, where the label of the merged structure is a pair trivially constructed by duplicating the label of the head:

(6)   Merge $(\{x, \{x, y\}\}, \{w, \{w, z\}\}) = \{<w, w>, \{\{x, \{x, y\}\}, \{w, \{w, z\}\}\}\}$

Note that all this does is essentially label specifiers and adjuncts as distinct.

Duffield (Chapter 7) argues that something like this distinction should be maintained in the grammar. He provides a contrast between two languages, Maltese Arabic and Irish, with construct state phenomena (see also Chapters 6 and 9, by Benmamoun and Hoekstra, respectively, for discussion of different aspects of this phenomenon). In the construct state, an N head raises over the possessor to the D position, and this gives rise to a number of effects (definiteness of the possessed element; phonological reduction of the head; no determiner). Maltese Arabic and Irish share these basic characteristics. However, Duffield's point is that the way that adjectives within a construct state behave in the two languages is very different. He gives arguments from adjective order, the behaviour of demonstratives and contrastive particles, and the appearance of definiteness agreement effects, amongst other things, to show that adjectives in Maltese Arabic are adjuncts, whereas in Irish they are specifiers. If this argument is correct, then the specifier/adjunct distinction must be maintained, and perhaps should be derived rather than stipulated in the theory.

The question of *how* specifiers contribute to the resultant merged structure is explored in Cann's contribution to the volume (Chapter 2). Cann argues that, when a term merges with a projected term, then, in some cases, *both* project information to the resulting structure. The information that is projected is the unification of features from the constituent parts. In this sense, specifiers act much like heads in that they project features. Cann shows how this system allows an analysis which can assume a unified lexical representation for passive and past participles, and for perfective and causative auxiliaries. His idea is that the specifier of the participial affix projects information to the mother node, which gives rise to different selectional properties. He also shows how such a system provides a more refined characterization of grammatical change, whereby a lexical head (termed by him a *contentive*) over time may be reanalysed as a specifier and then as a functional head.

Cann's system bears close similarity to the model argued for by Cormack (Chapter 3), who takes the further step of eliminating specifiers altogether. In her system, Merge builds up syntactic structure and semantic structure in tandem, where the structure-building operation is constrained by selectional features on the head. Cormack examines a number of structures where specifiers have been proposed, and shows that in each case the specifier can be thought of as one of the arguments of a (sometimes covert) two-place operator. An operator is simply a head with unsaturated syntactic requirements; for her, these are mainly selectional features. For example, the subject is not combined with the tensed VP as the specifier of TP; rather the head of the subject DP is a two-place operator combining with an NP predicate by Merge, with the result combining with the tensed VP. Semantically, this set of operations binds the external theta-roles of the NP and VP, giving the correct reading. The resulting system eschews the use of the notion specifier altogether, but extends the ability of functional heads to select two arguments.

3.2. *Attract*

Attract may be defined as follows:

(7)   A head H in a structure Σ with a feature f attracts a feature f' on a sub-structure of Σ, α iff:

    (i)   H c-commands α;
    (ii) f' is the closest feature to f (MLC);
    (iii) f is uninterpretable; and
    (iv) the sets of features on H and α are compatible.

For example, a *wh*-complementizer endowed with a D-feature (necessarily uninterpretable since D is on C, see condition iii) will attract a *wh*-DP (condition iv requires that the DP that is attracted bears a *wh*-feature) whenever the complementizer c-commands DP and there is no closer *wh*-DP (the Minimal Link Condition). The biconditional nature of the definition of Attract here encodes the Last Resort condition that movement is forced only to establish a feature-checking relation.

Manzini (Chapter 10) points out that this definition of Attract does not explain strong island effects such as the Condition on Extraction Domains effects (Huang 1982), or effects of the *that*-trace type. She redefines Merge so that it creates not set-theoretic structures but rather what she terms *dependencies*. A dependency is a generalization of the idea of checking relation which includes semantic dependencies, morphosyntactic dependencies, and pure feature-checking dependencies between heads. In order to deal with cases where a complex element is to be analysed as the specifier of another complex element, she adopts an assumption much like Cormack's idea that determiners are two-place operators. For Manzini, the determiner in a subject establishes a branching dependency between its NP and the tensed VP. Her solution to the strong island problem depends upon the idea that a trace must be connected to its antecedent by a minimal series of dependencies. Extraction from a specifier position is then ruled out because of the branching nature of specifier dependencies. Since dependencies are established between heads, the notion of head government, dispensed with by Chomsky, becomes a primitive of the theory, leading to a way of characterizing *that*-trace phenomena.

Simpson, in Chapter 12, also challenges the structure proposed for the strictly local nature of feature checking that is part of the definition of Attract.

Using data from Iraqi Arabic and Hindi, he argues that constraints on the licensing of *wh*-phrases in these languages cannot be captured by covert feature raising under the assumption that checking only takes place in specifier–head or head-adjoined configurations. He proposes instead to widen the set of feature-checking relations so that a *wh*-feature may be checked in situ in what he terms a *tensed domain*. The implications of this approach are that specifiers may not provide the unique environment for feature checking that Chomsky proposes, but that other types of dependency may be relevant as well.

Simpson's chapter reduces the need to appeal to covert movement for the checking of *wh*-features. Benmamoun (Chapter 6) takes this idea slightly further and argues that checking of Case features is *never* done in the covert component of the grammar because it essentially has only PF motivation. This leads to the very strong claim that Case checking always takes place in a specifier–head configuration before Spellout. Benmamoun argues for this conclusion by taking a case which seems to provide strong motivation for covert Case checking (the VSO/SVO word-order alternation in Arabic) and showing, using data from negation and existentials, that the subject in a VSO structure is outside the VP and has its Case features checked in a specifier–head configuration. This means that Chomsky's speculation that VSO structures arise because these languages have weak nominative case features cannot be correct (see McCloskey 1996 for an independent argument that the VSO language Irish also checks Case overtly on its subject in a specifier position). Benmamoun argues that the agreement system in Arabic provides evidence that the verb and the subject undergo a kind of merging operation in the morphological component, and that this, and not feature strength, explains why postverbal and preverbal subjects display different agreement patterns (see Adger 1997 for an argument that this merger is sufficient to license a subject). Benmamoun then extends this argument to construct state phenomena in Arabic and shows how the same conclusion follows.

Alexiadou and Anagnostopoulou (Chapter 5) explore the nature of the Extended Projection Principle (EPP) on Minimalist assumptions. The EPP in Government and Binding theory ensures that there is always a specifier of IP (a subject) in a clausal structure. These authors argue that a version of the EPP can be maintained within Minimalist assumptions as well, given the assumption that the EPP is a feature-checking operation that may be satisfied by overt checking not only in a specifier configuration, but also in a head-adjunction configuration. Their proposal is that null-subject languages instantiate this option, and that in these languages the verb raises to T, checking a nominal feature of T. This satisfies the EPP, even though there is no overt or covert specifier. They bring forward a battery of arguments that VSO orders in null-subject languages do not involve the merging of a covert expletive in [Spec, TP], as in Chomsky's analysis of existential constructions in English. Their proposal maintains a distinction between *pro*-drop VSO languages such as Greek and true VSO languages such as the Arabic cases discussed by Benmamoun, since in the latter, as Benmamoun shows, the subject has raised from VP to check features. Under Alexiadou and Anagnostopoulou's proposal, the raising of the verb in languages such as Greek and Spanish is sufficient to satisfy the features on T. Whereas Benmamoun argues that Case checking occurs always in a specifier position, Alexiadou and Anagnostopoulou argue that EPP checking may occur via overt head adjunction. If both of these chapters are correct, it follows that EPP checking and Case checking must be dissociated, as is assumed for independent reasons by Chomsky.

Also addressing the question of X^o versus XP movement, Nichols (Chapter 11) shows that there is a class of elements in Zuni that appear to undergo a clitic-like behaviour, in that they cluster at the start of the clause. She argues that the unifying characteristic of this set of elements is that they are syntactically weak, and that this is why they move. The class includes certain determiners, non-3rd person pronouns, and possessives. This challenges the definition of Attract that we assumed above, since it is the properties of the moved items rather than the properties of the moved-to position that motivates their displacement. Nichols shows that these elements are actually not clitics, because they are full phonological entities. Nor do they raise for reasons of Case (as the examples with possessives fronting show). It appears then that these elements are not raising to adjoin to a head position. Nichols proposes instead that they raise into available specifier positions, specifically specifiers within IP, their order being determined by Last Resort. Nichols contrasts their behaviour with the behaviour of *wh*-words. These occur in the opposite order to that predicted by Last Resort. The proposal is that *wh*-words move to multiple specifier positions of C while pronouns move to specifier positions of different heads within IP. If Last Resort is sensitive to this difference, the different orders follow. If Nichols is correct, then the theory must allow single specifiers of some heads and multiple specifiers of others, requiring a *rapprochement* between Kayne's and Chomsky's theories.

Hoekstra (Chapter 9) picks up on the proposal by Kayne, mentioned above, that there is a basic linear order of argument insertion and that surface word orders are derived by movements of arguments and heads to functional projections. Hoekstra's specific proposal is that the little-understood process normally termed '*of*-insertion'—as in

(8)   The smoking of cigars

—is best analysed as a raising construction, where *of* is a type of C, and *smoking* is generated as sister to *cigars* and then raises to [Spec, *of* P]. Evidence for this view comes from binding facts in nominalized infinitives in Dutch, which appear to have the same general form as other *of*-insertion constructions. The binding data shows that the XP immediately following the counterpart of *of* in these constructions is hierarchically superior to any following XP. This is only possible given a structure like the one Hoekstra proposes. One consequence of this analysis is that the dichotomy between free state and construct state nominals (see also Benmamoun's and Duffield's contributions) found in Semitic and Celtic is actually replicated in Germanic: free states correspond to *of*-insertion constructions and construct states correspond to N-to-D raising constructions. In this sense, Hoekstra's work relates closely to the point made by Alexiadou and Anagnostopoulou: there appears to be a systematic alternation between head adjunction and XP movement to specifier positions in various construction types, a point captured in the theory of Attract outlined above by the definition of checking relations as Spec–head or head–head relations (contra Simpson). Hoekstra extends his theory of nominalized infinitives to other constructions putatively involving *of*-insertion, and outlines a range of desirable consequences. He shows that this kind of theory allows the formulation of a constraint that regulates the relationship between the internal structure of a specifier and its related head, and that the effects of this constraint coincide with the Head Final Filter proposed by Williams (1981).

3.3. *Acquisition*

The hypothesis that the structures of UG are available to the language learner from the onset of the acquisition process is known as Continuity (Pinker 1984). One of the predictions of a strong interpretation of Continuity (see e.g. Whitman *et al.* 1990) is that the full range of functional projections is immediately available to the language learner. Given the view of movement described above, where functional categories attract other elements, this gives rise to a puzzle: why do children not display the full range of movement structures seen in adult grammars? That is, why are child grammars not immediately identical to adult grammars? One possibility is to deny Continuity, and claim that structure, principles, or operations of grammar mature in a child (see e.g. Radford 1986; Borer and Wexler 1987). Another explanation for the same data relies on a weaker interpretation of Continuity, which makes the emergence of structure dependent on triggering data.

However, recall that it is not the presence of functional categories alone that triggers overt movement operations in Minimalism, but rather the strength of the features of those functional categories. Language acquisition can then be seen as the process of setting the strength of features of pre-existing functional categories based on the incoming data. Setting certain features as strong will result in head movement, while setting others as strong will result in movement to specifier positions. The adult grammar is attained when all features of all categories are set. Note that, under this view, linguistic variation is confined to properties of features of functional categories.

Santelmann's contribution to this volume (Chapter 14) addresses the question of whether the two types of feature setting alluded to above are necessarily distinct. She shows that, in the acquisition of V2 constructions in Swedish, movement to [Spec, CP] and movement to the C position are acquired simultaneously, in contrast to other types of putatively related head and XP movement. This suggests, from a Minimalist perspective, that there is a single feature on C that is responsible for both movements, or that there is some obligatory feature agreement between the two features of C responsible for head and XP movement (a less attractive option, but one that bears on Hoekstra, Hyams, and Becker's chapter). This chapter is a good illustration of how acquisition studies can cast light on core properties of grammar that are difficult to ascertain by just studying the developed grammar.

Hoekstra, Hyams, and Becker (Chapter 13) also address the question of the role that specifier–head agreement plays in acquisition. They show that an interesting correlation holds between the stage in language development when root infinitives appear (that is, infinitive morphology in root contexts) and the stage when there is an underspecification of certain functional information in the nominal phrase. They assume that both the nominal and clausal projections contain a functional head Number, and that this functional head is responsible for number and definiteness information in DP and for finiteness in the clause. The Number functional head in DP usually receives its feature values from the content of the N itself (singular, plural), while the Number functional head in the clause receives its specification derivatively via specifier–head agreement from the subject. Given that there is a stage in the acquisition process when Number in DP is unspecified, the prediction is that at this same stage the Number head in the clause will also be unspecified, and the clause will be infinitival. The correlation is thus established, based crucially on the early operation of specifier–head agreement in language acquisition, an assumption which itself proceeds from Continuity, although not necessarily a strong interpretation of it. The almost identical configuration of nominal and clausal architecture is, of course, argued for by Hoekstra in his chapter.

Assuming Continuity, the initial state of the first-language learner contains a full array of featurally underspecified functional categories awaiting strength specification. The question for second-language acquisition is whether its initial state is the same. Schwartz (Chapter 15) argues that second-language learners do not have an underspecified grammar, but rather transfer the values of features from their native language to the target language. Her evidence is of two sorts: the acquisition of French clitics by English speakers, and the acquisition of VO order by a Turkish speaker. Schwartz makes crucial use of the specifier–head relationship in her analysis of both types of evidence. She argues that the delay in the acquisition of clitics by English speakers learning French can be reduced to the (erroneously transferred) strength of clitic projections in the learners' initial grammars, and that OV orders in the English spoken by a Turkish child arise from movement of the object to a preverbal position from its underlying postverbal site. This analysis of OV order is based on Kayne's claim that all clauses are underlyingly SVO (see Section 2.2 above). The movement operation is triggered by a strong feature on a functional head above V. The Turkish child transfers the value of this feature to English directly from its value in Turkish, giving rise to the observed structure. It is only later that the child learns to reset the feature to weak, thus acquiring the VO order of the target language.

REFERENCES

Abney, S. (1987), 'The English Noun Phrase in its Sentential Aspect', Ph.D., MIT.

Adger, D. (1997), 'VSO Order and Weak Pronouns in Goidelic Celtic', *Canadian Journal of Linguistics*, 42: 9–29.

Borer, H., and Wexler, K. (1987), 'The Maturation of Syntax', in T. Roeper and E. Williams (eds.), *Parameter-Setting and Language Acquisition*, Reidel, Dordrecht, 123–72.

Bresnan, J. (1972), 'The Theory of Complementation in English Syntax', Ph.D., MIT.

Chomsky, N. (1970), 'Remarks on Nominalization', in R. Jacobs and P. Rosenbaum (eds.), *Readings in English Transformational Grammar*, Blaisdell, Waltham, Mass., 184–221.

——(1981), *Lectures on Government and Binding*, Foris, Dordrecht.

——(1986a), *Barriers*, MIT Press, Cambridge, Mass.

——(1986b), *Knowledge of Language*, Praeger, New York.

——(1989), 'Some Notes on Economy of Derivation and Representation', *MIT Working Papers in Linguistics*, 10: 43–74.

——(1993), 'A Minimalist Program for Linguistic Theory', in K. Hale and A. Marantz (eds.), *The View from Building 20*, MIT Press, Cambridge, Mass., 1–52.

——(1995), *The Minimalist Program*, MIT Press, Cambridge, Mass.

Gazdar, G., Pullum, G., and Sag, I. (1982), 'Auxiliaries and Related Phenomena in a Restrictive Theory of Grammar', *Language*, 59: 591–638.

Hoekstra, E. (1991), 'Licensing Conditions on Phrase Structure', Ph.D., University of Groningen.

Huang, J. T. (1982), 'Logical Relations in Chinese and the Theory of Grammar', Ph.D., MIT.

Jackendoff, R. S. (1977), *X' Syntax: A Study of Phrase Structure*, MIT Press, Cambridge, Mass.

Kayne, R. (1994), 'The Antisymmetry of Syntax', MIT Press, Cambridge, Mass.

Koopman, H., and Sportiche, D. (1990), 'The Position of Subjects', *Lingua*, 85: 211–58.

McCloskey, J. (1996), 'Subjects and Subject Positions', in R. Borsley and I. Roberts (eds.), *The Syntax of the Celtic Languages: A Comparative Perspective*, Cambridge University Press, Cambridge, 241–83.

Pinker, S. (1984), *Language Learnability and Language Development*, Harvard University Press, Cambridge, Mass.

Pollock, J.-Y. (1989), 'Verb Movement, UG, and the Structure of IP', *Linguistic Inquiry*, 20: 365–424.

Radford, A. (1986), 'The Acquisition of the Complementiser System', *Bangor Research Papers in Linguistics*, 2, Department of Linguistics, UCNW, Bangor, 55–75.

Stuurman, F. (1985), 'X-Bar and X-Plain: A Study of the X-Bar Theories of the Phrase Structure Component', Ph.D., University of Utrecht.

Whitman, J., Lee, K.-O., and Lust, B. (1990), 'Continuity of the Principles of Universal Grammar in First Language Acquisition: The Issue of Functional Categories', in T. Sherer (ed.), *Proceedings of the North Eastern Linguistics Society* 21, GLSA, Amherst, 383–97.

Williams, E. (1981), 'Argument Structure and Morphology', *Linguistic Review*, 1: 81–114.

PART I
The Nature of Specifiers

2

Specifiers as Secondary Heads

RONNIE CANN

I. X-BAR THEORY

One of the important tasks of a syntactic theory is to provide an account of the different dependency relations that hold between elements in a phrase. In Dependency Grammar (following various traditional grammatical traditions (cf. Lyons 1968)), there are two basic types: complement and adjunct (or modifier). The first defines an obligatory relation between a functor (or head) and its argument and the second an optional modification of a category (or head). In Categorial Grammar, these two are the only types of relation allowed by the basic theory,[1] shown in (1), where X and Y are any category labels.[2]

(1) *Categorial Grammar*
    (i) $X/Y + Y \Rightarrow X$ (complement)
    (ii) $X/X + X \Rightarrow X$ (adjunct)

These two dependencies are easily reconstructed in phrase structure terms with complements introduced as (phrasal) sisters to a lexical category, both dominated by a phrasal category (2.i), and adjuncts introduced as sisters to a phrasal category, dominated by an instance of the latter (2.ii).

(2) *Phrase Structure Grammar*
    (i) $XP \rightarrow X + YP$ (complement)
    (ii) $XP \rightarrow XP + YP$ (adjunct)

In standard X-bar theory, a third type of dependency was introduced into phrase structure formalisms, the so-called specifier. Although interpreted in works such as Jackendoff (1977) as a linear relation to a head (precedence),

I am grateful to all those who commented on the earlier version of this chapter delivered as a paper at the Specifiers Conference at York University; to Mary E. Tait, with whom some of the ideas presented here were worked out; to a number of postgraduate students, particularly Diane Nelson and Martha Robinson; to Annabel Cormack for e-mail comments on one of the drafts; and to two anonymous referees. The usual caveats apply.
  [1] Modifications on the basic type of functional application are found that yield different structural relations, see Steedman (1988), among others.
  [2] In (1) and below, order of elements within rule schemata is immaterial to the discussion and so '+' should be interpreted as unordered concatenation.

the specifier relation is more commonly defined in structural terms as sister to a non-minimal head and daughter of a maximal projection (3.i). Within the standard version of X-bar theory (see e.g. Radford 1988), the complement relation (3.ii) is analysed in the same way as in the PSG rule in (2.i) except that the dominating node is defined as a category that is neither maximal (phrasal XP) nor minimal (lexical X)—namely X′.

(3)   *X-bar Theory*
        (i) $XP \rightarrow X' + Y$ (specifier)
        (ii) $X' \rightarrow X + YP$ (complement)

The introduction of the specifier relation enabled another traditional functional notion, that of the subject, to be reconstructed within Phrase Structure Grammar in a generalized (cross-categorial) way. Although the latter appears to have been the principal reason for its introduction in Chomsky (1970), the relation has in fact been used in various ways since that time to encompass minor grammatical formatives, operators, escape hatches for movement, and so on.

In X-bar theory, the adjunct relation has been somewhat problematic, but it has generally been assumed that a recursive schema, like that in (2.ii), is necessary to analyse adjuncts such as attributive adjectives and so on. Thus, the theory is extended to incorporate the schema in (4), where X^n ranges over levels of a category X and permissible values of n are defined for some variant of the theory.[3] This schema in effect adopts into X-bar syntax Harris's repeatable substitution equations (Harris 1951).[4]

(4) $X^n \rightarrow X^n + YP$ (adjunct)

These three dependency relations—complement, adjunct, and specifier—have been very fruitful in providing the theoretical vocabulary for discussing the syntactic behaviour of different types of expression. However, in the drive for explanatory adequacy, there remains a strong tendency to reduce the number of structural interpretations of these three relations. This is evident in the recent work of Kayne (1994) and Chomsky (1995a, b) (basically following e.g. Henk Verkuyl (1981), Frits Stuurman (1985), and others in the 1980s). In Kayne's work, there are two levels of projection, maximal (XP) and minimal (X), with the two basic relations of CG, complement and adjunct. Specifiers are subsumed under a restricted concept of adjunct, as in (5).

---

[3] In the 'pre-Minimalist' version of transformational grammar, n was restricted to 2 or 0, thus allowing only XP (maximal) or X (lexical) adjunction. In Chomsky's current theory, however, n is restricted to 0 only (Chomsky 1995b). It should be noted that Chomsky does not discuss adjunction that does not result from movement (like attributive modification) and specifically denies that 'there is any good phrase structure theory of' such matters (Chomsky 1995b: ch. 4, fn. 22). It therefore remains to be seen whether the extreme restriction to lexical adjunction is tenable.

[4] See Stuurman (1985: 16–26) for a discussion of the resemblances between Harris's and Chomsky's proposals.

(5)   *Kayne (1994)*
      (i) XP → X + YP   (complement)
      (ii) XP → YP + XP   (adjunct/specifier)

Multiple adjunction is prohibited in this theory through the operation of the *Linear Correspondence Axiom*, which is taken to derive word order from hierarchical relations (asymmetric c-command). A consequence of this (controversial) move is that all movement must take place to, and through, a unique adjunct/specifier position, leading to a proliferation of (often null) functional heads to provide the necessary positions.

In Chomsky (1995*a*, *b*), all bar levels are eschewed and the specifier relation is defined by the same structural relation to the head as a complement, as in (6.i), where x and y are labels derived from lexical expressions (this is discussed below), and y is the non-head variously interpreted as specifier, complement, or adjunct. Pure adjuncts, on the other hand, are restricted to lexical adjunction.[5] Since multiple specifiers are not disallowed in principle (as in Kayne), phrasal adjuncts are defined by the same basic relation to the head as complements and specifiers.

(6)   *Chomsky (1995a)*[6]
      (i) $x \rightarrow x + y$ (complement/specifier/adjunct)
      (ii) $<x, x> \rightarrow x + y$ (adjunct (lexical))

Although the basic structural definition of complementation, specification, and (phrasal) adjunction is the same, the distinction between complements and specifiers/adjuncts is defined in terms of locality to a head. A complement is the most local (least embedded) expression to a head and a specifier is anything else in the structural domain of the head. If the notions specifier and complement continue to have content (as they do in Chomsky (1995*b*), since only specifiers can check features), then these assumptions simply reconstruct X-bar theory. Although this theory does so without the postulation of extra features such as bar levels, it still ascribes different properties to different levels constructed by the same operation, Merge. The checking operation must, therefore, be able look inside a tree—that is, beyond the local domain—in order to ascertain whether a term x is minimal or not (since x as a term and x as a label are non-distinct). While this may not seem to be much to propose in order to maintain a purely minimal definition of structure building, it is not clear why the distance between a head and its complement/specifier should

---

  [5] The notation, $<x, x>$ in (6.ii) indicates a two-segment category which is not a term of a phrase marker and so not visible at LF.
  [6] Chomsky uses a set-theoretic notation for the structures induced by the tree-building operation 'Merge' so that the rule schemata in (6.i) and (6.ii) are represented as (i) and (ii), respectively. For the purposes of this chapter, there are no consequences of the differences in notation.

(i) $\{x, \{x, y\}\}$
(ii) $\{<x, x>, \{x, y\}\}$

Ronnie Cann

have such significance nor why only non-local expressions (specifiers) enter into checking relations. Further problems, of course, arise with the consideration of adjuncts—all specifiers according to Chomsky, but differing in their syntactic properties. Despite the interesting attempts of Chomsky and Kayne to reduce the number of distinct X-bar relations, the differences between complements, specifiers, and adjuncts remain significant and still need to be stated independently. There is as yet no reason to suppose that the differences do not reside in differences in their structural realization.

2. SPECIFIERS AND COMPLEMENTS

It is well known that a construction containing a specifier typically has a distribution that differs from those of either of its subconstituents on their own and that properties of the specifier may be selected or otherwise determined by a higher governing head (cf. e.g. Chomsky 1986). In Cann (1993), it is suggested that this observation be adopted into the grammar by allowing two expressions, a specifier and its head, to combine to form a constituent that has more grammatical properties than either expression on its own. This is done by requiring that the category of a local tree consisting of a specifier and a head be determined by the unification of the categories of its immediate subconstituents. The statement in (7) is interpreted there as forming part of the phrase structure component and has the effect of making specifiers secondary heads.

(7)   If α is a specifier of β then the category of the minimal tree, T containing α and β, is given by the unification of the categories of α and β.

If one puts this into the terms of Chomsky's Bare Phrase Structure (Chomsky 1995*a*), we replace the definition of specifier in (6.i) with (8) (where the relation $\cup$ is to be made more precise below).

(8) $x \cup y \rightarrow x + y$ (specifier)

Chomsky observes that the construction of the label of a mother node from the union of the labels of both its daughters is logically possible, but dismisses the idea out of hand:

The label [of a phrase marker] must be constructed from the two constituents α and β. Suppose these are lexical items, each a set of features. Then the simplest assumption would be that the label is [one of]:

i   the intersection of α and β
ii the union of α and β
iii one or the other of α, β

The options [i] and [ii] are immediately excluded: the intersection of α, β will generally be irrelevant to output conditions, often null; and the union will not only be irrelevant but contradictory if α, β differ in value for some feature, the normal case. (Chomsky 1995a: 397)

Chomsky does not attempt to show that the 'normal case' is, in fact, for α and β to differ in the value for some feature and thus that their union is contradictory.[7] Presumably, he would base his claim on his hypothesis that, since α and β are labels projected from lexical items, they contain phonological features whose union is likely to lead to contradiction. However, if we restrict our attention to syntactic features (I will return below to the question of phonology), then it is not true that the union of two labels will generally lead to contradiction. If, as sometimes suggested, functional categories are not inherently verbal or nominal, then incoherence will not normally arise where one of the unified labels is a functional expression.[8] For example, if the formal features of *the student* and *Agr* are as in (9a) and (9b) then the union of the two items is the non-contradictory set in (9c) (assuming for the moment that $\cup$ is to be interpreted simply as set union of formal, syntactic, features).

(9) (*a*)   the student: {Det:def,3,sg}
   (*b*)   Agr: {3,sg}
   (*c*)   the $\cup$ Agr: {Det:def,3,sg}

Indeed, the compatibility of formal features is a *sine qua non* for specifier–head agreement (and consequent feature checking) and must hold not only of noun phrases in the specifier position of Agr (assuming the independence of this node, *pace* Chomsky 1995b), but also in operator positions in order to allow the satisfaction of the Neg and *Wh*-criteria (see Rizzi 1990b; Haegeman and Zanuttini 1991).

In terms of tree-building operations, then, I am suggesting a new operation for syntactically induced dependencies like those generally ascribed to specifiers. This does not involve simple substitution of a tree for a (c-selected) node, like Chomsky's Merge, but the combination of two trees (simple or complex) and the creation of a new categorial label for the mother, determined by the union of the root labels of the two trees combined by the process. This process of union may also be seen as a validation of the syntax–lexicon interface: checking in Chomsky's terms. If contentives come out of the lexicon with their morphosyntactic features fully specified (perhaps as part of the numeration process, as suggested in Chomsky 1995b: 225 ff.), and if functional categories

---

[7] Notice that Chomsky is assuming not that it is the simple union of feature sets that is ill formed, but that the resulting set contains instances of the same feature with different values: an incoherent category, rather than an incoherent set. See Gazdar *et al.* (1985) for discussion of such matters.

[8] Even if all labels carry N and V features, however, it will often arise that the union of two labels will not be incoherent.

are essentially syntactic constructs, then matching of features becomes essential to maintain congruence between the two domains. The union process can
thus be viewed as ensuring compatibility between lexically and syntactically
derived feature specifications.

Technically, this can be quite easily achieved if we treat ∪, not as set union,
but as category unification as commonly construed (see Pollard and Sag 1994:
19, and much other literature). Assume that certain features in lexical entries,
those that have syntactic significance like Tense, AGR, etc., have values that
are variables which range over a restricted subset (possibly unary) of the values
associated with the feature. Feature checking can then be viewed as instantiation of this variable with a particular value as determined by a particular tree
configuration. Such a checking procedure will be necessary under the natural
assumption that feature variables are not interpretable at LF.

Let us consider first feature checking through head movement, taking as
example the movement of a verb to a participle head position. Following Cann
and Tait (1995), participles in English may be analysed as realizations of a
(language-specific) functional category which we may label PRT. This has two
variants, which can be encoded by letting PRT take one of two values, EN (for
the passive/perfect participle) and ING (for the present participle).[9] A participle verb form, such as *kicked*, may then be analysed as including, as part of
its label, the feature PRT with a variable value, which we may represent as *en*,
that ranges over only the single passive/perfect value of PRT, EN. This variable
value of PRT on the verb must be instantiated during the derivation, which can
be achieved directly through head movement if this operation does not create
a lexical adjunction structure like that in (6.ii), but unifies the features of the
target node with that of the moved element. Thus, abstracting away from
irrelevant details, the movement of *kicked* to the participle head involves the
creation of structures like that in (10), which shows the way the variable value
en associated with the label of the verb is identified with the given value EN of
the functional head. In this way, morphological features are straightforwardly
checked against syntactic ones.

(10)

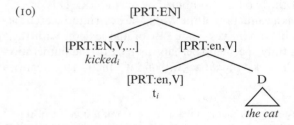

Exactly the same process of feature instantiation can be used to account for

---

feature checking in typical specifier constructions, reinterpreted here as doubly headed structures formed through the unification (as opposed to union) of the labels of the two heads.[10] The creation of tree structures involving the process envisaged in (8) will thus instantiate variable feature values. Consider *wh*-movement, for example. To ensure that *wh*-elements move to the complementizer position within the Minimalist framework, it is necessary to assume that a *wh*-phrase contains a C feature that must be checked (pre- or post-Spellout depending on strength). Let us assume (following suggestions in Gazdar *et al.* 1985; Pollard and Sag 1994, etc.) that *C* is a feature that may take a number of values, depending on whether the clause is a question (Q), relative (R), etc. As part of the label of the *wh*-expression, the feature C takes a variable value, *rq*, ranging over (at least) the two values Q and R,[11] which will need to be instantiated during the course of a derivation to ensure convergence. The *wh*-expression moves and combines with the complementizer clause that contains it. The latter may itself contain a variable feature value for WH ranging over + and − (to distinguish constituent questions from root questions and *wh*-relatives from those with just a complementizer).[12] As part of the combination of the two trees the formal features of the labels at their roots are unified, instantiating the variable feature values with fully specified ones, as shown in (11), where the arrows relate the instantiated feature values with the appropriate variables (irrelevant details are omitted or simplified, so whatever is under C is just labelled 'IP' for convenience).[13]

(11)   ([D,C:rq,WH:+] ∪ [C:R,WH:~]) = [D,C:R,WH:+]

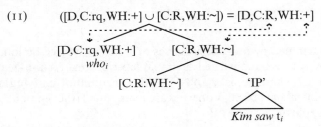

Thus, feature checking can be specified as a single process: the instantiation of variable feature values through unification. There are, however, two operations that involve it: substitution head movement, interpreted as unification of

---

[10] Note that the process must be unification and not union here since [PRT:en] and [PRT:EN] are different formal objects whose union would be {[PRT:EN], [PRT:en]} but whose unification is [PRT:EN].

[11] Some *wh*-expressions, such as *what*, may be lexically specified as taking a more restricted value for C which ranges only over Q, thus disallowing them from appearing as relative markers. There are, however, dialects of English that allow relative *what*, so that this property does seem to be truly lexical and so open to dialectal variation.

[12] This could be seen as an analogue of Cormack's double selection of C for its specifier and WH for C (see Ch. 3, this volume). This is not a necessary assumption for my purposes.

[13] In fact, the tree in (10) would never appear as such, since the process of unification instantiates all instances of the relevant variables throughout the tree.

one lexical node with another;[14] and phrasal movement, interpreted as the
'specifier' tree-building operation in (8), for the validation of syntactic dependencies. In both cases, however, the moved element becomes a head, singulary
in the case of head movement, and secondary in phrasal movement.

Returning to Chomsky's headed schema in (6.i), repeated in (12*a*), we may
now interpret the structures induced by this in a rather different way to produce a coherent difference between complements and other expressions. In
Chomsky's schema, the head is a unique lexical element and so structures
based on it may be considered to define the lexical domain of that head—that
is, its theta-marking and c-selectional domain (cf. Grimshaw 1990). Hence, a
lexical entry like that in (12*b*) will induce a tree structure like that in (12*c*),
which may be construed as the syntactic realization of the lexical structure of
the verb in that independent properties of the lexical item (such as theta-roles)
are mapped into nodes (merge sites) with the head determining part of the
label of each lexically determined dependency. Functional categories just
project their c-selected complements.[15]

(12) (*a*) $x \rightarrow x + y$ (lexical projection)
   (*b*)   {give, V, <Goal, Theme, Agent>}
   (*c*)

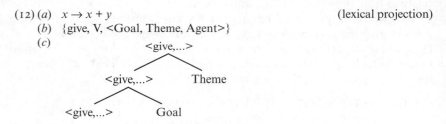

Where a tree is determined by lexical properties of a head, the tree-building
operation, Merge, may thus be construed as simple substitution of a non-head
node by another tree (as in Chomsky 1995*b*), with concomitant unifying of
node labels to guarantee that lexical properties are maintained (the remnant of
the Projection Principle of earlier work).

---

[14] I am here making no claims that all head movement is substitution. It may be that lexical
adjunction remains a necessary operation within the grammar. For example, in the theory es-
poused below, the analysis of Subject–Auxiliary Inversion as involving I-to-C movement is not
tenable if the movement is substitution, at least in *wh*-questions, since this would exclude the
fronting of a plural *wh*-phrase with a singular auxiliary (e.g. *Which students does Mary like?*). It
may be that I adjoins to C in these cases to allow number (and person) mismatches between the
wh-specifier and auxiliary, or that the auxiliary moves to a position between I and C. However,
whatever the correct account, the current theory predicts that the movement of auxiliary in these
cases does not involve checking of a *wh*-feature with the *wh*-expression and that other factors must
be involved to derive such movement. This is a matter for further research.
[15] One could use Cormack's (Ch. 3, this volume) categorial notation to encode c-selectional
properties of both contentive and functional expressions. This sort of lexical projection is also
reminiscent of HPSG (see Pollard and Sag 1994). See also Tait (1991) for a discussion of lexically
induced trees and Fukui (1986) for arguments that contentive categories realize arguments within
X′ domains.

3. SELECTING SPECIFIERS:
THE PASSIVE/PERFECT PARTICIPLE

Specifiers may appear not just to check features, however. They may be introduced to satisfy lexical dependencies that would not otherwise be satisfied. Cann and Tait (1995) use the treatment of specifiers as resulting from the unification of two heads to provide a new account of the passive and perfect constructions in English. They take as their point of departure the hypothesis that, for grammatical elements, morphological identity entails syntactic (categorial) identity. For example, it is common in syntactic theory to treat the perfect and passive participles in English as the realization of separate morphemes, despite the fact that there are no differences in the morphological forms of verbs, even down to suppletion, whether they appear in passive or perfect constructions.[16] In other words, passive and perfect participles are treated as homonyms, morphophonologically identical realizations of different morphemes. However, there is no a priori reason to suppose that the use of the single form in both constructions in English is purely accidental nor that the labels traditionally given to these syntactic constructions by linguists are anything but a terminological convenience.[17] It is at least an interesting hypothesis that minimalist expectations apply also in the functional lexicon and that homonymy of grammatical elements is not tolerated.[18] Cann and Tait, therefore, analyse both the passive and the perfect participles as projections of a single category, which they label *en* after Chomsky (1957). It follows from this assumption that the differences in the distribution (and interpretation) of *en*-participles in English must derive from the expressions with which they combine.

The data in (13*a*)–(13*h*) illustrate some of the different contexts in which the perfect/passive participles can appear in English.

(13) (*a*) Harassed by the students, the lecturer finally left.
　　 (*b*) *Be harassed by the students, the lecturer finally left.
　　 (*c*) The lecturer was harassed by the students.
　　 (*d*) The students have harassed the lecturer.
　　 (*e*) *The lecturer was harassed the students.
　　 (*f*) *The students have harassed by the lecturer.

---

[16] Warner (1993) uses a feature +EN to identify the past (*sic*) and passive participles, but still differentiates them by the use of the feature ±PRD (predicative), the first being –PRD and the second +PRD.

[17] Note that the claim made here is strictly with reference to (certain dialects of) English. No claim is being made that the passive and perfect morphemes are universally identical. Indeed, most languages that have both passive and perfect do differentiate them morphologically, in which case the constructions will necessarily be distinct in analysis. Thus, in the discussion that follows, the specifics of the analysis pertain only to English, while only the general mechanisms are considered to be universal in any meaningful sense.

[18] There is strong psycholinguistic evidence for this hypothesis with respect to functional elements (see Cann 1996 for discussion).

    (*g*)   *The lecturer might harassed by the students.
    (*h*)   *The students might harassed the lecturer.

In (13*a*), the participle is in an adjectival context (cf. *Angry with the students, the lecturer finally left*), where no auxiliary can appear (13*b*); in (13*c*) and (13*d*), the participle appears in verbal contexts, passive in (13*c*) and perfect in (13*d*); (13*e*) and (13*f*) illustrate that the syntactic (case-assigning) properties of the participle are dependent on which auxiliary appears; and (13*g*) and (13*h*) show that the auxiliary verbs are obligatory in situations where there is an element (like tense, modal, or another instance of the participle) that requires a following verb.

    Cann and Tait explain these differences as deriving from an analysis in which the auxiliaries appear as specifiers to syncategorematic *en* in the syntax where specifiers unify their properties with heads as suggested above. Revising the structures they suggest in the light of Chomsky (1995*a*), the basic structure of the perfect and passive constructions, differing only in which auxiliary is chosen, is as given in (14).[19]

(14)

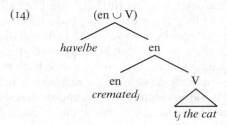

The grammaticality of participial expressions without an auxiliary as in (13*a*) shows that the auxiliary does not appear in (14) to satisfy any of the properties of the participial head: it is neither selected by *en* nor checks any of its features. It must, therefore, by economy principles, appear in order to satisfy the requirements of some other element. Apart from feature checking, the other principal mechanism that drives minimalist derivations is selection, determined by the merging of one tree with a node lexically projected from the label of some head, as noted above. For selection to have significance, any property of the merge site must be a property of the root node of the tree to be merged. In other words, if a head selects a verb, then the root node of any tree that satisfies this selectional property must be verbal.[20] Since the *en* morpheme

---

[19] Where (en ∪ V) may be construed as [PRT:EN,+V,–N]. Note that if *en* has any major features, then this may only be [+V] with N undefined to allow for the participle to appear in both verbal and adjectival contexts.
    In (14) and the following examples, I have not shown the original position of subjects in order not to commit to, or deny, the VP-Internal Subject Hypothesis.

[20] Thus, the relation between the categories of the root and merge sites is one of extension as defined in Gazdar *et al.* (1985: 39).

(PRT:EN) is syncategorematic, it has no verbal features (or only incompletely specified features, see note 19) and so cannot satisfy the selectional properties of a tense or modal node. This automatically accounts for the ungrammaticality of (13g) and (13h) where no auxiliary appears in such contexts. However, the appearance of an auxiliary to give the structure in (14) means that the root now has a verbal specification (through the unification of the properties of the auxiliary with those of the participial head) which can locally satisfy the selection property of tense/modal, as shown in (15).

(15)

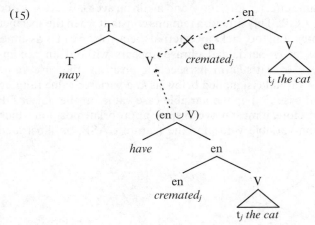

The grammaticality of (13a) thus follows from the fact that the participle is in a position where a verb is selected, while the ungrammaticality of (13b) results from the lack of any licenser for the auxiliary.

The different case-assigning properties of the two constructions (illustrated in (13c)–(13f)) are fairly straightforwardly derived under the current analysis. Burzio's generalization states that a verb assigns object case if, and only if, it assigns an external theta-role (Burzio 1986). Within the current framework, we may interpret this statement as providing a means of licensing an expressed case value on some functional head, which I shall here take to be AGR.[21] Thus, I assume that certain functional heads will normally be generated with certain features having a variable value which can only be instantiated as a non-variable value when something else licenses that value. While we may assume that person and number are inherent features of AGR (or D), and that such features have values instantiated as part of the numeration, the case value is dependent on the position of the node in the tree. Nominative (subject) AGR

---

[21] Unlike Chomsky (1995b), it is necessary in the current framework for case to be checked by an independent functional head. This is because a DP specifier of a VP is impossible, since the unification of these two categories gives rise to an incoherent category (one that is both nominal and verbal).

gets its case value by virtue of its selection of Tense as a complement. Accusative (object) AGR, however, requires something else to determine its case value, which, by Burzio's generalization, is the ability of an immediately dominating element to assign an external theta-role.

Hence, as the functional head, *en*, does not itself assign an external theta-role,[22] it does not license an accusative case value on AGR in its complement position. When V moves to *en*, its external theta-role is absorbed (see Haegeman 1991 and references cited therein, and, with very different assumptions leading to the same effect, Cann 1995) and again an accusative case value fails to be licensed on AGR. This situation remains constant when the specifier is *be*, because this expression, too, lacks an external theta-role. We may assume, therefore, that where an *en*-participial phrase appears without an accompanying auxiliary verb or with *be* in its specifier position, the case value on AGR remains as a variable (signalled below as *k*, a variable value ranging over any grammatical case).[23] For the variable case value on the object DP to be instantiated, therefore, it must move to some appropriate position which contains a proper non-variable value for the feature CASE, as illustrated in (16).

(16)

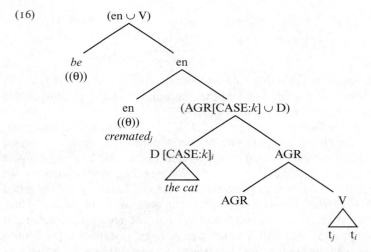

On the other hand, *have* does assign an external theta-role (on the assumption that perfective *have* is the same as main verb *have*, see Section 4). Although *have* itself does not immediately dominate the AGR projection, its properties are shared with the node that does (*en*) through the unification operation.

---

[22] This stance differs from that taken in Cann and Tait (1995).
[23] It is possible, of course, that it is the AGR projection itself that is licensed by the external theta-role, in which case it will simply not appear in the stated structures. The effect will be the same.

Hence, an accusative case value is licensed on AGR. Since the object noun phrase can instantiate (check) its case variable in the specifier position of AGR, it will move no further, as shown in (17).[24]

(17)

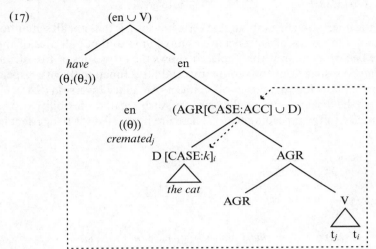

4. DOUBLE- VERSUS SINGLE-HEADED STRUCTURES: CAUSATIVE AND PERFECT *HAVE*

The analysis of auxiliaries as specifiers interpreted as secondary heads has further advantages in analysing other constructions involving the verb *have* in English. As is well known, this verb appears in a wide range of constructions that, from a semantic point of view, can be divided up into contentive (main verb) uses (18a) and functional (grammatical) ones (18b).[25]

(18) (a)   *Contentive*
     (i)   *Possessive*:   Jo has three books.
     (ii) *Relational*:   Jo had a sister once.
     (iii) *Inalienable Possession*:   Jo has blue eyes.
     (iv) *Experiencer*:   Jo had a headache.
     (v)   *Process*:   Jo had the new boy last night.

---

[24] The structure in (17) embodies a number of further assumptions that I do not have space to go into here. The principal one of these is that head movement takes place into the nearest available compatible position, as in Rizzi (1990a). V cannot move into AGR in (17) since its feature specification would not unify with that of the DP in the specifier position. Another aspect of this analysis that is not discussed here is the way the external theta-role of the verb is identified with the subject. This matter is discussed in Cann (1995).

[25] For discussion of properties of *have* and different ways to analyse them, see Cowper (1992), Kayne (1993), and Ritter and Rosen (1997), among many others.

   (*b*) *Functional*
      (i)   *Perfect*:   Jo has gone home.
      (ii) *Causative*:   Jo had the cat cremated.
      (iii) *Modal*:   Jo has to go home.

One of the interesting facts about this verb, however, is that not all semantic-ally functional instances of *have* behave as auxiliaries and not all uses of the contentive behave as main verbs. Table 2.1 shows the properties of five of the different *have* constructions (two contentive and three functional) with respect to four normal tests for auxiliaryhood: Subject–Auxiliary Inversion (SAI), *n't* cliticization, the disallowance of the 'dummy' verb *do*, and the ability of the verb to cliticize to the preceding word. These are illustrated for the perfect in (19*a*)–(19*d*).[26]

    (19) (*a*) Has Jo cremated the cat?
         (*b*) Jo hasn't cremated the cat.
         (*c*) *Jo does have cremated the cat.
         (*d*) Jo's cremated the cat.

TABLE 2.1. *Auxiliary properties of* have *constructions*

	SAI	*n't*	~*do*	Clitic
Possessive	+	+	−	+
Process	−	−	−	−
Perfect	+	+	+	+
Modal	%	%	−	?−
Causative	−	−	−	−

The pattern in Table 2.1 shows the cline in auxiliaryhood shown in (20) from the main verb properties of the process and causative to the most auxiliary-like behaviour of the perfect. The modal construction appears in the middle and is most subject to idiolectal variation.

    (20)   Process/Causative > Modal > Possessive > Perfect

As with the perfect/passive participles, this variability in the properties of constructions based on a single morph might be analysed by postulating homonymy—that is, distinct lexical entries for the different uses of the verb. However, such an approach fails to explain the apparent binary distinction be-tween the constructions (ignoring the modal construction for convenience)—

---

[26] The % for the modal use indicates variation in acceptability of such examples as (British English) *Has Lou to go home?*, *Lou hasn't to go home* versus the much more marginal *?Lou's to go home*. (All of these are grammatical in the author's idiolect.)

that is, an apparently straight main verb/auxiliary split—and fails to account for why this distinction should cut across the contentive/functional divide.

The observation of the syntactic differences in *have* constructions shows an interesting link with studies of grammaticalization processes, as described, for example, in Hopper and Traugott (1993). Grammaticalization is analysed by Hopper and Traugott as the development of a grammatical item ('bleached' of its contentive interpretation) from a single (contentive) expression via a polysemous stage where emerging grammatical and contentive uses are active side-by-side through a process of pragmatic enrichment. Given that the development of auxiliaries in this framework is analysed as the grammaticalization of main verbs, the variability shown above indicates that *have* is currently in the middle, polysemic, period in English. If this is the case, an explanation needs to be found for why the different polysemes should have different syntactic properties, since normally a polysemous item maintains its syntactic properties in its different interpretations.

If *have* is treated as a single polysemous expression and morphemes are treated monadically in the syntax, then the differences in the syntactic properties of the constructions must be explained in terms of the structures they induce. The structure for perfective *have* was given in (14) above, in which the auxiliary verb acts as a second head with the participle, unifying its properties with those of the participial head. In this construction, *have* exhibits strictly auxiliary behaviour, as indicated in Table 2.1. Causative *have*, on the other hand, exhibits only main verb characteristics: it does not allow SAI (**Had Jo the cat cremated?*) or *n't* cliticization (**Jo hadn't the cat cremated*); cannot cliticize to the subject (**Jo'd the cat cremated*); but does permit '*do*-support' (*Jo did cremate the cat*). Under the assumption that main verbs, which all display the same behaviour, are analysed as singular heads, *have* in its causative manifestation may also be analysed as an ordinary head taking a participial complement, as shown in (21).

(21)

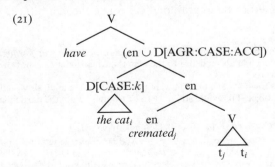

This structure differs significantly from that in (14). In the first place, *have* is an independent element heading its own, uniquely determined, projection and thus it requires its c-selectional properties to be satisfied (taken here to be D, something that can be assigned an appropriate theta-role). The *en*-complement alone cannot satisfy this requirement and so before Merge creates the structure in (21) a noun phrase must unify with it to yield a tree rooted in $(D \cup en)$ which is of the appropriate type (D) to satisfy the selectional property of *have*.[27] Since *have* does not unify its case-assigning properties with the participle in this construction, the direct object is not case-licensed in situ and so must move. The nearest position in which the case of the object can be checked is the specifier position of the participle, to which the object raises as observed.[28]

No attempt can be made here to give a full account of the observed syntactic differences between *have* instantiated as an independent head, as in the causative, and as a second head, as in the perfect. However, the analysis sketched above suggests that overt movement of V to C in English—and perhaps elsewhere—involves the movement of auxiliary V through the *specifier* of T rather than through the head position.

In the doubly headed structures created by the unification operation, the status of both subconstituents remains maximal, under the assumption that movement applies only to maximal or minimal elements. The 'specifier' expression must be maximal, since it may be moved from such a position in topicalization and *wh*-constructions, etc.—for example, (22*a*). On the other hand, its sister constituent, the 'head' expression, is also maximal, since, for example, the participle can be topicalized as in (22*b*). This follows from the fact that $x \cup y$ is not equivalent to either x or y; that is, it is not strictly a projection of either one of them.

(22) (*a*) [$_{WH}$ which books]$_i$, did Jo think [$_{(WH \cup C)}$ t_j C [he lost t_j]]
    (*b*) [$_{en}$ cremated the cat]$_i$, Jo thought he [$_V$ had]$_j$ [$_{(V \cup en)}$ t_j t_i]]

The maximality of both constituents in the specifier construction accounts directly for why main verbs in English cannot appear in COMP (or preceding adjuncts, etc.). If the Uniform Chain Condition of Chomsky (1995*b*) is valid, then (23*b*) is correctly predicted to be ungrammatical, since the chain (t_j, t_j')

---

[27] The causative meaning is maintained if the participial form is *ing* as in *Jo had the cat howling, Jo had the cat eating smoked tofu*, which lends credence to the idea that the participle is not the 'real' (selected) complement of the verb.

[28] A full AGR projection is not shown in (21), but if it were there as in (i), the analysis would not be materially affected, since the object DP would still have to be fronted before the participle to have its case checked.

(i)   [$_V$ have [$_{(AGR \cup D)}$ [$_D$ the cat]$_j$ AGR [$_{(en \cup D)}$ t_j' [$_{en}$ cremated] [$_V$ t_i t_j]]]]

Notice that the satisfaction of the selecting head, *have*, by a moved noun phrase requires that Merge has to apply to the tree [$_{en}$ [$_{[en, V]}$ *cremated*] [$_{VP}$ t [$_{DP}$ *the cat*]]] to raise the DP prior to the combination of the participle with the verb. Otherwise, selectional properties could be satisfied by covert (F-)movement after Spell-Out. It must therefore be the case that Merge immediately satisfies lexical dependencies, as noted above. Since on this account movement must take place before the satisfaction of lexical selection, this analysis provides a further argument against the significance of D-structure as a level of representation.

involves a maximal head and a minimal tail (as more clearly shown in the tree (11)).[29] Example (23a), on the other hand, involves a chain that is uniformly maximal in Chomsky's terms and so the construction is grammatical. It could therefore be a matter of parameterization whether verb movement occurs through the specifier or the head of the Tense projection, leading to differences in the ability of verbs to front.

(23) (a) $[_C [_C [_V \text{has}]_j C] \text{Jo} [_{(T \cup V)} t_j T [_{(en \cup V)} t_j' \text{cremated the cat}]]]$

(b) $*[_C [_C [_V \text{has}]_j C] \text{Jo} [_{(T \cup V)} t_j T [_V t_j' \text{the cat cremated}]]]$

(c)

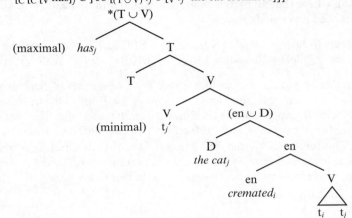

Auxiliary cliticization is also explicable in these terms. In this case, whatever syntactic position is correct for an auxiliary clitic, it is, under all accounts, a maximal one, and so movement of the auxiliary from the secondary head position in T to this position does not violate uniformity, as illustrated in (24a). In the case of *have* in singulary head position, where the tail is minimal, the UCC predicts ungrammaticality in the same way as for (23b), as shown in (24b).

(24) (a) $[_D [_D \text{Jo}] \text{'d}_j] [_{(T \cup V)} t_j T [_{(en \cup V)} t_j' \text{cremated the cat}]]$

(b) $*[_D [_D \text{Jo}] \text{'d}_j] [_{(T \cup V)} t_j T [_V t_j' [_{(en \cup D)} \text{the cat cremated}]]]$

There are a number of ways in which examples with negative clitics can be analysed, depending on one's general treatment of negation in the syntax. Because of the restriction of this process to finite contexts (**Kim wants to-n't go*), it is clear that *n't* must be associated with tense in some way. One possible

---

[29] Covert F-movement of the tense feature of a main verb may then be analysed as movement to the head of T. It is possible that all covert movement should be analysed as F-movement to a head position. In the theory of this chapter, since features are checked in the same way for both phrasal and head movement, no further operations need be defined and no extra structure need be created post-Spell-Out.

analysis appears in (25*a*).[30] This adopts the analysis of Gazdar *et al.* (1982), where it is argued that verbs are specified lexically for the clitic, on the grounds of lexical variation (like *won't* for **willn't*, *ain't* for *%amn't*, etc.), and is consistent with the arguments in Zwicky and Pullum (1983) concerning the treatment of *n't* as an inflection rather than a clitic. In the analysis here, the verb contains a variable NEG value that needs to be checked against the NEG head, before movement to the T projection to check tense. The resulting chain is uniformly maximal, unlike that formed by the movement in the causative example in (25*b*), where the tail of the chain is minimal and its head is maximal, as in the analyses presented above.

(25) (*a*) [$_D$ Jo] [$_{(T \cup V)}$ hadn't$_j$ T [$_{(NEG \cup V)}$ t_j NEG [$_{(en \cup V)}$ t_j' cremated the cat]]]
  (*b*) *[$_D$ Jo] [$_{(T \cup V)}$ hadn't$_j$ T [$_{(NEG \cup V)}$ t_j NEG [$_V$ t_j' [$_{(en \cup D)}$ the cat cremated]]]]

Whether or not the suggestions above for the analyses of SAI, auxiliary, or *n't* cliticization are the best that can be made for English is not important for the current argument, however. What is significant is that the two exemplar constructions, causative and perfect, involve two different structural realizations. This means that some syntactic account of their differing properties can be given without assuming that there are two (or more) different verbs, *have*, or two different morphemes, Passive and Perfect in English.

5. GRAMMATICALIZATION

In addition to providing a structural difference between main verb and auxiliary-type uses of *have* in English, the hypothesis that certain verbs may appear as secondary heads (specifiers), provides a way to account for the diachronic process of grammaticalization. Example (26*a*) shows the hypothesized grammaticalization of verbs according to Hopper and Traugott (1993). This is clearly a more articulated development than that implied by current formal ideas about structure which only provide two contrasts: between contentive and functional heads (26*b*). The current hypothesis, however, provides a third

---

[30] Other analyses are possible. For example, (i) gives an analysis in which the negative clitic undergoes head movement from NEG to T with movement of the auxiliary to the secondary head (specifier) position of T. The analysis in (ii) treats the negative clitic as a secondary head of NEG which moves to become a secondary head of T. The auxiliary then moves to a second specifier position (yielding a construction with three heads). Only the analysis in (25*a*), however, provides a straightforward treatment of fronted negative auxiliaries, since only in this analysis do the auxiliary and the negative clitic form a constituent. (But see Section 6 for a suggestion that would solve this in the phonology.)

(i)   [$_D$ [$_D$ Jo]] [$_{(T \cup V)}$ had$_j$ [$_T$ n't$_i$] [$_{NEG}$ t_i [$_{(en \cup V)}$ t_j' cremated the cat]]]
(ii)   [$_D$ [$_D$ Jo]] [$_{((T \cup NEG) \cup V)}$ had$_j$ [$_{(T \cup NEG)}$ n't$_i$ T [$_{NEG}$ t_i NEG [$_{(en \cup V)}$ t_j' cremated the cat]]]]

position in the development midway between the two heads, the specifier of a functional head, (26c).

(26) (a)   Full Verb > Auxiliary > Clitic > Affix
    (b)   C-Head > F-Head
    (c)   C-Head > Specifier > F-Head

We have seen above how the development of auxiliaries as clitics is accounted for in the theory presented in this chapter, but the syntactic development into an inflection/functional head also follows naturally from the analysis of dependent auxiliaries as secondary heads. A specifier associated with a particular functional head (with a particular meaning) is dissociated from other instances of the original verb through phonological reduction, etc. At some point, the specifier merges completely with the functional head, with which it combines to give a 'composite' category, maintaining a semantics based on the earlier specifier phase but now 'bleached' of any information independent of the construction. An example that can be analysed in this way is the development of the Romance future from the Latin periphrasis *habere*-plus-infinitive construction. This is discussed by Hopper and Traugott (1993)[31] in terms of the reanalysis of an independent infinitival complement as part of the verb complex involving *habeo* 'have' with subsequent morphological changes, (27) (Hopper and Traugott 1993: 44, example 13).

(27)   *Classical Latin*: [[cantare] habeo] >
        Late Latin: [cantare habeo] >
        French: [chant-er-ai]

In the current theory, this reanalysis has a natural reconstruction in terms of the development noted in (26c). Simplifying and abstracting away from complex functional systems, the independent Latin verb *habeo* plus infinitival complement in (28a) is reinterpreted in later Latin as a doubly headed verb plus infinitive construction (28b). In the final stage, (28c), the properties of the verb and those of the infinitival projection have fully merged to give a single inflectional category (shown as *habere-Inf* below) interpreted as future tense.

(28) (a)   *Classical Latin*

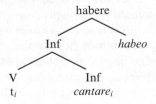

---

[31] And see Roberts (1993) for an analysis within the Principles and Parameters framework that differs substantially from that proposed below.

(*b*) *Late Latin*

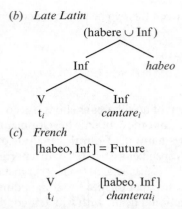

(*c*) *French*
[habeo, Inf] = Future

Analysing specifiers as secondary heads, therefore, not only provides a means of maintaining a minimal grammatical lexicon of one morph/one meaning, but provides a theoretical means of accounting straightforwardly for the process of grammaticalization.

6. UNIFYING LABELS

To end, I briefly return to the concept of unification as it applies to syntactic labels. As mentioned above, Chomsky rejects the idea that $x \cup y$ is coherent where x and y are lexical labels. In the discussion above, the operation was taken to be unification of formal syntactic features, thus excluding the semantic and phonological information that also comprises a lexical label. Treating $x \cup y$ in this way already puts some constraint on specifiers: only categorially compatible elements may appear in doubly headed (specifier–head) constructions. This is sufficient to rule out, for example, noun phrases unifying with verbal heads (all arguments must therefore be complements) or adjectives with nouns. Indeed, except for expressions of the same major category, the operation $x \cup y$ will tend to require one of x, y to be a functional category of a compatible sort.

Consideration of phonological information reinforces this restriction, given certain assumptions. Chomsky (1995*b*) takes the position that inflectional functional categories do not themselves contain phonological material (as was assumed in earlier work, e.g. Baker 1988), but that contentives appear in a numeration either fully morphologically determined (for number, tense, person, etc.) or with sufficient information that their morphological form can be determined by some morphological component. Assuming that phonological information is in the domain of the unification operation (as it should be if labels are determined by lexical expressions), and that the unification of the phonological matrices of two expressions is incoherent, then $x \cup y$ will be coherent if (and only if) one of x or y contains no phonological information; that is, if one of the expressions is phonetically null. The constraint in English against doubly filled COMP positions follows automatically from this assumption.[32]

This will again tend to favour combinations where one of the combining constituents is an inflectional functional category (normally phonologically null). This would, however, rule out both of the alternative analyses of *n't* cliticization in footnote 30, because a phonologically realized auxiliary appears with a phonologically realized negation element, a conclusion that would support the analysis in the text. However, it could be that certain elements phonologically specify a position that can be unified with the phonology of another element. For example, the negative clitic could have a phonological structure $/\phi+nt/$, where ϕ is a phonological variable. This variable would then be instantiated as part of the unification with an auxiliary verb—that is, $/hæd/ \cup /\phi+nt/$ gives $/hæd^\vartheta nt/$. This matter must be left open here, but whether or not phonological unification is allowed, it is likely to be very restricted (perhaps just to clitics) and is unlikely to be a property associated with contentives.

Finally, there is the status of the semantic features of a label to be considered with respect to the unification operation. The hypothesis that there is only one verb *have* in the causative and perfect constructions requires an account of the different interpretations of the two constructions, derived from some basic meaning of the item, possibly with pragmatic enrichment as suggested by Hopper and Traugott. The assumption that $\cup$ applies to the semantic structure of a label as well as its syntax and phonology provides the necessary means to achieve this. In other words, in $x \cup y$ the argument structures of two expressions merge into a single object with shared arguments and combined properties (cf. Grimshaw and Mester 1988). For the causative/perfect distinction, the difference in interpretation is thus due to the different way in which *have* combines with the participial phrase. In the causative, the participial (plus DP) phrase functions as the full argument of *have*, whereas in the perfect the argument structures of the verb and the participle merge so that the internal argument of *have* is not the whole participial phrase, but the verb itself. Cann (1995) shows that this distinction is sufficient to derive the basic semantic interpretation of the causative and the perfect constructions in English based on a single interpretation for both *have* and the participle morpheme *en*. In this paper, a minimal semantics is assigned to *have* that captures the facts that: the event denoted by an expression involving the verb depends on its complement (*Jo has a headache*—state, *Jo has a party*—activity); the external argument of *have* has an underspecified theta-role which is dependent on the semantic content of the Theme (*Jo has a headache*—Experiencer, *Jo had a baby*—Agent, *Jo has a table*—Possessor); and the external argument bears a locative relation

---

[32] Where languages allow the equivalent of expressions like *the students who that I saw*, it further follows that the *wh*-expression cannot combine with the complementizer as a specifier.

to the theme (cf. Kayne 1993, etc.). The participle head *en* is interpreted as denoting a state and having an internal event argument (associated with the verbal stem) that is contiguous with that state (and so may be pragmatically interpreted as cause of, or temporally prior to, the state).

In the causative construction (e.g. *Jo had the cat cremated*), the semantics of *have* and *en* are independent and the participial phrase is interpreted as the Theme of the verb. The event denoted by the *have*-phrase and the thematic role of the subject is thus determined by the semantics of the participial phrase. The latter denotes a state resulting from the activity of someone's cremating the cat and gives rise to the interpretation of the whole sentence as involving some independent event that leads to a state of a cremated cat. The least-marked relation between this event and the state is one of causation and we get the intended reading with an interpretation of the external argument of *have* as the Agent of the causing event.

In the perfect, however, the semantic structure of the participle head and the verb, *have*, are unified, so that the internal argument of *have* is identified as that of the participle (i.e. the event denoted by the verbal stem), and the state denoted by the participle head is identified as the eventuality denoted by the verb. This means, first, that there are just two eventualities in the perfect construction, not three as in the causative: the eventuality associated with the verb stem and the state that follows on from that, the classic structure of the perfect. Secondly, the role of the external argument of *have* is determined by the semantics of the verbal stem. Since the external theta-role has not been assigned directly (because of absorption by the participle head), it is a short step to identifying the unassigned role as being that of the external argument of the auxiliary. This identification is reinforced by the locative relation between the arguments of *have* which require the subject to be 'located at' (i.e. a participant in) the event denoted by the verbal stem.

If the reasoning outlined above is correct, then, semantically, the specifier relation provides a means of deriving pragmatically enriched interpretations that are compositionally determined by the semantics of two elements. It follows that doubly headed constructions will again tend to favour one of the constituents being a functional category and the other an expression whose interpretation is open to pragmatic enrichment (i.e. one that is starting to lose its independent contentive status).

Summarizing, the unification operation has the consequence that the combination of two expressions in a doubly headed construction is restricted as set out in (29).

(29) $x \cup y$ is valid iff
     (i)   the formal features of x and y are non-contradictory;
     (ii) either x or y is phonologically null; and
     (iii) the argument structure and associated thematic structure of x and y
            can merge coherently.

Notice that (29) is not a stipulation, but follows from a number of straightforward assumptions. Furthermore, these conditions do not impose any total constraint on the inherent nature of x and y. Thus, while they tend to favour one of the combining constituents being a functional category, they do not absolutely require it. This will allow some freedom (often missing from formal or semi-formal theories of syntax) for the development of grammatical expressions from contentive ones, as envisaged above.

Clearly, this analysis of specifiers as secondary heads and of the conditions imposed on the relation by the unification operation has wide-ranging consequences that require further exploration. For example, the theory disallows movement from leaving a full copy of a moved constituent. Otherwise, expressions like *who$_i$ did the student say* [$_{(C \cup WH)}$ t_i' *that the lecturer was harassing* t_i] would be ungrammatical, as the phonological information of the trace t_i' would be required to unify with that of the phonologically overt complementizer. Another important consequence is that the theory of word order to be found in Chomsky (1995a) (and Kayne 1994) is impossible under these assumptions. Since, as noted above, x and y in $x \cup y$ structures are both maximal and since $x \cup y$ is non-distinct from both x and y, notions of asymmetric c-command are problematic. Where only one of the expressions is minimal, then in the theory of Chomsky (1995a) there will be no problem: the minimal expression will asymmetrically c-command, and so precede, the minimal elements in the other (although this is a problem for Kayne). Where both x and y are non-minimal (or both minimal), c-command relations will not be asymmetric, however defined, and there will need to be something more required to define ordering relations.

Furthermore, once two constituents have been merged through unification, it is impossible to tell the difference between them with regard to their status as heads (or specifiers). It is not clear that anything, in fact, follows from this. Since both expressions (where one does not have a trace embedded in the other) are 'maximal' from the point of view of further movement, the fact that one might be labelled as the head is not significant for this operation. From the semantic point of view, the unification of the semantics of the two elements again renders the headedness of the subexpressions of the construction irrelevant. However, if one wants to define a notion of primary headedness within 'specifier–head' constructions, then it should be possible to do so, as the two subexpressions will in general differ in one of two ways, as specified in (30a) and (30b). The first distinguishes 'specifiers' from co-structures into which they have a thematic dependency, while the second defines headedness in terms of selection (a typical pre-theoretical property ascribed to heads, cf. Zwicky 1985). Notice that on many occasions both properties will pick out a single expression (e.g. where X is C and Y is DP). On other occasions, as in the auxiliary construction in English, selection may be the principal property, as for example in the perfect, where *have* is selected as the primary head in *have* ∪ *en*, again in conformity with pre-theoretical expectations.

(30) (*a*) In {*x* ∪ *y*, {*x, y*} }, if *x* contains the trace of *y*, then *x* is the primary head.
      (*b*) In {*x* ∪ *y*, {*x, y*} }, if *x* is selected, then *x* is the primary head.

Whatever solutions are found for the apparent problems noted above, the introduction of a second tree-building operation utilizing unification provides an interesting theoretical model that appears to be able to analyse common constructions straightforwardly with the minimum of ancillary assumptions; provides a theoretical account of the process of grammaticalization; and allows selectional (and other) dependency relations to be satisfied strictly locally.

REFERENCES

Baker, M. C. (1988), *Incorporation: A Theory of Grammatical Function Changing*, Chicago University Press, Chicago.

Burzio, L. (1986), *Italian Syntax*, Reidel, Dordrecht.

Cann, R. (1993), 'Patterns of Headedness', in G. Corbett, N. M. Fraser, and S. McGlashan (eds.), *Heads in Grammatical Theory*, Cambridge University Press, Cambridge, 44–72.

——(1995), 'Grammaticalization, Compositionality and *Have* in English', unpublished Ms., University of Edinburgh.

——(1996), 'Categories, Labels and Types', *Edinburgh Occasional Papers in Linguistics*, 96(3).

——and Tait, M. E. (1995), 'Raising Morphology', in C. S. Rhys, D. Adger, and A. von Klopp (eds.), *Functional Categories, Argument Structure and Parametric Variation*, Edinburgh Working Papers in Cognitive Science, vol. 9, Centre for Cognitive Science, University of Edinburgh, 1–23.

Chomsky, N. (1957), *Syntactic Structures*, Mouton, The Hague.

——(1970), 'Remarks on Nominalisation', in R. A. Jacobs and P. S. Rosenbaum (eds.), *Readings in English Transformational Grammar*, Ginn, Waltham, Mass., 184–221.

——(1986), *Barriers*, MIT Press, Cambridge, Mass.

——(1995*a*), 'Bare Phrase Structure Theory', in G. Webelhuth (ed.), *Government and Binding Theory and the Minimalist Program*, Basil Blackwell, Oxford, 385–439.

——(1995*b*), 'Categories and Transformation', in *The Minimalist Program*, MIT Press, Cambridge, Mass., 219–314.

Cowper, E. A. (1992), 'Infinitival Complements of Have', *Canadian Journal of Linguistics*, 37: 115–35.

Fukui, N. (1986), 'A Theory of Category Projection and Its Applications', unpublished doctoral dissertation, MIT.

Gazdar, G., Pullum, G. K., and Sag, I. A. (1982), 'Auxiliaries and Related Phenomena in a Restricted Theory of Grammar', *Language*, 58: 591–638.

——Klein, E., Pullum, G. K., and Sag, I. A. (1985), *Generalized Phrase Structure Grammar*, Basil Blackwell, Oxford.

Grimshaw, J. (1990), *Argument Structure*, MIT Press, Cambridge, Mass.

——and Mester, A. (1988), 'Light Verbs and θ Marking', *Linguistic Inquiry*, 19: 205–32.

Haegeman, L. (1991), *Generative Syntax*, Basil Blackwell, Oxford.

——and Zanuttini, R. (1991), 'Negative Heads and the NEG Criterion', *The Linguistic Review*, 8: 233–52.

Harris, Z. (1951), *Methods in Structural Linguistics*, Chicago University Press, Chicago.

Hopper, P. J., and Traugott, E. C. (1993), *Grammaticalization*, Cambridge University Press, Cambridge.

Jackendoff, R. (1977), *X' Theory*, MIT Press, Cambridge, Mass.

Kayne, R. (1993), 'Towards a Modular Theory of Auxiliary Selection', *Studia Linguistica*, 47: 3–31.

——(1994), *The Antisymmetry of Syntax*, MIT Press, Cambridge, Mass.

Lyons, J. (1968), *An Introduction to Theoretical Linguistics*, Cambridge University Press, Cambridge.

Pollard, C., and Sag, I. A. (1994), *Head-Driven Phrase Structure Grammar*, Chicago University Press, Chicago.

Radford, A. (1988), *Transformational Grammar*, Cambridge University Press, Cambridge.

Ritter, E., and Rosen, S. T. (1997), 'The Function of *Have*', *Lingua*, 101: 295–321.

Rizzi, L. (1990*a*), *Relativized Minimality*, MIT Press, Cambridge, Mass.

——(1990*b*), 'Speculations on Verb Second', in M. Nespor *et al.* (eds.), *Grammar in Progress: A Festschrift for Henk van Riemsdijk*, Foris, Dordrecht, 375–86.

Roberts, I. (1993), 'A Formal Account of Grammaticalization in the History of Romance Futures', *Folia Linguistica Historica*, 13: 219–58.

Steedman, M. (1988), 'Combinators and Grammars', in R. T. Oehrle, E. Bach, and D. Wheeler (eds.), *Categorial Grammars and Natural Language Structures*, Kluwer, Dordrecht, 417–42.

Stuurman, F. (1985), *Phrase Structure Theory in Generative Grammar*, Foris, Dordrecht.

Tait, M. (1991), 'The Syntactic Representation of Morphological Categories', unpublished Ph.D. dissertation, University of Edinburgh.

Verkuyl, H. (1981), 'Numerals and Quantifiers in X-Bar Syntax and Their Semantic Interpretation', in J. A. G. Groenendijk, T. M. V. Janssen, and M. B. J. Stokhof (eds.), *Formal Methods in the Study of Language*, Mathematisch Zentrum, Amsterdam, 567–99.

Warner, A. R. (1993), *English Auxiliaries: Structure and History*, Cambridge University Press, Cambridge.

Zwicky, A. (1985), 'Heads', *Journal of Linguistics*, 21: 1–30.

——and Pullum, G. K. (1983), 'Cliticization versus Inflection: English *n't*', *Language*, 59: 502–13.

3
Without Specifiers

ANNABEL CORMACK

1. ABSTRACT

I argue that UG does not make use of any special specifier projection related to a head. Rather, putative specifiers have various alternative descriptions. It is argued that because every instance of structure building (i.e. Merge) must be licensed under selection, functional heads and minor category heads must project doubly headed structures. Under these assumptions, there is no place for a Spec–head relation: instead, head–complement or head–head relations must and may suffice.

I consider specifiers of lexical heads in some detail, including Icelandic transitive expletives. I then indicate briefly how *wh*-specifiers of C, and topicalized phrases, may be accounted for.

2. INTRODUCTION

Under the Minimalist Programme of Chomsky (1995), any syntactic construct whose presence is not determined by either the articulatory–perceptual or the conceptual–intentional interface is suspect. I argue here that the notion of specifier is not so determined, that it is not useful, and that dispensing with it gives better explanations of various phenomena it has been used to explain.[1]

I take it as a fundamental principle that every instance of structure building is licensed; and the primary licensing condition for Merge is selection.[2] It follows that there are no adjunction structures as such. However, functional and minor categories do not project in the same way as lexical categories, but are to be seen as one- and two-place operators. It is the two-place operators that give rise to the bit of structure which is most usually called a specifier. This allows us to correct a long-standing error in the treatment of subjects,

---

I wish to thank Neil Smith, Rita Manzini, and two anonymous reviewers for comments and advice. Some of this work was done while I was in receipt of a grant from the Leverhulme Trust, to which I am grateful.

[1] A specifier seems to be the one (or more) non-adjunct sister to any projection of a head other than X^0 (Chomsky 1995: 245).

[2] See Cormack and Breheny (1994) and Cormack and Smith (1994).

which was based on an inadequate understanding of natural language determiners.

What I offer is the outline of a proposal; I shall have to make a number of claims for which I have argued elsewhere and which I cannot justify here for lack of space, and I will simplify by ignoring scope. After two sections introducing some background assumptions, I discuss first putative specifiers of minor categories and lexical heads, and then some putative specifiers of functional heads.[3]

3. COMPOSITIONALITY

In this section, I give some preliminary motivation for the tools I shall be using. All the relevant notions will be taken up again in later sections.

One of the recurring themes in syntactic explanation has been that of locality, in the sense that certain relations must be licensed locally. The strongest version of this would stipulate that checking of a feature that needs to be checked must take place at the Merge which introduces the relevant feature, and can only involve the two items merged: checking is strictly local and fully compositional. This extreme is untenable, but as a working hypothesis all checking and licensing should be assumed to take place locally and compositionally unless it can be shown in a particular instance that this is untenable.

As an example, consider the position when a verb phrase such as [*saw Mary*] has been constructed by Merge.[4]

(1)   [$_{VP}$ saw Mary]
(2) (*a*)   [$_T$ PAST [John [$_{VP}$ saw Mary]]]
     (*b*)   [John [$_T$ PAST [$_{VP}$ saw Mary]]]

The VP s-selects externally for an entity-type argument, to be realized as a noun phrase. But if an np is merged next, as under the Internal Subject Hypothesis, and as apparently demanded by the verb, it will not be Case-licensed. Minimalist economy considerations should lead us to reject the notion of merging incorrectly and rectifying the situation later.[5] The first conclusion should be that the np is not merged immediately, as in (2*a*), but must wait until

---

[3] The aim is to show that we can and should eliminate the construct 'specifier', rather than to show empirical consequences of the claim. There are empirical consequences, such as the prediction of the contrast in (19).

[4] The notation and the omission of some functional categories is for clarity. For convenience, I initially use the abbreviation 'vp' to refer to some projection of V, perhaps including T, and 'np' to refer to the conventional noun phrase, including D. VP and NP refer to projections of V and N, respectively, lacking just the external argument, without the functional heads T or D. For a functional head F, FP is an abbreviation for the first node at which F has all its selections discharged. A more formal bare notation derived from that of Chomsky (1995: ch. 4) is introduced below.

[5] Cormack and Smith (1997) show how to eliminate head movement.

after the Case-assigner (say, finite T) is present, as in (2*b*). The second conclusion is that the s-selection of the VP must in some sense be discharged by
T, otherwise we have unchecked s-selection in the merger. Thirdly, since there
is as yet no external argument to the VP, the merged constituent itself must
now s-select for an entity-type np. These conclusions are, I believe, correct, and
I will expand on the matter below. Any objection to this order of Merge is likely
to be implicitly semantic: intuitively, T should be combined with a saturated V
projection.[6] Since the semantically natural order of combination has been
scrambled in (2*b*), as opposed to (2*a*), it is clear that something has to be said
about the semantics. For this reason, semantic information about Merge needs
to be supplied.[7]

The standard way of putting two constituents together can be interpreted as
function-argument application in both syntax and semantics. We may
designate the operator, or combinator, that does this putting together as **A**, for
'application'. In order to account for the merging of finite T and the VP, to
derive the TP in (2*b*), it is impossible to use **A**. What is required might be
notated using Williams's (1989 and earlier) Vertical Binding index percolation.
However, the semantics is explicit if we use instead the combinator **B**, function
composition. This has exactly the syntactic and semantic 'rebracketing' effect
required, since $(\mathbf{B}\,fg).x = f.(g.x)$. Here, as is more usual, the unmarked combinator, application, is shown with an infix dot (on occasion, it may be shown
with no sign in such formulae). To verify the correctness of using **B**, put finite
T, say PAST, for f; put (*saw Mary*)' for g, and *John*' for x. For a discussion of
the categorial syntax of the combinators, see Cormack (1995).

Somewhat similarly, consider how [*John*] may be merged in (3).

(3)   John seems foolish

It is finite T which Case-licenses [*John*], so despite the fact that *foolish* s-selects
for an external argument, [*John*] cannot properly be merged until after the T
has been merged. We must, therefore, first merge *seems* with *foolish*, as in (4*b*),
rather than *John* with *foolish*, as in (4*a*).

(4) (*a*)   [seem [John foolish]]
    (*b*)   [John [seems foolish]]

Again, we must have some combinator which does the required job in the
merger of *seem* and *foolish*, since function application is appropriate for (4*a*) but
not for (4*b*). Williams's (1994) characterization of his Vertical Binding as function composition amounts to using **B** here, as well as in (1) above; and Jacobson

---

[6] For suggestions as to how long-distance agreement and quirky case can be accommodated in
a framework without np movement, see Cormack (1995).

[7] In addition, many syntactic arguments are based on semantic intuition, and it is useful to
make the assumptions overt. Notions like that of expletive items are irrevocably semantic.

(1990) explicitly uses function composition for Raising. However, Cormack and Smith (1994) argue that lexical heads always select externally, even if the associated theta-role is semantically vacuous.[8] In this case, we require something more elaborate than **B**, and make a distinction between combinators available to lexical and functional heads at Merge. The required combinator is **R**, where **R** has the effect of associating the theta-role assigned by *foolish* with the nil external selection of *seem*.[9] The result is that the argument, [*John*], binds both these roles. The semantics of **R** is given by: $\mathbf{R} \, fg = \lambda x([f.(g.x)].x)$.

The more familiar invocation of compositionality is semantic. The normal unit of syntactic well-formedness used to be the sentence, and despite changes in syntax it is still often taken to be the minimum unit to which semantic interpretation is required to apply. It is easy to see that this is not right. Phrases are normally interpretable. In particular, vps such as (5) and (6) are readily interpreted.

(5)   to admire oneself

(6)   pursued *t* (by a bear)

But in current practice, this will not be so.[10] Both the anaphor in (5) and the np-trace in (6) are standardly given their reference with respect to their antecedent—and there is no antecedent present.

The solution here is that the np-trace and the anaphor should instead be associated with the external selection of the head verb, rather than with whatever fulfils that selection. Thus in (5), what we know is that the person admired is identical to the person who does the admiring—even though we do not yet know who that person is. Similarly, in (6), we know that the person pursued is identical to whatever turns out to satisfy the external role of *pursued* (about which the verb, being passive, says nothing).[11] The meanings for *oneself* and the np-trace do not concern us here, but it should be clear that what will be needed is some legitimate way of combining the verb with each of these, quite independently of the value of any potential antecedent. Again, we need combinators. In the case of the reflexive, the combinator is possibly incorporated into the meaning (Szabolcsi 1990); in the case of np-trace, I have argued in Cormack (1995) that it is possible to give np-trace a meaning such that **R** serves the purpose.

At this point, the exact meaning of the combinators is less important than the fact that such things exist, and can do the designated syntactic and semantic jobs in parallel. Combinators have, furthermore, one suitably 'minimalist'

---

[8] See also Cormack and Breheny (1994) and Cormack (1995).

[9] This procedure requires that the Internal Subject Hypothesis is rejected. See Section 6.1 for discussion.

[10] Williams's position, as in Williams (1989), where the external argument index on a category 'serves as a sort of lambda abstractor' (p. 431), is of course compatible with the data.

[11] For further argument along these lines, see Cormack (1989).

property. They neither introduce nor require variables or indexing, although they mimic the effects of movement with coindexing.

I have pointed to one kind of syntactic and one kind of semantic anomaly in current Principles and Parameters theory. The proposal that I have put forward gives the same sort of treatment to both. In each case, properly licensed constituents are put together by Merge in somewhat non-standard ways, using combinators.

It may be observed that the emphasis on compositionality determines that for each of the heads *saw*, *foolish*, *admire*, and *pursued*, in the examples above, our attention is necessarily directed not to the specifier of the head, but rather to its external selection. I shall argue that the notion specifier is redundant.

4. SELECTION

I assume that selection is coded in a lexical entry by a feature mechanism. The idea is that selection features are arranged hierarchically, in a stack, and that they are deleted as they are checked, rendering the next feature accessible to checking, as in a categorial grammar.[12] Selection features are identified by the preceding slash '/'.

Consider a lexical head. Lexical heads encode the conceptual category of a relation. That is, a lexical head if saturated with the appropriate number of arguments encodes a proposition which is true if the encoded relation holds between those arguments. Hence, if all the selection features of a lexical head X have been deleted, we will have a phrase, of category X and type $<t>$—that is, we will have a complete proposition, which is a projection of X.[13] For example, for a verb like *think*, the c-selection and s-selection could be shown as a complex feature as in (7a). Note that I generally use a bare notation which refers simply to selection for C (the head) rather than for CP, and so on, and that there is selection for the category of the internal and external arguments.[14] The types $<e>$ and $<t>$ are the s-selection labels for the appropriate semantic kinds: entities and propositions, respectively.[15] If a clausal CP object is supplied, the C and $<t>$ features are checked and deleted, leaving the selection as in (7b). This is identical to the selection by an intransitive—just the subject is still needed.

---

[12] Svenonius (1994) argues for c-selection as a checking relation between a head and the head of its complement.

[13] I abstract away from the underdetermination which pragmatic processes determine, such as reference assignment.

[14] It may be possible to dispense with categories, but I doubt it; nor do I see any particular advantage in doing so. However, a more elaborated s-selection system than just the $<e>$ and $<t>$ types I use here is undoubtedly needed.

[15] The types $<e>$ and $<t>$ may be interpreted as giving the 'categories' of the Language of Thought, into which NL must be translated, as an alternative to the standard model theoretic semantics interpretation.

(7) (a)   think V$<t>[/D<e>/C<t>]$[16]
  (b)   think that it is raining V$<t>[/D<e>]$

In line with Cormack (1995), I assume that every internal argument, but not the external argument, is Case-licensed by the lexical head Case: either [+Case], or [–Case] (see further below). The notion of syntactic Case, like Category, seems to be a genuine UG construct. An external argument is simply that argument which binds the last (innermost) selection on the stack. It is 'external' only in the sense that it is Case-licensed externally, being assigned neither [+Case] nor [–Case] by the lexical head. Subject–object asymmetries should follow just from these two properties of external arguments.

A category with the type shown in (7b) is a semantic predicate, a useful thing in its own right. Let us refer to a projection of a lexical head X which has no unchecked Case feature as an XP. The XP will necessarily have all its internal selections saturated by licensed arguments, and will have type $<t/\alpha>$ for some $<\alpha>$.[17]

5. SPECIFIERS OR ADJUNCTS?

When the notion of 'specifier' was first introduced (in Chomsky 1970 and Jackendoff 1977), the position was used not just for subjects, but for various other items which occurred in a pre-head position, including for instance the items shown in bold in the examples in (8a), (8b), and (9a), relative to the itali-cized heads.[18] It has also been suggested by Sportiche (1994) that in a structure comparable to (9b), the initial clause is the specifier of the projection of the head *because*.

(8) (a)   **very** *hot*
  (b)   **must** *eat* the apple

(9) (a)   **so** *hot* that I burned my tongue
  (b)   [**John left** [*because* [he was hungry]]]

I claim that the structures in (8) and (9) are licensed by operator heads, re-spectively one- and two-place. In Cormack and Breheny (1994) and Cormack (1995), it is argued that minor category heads along with functional heads are syntactically as well as semantically one- or two-place operators. The under-lying premiss is that the notion of an operator is a conceptual primitive, as is the notion of a relation. An operator is a function whose output is of the same kind as its input(s) (= operands), whereas a relation is a function such that its

---

[16] The notation X[/P/Q/R] is to be read as equivalent to ((X[/P])[/Q])[/R]. Notice that the selec-tion with the most brackets is the external one, contrary to the notation used by Grimshaw (1990), who also argues for a hierarchical structure for theta-selection.

[17] $<\alpha>$ may be <nil>—see Section 6.2.

[18] The major omission here is that of possessives. This is too large an issue to discuss here.

output is a truth value, whatever the kind of its input(s) (= arguments). The Merge notation which I suggest below simply reflects the basic properties of operators: they combine with their operand(s) and become saturated according to selection, and the result has the category of the operand.

Below, I generally give the minor categories the category $_1M$ (for a one-place operator) and $_2M$ (for a two-place operator).[19] The semantic type for one- and two-place operators will be $<\alpha/\alpha>$ and $<<\alpha/\alpha>/\alpha>$, for some $<\alpha>$. Notice that where $<\alpha> = <t>$, it is not possible to tell by inspection whether we have a relation or an operator, and an NL may choose either encoding.

A head selects for its arguments hierarchically. As each set of selection features is checked, it is deleted. Given this, the suggested Merge trees for (8a) and (8b) are as in (10a) and (10b), respectively.

(10) (a)   {$_1M$, A} = MP = AP   (b)   {$_1I$, V ...} = IP = IVP

    $_1M[/A]$*very*   AP*hot* $_1I[/V]$*must*   VP*eat the apple*

The mother category label in (10a) is to be read as follows: the lexical category is A, and the operator head is $_1M$. The whole is the maximal projection of $_1M$ in the sense that $_1M$, whose selection properties licensed the whole projection, is now saturated; for this reason it is sometimes convenient to refer to the projection as MP (or, in other circumstances, as AP). The AP, which determines the lexical category of the whole, is the HOST phrase to the operator $_1M$. Note that the set {$_1M$, A} is a pair (of sets of features), not the union of the features of the two heads.[20] Similarly, in (10b), the lexical head is V (of VP), and the operator head is $_1I$ (Infl). To simplify, we may refer to the saturated projection of a one-place functional head like Infl as IP, instead of the full {I, . . . V}. The host category in (10b) is VP; because of the special status of Infl, we may conveniently refer to the whole as IVP, but not as VP.[21]

Because many such operators are closely related to sentential adjuncts, I shall assume that the correct type for the *very* in (10a) is $<t/t>$. The full c- and s- type for *very* is thus $_1M<t>[/A<t>]$. The operand AP in (10a) is of type $<t/e>$ rather than $<t>$, which means that we must use function composition, **B**, to obtain the correct output. The free availability of composition will be taken as

---

[19] It seems possible that minor categories are never selected for as such, though particular instances may be selected (e.g. projections of M*so*, below), and perhaps particular subclasses such as adverbs of motion. Distinct category labels might, however, turn out to be necessary.

[20] See discussion in Chomsky (1995: 244), where union is rightly rejected as a possibility. For a special class of exceptions, see Cann (Ch. 2, this volume). Pair construction with three heads would give {X,{Y, Z}}, not {X, Y, Z}; if all heads were projected, this would simply reiterate the tree structure. For two heads with feature sets {$f_1 \ldots f_n$} and {$F_1 \ldots F_m$}, respectively, the result would be { {$f_1 \ldots f_n$}, {$F_1 \ldots F_m$} }, not {$f_1 \ldots f_n$, $F_1 \ldots F_m$}.

[21] It is likely that tensed Infl, or T, is a binder of a temporal index, in a more articulated type system, and similarly that C may be a binder, possibly of a world index. A VP without an Infl is unlicensed, since the morphological features on V cannot be checked.

characteristic of functional heads. The proper type for $_I must$ in (10*b*) is outside the scope of this chapter, since it involves temporal matters, but we may take it as $<t/t>$ without distortion of the simplified types.

For (9*b*), our intuitive semantics tells us that *because* gives a relation between two propositions, so that it has a type $<<t/t>/t>$. However, since the *because*-phrase functions as an adjunct to a projection of V, the *because* must be coded linguistically as an operator. We need a structure which is licensed by a two-place operator, as shown in (11).[22]

(11)

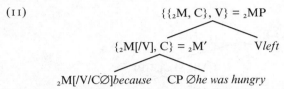

$$\{\{_2M, C\}, V\} = {}_2MP$$
$$\{_2M[/V], C\} = {}_2M' \qquad V\textit{left}$$
$$_2M[/V/C\emptyset]\textit{because} \qquad CP \, \emptyset\textit{he was hungry}$$

It has been assumed here as in (10) that the $_2M$ operator is fully head-initial.[23] It has also been assumed that the 'adjunct' is in this instance attached at the V° level.[24] The head $_C\emptyset$ is the empty complementizer corresponding to $_C that$. The word order will be rectified provided that there is some higher head to which the verb moves (perhaps the μ of Johnson 1991).[25] The host phrase is $_V left$.

Here, it is intuitively clear that what we have is lexically a projection of $_V left$, and that it is an operator projection of $_2M because$: *left* and *because*, and only these, are the heads of the projection. CP abbreviates at least $\{C\{I, V\}\}$, but neither C, nor the V and I embedded under C in CP are heads of the whole. If the host had more than one head already, then it would contribute more than one to the total of heads of the projection.

No useful generalizations are captured by identifying the host V projection as a 'specifier' of $_2M because$: for instance, it is not this constituent which is opaque to extraction, but the operator category $_2M'$, the conventional adjunct. The importance of this observation is that it is always the non-host operand which is opaque, as we shall see in further examples below. It is a theorem of combinatorial logic that, using the combinators **A** and **B**, it is possible to extract from the final, but not from the initial, operand of a two-place operator.[26]

---

[22] The structure here is comparable to the branching dependencies discussed in the section on Connectedness by Manzini (Ch. 10, Sect. 3, this volume). Note however that as well as providing the semantic information, the structure suggested here is inherently asymmetric with respect to the two operands of the head.

[23] In this framework, the linearization proposals of Kayne (1994) must be rejected.

[24] See Stroik (1990) for arguments that adjuncts may attach to projections of V as low as V°.

[25] I assume that μ attracts a category with the feature [V], (for example, $\{D, V\}$), not necessarily a V°. Then we may also obtain 'Light Predicate Raising' effects (Larson 1988), allowing for examples like *Kim [left the party] because he was hungry*.

[26] Suppose we have the two-place operator F[/P/Q]. We can combine this with the gapped constituent Q[/X], by **B**, to give F[/P/X]; but we cannot combine this with P. It is also possible to extract from both operands simultaneously, giving a parasitic gap construction. This requires the use of the combinator **S** (see Steedman 1988 or 1993).

Thus the facts here are consistent with the assumption that what we have is indeed a two-place operator, with the 'adjunct' as the initial operand, and that this in itself explains the opacity of adjuncts.

For (9a), *so hot that I burned my tongue*, there must also be some two-place operator head, but I suggest that this is not *so*, but rather the covert subordinating conjunction operator $. I assume here that this operator selects its second operand to the left (note the positions of the $ projections).[27] The semantics, like that of *very hot*, requires composition where the operator ($_2$M′, in this instance) is merged with *hot*.

(12) $\{\{_2M, CP\}, \{_1M, A\}\} = {}_2\$P$

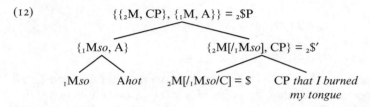

$\{_1Mso, A\}$ $\{_2M[/_1Mso], CP\} = {}_2\$'$

$_1Mso$ $Ahot$ $_2M[/_1Mso/C] = \$$ CP *that I burned my tongue*

Here, considering the final constituent, the operator head is $_2M$ $, and the host category is $\{_1M, A\}$. The heads of the whole are thus $, *so*, and *hot*. Nothing in the CP is a head of $\{\{_2M, CP\}, \{_1M, A\}\}$.

As with $_2Mbecause$, the category $_2\$'$ is opaque to extraction, whereas the host may be transparent, as we see from (13).

(13) (a)   Which child is Mary so fond of *t* that she spoils?
     (b)   *Which bicycle is Mary so fond of Jim that she gave him *t*?

For lexical heads, the selection discharged last is distinguished as lacking any Case-licensing feature, where Case licensing is implicated in selection discharge. For minor and functional heads, the final selection is distinguished as giving the lexical category of the maximal projection of the head. These two final selections give rise to the distinguished constituents 'subject of' and 'host of', respectively, relative to a head.

6. SPEC OF LEXICAL HEAD

6.1. *External selection and the Internal Subject Hypothesis*

One of the reasons for the attractiveness of the Internal Subject Hypothesis (ISH) is that it gives a natural expression to the fact that the subject associated

---

[27] The correct position is probably to the left, with movement of the *so*P to $, so that the operator is fully left-headed, like the other two-place operators. The motivation for the movement would be to give the canonical iconic order of the two operands which is consistent with the cause–effect interpretation of the conjunction $ (see Cormack and Smith 1994 for discussion).

with a lexical head is canonically related to that head semantically in just the same way as the internal arguments are, despite the fact that it may appear separated from the lexical head by other heads such as raising verbs. However, in the formalism suggested above, this relation will be directly given in the syntax and semantics associated with the external theta-selection. For example, a transitive verb like *think* is not entered in the lexicon with only its internal argument given, in the traditional manner, as '—CP', but as having a selection specification $V<t>[/D<e>/C<t>]$. Thus, provided that our syntax and semantics are appropriately compositional, whatever argument eventually binds the external theta-selection will necessarily be properly associated with the V and its meaning. The ISH is not necessary in order to capture this fact.

Further, the ISH is an obstacle to a proper understanding of compositional semantics. Consider for instance (14).

(14)   John left the room angry

Since nothing overt selects for the adjective, and Merge must be licensed by the discharge of selection features, it must be selected for as one of the two operands of a covert two-place operator, the conjunction head \$. The ISH requires that we have an external argument PRO inside the AP *angry*, coindexed with [*John*]. This entails that this second operand has type $<t>$ level. But if we follow Cormack and Smith (1994) in assimilating these structures to serials, and Collins's (1997) arguments for 'object sharing' in serial structures, then this is incorrect: the \$ conjunction must be at the $<<t/\text{nil}>/e>$ level, conjoining the unaccusative $A°$ *angry* to the unaccusative $V°$ *left the room* (see Section 6.2). This Merge takes place before T[PAST] and [*John*] are merged, so we avoid both of the undesirable artefacts of PRO and coindexing.

It is not even the case that every external theta-selection is bound by an argument. For example, within a noun phrase, such as [*every dog*], there is an NP, [NP dog], which is a predicate. But this predicate does *not* have a subject: its external selection is discharged by being bound by the determiner [*every*] (see further below).

The conclusion, then, is that there is no specifier *content* associated directly with the projection of a lexical head.[28]

6.2. *Empty specifiers of lexical projections*

One of the uses of an empty specifier position is to act as a landing-site for raising. It has been suggested above that a lexical head always selects externally for a category D;[29] this selection must have a type. The hierarchical ordering

---

[28] One more argument against the ISH is noted in Section 7.1 below. Other arguments against the ISH are given in Bobaljik (1995) and Koizumi (1995).

[29] It follows that subject clauses are headed by D (phonologically null in English, but overt in modern Greek for instance).

of selection offers a straightforward way of encoding this: we take it to act like a place-value system, with zero as a place holder. Consider an unaccusative head. An unaccusative lexical head is one whose sole argument behaves like an object rather than a subject. It must select like a transitive, but the meaning postulates associated will have nothing to say about the external role, which remains vacuous. Cormack and Smith (1994) notate such a role with the type <nil>. Unaccusative *arrive*, then, can have a meaning *arrive″* related to a one-place conceptual meaning *arrive′* as follows:

(15)   arrive″ = $\lambda x \lambda y (\text{arrive}'(x))$

It will have selection given by V<*t*>[/D<nil>/D<*e*>], with the internal selection having a [–Case] feature. The idea that every lexical head 'has a specifier' is reduced to the requirement that every lexical head has a final selection without a Case feature—but this selection may be semantically nil. Internal arguments can equally be given <nil> roles—I argue in Cormack (1995) that a 'raising to (<nil>) object' is how ECM and SC subjects are licensed.

7. SUBJECTS

The next question then is the overt position of a subject in a tensed clause. We ignore the split-Infl hypotheses, and assume that Infl is a one-place operator on VP. If subjects are not in the Spec of IP, then it must be that IP is within the selection of the head of the subject (i.e. of D). Determiners are semantically two-place binding operators (Barwise and Cooper 1981). The null hypothesis is that they will be two-place binding operators syntactically as well, which is what is needed.[30] In a variable-free notation, they canonically bind a pair of predicate operands: an NP and an XP.[31] Thus a noun phrase is not a DP, but more properly a D′, which is a complex operator category with the meaning of a generalized quantifier. Simplifying, a subject noun phrase will be the operator category [$_{\{D, N\}}$ D NP] within the whole D projection [$_{\{\{I, V\}, \{D, N\}\}}$ [$_{\{D, N\}}$ D NP] I VP]], where NP and VP are predicates. A noun phrase may usefully be referred to as a DNP, and the second operand as IVP. The determiner binds the external selection in both the predicates, and is the functional head of the V-headed lexical projection. In the diagram in (16), NP and VP abbreviate N<*t*>[/D<*e*>] and V<*t*>[/D<*e*>], respectively.

---

[30] Manzini (Ch. 10, this volume) also takes D to have two operands.

[31] In a variable-free notation, two-place binders have types such as <<*t*/<*t*/*e*>>/<*t*/*e*>>, which is not an operator type by the earlier definition, but only under a definition whereby they map functions into functions. It is convenient to refer to them as operators, since they have properties in common with ordinary operators.

(16)

$$\{\{{}_2D, N\}, \{{}_1I, V\}\} = {}_2DP$$

$\{{}_2D[/VP], N\} = D' = DNP \qquad \{{}_1I, V\} = IP = IVP$

${}_2D[/VP/NP] \qquad NP \qquad {}_1I[/VP] \qquad VP$

every   *dog*   **pres**   *barks*

Note: *every* is a two-place binding operator of type D<t>[/VP<t/e>/DP<t/e>].

Notice that just as we cannot extract from the first operand of a ${}_2M$ head, so we cannot (in general) extract from DNP, which is the first operand of a ${}_2D$ head, as seen in (17).[32]

(17)   *Which problem did you dispute [the [claim that Alice had solved *t*]]?

It is not the case that all nps are headed by binding ${}_2D$. In particular, this is not true of predicate nps, such as the bracketed one in (18), where the D *no* must be a non-binding one-place operator, ${}_1D$.

(18)   Ursula considers Gerald [no fool]

In such cases, the prediction will be that the np is not opaque to extraction. This prediction is borne out, as we see from the contrast in (19). In (19*a*), the bracketed np is an argument, and must be headed by ${}_2D$; in (19*b*), with raising *be*, a predicational np is headed by ${}_1D$.

(19) (*a*)   *Which mountain did you meet [the first man to climb *t*]?
    (*b*)   Which mountain was Tensing [the first man to climb *t*]?

If a subject DNP is defined as a 'specifier' of IP, then it is possible to set up a 'Spec–head' relation, which may be for instance a checking configuration. If the correct result of Merge is as in (16), we have an alternative. First, we may take the head D of DNP, rather than DNP, to be first member of the relation. Secondly, D is related to at least V (and N) by selection, and to both Infl and V (and N) by the relation 'head of complement'. This means that there is a head–head relation between D and Infl, which can be exploited in checking. Thus, once we have D as a two-place operator, we can use more primitive relations in place of the Spec–head relation.

7.1. *Binders and Case licensing*

I shall assume (as in Cormack 1995) that the discharge of a lexical selection is mediated and additionally licensed by a functional head AGR, which must be

---

[32] I claim, then, that examples like that in (i) must have an alternative syntactic structure.
(i)   Who did you say you met [the [father of *t*]]?

local to ensure compositionality. AGR has semantic content. It may have as its semantic content the combinator $\underline{A}$ or the combinator $\underline{R}$. Of these, $\underline{A}$ (function-argument application) induces binding of the theta-selection by a saturated complement. The raising combinator $\underline{R}$ induces a semantic equivalent of a generalized raising, so that the binding of the external selection of the complement (which may be np-trace) is deferred. It will be bound along with the next theta-selection of the head. The choice between $\underline{A}$ and $\underline{R}$ is determined by the Case properties of the local projection of a lexical head, with [+Case] being checked by $\underline{A}$ and [–Case] being checked by $\underline{R}$. Lexical XP has no Case feature, as noted above. In consequence, we must assume that a determiner as in (16) above is not of itself licensed to combine by $\underline{A}$ with its second operand, unlike normal operators, although it is licensed to combine by $\underline{A}$ with its first operand.

This has two consequences which are relevant here. First, object DNPs can have essentially the same structure as subject DNPs, with the D selecting for NP and a projection of a lexical category, X^n. The local licensing by AGR will give rise to structures with the form of (20).

(20) $[_{AgrP} \underline{A}\text{-ate} [_{2D} \text{the} [_{NP} \text{bread}]] [_V t]]$

We may suppose that the movement of the verb to AGR is forced by the checking requirements of AGR with respect to the Case licensing on the verb. This AgrP is a properly licensed predicate, with a well-formed semantic interpretation. Notice that the DNP [*the bread*] is functioning with respect to the transitive [*ate*] (reconstructed), just as a subject acts with respect to a predicate, as in (16). Any one projection of a lexical head, with its single accessible selection, permits just one binder of this kind, imposing binary branching and partially paralleling the 'single complement' suggestion of Larson (1988).

Secondly, if we take into account AGR, and take finite C rather than finite I as the [+Case] licenser for subjects,[33] we get the more elaborated structure in (21), where C will have null phonological content in root sentences in English.

(21) $[_{AgrP} \underline{A}\text{-that} [_D \text{every} [_{NP} \text{dog}]] [_C t [_I \textbf{pres} [_{VP} \text{barks}]]]]$

Here, the subject cannot be merged unless the [+Case] operator C has been merged. This provides another reason for rejecting the ISH.

It is an $\underline{R}$ content of AGR which allows for subjects separated from their theta-assigners by other lexical heads. For example, if we have an intervening

---

[33] I depart here from Cormack (1995). Given a uniform attraction of the [+Case] head to AGR, the Case-licenser for subjects cannot be one which hosts auxiliaries in uninverted clauses. Haegeman (1992) argues for C as the nominative Case-licenser in West Flemish, as does Platzack (1986) for Germanic generally (but specifically excluding English).

head *seems* in (21), because *seems* Case-licenses **R** on its internal selection and selects for an IVP with *to*, we have the structure in (22).

(22)   [$_{AGR}$ **A**-that [$_D$ every [$_{NP}$ dog]] [$_C t$ [$_I$ **pres** [$_{AGR}$ **R**-seems [$_{VP}$ vt [$_{IVP}$ to bark]]]]]]]

The combinator **R** composes [*seems*] with [*to bark*], with the effect that the binder of external selection of the whole discharges both the external (nil) selection of *seems* and the external type $<e>$ selection of *bark*. The AgrP itself has type {AGR, V}$<t>$[/D$<t>$]. No subject np-trace or coindexing is required for this process, which is simply a form of Merge (see Cormack 1995 for discussion). Again, the absence of Spec positions in the two vps does not prevent the correct semantics being induced.

Descriptively, as well as theoretically, the term 'specifier' is unnecessary. We already have 'subject of', which will apply, twice, to [*every dog*] in (22). We still might wish to distinguish that argument which is Case-licensed by C, so that the subjects of small clause and ECM predicates would be excluded; but this can be referred to as 'subject of the clause'.

7.2. *Icelandic transitive expletives*

The basic idea for expletives is that the expletive occupies a position to which a normal theta-role is not assigned: the head verb assigns a nil role externally. In English, *there*-type expletives are licensed if and only if the verb is unaccusative or passive.[34] An unaccusative verb selects for an external argument, but assigns no semantic role to that argument. For a verb like *fall*, the type will be as in (23).

(23)   V$<t>$[/D$<$nil$>$/D$<e>$]

We may assume that the general unaccusative licensing a *there*-expletive will be as in (24). Such a type could arise for instance from passivization of a ditransitive.

(24)   X$<t>$[/D$<$nil$>$/D$<e>$/J$<j>$/K$<k>$/ . . .]
         where J, K, . . . and *j, k*, . . . are variables over categories and their associated types, respectively.

There-type expletives must also have a local associate DNP, generally an indefinite. Since Icelandic permits transitive expletives, the natural conclusion is that transitive verbs in Icelandic must be (at least in these structures) unaccusative in this sense. That is, the agent discharges the second selection, not the first external one.

There seem to be two ways this might arise. First, the lexical entry for all

---

[34] There are apparent exceptions to this generalization which I will ignore here.

verbs might provide the extra place. Perhaps is it designated for a topic, with the subject being able to move to that position. Alternatively, the extra selection is constructed by means of a semantic–syntactic operator which appears in a Merge tree.[35] There is evidence that such an operator is needed, at least for some Scandinavian languages.

Consider the Swedish pseudo-coordination[36] example in (25), from Josefsson (1991), and the parallel examples from the Trøndelag dialect of Norwegian (data from Tor Åfarli, personal communication, 1996) in (26).

(25)   I köket står det en kwinna och lagar middag
       in the-kitchen stands there a woman and cooks dinner
       'In the kitchen, there stands a woman and cooks dinner.'

(26) (a)   Det kom en mann og reparerte bilen min
           'There came a man and repaired my car.'

     (b)   Det satt et menneske og leste avisen
           'There sat a person and read the newspaper.'

In (25), [*står*] must be unaccusative to license [*det*] 'there'. But conjunction will only be licensed if the conjuncts have the same selection features; that is, both [*står*] and [*lagar middag*] must be either regular or unaccusative predicates. However, transitive expletives are ungrammatical in Swedish, so presumably the conjunct [*lagar middag*] is not unaccusative. We must assume then that the $P conjunct phrase is a regular predicate, but that it stands in the scope of an operator NIL1 which provides a joint extra nil external selection, licensing the [*det*]. The conjunction in (25) is subordinating, asymmetric conjunction, as can be seen by the fact that the initial verb, the host, may be extracted to raise to C. This allows us to explain the licensing of NIL1. NIL1 is licensed if it is in a checking relation with a potentially unaccusative verb, and the relevant checking configuration is sensitive just to the head verb of the asymmetric conjunct, [*står*].[37] The same must apply to license the Norwegian examples.

The properties of the semantic/syntactic NIL1 operator are quite straightforward. It is clear that the operator has the phrase [*lagar middag*] not just the verb *lagar* in its scope. Before the application of the operator, this phrase has a type $<t/e>$, because it is a predicate. The verb *står* must have the same type—that is, its basic conceptual monotransitive type. The operator turns a verb of type $<t/e>$ into one of type $<<t/\text{nil}>/e>$, simply by adding a vacuous lambda-abstraction. Its semantics is $\lambda V \lambda x \lambda y (V.x)$. Syntactically, the new head is now

---

[35] See Cormack and Smith (1997) for a treatment of the passive by means of a somewhat similar operator.

[36] Johannessen (1993) calls this 'unbalanced' coordination. Like the English *run and . . .* examples, extraction of the object is allowed, in apparent violation of the across-the-board requirement.

[37] The checking relation in this case is probably selection.

transitive (of the unaccusative subspecies), so permitting the associated expletive in the subject position.

Then Icelandic would be differentiated from Swedish and Norwegian by the licensing conditions on this operator NIL1. In Icelandic, it would be freely available, applying optionally to all intransitives, and to transitives; but in Swedish, it is licensed only if it is in a checking relation to a verb belonging to the appropriate subclass of intransitives (i.e. the unaccusatives).[38]

Chomsky's suggestion (Chomsky 1995: 354ff.) amounts to admitting an extra specifier position for T in the syntactic structure, just for languages with Transitive Expletive Constructions. The 'multiple-checking' parameter seems to have few other uses, though Collins (1995) applied it to serial verb morphology.[39] Mine amounts to using the NIL1 operator, which is available in all languages, to construct an extra position in the theta-structure of the verb phrase. The parameter relates to the selection properties of the NIL1 operator. There are possibly empirical differences between the two positions, and the consequences of my suggestion need further investigation.

8. SPEC OF FUNCTIONAL HEAD

8.1. *Spec of C:* wh-*elements*

In a theory not admitting specifiers, since C in a root sentence is a one-place operator, and may host an inverted auxiliary, *wh*-phrases must be headed by some other category. I postulate a head, say W, which may host a one- or a two-place operator, and which selects for CP. It is probably the case that the W is a feature on some other category—for example D, in the instances discussed here—rather than an independent category. If so, then this feature will be selected for instance by *ask*, and must itself be allowed to select for C. I shall continue to use W as a category for simplicity of exposition.

Who, for instance is a one-place binding operator, whereas *which* is a two-place binding operator. In a variable-free format, as with quantifiers, the operands need to be predicates. The final operand in each case needs to be a predicate based on a CP.[40] We will come to the treatment of the gap or trace in a moment.

(27) (*a*) I know [[$_{2}$W which [$_{NP}$ man]] [$_{CP}$ John saw *t*]]
    (*b*) I know [[$_{1}$W who] [$_{CP}$ John saw *t*]]

---

[38] The parameter will also need to determine whether NIL1 is optional or obligatory in these languages when there is an unaccusative verb. I leave the question open here.

[39] See Cormack and Smith (1997) for an alternative account of the required checking parameter.

[40] *Wh*-in-situ must not of course select for C, but simply for V; we may assume this is regulated by the fact that it has a feature marking it as dependent (on the higher W).

We will have the structure in (28) for the embedded clause in (27*a*), where ∅ is an empty [+finite]C.

(28)

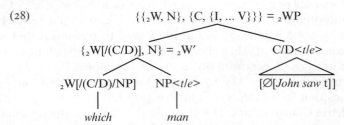

$$\{\{_2W, N\}, \{C, \{I, ... V\}\}\} = {}_2WP$$

$$\{_2W[/(C/D)], N\} = {}_2W' \qquad\qquad C/D<t/e>$$

$$_2W[/(C/D)/NP] \qquad NP<t/e> \qquad\qquad [\varnothing[John\ saw\ t]]$$

which   *man*

Note that, as with the other two-place operators, the first operand is opaque to extraction. Note also that there is a head–head relationship between the W head and the C of its second operand, so that this will serve instead of the usual Spec–head relation.

I shall only consider two cases here: object gap and subject gap. Let us consider object gaps first. In a standard Combinatorial grammar, where constituents are canonically combined with function application, *wh*-movement is modelled by replacing function application with composition of functions. In the grammar proposed in Cormack (1995), we have **R**, as well as **A**. Suppose the CP is constructed by replacing each instance of **A** or **R** with its composing analogue, **B** or **R***, respectively.[41] Then we get the right result, that is, a constituent of type <*t/e*>, for say [∅ *John saw*], but the [+Case] feature on the final word *saw* has not been checked. It can only be checked by offering an 'internal' argument, and adding the appropriate AGR**A**. The constituent thus produced is suitable for a Right Node Raising structure like that in (29), where [*the rabbit*] is an in situ object of the *but* conjunction of two composed phrases.[42]

(29)   I think [[(that) John saw] but [(that) Mary didn't see]] the rabbit

Suppose then that to obtain *wh*-movement, the [+Case] feature which ensures a local argument is suppressed.[43]

(30)   X[+Case][/D] may freely appear as X[/D], where X is lexical.

We do not need to make any stipulation as to where the [/D] feature is saturated, if we assume that WP is not only selected in embedded questions, but is

---

[41] The composing analogue of **A** is **B**, defined by **B** $fg = \lambda x.f(g(x))$. For **B**^{n}, the generalized composition combinators, see e.g. Steedman (1988, 1993). The composing analogue of **R** is say **R***, defined by: **R*** $fg = \lambda x\mathbf{R}\ f(g(x))$; see Cormack (1995).

[42] Recollect that the Case-licenser is attracted to AGR. I assume that in a composed structure, pied-piping of the whole is obligatory.

[43] We may ensure that the correct combinator is chosen by stipulating that if the head has two non-Case-licensing selections, then the composing combinator is selected; normally, only the external selection is marked for neither [+Case] nor [–Case]. Island effects will need to be accounted for: see Szabolcsi and Zwarts (1990) and Steedman (1996) for discussion.

checked locally in root questions. Let us assume an interpretable [+Q] feature on C, in root questions, with a strong V feature to attract a verb, which for independent reasons must be an auxiliary in English.

Concomitantly, the two-place operator *which* must be defined to combine with its final operand by $\underline{A}$, just as non-binding operators do. This is in contrast to regular determiners, which license no combinator for their final operand, as noted in Section 7.1. If we mark the $\underline{A}$-licensing on the selection marker, then a *wh*-two-place binder will have category $W[/_{\underline{A}}CP/_{\underline{A}}NP]$, whereas an argument determiner has category $D[/XP/_{\underline{A}}NP]$.

The provision of (30) can be generalized to CP gaps, and to indirect argument gaps. But it is clear that it simply does not allow subject gaps: subjects are not licensed by a lexical X, but by C, and C[+Case] does not fit the format of (30) since its selection is for [/V]. In consequence, there will be no subject gaps unless special provision is made in the functional lexicon, and in particular by allowing variants of the C[+Case] complementizers such as *that* or *for*.

Since subject gaps in embedded clauses are desirable, some languages offer variant complementizers which permit subject gaps. In English, there is a $_C\varnothing$ which is like $_C that$ (in features and meaning) except that is assigns no [+Case] feature; in French, there is a $_C qui$ which is like $_C que$ except that it assigns no [+Case] feature. It will select simply for IVP, and the external selection will be passed compositionally up the tree, as required.[44] There appears to be no subject-gap equivalent of $_C for$ in English, as we see from (31).

(31)   *What does the cat long (for) to appear in her dish?

In root subject questions, a *wh*-NP must select for C without Case licensing, since it supplies the combinator $\underline{A}$ (to discharge the external role) itself. The structure formed will be of the form shown in (32). Notice that V-to-C movement will be string-vacuous, as required.

(32)   [$_{WP}$ [$_W$ which [$_{NP}$ man]] [$_{CP}$ $_C\varnothing$ [$_{IVP}$ saw the dog]]]

8.2. *Topics*

In English, arguments may be topicalized. The provision of (30), and the variants of C, will already almost allow this. The tree in (28) will be well formed if the *wh*-NP is replaced by a DNP, provided that the D's second operand may be of category C[/D] and that, like a *wh*-NP, it may be licensed to combine with its final operand by $\underline{A}$. If, as suggested in Section 8.1, W is a feature on D, rather than a category, then we would expect topicalization to be possible unless the two properties mentioned above were specifically restricted to Ds with the [+W] feature.

---

[44] Complementizers with and without the [+Case] feature select with $/_{\underline{A}}$.

However, the unrestricted application of this mechanism would allow the selection released from Case licensing to be saturated by a DNP anywhere in the tree c-commanding its usual place, and also would allow any number of such displaced DNPs.[45] Suppose we require that the DNP be of type $<t/<t/e>>$. Then this means that when it binds, there is only one unbound selection. This will give topicalizations corresponding to the *wh*-binders above. We can impose this restriction on the relevant DNPs, since they must in any case be different from ordinary Case-licensed DNPs. We simply require the D to have only the canonical type $<<t/<t/e>>/<t/e>>$. If the new provision applies to *wh*-heads as well then it will only be possible to have one *wh*-item in a raised position.

If subjects obtain their AGR licence from C[+Case], then a topicalized object should appear outside C. Consider the examples in (33).

(33) (*a*)   *What will if there is no food in the house Mary eat?
     (*b*)   ?What, if there is no food in the house, will Mary eat?
     (*c*)   If there is no food in the house, what will Mary eat?

These root questions have movement of C[+Case] to AGR, and V to C, so that *will* marks the AGR position. The example (33*a*), where AGR-C is not adjacent to the subject *Mary*, is sharply ungrammatical, as we would expect. In Modern Greek, the same word order is available in embedded clauses, as in (34) (from Tsimpli 1990), but the English equivalent is ungrammatical, as can be seen from the gloss.

(34)   Mu-ipe to vivlio oti edhose sti Maria
       me-said the book that gave-3S to-the Maria
       'He said to me that he gave the book to Maria' (where 'the book' is focused).

Let us assume that in English, a lexically selected complementizer must be the adjacent head to its selector.[46] In order to accommodate topicalization in embedded positions, we must postulate CP recursion (Rizzi and Roberts 1989) or the 'split C' of Rizzi (1997). Let us suppose $_C$*that* may select for $_C$∅[+Case], where $_C$*that* must have no Case feature. This also gives the head position required for V to C in embedded clauses like that in (35).

(35)   He claimed that never before had he eaten such a dreadful meal.

The claim of this section, then, is that topicalization does not involve a separate Topic head.[47] The displaced phrase is just what it looks like: a DNP, in

---

[45] Such movement might correctly characterize scrambling in some languages.

[46] This is not string-adjacency: a head will be 'head-adjacent' to the highest of the heads of its complement. Note that in general, I have been assuming (unlike Manzini in Ch. 10 of this volume) that a head may check, e.g. for selection, any of the heads of its complement, not just the adjacent one.

[47] Rizzi (1997) shows that in Italian structures with split C, the structure . . . C (Top*) (Foc) (Top*) C . . . is licensed. The 'Top' phrases are due to Clitic Left Dislocation and are not binders; it is the 'Foc' phrases that correspond to English topicalization. The distribution is as expected

the examples above. It further follows that there is no special 'topicalization' semantics involved, and that whatever pragmatic effect is obtained is obtained simply by virtue of the early and non-canonical presentation of the DNP content to the hearer. Once such a DNP has been presented, the rest of the provisions, such as the **A** combinator licensing, and special versions of C or V, must follow, if the sentence is to be grammatical. Thus, provided that topicalization is to the left, there seems to be no need for any other device to explain the 'optional movement' of the DNP.[48]

In the preceding subsections, I have offered some alternatives that are available to serve instead of specifiers of functional heads. The discussion has been restricted to the rudiments of A′-binding of canonically [+Case]-licensed selections. This leaves [–Case]-licensed selections, and adjuncts, not discussed at all.

8.3. *Other pre-IP heads*

One advantage of the assumption of separate heads C and W is that selection is better articulated. It also immediately raises questions as to whether the head for relative clauses or exclamatives is the same as that for questions, and whether there is a separate head for conditionals. Since it is necessary to account for such UG possibilities as the Dutch in (36),[49] we may assume that there are at least three possible pre-IP heads, corresponding to *wh*-relative, conditional, and complementizer items.

(36)   Hij weet welke jongen of dat je gezien hebt.
        he knows which boy if that you seen have
        'He knows which boy you have seen.'

Then for instance conditional inversion in English, as in *Had it t rained, I would have got wet*, would have V raising to the Conditional head, rather than to C.[50] Because of semantic similarities between the various traditional *wh*-Spec CP operators, we might assume that the differentiation is made by features. So for instance if W may contain a semantic feature [+Q] for a question, [+Exc] for an exclamative, or [+Rel] for a relative, we can let verbs like *ask* select for [+Q], where this will include W[+Q] and Cond[+Q]. Similarly, *easy* may make a selection for {W[Op], C*for*}, where Op is the empty operator.[51] Because there

---

under my characterization of topicalization: a topicalized/focused DNP can be realized anywhere between the two C heads, and hence can interrupt a sequence of CLD phrases.

[48] A special feature could of course be imposed on the head of these displaced phrases. Notice that even under an 'economy' constraint (Chomsky 1991), no violation will occur, since because displaced and Case-licensed DNPs are headed by Ds with distinct properties, the numerations would differ in topicalized and non-topicalized structures.

[49] The example is from Eric Hoekstra via Christer Platzack, thanks to the Linguist List.

[50] See also Rizzi (1997).

[51] The semantics required for $_W$Op is simply the identity function $\lambda P.P$.

is no subject-gap-licensing version of $_C for$, structures with the empty operator correctly have non-subject gaps (unless there is further clausal embedding).

9. CHECKING

If there are no specifiers, then there is no Spec–head checking. Chomsky (1991) noted that checking for Case at that time took place in two configurations: Spec–head and head–complement. Despite saying at the time that the latter was the more basic relation, he opted to uniformize the checking so that both were licensed in Spec–head configurations. This was necessitated by the current analysis of subjects as having $_1D$ instead of $_2D$ heads. A better account of ECM structures came as a side-effect.

Under the proposals above, Spec–head checking can and must be replaced by some variety of head–head checking. This checking is not under head–head adjunction. It is either between a head and some head of its complement, or may need to be 'at a distance' as argued for on independent grounds in Cormack and Smith (1997). Where currently covert movement is employed, head–head checking when the constituent is in situ will equally serve. A 'raising to object' account of ECM structures is made available again by the postulation of nil roles (Cormack 1995), so that here too an explanation comes as a side-effect.

10. CONCLUSIONS

What I have proposed seems to me to be a simplification of the current theory, and one which permits a more natural relation between syntax and semantics. From the point of view of syntax, the suggested changes demand the reformulation of a number of principles. In some instances, this would be fairly trivial, but it is my hope that in other instances the move would provide new results and insights.

In sum, I claim that dispensing with both specifiers and adjuncts leads to analyses that are both syntactically simpler and semantically more transparent, adding explanatory content without loss of descriptive power.

REFERENCES

Barwise, J., and Cooper, R. (1981), 'Generalised Quantifiers and Natural Language', *Linguistics and Philosophy*, 4: 159–219.

Bobaljik, J. D. (1995), 'Morphosyntax: The Syntax of Verbal Inflection', Ph.D. dissertation, MIT.

Chomsky, N. (1970), 'Remarks on Nominalization', in R. A. Jacobs and P. S. Rosenbaum (eds.), *Readings in English Transformational Grammar*, Ginn, Waltham, Mass., 184–221.

——(1991), 'Some Notes on Economy of Derivation and Representation', in R. Freidin (ed.), *Principles and Parameters of Comparative Grammar*, MIT Press, Cambridge, Mass., 417–54.

——(1995), *The Minimalist Program*, MIT Press, Cambridge, Mass.

Collins, C. (1995), 'Serial Verb Constructions and the Theory of Multiple Feature Checking', Ms., Cornell University.

——(1997), 'Argument Sharing in Serial Verb Constructions', *Linguistic Inquiry*, 28: 461–97.

Cormack, A. (1989), 'The Syntax and Semantics of Definitions', Ph.D. dissertation, London (forthcoming 1998, Garland).

——(1995), 'The Semantics of Case', *UCL Working Papers in Linguistics*, 7: 234–76.

——and Breheny, R. (1994), 'Projections for Functional Categories', *UCL Working Papers in Linguistics*, 6: 35–61.

——and Smith, N. (1994), 'Serial Verbs', *UCL Working Papers in Linguistics*, 6: 63–88.

————(1997), 'Checking Features and Split Signs', *UCL Working Papers in Linguistics*, 9: 223–52.

Grimshaw, J. (1990), *Argument Structure*, MIT Press, Cambridge, Mass.

Haegeman, L. (1992), *Theory and Description in Generative Syntax: A Case Study in West Flemish*, Cambridge University Press, Cambridge.

Jackendoff, R. (1977), *X-Bar Syntax: A Study of Phrase Structure*, MIT Press, Cambridge, Mass.

Jacobson, P. (1990), 'Raising as Function Composition', *Linguistics and Philosophy*, 13: 423–76.

Johannessen, J. (1993), 'Coordination: A Minimalist Approach', Ph.D. dissertation, Oslo.

Johnson, K. (1991), 'Object Positions', *Natural Language and Linguistic Theory*, 9: 577–636.

Josefsson, G. (1991), 'Pseudocoordination: A VP + VP Coordination', *Working Papers in Scandinavian Syntax*, 47: 130–56.

Kayne, R. S. (1994), *The Antisymmetry of Syntax*, MIT Press, Cambridge, Mass.

Koizumi, M. (1995), 'Phrase Structure in Minimalist Syntax', Ph.D. dissertation, MIT.

Koopman, H., and Sportiche, D. (1991), 'The Position of Subjects', *Lingua*, 85: 211–58.

Larson, R. (1988), 'Light Predicate Raising', Ms., MIT.

Platzack, C. (1986), 'COMP, INFL, and Germanic Word Order', in L. Hellan and K. K. Christensen (eds.), *Topics in Scandinavian Syntax*, Reidel, Dordrecht, 185–234.

Rizzi, L. (1997), 'The Fine Structure of the Left Periphery', in L. Haegeman (ed.), *Elements of Grammar. A Handbook of Generative Syntax*, Kluwer, Dordrecht, 281–337.

——and Roberts, I. (1989), 'Complex Inversion in French', *Probus*, 1: 1–30.

Sportiche, D. (1994), 'Adjuncts and Adjunction', *GLOW Newsletter*, 32: 54–5.

Steedman, M. (1988), 'Combinators and Grammars', in R. T. Oehrle, E. Bach, and D. Wheeler (eds.), *Categorial Grammars and Natural Language Structures*, Reidel, Dordrecht, 417–42.

——(1993), 'Categorial Grammar', *Lingua*, 90: 221–58.

——(1996), *Surface Structure and Interpretation*, MIT Press, Cambridge, Mass.

Stroik, T. (1990), 'Adverbs as V Sisters', *Linguistic Inquiry*, 21: 654–61.

Svenonius, P. (1994), 'C-Selection as Feature-Checking', *Studia Linguistica*, 48: 133–55.

Szabolcsi, A. (1990), 'Combinatory Grammar and Projection from the Lexicon', in I. Sag and A. Szabolcsi (eds.), *Lexical Matters*, CSLI, Stanford, Calif., 241–68.

——and Zwarts, F. (1990), 'The Semantic Properties of Composed Functions and the Distribution of Wh-Phrases', in M. Stokhof and L. Torenvliet (eds.), *Proceedings of the Seventh Amsterdam Colloquium*, Institute for Language Logic and Information, Amsterdam, 529–55.

Tsimpli, I. M. (1990), 'The Clause Structure and Word Order of Modern Greek', *UCL Working Papers in Linguistics*, 2: 226–55.

Williams, E. (1989), 'The Anaphoric Nature of Theta-Roles', *Linguistic Inquiry*, 20: 425–56.

——(1994), *Thematic Structure in Syntax*, MIT Press, Cambridge, Mass.

4

Filling and Licensing Multiple Specifiers

EDIT DORON and CAROLINE HEYCOCK

1. INTRODUCTION

The uniqueness and obligatoriness of the clausal subject (Spec-TP) that characterizes languages such as English does not hold across all languages.[1] It has recently been argued (Ura 1994, 1996; Chomsky 1995) that specifiers may be generated recursively. Together with the assumption that in certain languages nominative case may be licensed on more than one element, this provides the necessary positions for 'multiple-subject' constructions (MSCs, henceforth) as they exist in languages such as Japanese and, we will argue, also the Semitic languages of Modern Hebrew and Modern Standard Arabic. However, this proposal raises in turn a number of issues concerning the elements filling these positions. In this chapter we address the related questions of how these positions are filled and how the resulting structures are interpreted.

2. THE EXISTENCE OF MULTIPLE SPECIFIERS

2.1. *Examples of the construction*

2.1.1. *Japanese*

The existence of what have variously been called multiple subjects and multiple nominatives is uncontroversial in Japanese. Two examples are given in (1).[2]

We would like to thank all those who helped us with the Semitic data, especially Rana Fahoum, Othman Naamne, Aryeh Levin, and Shraga Assif, and with the Japanese data, especially Naoki Fukui, Hiroshi Hasegawa, Etsuko Hayashi, Kuniyoshi Ishikawa, Lizanne Kaiser, Mariko Kondo, Hiromu Sakai, and Takashi Toyoshima. We would also like to thank audiences at the Specifiers Conference at the University of York and at the Jersey Syntax Circle at Rutgers University for their valuable comments. We are grateful to the British Council for a travel grant to the second-named author which partially funded her visit to Jerusalem in 1995, and to the Hebrew University for extending the use of its facilities to her as a Summer Visitor.

[1] We take T[ense] to be the functional head of the clause, as in Chomsky (1995), as we do not assume independent Agr heads. There may be languages in which T is split into separate Tense and Aspect heads. In fact, Arabic may be one such language, as suggested in Fassi Fehri (1993).

[2] Note that throughout this chapter the translations are intended only to give a rough idea of

(1) (*a*) mary-ga   kami-ga   nagai (koto)
           Mary-NOM   hair-NOM long   (fact)
           'Mary has long hair.'

    (*b*) yoi   otya-ga   nihonzin-ga   kononde nomu (koto)
           good green-tea-NOM Japanese-NOM enjoying drink (fact)
           'Good green tea, Japanese people drink [it] with pleasure.'

2.1.2. *Semitic*

The existence of multiple subjects in Modern Standard Arabic and Modern Hebrew (which for convenience we will refer to collectively in this chapter as 'Semitic') is more controversial. The basic structure of Arabic sentences is VSO, as shown in (2).[3] We assume that VSO is due to a weak D-feature of T, as suggested in Chomsky (1995).[4]

(2)   yuqa:bilu   T-Tulla:b-u   hind-an
       meet(3M)   the-students(M)-NOM   Hind(F)-ACC
       'The students are meeting Hind.'

Yet there are sentences where one or more nominative noun phrase appears sentence-initially:

(3) (*a*) hind-un   yuqa:bilu-ha   T-Tulla:b-u
           Hind-NOM   meet(3M)-her   the-students(M)-NOM
           'The students are meeting Hind.'
           Literally: 'Hind, the students are meeting her.'

    (*b*) ?al-bayt-u   ?alwa:n-u-hu   za:hiyat-un
           the-house-NOM   colours-NOM-its   bright-NOM
           'The house has bright colours.'
           Literally: 'The house, its colours are bright.'

Although contemporary linguists of Arabic usually treat examples like (3) as left-dislocations, corresponding to the literal gloss, we will argue that all sentence-initial nominative noun phrases like those above are subjects, as was

---

the meaning; since English does not allow MSCs the structure of the translations cannot correspond to the originals. In particular, translation as a left-dislocation should not be taken to imply that this is the structure of the original sentence.

In the Japanese examples *koto* (fact) is added so that the sentence is read as an embedded clause; this is done to avoid the awkwardness that can occur when a matrix sentence does not have a *wa*-marked topic.

[3] For a different view on the base position of subjects in Arabic, see Benmamoun (Ch. 6, this volume).

[4] In Standard Arabic, when the verb precedes the thematic subject it agrees with it only in person and gender. We take the apparent singular number morphology to be in this case a default, and to indicate lack of number agreement. In the glosses we indicate this lack of number agreement by giving no specification for number. Thus (3M) indicates a non-agreeing 3rd person masculine form; when there is actual singular agreement the gloss is given as (3MS).

argued in Doron (1996) (the rest of the sentence being a 'sentential predicate').[5]

A similar construction occurs in Hebrew:

(4) (a) ruti yeS la savlanut
        Ruti there-is to-her patience
        'Ruti has patience.'

   (b) ruti sof-a le-naceax
        Ruti end-hers to-win
        'Ruti will end up winning.'

This construction is treated essentially as left-dislocation by Nahir (1955), Peretz (1961), and Blau (1966), but we will argue that the initial noun phrase is not dislocated, but a syntactic subject, as claimed already by Rosén (1977) and Ornan (1979) (whose analyses, however, differ considerably from ours).

2.2. *The initial phrase is a subject*

In this section we will demonstrate that the initial nominative noun phrase in these constructions has in all cases the properties normally associated with subjects in the relevant languages. In particular, we will demonstrate that it is neither a dislocated phrase nor in a designated focus position (these being the two standard counteranalyses in Semitic and Japanese respectively). Rather, it is a subject which combines with a 'sentential predicate', that is, a phrase that semantically denotes a property, though syntactically it is a full clause which already contains a subject.

2.2.1. *Case marking, Exceptional Case Marking, and raising*

Many authors have argued that in Japanese these initial phrases (henceforth 'Broad Subjects') behave like thematic subjects ('Narrow Subjects') (see e.g. Kuno 1973; Kuroda 1986; Heycock 1993, and references contained therein). Most obviously, in Japanese the Broad Subject is marked with *ga*, which is generally considered to be the realization of nominative case. Topics in Japanese, on the other hand, are marked with the particle *wa*.

Further, as pointed out by Kuno (1978), Broad Subjects in the complement

---

[5] It is also possible for the thematic subject to appear in sentence-initial position:

(i)   ?aT-Tulla:b-u   yuqa:bilu-una hind-an
        the-students(M)-NOM meet(3M)-P   Hind-ACC
        'The students are meeting Hind.'

In this case, the verb agrees in number, as well as person and gender. The status of this thematic subject is somewhat different from the non-agreeing subjects; the reasons for this will be discussed extensively in Section 3.

clause of what have been analysed as ECM verbs can alternate between nominative and accusative marking, just as Narrow Subjects can:[6]

(5) boku-ga john-o/-ga   imooto-ga kirei-da   to   omowu
    I-NOM   John-ACC/NOM sister-NOM beautiful-be that think
    'I think that John's sister is beautiful.'

In Semitic also, the Broad Subject occurs in nominative case, and MSC constructions (in contrast to dislocated sentences) can be embedded under ECM verbs, as illustrated by the Arabic example (6a). This is of course impossible for left-dislocation in English, as illustrated in (6b).

(6) (a) dhanan-tu l-bayt-a   ?alwa:n-u-hu   za:hiyat-un
       thought-IS the-house-ACC colours-NOM-its bright-NOM
       'I believed the house to be of bright colours.'

    (b) *I believed John, him/he to be a hero

It should perhaps be noted that while the Arabic MSC construction differs from English left-dislocation in its ability to be embedded under an ECM verb, topicalization structures are as bad in this context in Arabic as they are in English. This can be seen clearly by the contrast in acceptability of the minimal pair in (7a, b), where (7a) is a grammatical embedded MSC construction and (7b) is an ungrammatical embedded topicalization (distinguishable by the lack of a clitic on the verb); (7c) is the corresponding grammatical matrix topicalization.

(7) (a) dhanan-tu hind-an   yuqa:bilu-ha T-Tulla:bu
       thought-IS Hind-ACC meet(3M)-her the-students
       'I believed Hind to have been met by the students.'

    (b) *dhanan-tu hind-an   yuqa:bilu T-Tulla:bu
       thought-IS Hind-ACC meet(3M) the-students
       Intended: 'I believed Hind to have been met by the students.'

    (c) hind-an   yuqa:bilu T-Tulla:b-u
       Hind-ACC meet(3M) the-students
       'Hind, the students are meeting.'

There is, therefore, no reason to hypothesize that Arabic is somehow just generally more liberal in what can appear in an ECM context.

2.2.2. *Coordination*

An additional respect in which Broad Subjects behave like other subjects is that in a coordination a single noun phrase may be 'shared' between two conjuncts, in one of which it functions as the Broad Subject, and in the other as the Narrow Subject. An example from Arabic is given in (8).

---

[6] A possible alternative is that these verbs involve control: the point here is unaffected, as only subjects can be controlled.

(8) sayya:rat-i [[lawn-u-ha   za:hiyy-un]   wa- [maftu:Hat-un min
     car(F)-my colour(M)-NOM-its bright(M)-NOM and open(F)-NOM   from
     al-a'la]]
     above
     'My car has a bright colour and is a convertible.'

Here, according to our analysis the sequence *lawn-u-ha za:hiyy-un* (colour-its
bright) is a predicate; as such it is expected that it be conjoined with another
predicate: *maftu:Hat-un min al-a'la* (open from above). Note that the latter,
being a predicate AP, is undoubtedly a predicate and not a sentence with a null
subject, since predicate APs do not license *pro*-drop in this language. Similar
examples of coordination can be given for Hebrew and Japanese.

2.2.3. *Non-peripheral position*

Although Broad Subjects obligatorily occur outside Narrow Subjects in all the
languages under consideration (see Section 3.1 for discussion) they do not
occur in the kind of peripheral position that left-dislocated phrases do. For example, in both Semitic and Japanese, Broad Subjects occur freely in embedded
contexts, in contrast to left-dislocations (and to *wa*-phrases in Japanese). This
is already illustrated for Japanese in the examples that have been given, which
have all been complements of the nominal head *koto* rather than matrix clauses
(see footnote 2).

In Arabic, example (6) above showed a Broad Subject embedded beneath an
ECM verb. Further, in clauses that include the auxiliary *ka:n* (be), the Broad
Subject may follow the auxiliary:

(9) ka:na   l-bayt-u   ?alwa:n-u-hu   za:hiyat-un
     was(3M) the-house(M)-NOM colours-NOM-its bright-NOM
     'The house was of bright colours.'

In Hebrew, the example in (10) shows that a Broad Subject may occur to the
right of an adjunct, which a left-dislocated phrase may not.

(10) be-anglit   kol miSpat   yeS   l-o   nose
      in-English each sentence there-is to-it a-subject
      'In English each sentence has a subject.'

Compare the ungrammatical English example in (11*a*), in which a left-
dislocated phrase follows an adjunct (contrasting also with the grammatical
example in (11*b*), where the left-dislocated phrase is in the peripheral position).

(11) (*a*) ?*In English a sentence like that, it would have a subject
     (*b*) A sentence like that, in English it would have a subject

2.2.4. *Quantified subject*

A further property that distinguishes Broad Subjects from topics and dislocated phrases is that Broad Subjects can be *wh*-phrases and bare quantifiers.
Example (12) is an example of a *wh*-phrase from Japanese.

(12)   dare-ga   me-ga   aoi   no-desu-ka?
        who-NOM   eyes-NOM   blue   qu
        'Who has blue eyes?'

The corresponding topicalized sentence is only marginally acceptable:

(13)   ??dare-wa   me-ga   aoi   no-desu-ka?
         who-TOP   eyes-NOM   blue   qu
        'Who has blue eyes?'

Example (14) shows a universally quantified Broad Subject in Arabic, and (15) a downward-entailing quantifier Broad Subject in Hebrew.

(14)   kull-u   ?insa:n-in   tuHibbu-hu   ?umm-u-hu
        every-NOM   man-GEN   love(3F)-him   mother-NOM-his
        'Everyone's mother loves him.'
        Literally: *'Everyone, his mother loves him.'

(15)   af   exad   eyn   be-yad-o   la'azor   le-rina
        no   one   it-isn't   in-power-his   to-help   Rina
        'No one has it in his power to help Rina.'

2.2.5. *Broad Subjects are not in a focus position*

In Semitic it is clear that Broad Subjects are not licensed by Focus: like Narrow Subjects, they may have the discourse function of either topic or focus, and in fact typically do not carry focal intonation. For Japanese, however, it has occasionally been claimed that Broad Subjects are in some designated focus position (Kiss 1981). The reason for this is presumably the fact that when the Broad Subject appears in a matrix clause, it is often interpreted as being in focus. However, as argued by Kuroda (1986) and subsequently by Heycock (1993), Broad Subjects behave no differently in this respect than the subjects of individual-level predicates, and, like them, can be interpreted without focus in a number of contexts—in particular, in non-root clauses. Further, if we leave out of consideration the type of sentence that we are considering in this chapter, in order not to beg the question of how it is to be analysed, there is a clear generalization that only a focused subject appears with *ga*: thus, when the object of an ordinary transitive verb is questioned the *wh*-phrase (and the corresponding constituent in the answer) take the accusative case marker *o*; *ga* would be unacceptable. Thus the proposal that *ga* is a focus marker (or appears on phrases in a focus position) is not well motivated.

2.3. *Other subject properties of the Broad Subject*

In addition to the data given above, which clearly indicate that the Broad Subject is neither left-dislocated nor in some designated focus position, there are various other diagnostics in the languages we are considering which demonstrate that the Broad Subject has the properties of a subject (properties presumably associated with the Spec-TP position).

2.3.1. *Subject-oriented reflexives in Japanese*

Broad Subjects can bind the reflexive *zibun*, as illustrated in (16).

(16)   sono hito$_i$-ga   kodomo-ga zibun$_i$-yori atama-ga ii   (koto)
         that person$_i$-NOM child-NOM self$_i$-than head-NOM good (fact)
         'That person$_i$ [is such that his/her] child is more intelligent than him$_i$/her$_i$.'

The possibility of this binding is relevant in two respects, as argued by Heycock (1993). First, it suggests that the Broad Subject is in an A-position, given the general assumption that binding of anaphors is only possible from A-, rather than A'-positions. Secondly, it constitutes another instance of the Broad Subject behaving like a Narrow Subject, as *zibun* is known to be a subject-oriented reflexive.

It has been argued that when *zibun* has a long-distance antecedent it can function as a logophoric pronoun (Kuno 1972; Kuno and Kaburaki 1977; Kameyama 1984, 1985; Sells 1987), in which case its antecedent may be a non-subject. However, a Broad Subject can also be the antecedent for the anaphor *zibun-zisin*, which is strictly a local subject-oriented anaphor (Kurata 1986; Katada 1991):[7]

(17)   john$_i$-ga   zibun-zisin$_i$-no hisyo-ga   kubi-ni natta (koto)
         John$_i$-NOM self$_i$-GEN   secretary-NOM was-fired   (fact)
         'John$_i$ [is such that] his$_i$ secretary was fired.'

2.3.2. *Arabic*

In addition to the arguments already given, there are other indications in Arabic that the MSC is not a case of left-dislocation. For one, a sentential predicate behaves with respect to control exactly like a simple predicate. Consider for example a verb of obligatory control such as *tajarra?a* (dared) in sentence (18).

(18)   qa:la   muHammad-un ?inna zayd-an   qad tajarra?a   ?an
         said(3M) Mohammad-NOM that Zayd-ACC had dared(3MS) to
         yuqa:bila l-mu'allim-a
         meet(3MS) the-teacher-ACC
         'Mohammad said that Zayd had dared to meet the teacher.'

---

[7] It has sometimes been claimed (see e.g. Ura 1996: 141) that *zibun-zisin* cannot be bound by a Broad Subject. Ura gives the following example:

(i)   *john$_i$-ga   imooto$_j$-ga zibun-zisin$_{*i/j}$-no heya-de korosareta (koto)
        John$_i$-NOM sister$_j$-NOM self$_{*i/j}$-GEN   room-in was-killed (fact)
        'John$_i$'s sister$_j$ was killed in self$_{*i/j}$'s room.'

However, it appears to be the intervening subject that makes the binding by the Broad Subject unavailable; as the grammaticality of the binding in (17) shows, the Broad Subject is otherwise available as an antecedent.

According to (18) it is Zayd who is to meet the teacher, not Mohammad. This locality requirement on the anaphoric link in (18) is explained if it is indeed control. Obligatory control is local, unlike the antecedent–pronominal relation. But if obligatory control is involved here, it means that the clause *yuqa:bila l-mu'allim-a* is a predicate. The same holds of predicates abstracted on the object, as shown in (19).

(19)   qa:la   muHammad-un   ?inna zayd-an   qad tajarra?a   ?an
          said(3M) Mohammad-NOM that   Zayd-ACC had dared(3MS) to
          yuqa:bila-hu   l-mu'allim-u
          meet(3M)-him the-teacher-NOM
          'Mohammad said that Zayd dared to be met by the teacher.'
          Literally: 'Mohammad said that Zayd had dared [for] the teacher to meet him.'

In (19), it is understood that the teacher will meet Zayd, not Mohammad. The locality of the anaphoric link between the antecedent *Zayd* and the suffix *-hu* again demonstrates that it is not an antecedent–pronominal relation but control. In other words, *yuqa:bila-hu l-mu'allim-u* is a predicate.

Another indication of the status of this construction is that the sentential predicate can be used not only predicatively, but also attributively (in the construction called *na't sababiyy* (indirect attribute)). Consider the sentential predicate in (20*a*), *bint-u-hu jami:lat-un* (daughter-his beautiful). This same phrase is used attributively in (20*b*), *jami:la bint-u-hu* (beautiful daughter-his), to modify the noun *?ar-rajul* (the man).

(20) (*a*)   ?ar-rajul-u   bint-u-hu   jami:lat-un
            the-man-NOM daughter-NOM-his beautiful-NOM
            'The man has a beautiful daughter.'
            Literally: 'The man, his daughter is beautiful.'

       (*b*)   qa:bal-tu r-rajul-a   l-jami:lat-a   bint-u-hu
            met-1S   the-man-ACC the-beautiful-ACC daughter-NOM-his
            'I met the man whose daughter is beautiful.'

The sentential predicate is treated here just like a simple adjectival phrase, which can typically be used both predicatively and attributively.

Note that the *na't sababiyy* is not a relative clause but a regular adjectival modifier. Its head agrees in Case and definiteness with the noun it (indirectly) modifies: in (20*b*), the adjective *jami:la* is definite and accusative, just like the noun *rajul*. There is of course no such agreement between a head noun and parts of a relative clause.

2.3.3. *Hebrew*

In Hebrew there are additional subject-oriented constructions which treat Narrow Subjects and Broad Subjects alike. For example, there is a particular cleft construction which applies to subjects only:

(21) (*a*) dani hu Se- 'azar le dina
          Dani he that helped to Dina
          'It is Dani who helped Dina.'

     (*b*) *dina hi Se- dani 'azar l-a
          Dina she that Dani helped to-her
          'It is Dina that Dani helped.'

As we would now expect, Broad Subjects can also be clefted in this construction. The following example is from Amatzia Porat's Hebrew translation of Faulkner's *Absalom, Absalom!*, published by Am Oved Publishers, Tel Aviv, 1983:

(22)   Se-harey elen hi be-ecem Se-haya   l-a   sade panuy
        since   Ellen she in-reality that-there-was to-her field free
        'Since it was really Ellen who had the free field.'

3. THE DERIVATION: MOVEMENT OR MERGING?

On the basis of the evidence that we have introduced from all the languages under consideration, we take it to be established that Broad Subjects are indeed subjects. Nevertheless, there are a number of respects in which Broad Subjects differ from Narrow Subjects. We shall now argue that the principal difference between Narrow Subjects and Broad Subjects is that while Narrow Subjects are base-generated within the VP, so that their occurrence in Spec-TP is due to movement, Broad Subjects are *merged* at Spec-TP; that is, they are base-generated in that position, and do not form a chain with a trace within VP.

3.1. *Broad Subjects and feature checking*

The first piece of evidence that Broad Subjects are merged at Spec-TP, while Narrow Subjects are moved, is that in Arabic only Narrow Subjects induce verbal agreement:

(23) (*a*) ?aT-Tulla:b-u   yuqa:bilu-una hind-an
          the-students(M)-NOM meet(3M)-P   Hind(F)-ACC
          'The students are meeting Hind.'

     (*b*) hind-un   yuqa:bilu-ha T-Tulla:b-u
          Hind(F)-NOM meet(3M)-her the-students(M)-NOM
          'The students are meeting Hind.'
          Literally: 'Hind, the students are meeting her.'

We follow the proposal of Chomsky (1995), according to which an element cannot check off features (such as agreement) of the head if it is merged as the specifier of that head. Thus the facts in (23) follow straightforwardly. Broad Subjects are merged at Spec-TP, and hence cannot check agreement features

there. Narrow Subjects, on the other hand, are merged at Spec-VP.[8] In example
(23a) above, and (24) below, the external argument of *meet* is generated in
Spec-VP.

(24)   yuqa:bilu T-Tulla:b-u   hind-an
        meet(3M)   the-students(M)-NOM Hind(F)-ACC
        'The students are meeting Hind.'

In order to account for the variable appearance of agreement morphology, and
its correlation with movement of the subject, we adopt the proposal of Doron
(1996), according to which there are two types of number agreement feature in
Arabic: strong—which is marked overtly on the verb—and weak. In (24) the
weak form occurs: thus the subject remains within the VP by *Procrastinate*. In
(23a), the strong form occurs, and hence raising of the subject to Spec-TP is
obligatory.

The assumption that number agreement may be a strong feature in Arabic
is not completely uncontroversial. It has been noticed by Demirdache (1989)
that *pro*-drop sentences obligatorily exhibit number agreement features not
only on the main verb, but also on the auxiliary *ka:n* (be), as in (25). This point
is raised by Benmamoun (1996) as a criticism of the view that overt number
agreement is a strong feature. For why should overt number agreement be obligatory with *pro* more than the once required for the identification of *pro*?

(25)   ka:nu-u   /*ka:na   yuqa:bilu-una hind-an   fi s-sa:Hat-i
        were(3M)-P /*was(3M) meet(3M)-P   Hind(F)-ACC in the-yard-GEN
        'They used to meet Hind in the yard.'

We do not think that this objection is compelling, however. The double agreement in (25) can be accounted for if the auxiliary *ka:n* (be) is in the head whose
specifier is the Case-checking position for Nominative. Assuming with Rizzi
(1986) that *pro* can only be identified by occupying a Case position by Spellout
(to translate his proposal into the terminology of Chomsky 1995), it must raise
overtly to the specifier of *ka:n-* in (25). In order for this to be possible, some
feature in the specifier must be strong. We know that Nominative Case in
Arabic is weak, so some other feature in this position—Agreement—must be
strong.

A further advantage of our proposal that Broad Subjects are merged at
Spec-TP, coupled with the assumption that number agreement is a strong
feature in Arabic, is that it can account for the rigid ordering constraints: the
(non-agreeing) Broad Subject must precede the Narrow Subject, as illustrated
in (26).

---

[8] Note that in these languages nominative case differs from agreement in allowing checking
even in the position of merger. We take this to reflect the difference between strong and weak features. Case, being weak in these languages, is checked by a head–head relation at LF rather than
by a specifier–head relation.

(26) (*a*) hind-un   ?aT-Tulla:b-u   yuqa:bilu-una-ha
      Hind(F)-NOM the-students(M)-NOM meet(3M)-P-her
      'The students are meeting Hind.'

      Literally: 'Hind, the students are meeting her.'

   (*b*) *?aT-Tulla:b-u   hind-un   yuqa:bilu-una-ha
      the-students(M)-NOM Hind(F)-NOM meet(3M)-P-her
      'The students are meeting Hind.'

      Literally: 'The students, Hind, (they) are meeting her.'

The explanation for the obligatory position of the Broad Subject to the left of
the Narrow Subject again lies in the fact that it is merged rather than moved.
Being merged, it cannot check strong agreement features itself. However, using
the definition of *closeness* in Chomsky (1995: 358), because the Broad Subject
is closer to T than the Narrow Subject in (26*b*), it prevents the latter from being
attracted to a second Spec-TP.

Thus, when strong agreement features are present, the only possible order is
the one in which the Narrow Subject moves first to check them off, and then
the Broad Subject is merged. If, on the other hand, the weak form of number
agreement occurs, here, just as in a sentence like (23*b*), the Narrow Subject will
have to remain in situ (again, by Procrastinate) and the order Narrow Subject–
Broad Subject will still not occur.

In Hebrew there is no evidence for strong agreement features. However,
Hebrew does have a strong feature that forces some XP (not necessarily a DP)
into clause-initial position. Thus for example the Hebrew equivalent to the
well-formed verb-initial Arabic sentence in (24) is ill formed. See (27).

(27)   *nifgaSim ha-talmidim 'im ruti ba   gina
        meet   the-students with Ruti in-the yard
        'The students meet with Ruti in the yard.'

We will refer to this feature (which may be the same as the feature which forces
movement of some XP to initial position in verb-second languages) as the XP-
feature. Again, on the assumption that the Broad Subject is merged rather than
moved, we predict that it cannot check this feature: a prediction that is borne
out by the ungrammaticality of the example in (28*a*), where the Broad Subject
stands alone before the verb. The minimally different example in (28*b*), on the
other hand, is fully grammatical because the Narrow Subject has moved and
checked off the XP-feature.

(28) (*a*) *kol   sar   'omed Somer roS-o   leyad mexonit-o
        each minister stands body guard-his by   car-his

   (*b*) kol   sar   Somer roS-o   'omed leyad mexonit-o
        each minister body guard-his stands by   car-his

        Both: 'The bodyguard of each minister stands by his car.'

3.2. *The distribution of* pro *and trace*

Since in our analysis the Broad Subject does not occupy a position to which the verb assigns a theta-role, nor has it moved from such a position, it follows that the element that occupies the argument position in Hebrew and Arabic and is coindexed with both the Broad Subject and the agreement clitic on the verb is the null pronoun *pro* rather than a trace. This is a desirable consequence, since the argument positions in which *pro* occurs under our analysis are those in which it is standardly taken to appear in simple sentences; conversely, since these are Case positions, under normal assumptions traces are not expected to be able to occur there. For example, consider the MSC in (29), which under our hypothesis contains a *pro* in the position indicated.

> (29) ha-arye [mekor-o *pro*] be-africa
>   the-lion origin-his   in-Africa
>   'The lion originates in Africa.'

Our assumption that there is a *pro* in this sentence is based on prior analyses of simple sentences like (30).

> (30) xakarti   et   toldot ha-arye. [mekor-o *pro*] be-africa
>   researched(1S) ACC history the-lion   origin-his   in-Africa
>   'I researched the history of the lion. It (the lion) originates in Africa.'

Note that -*o* is not a fully fledged pronoun but rather a marker of agreement, as shown by the fact that it occurs together with a full noun phrase possessor (see e.g. Borer 1984; Engelhardt 1996):

> (31) [mekor-o Sel ha-arye] be-africa
>   origin-his GEN the-lion in-Africa
>   'The origin of the lion is in Africa.'

Nevertheless, (30) is fully felicitous, unlike a discourse containing a sentence where a 3rd person subject is missing, such as (32). In Hebrew *pro* cannot appear in subject position in non-embedded contexts if the subject is 3rd person (Borer 1989).

> (32) xakarti   et   toldot ha-arye. *higi'a   me-africa
>   researched(1S) ACC history the-lion   arrived from-Africa
>   'I researched the history of the lion. It(?) arrived from Africa.'

The contrast between examples like (30) and (32) is the basis for maintaining that there is a *pro* in the former.[9]

The null hypothesis is therefore that there is also a *pro* in the MSC given in (29). If instead we were to propose that the Broad Subject had moved from the

---

[9] The second sentence in (30) cannot be analysed with a trace in the place of *pro*, with *pro* itself as a Broad Subject, since we know from (32) that 3rd person *pro* cannot occur in subject position.

argument position, we would be positing movement from a Case position to a Case position—and in fact in many cases movement of the possessor from within a noun phrase—types of movement that are generally impossible.

3.3. *Islands for movement*

As just stated, any analysis of MSCs in terms of movement of the Broad Subject from a VP-internal argument position will have to explain how such movement can freely violate island constraints: in particular, how it can allow movement of a possessor out of a containing noun phrase. Ura (1996) proposes an analysis which accounts for such movement: but only in one special case. Under his account A-movement of a possessor out of a noun phrase can occur, but is limited to movement from one specifier of a head H to form a higher specifier of H. So, for example, in a language that allows multiple subjects, a possessor inside one subject (in Spec-TP) may raise to become the next-higher specifier of TP.[10]

This analysis, therefore, would allow for a movement account of examples like the Hebrew (29) or Arabic (3b). It would not, however, extend to Hebrew examples like (33), or Arabic (34), where possessor raising would have to have taken place from out of the (unmoved) object.

(33)   af bamay zar   lo makrinim et   srat-av   le-lo   targum
        no director foreign not show(3MP) ACC films-his without translation
        'No foreign director has his films shown without subtitles.'

(34)   ayy-u   muxrij-in   ?ajnabiyy-in la nu'riD   ?afla:m-a-hu
        any-NOM director-GEN foreign-GEN not show(1P) films-ACC-his
        min-du:n-i tarjamat-in
        without   translation-GEN
        'No foreign director has his films shown by us without subtitles.'

Since these cannot be analysed in terms of movement, but must involve merging of the Broad Subject at Spec-TP, we assume that this is true in all cases.

---

[10] Briefly, Ura's argument is as follows: What generally prevents A-movement of a possessor out of the containing noun phrase is the locality built into Attract: as mentioned before, Attract is defined to affect the phrase with the relevant features that is *closest to the attracting head*. Since the noun phrase containing a possessor will always be closer to an external head than the possessor is, the latter can typically not be 'attracted' out of the noun phrase. However, there is one circumstance where this will not hold: precisely in languages that allow multiple specifiers. By hypothesis, a language allows multiple specifiers for a particular head H if that language allows multiple checking of some feature [F] of H, and multiple violations of Procrastinate. Suppose that a noun phrase with a feature [F] of this type, containing a possessor also bearing [F], is attracted: it can check its feature against H, and its copy of the feature then deletes. But now the possessor within the noun phrase is the closest [F] element to H; it is therefore free to be attracted, and can move to a higher specifier position in order to check its [F] feature (Ura 1996: 127ff.). Thus A-movement of a possessor out of a noun phrase can occur, but is limited to movement from out of one specifier of a head H to a higher specifier of H.

In Japanese, too, the Broad Subject may correspond to the possessor of an unmoved object:

(35)   sono sakka-ga   minna-ga   sakuhin-o yomi-tagatte-iru (koto)
        that author-NOM everyone-NOM works-ACC read-wants-be   (fact)
        'That author [is such that] everyone wants to read [his] books.'

Again, rather than positing two distinct constructions, we conclude that since some Broad Subjects can only have been base-generated in sentence-initial position, this is true of all.[11]

3.4. *Idioms*

A standard illustration of the difference between raising and control is that phrases that are themselves idiomatic, and hence do not refer in the normal way, can be raised, but cannot act as controllers:

(36) (*a*) The cat seems to be out of the bag   (idiomatic)
     (*b*) The cat tried to be out of the bag   (literal only)

As suggested by Ura (1996: 106 ff.), we can apply this test to MSCs: if they involve raising, we would expect to find the pattern in (36*a*). While it is difficult to establish that there are *no* idioms that exhibit the pattern in (36*a*), we have found that the evidence supports our hypothesis that the MSC does not involve movement. Consider for example the Hebrew idiom *to blunt someone's teeth* meaning *to scold someone*, as in (37).

(37)   kvar   hikheti   et Sin-av   Sel dani pe'amim rabot
        already   blunted(1S)   ACC teeth-his GEN Dani times   many
        'I have scolded Dani many times.'

        Literally: 'I have blunted Dani's teeth many times.'

The phrase *Sin-av Sel dani* (Dani's teeth) can undergo A-movement, as shown by its ability to passivize:

---

[11] In order to deal with the problem for his movement analysis posed by examples like (35), Ura proposes precisely that there are two MSCs in Japanese, only one of which involves movement. His principal empirical argument for this distinction is the claim that there can be only one base-generated Broad Subject in a clause, while Broad Subjects formed by raising an inalienable possessor can iterate. However, we find that there is no such difference: Broad Subjects that are not inalienable possessors can also iterate:

(i)   oranda-no   sakana-ga huyu-ga   nisin-ga   yoi
        Holland-GEN fish-NOM   winter-NOM herring-NOM good-is
        'Fish in Holland [are such that] [in] winter herring is the best.'

Neither of the Broad Subjects *oranda-no sakana* (fish in Holland) or *huyu* (winter) is an inalienable possessor; hence by Ura's own assumptions both must be base-generated. (An example similar to (i) is cited by Ura (1996: 104, (4.8)) as ungrammatical; although less acceptable, some of our informants find that example grammatical as well.) We conclude that there is no independent empirical basis for two distinct MSCs in Japanese.

(38) Sin-av   Sel dani kvar   hukhu   pe'amim rabot
     teeth-his GEN Dani already were-blunted times   many
     'Dani has been scolded many times.'
     Literally: 'Dani's teeth have been blunted many times.'

However, the same phrase cannot retain its idiomatic interpretation as a Broad Subject:

(39) Sin-av   Sel dani kvar   hikheti   ot-an   pe'amim rabot
     teeth-his GEN Dani already blunted(1s) ACC-them times   many
     'Dani's teeth, I have blunted them many times.'   (literal only)

The same pattern is found in the idiom *to hang the collar round someone's neck* meaning *to blame someone*:

(40) (*a*) tamid tolim   et ha-kolar be-cavar-o Sel ha-nasi
            always hang(3MP) ACC the-collar at-neck-his GEN the-president
            'One always blames the president.'
            Literally: 'One always hangs the collar round the president's neck.'

     (*b*) ha-kolar   tamid nitle   be-cavar-o Sel ha-nasi
           the-collar always is-hanged   at-neck-his GEN the-president
           'One always blames the president.'
           Literally: 'The collar is always hung round the president's neck.'

     (*c*) ha-kolar   tamid tolim   ot-o be-cavar-o Sel ha-nasi
           the-collar always hang(3MP) ACC-it at-neck-his GEN the-president
           'The collar, one always hangs it round the president's neck.'
                                                                  (literal only)

3.5. *Lack of scope ambiguity*

A further empirical difference between Broad and Narrow Subjects which can be explained by our proposal is the difference in their scope behaviour. A Narrow Subject can be construed under the scope of a quantifier in the predicate, whereas a Broad Subject always has scope over a quantifier in the predicate. Examples (41*a*, *b*) are from Arabic.

(41) (*a*) fata:t-un Tawi:lat-un raqasat   ma'a kull-i   Sa:bb-in
            girl-NOM   tall-NOM   danced(3FS) with every-GEN boy-GEN
            'A tall girl danced with every boy.'   (ambiguous scope)

     (*b*) fata:t-un Tawi:lat-un 'arraftu-ha   bi-kull-i   Sa:bb-in
            girl-NOM   tall-NOM   introduced(1s)-to-her every-GEN   boy-GEN
            'I introduced all the boys to a (specific) tall girl.'

If *tall girl* is base-generated within the predicate in (41*a*) and moved to Spec-TP, it is predicted to have either scope relative to quantifiers in the VP. This conforms with the two possible readings of (41*a*): *tall girl* may be interpreted as having either wide or narrow scope relative to *every boy*. In (41*b*), on the other hand, *tall girl* is base-generated as a Broad Subject, and thus has wide scope over a quantifier in the VP. This corresponds to the only interpretation of (41*b*), where *tall girl* must have wide scope over *every boy*. Data from Classical Arabic that establish the same point can be found in Fassi Fehri (1993).

The same scope differences appear in Hebrew. Narrow Subjects have ambiguous scope with respect to other quantifiers, whereas Broad Subjects have wide scope only. In (42*a*), the subject has either wide or narrow scope relative to the adverb *every now and then*. In (42*b*), on the other hand, the Broad Subject has unambiguously wide scope.

(42) (*a*) hacagot tovot 'olot   midey pa'am
           plays   good are-performed every now and then
           'Good plays are performed every now and then.'   (ambiguous)

     (*b*) hacagot tovot ma'alim   ot-an   midey pa'am
           plays   good perform(3MP) ACC-them every now and then
           'Good plays are performed every now and then.'   (unambiguous)

Similar data exist also in Japanese. Sakai (1994) notes that an example like (43)—his (13*a*)—is ambiguous as to the scope of the universal quantifier: it may take scope only within the relative clause, or over the whole clause.

(43)   daremo-ga   kinoo-made   tukatte-ita konpyuuta-ga
         everyone-NOM yesterday-until used   computer-NOM
         kowarete-simatta (koto)
         broke-down   (fact)
         'The computer which everyone used has broken.'   (only one computer)
         Or 'For each person, the computer which he used has broken.'

He argues that this is so because the initial nominative *daremo-ga* (everyone-NOM) could be interpreted as being either inside the relative clause (hence the lower scope) or in our terms a Broad Subject of the whole clause (hence the higher scope). Sakai demonstrates that if the nominative quantifier is unambiguously inside the relative clause, only the lower scope is possible (note that this rules out the possibility that the scope ambiguity is due to scope interactions of the quantifier and some null relative operator within the relative clause). What he does not discuss is what readings are available if the nominative is unambiguously outside the relative—that is, a Broad Subject. It turns out that, just as we would expect from our analysis and from what we have seen in Semitic, the Broad Subject unambiguously has wide scope:

(44)   daremo-ga   kesa   kinoo-made   tukatte-ita
         everyone-NOM this-morning yesterday-until used
         konpyuuta-ga kowarete-simatta (koto)
         computer-NOM broke-down   (fact)
         'This morning, for each person, the computer which s/he had used until yesterday was broken.'

Again, the lack of ambiguity argues for an analysis in terms of merging rather than movement. It is well known that scrambling in Japanese results in scope ambiguity: the scrambled phrase can have either the scope associated with its scrambled position or that of its original position. If the Broad Subject in (44) had been moved out of the relative clause (as Sakai proposes) we would expect that it too would be ambiguous in its scope, contrary to fact.

4. INTERPRETATION

As we have just seen, our proposal has consequences for the semantic analysis of multiple-subject constructions. We now turn to look in more detail at the interpretation of Broad Subjects, demonstrating the difference of interpretation between a Broad Subject and a left-dislocated noun phrase on the one hand, and between a Broad Subject and a Narrow Subject on the other.

The first difference between a Broad Subject and a left-dislocated element concerns discourse structure: a left-dislocated noun phrase (and we include here a *wa*-marked phrase in Japanese) has a fixed pragmatic role of topic, whereas the Broad Subject, like any subject, may be (part of) the focus.

The second, related, difference has to do with denotation. A left-dislocated noun phrase must be referring, that is, denote an individual (or a group of individuals). It must therefore be a name or a definite description or at least a quantifier with a 'witness set', that is, upward-entailing. The clause which follows a left-dislocated element denotes a full proposition, not just a property: the proposition is related to the reference of the left-dislocated noun phrase by general discourse processes. One way that the proposition can be taken to relate to the left-dislocated topic is through containing a pronoun which serves to pick up the reference of the noun phrase, either by pragmatic coreference or by the e-type mechanism. In other words, this pronoun does not serve as a bound variable or a pronoun of laziness, but as a marker of coreference. In other cases (such as those that have been extensively documented for Japanese) an 'aboutness' relation may be established without any coreferential pronoun.

In MSCs, on the other hand, there exists a relation of predication between the Broad Subject and the clause following it. The clause denotes not a proposition but a property. One way of achieving a property denotation is through abstracting on a pronoun in the clause (a 'resumptive' pronoun).[12] A Broad

---

[12] In Japanese, there is not necessarily such a pronoun, and abstraction could be on the implicit Davidsonian argument. Thus for example the following (from Saito 1982) is possible in Japanese, but there is no equivalent in Semitic:

(i)   natu-ga   biiru-ga   umai
        summer-NOM beer-NOM   good
        '[It is in] summer [that] beer tastes good.'

Ornan (1979) cites some examples in Hebrew of MSCs without an overt pronoun—all, however, from the work of a single author, Shmuel Yossef Agnon. In contrast to the Japanese example in (i), in each case there is a grammatical alternate with an overt pronoun.

Subject may therefore be a quantifier, including downward-entailing quantifiers, unlike a left-dislocated noun phrase; this was shown in Section 2.2.4. The Broad Subject binds the resumptive pronoun in the same way as the Narrow Subject binds its trace in the VP.

As we have just seen, a Broad Subject is like a Narrow Subject in the range of quantifiers that it allows. Nevertheless, there are semantic differences between a Broad Subject and a Narrow Subject. Recall that in Section 3.5 we saw that a Broad Subject cannot take narrow scope with respect to other quantifiers in the sentence; we argued that this followed from the fact that, not having a trace internal to the VP, Broad Subjects could not be interpreted in a lower position at LF. According to many analyses that follow the basic insights of Kratzer (1989, 1995) and Diesing (1992), the position in which a phrase is base-generated determines whether it will fall within the restrictive clause or the nuclear scope of any operators in the sentence, including the generic operator. Consequently, our hypothesis that the Broad Subject is merged at Spec-TP predicts that it should be able to occur only within the restrictive clause. This prediction is met. Consider the following two Hebrew examples, where the second is an MSC:

(45) (a) ba-　　boker　　Sotim　　　kafe　tov
　　　　　in-the　morning　drink(3MP)　coffee　good
　　　　　'In the morning, one drinks good coffee.'

　　　(b) kafe　tov　　Sotim　　　ot-o　　ba-　　boker
　　　　　coffee　good　drink(3MP)　ACC-it　in-the　morning
　　　　　'Good coffee, one drinks it in the morning.'

In (45a), where the bare noun phrase *kafe tov* (good coffee) is in the argument position within the VP, it can be interpreted either existentially or generically; in (45b) on the other hand, where it is generated as a Broad Subject, it can only be interpreted generically. Note that while we have translated (45b) as an English left-dislocation (English not allowing MSCs), in Hebrew there is at least one derivation of this sentence where the initial phrase is a Broad Subject, as shown by the following coordination (as there is no *pro*-drop in the present tense in Hebrew, the second conjunct is unambiguously a predicate, so that this is not coordination of two full sentences):

(46)　　kafe　tov　　Sotim　　　ot-o　　ba-boker　　　ve　maSpi'a　kol
　　　　coffee　good　drink(3MP)　ACC-it　in-the-morning　and　effects　all
　　　　ha-yom
　　　　the-day
　　　　'Good coffee, one drinks it in the morning and [it] has an effect all day.'

The following examples demonstrate that the lexical predicate need not be individual-level, or even stative, but can be episodic:

(47) (*a*) hor-av   Sel adam ben Siv'im nifteru
         parents-his of man aged seventy died
         'The parents of a seventy-year-old died.'

     (*b*) adam ben Siv'im hor-av   nifteru
         person aged seventy parents-his died
         'A seventy-year-old has parents who have died.'

The same is known to be true of MSCs in Japanese, as illustrated in (17), repeated here as (48).

(48)   john$_i$-ga   zibun-zisin$_i$-no hisyo-ga   kubi-ni natta (koto)
       John$_i$-NOM self$_i$-GEN   secretary-NOM was-fired   (fact)
       'John$_i$ [is such that] his$_i$ secretary was fired.'

In (48), the property which is predicated of John is implicated from the particular event of the firing, which is an episodic eventuality; similarly for the Hebrew example (47*b*). We will not elaborate on the semantics of this implication, but it is much the same as is sometimes needed for interpreting the habitual operator in English. Thus, the following sentence can be judged true on the basis of an episodic event of John having signed a contract with a big company (Carlson and Pelletier 1995):

(49)   John sells vacuum cleaners

The event must be 'crucial' in that it determines the property. This is why, for example, Japanese speakers judge the following to be odd:

(50)   #john-ga musuko-ga waratta (koto)
       John-NOM son-NOM   laughed (fact)
       'John [is such that] his son laughed.'

5. CONCLUSION

In this chapter we have argued that the hypothesis that certain heads may allow multiple specifiers allows for an insightful analysis of constructions involving multiple nominative phrases both in Japanese and in Semitic. On the one hand we have given evidence concerning the syntax, semantics, and pragmatics of these constructions that demonstrates that they are not instances of left-dislocation or focus movement. The possibility of multiple specifiers of TP and of multiple checking of nominative case provides the necessary left-peripheral A-positions for these nominative phrases.

On the other hand we have also demonstrated that these 'Broad Subjects' have some syntactic and semantic properties that distinguish them from Narrow Subjects: in particular, they do not induce verbal agreement and cannot take narrow scope with respect to any other quantifier in the sentence. We have argued that these differences arise because specifiers can be the result of two different operations: Merge and Move. Specifically, Broad Subjects are merged at Spec-TP while Narrow Subjects are merged at Spec-VP and achieve their Spec-TP position by movement. Granted Chomsky's proposal that strong features cannot be checked by a phrase in the position in which it is merged, the lack of agreement with Broad Subjects follows immediately, as does their ordering with respect to the Narrow Subject. With respect to their interpretation, the obligatorily broad scope and typically generic interpretation of Broad Subjects follows directly from their lack of a VP-internal trace, given widely held assumptions concerning the correspondence between syntactic structure and semantic partitioning.

In order to satisfy Full Interpretation, there must be some interface role which Broad Subjects assume. This role cannot be any thematic role assigned by the clause's main predicate, since a Broad Subject does not have a trace in the argument position of any lexical predicate. What the MSC achieves syntactically is the construction of a new predicate for the Broad Subject. This predicate is interpreted as a new complex property which assigns an argument role, albeit not a thematic role in the lexical sense.

REFERENCES

Benmamoun, E. (1996), 'Agreement Asymmetries and the PF Interface', Ms., SOAS.
Blau, Y. (1966), *Yesodot Hataxbir*, Hamaxon Haivri Lehaskala Bixtav Beisrael, Jerusalem.
Borer, H. (1984), *Parametric Syntax*, Foris, Dordrecht.
——(1989), 'Anaphoric AGR', in O. Jaeggli and K. Safir (eds.), *The Null Subject Parameter*, Kluwer, Dordrecht, 69–109.
Carlson, G., and Pelletier, F. (1995) (eds.), *The Generic Book*, University of Chicago Press, Chicago.
Chomsky, N. (1995), *The Minimalist Program*, MIT Press, Cambridge, Mass.
Demirdache, H. (1989), 'Nominative NPs in Modern Standard Arabic', Ms., MIT.
Diesing, M. (1992), *Indefinites*, MIT Press, Cambridge, Mass.
Doron, E. (1996), 'The Predicate in Arabic', in J. Lecarme, J. Lowenstamm, and U. Shlonsky (eds.), *Studies in Afroasiatic Grammar*, Holland Academic Graphics, Leiden, 77–87.
Engelhardt, M. (1997), 'The Licensing of Subjects in Noun Phrases', in E. Doron and S. Wintner (eds.), *Proceedings of the Twelfth Annual Meeting of the Israeli Association for Theoretical Linguistics*, 1996 (IATL 4), Akademon, Jerusalem, 41–54.
Fassi Fehri, A. (1993), *Issues in the Structure of Arabic Clauses and Words*, Kluwer, Dordrecht.
Heycock, C. (1993), 'Syntactic Predication in Japanese', *Journal of East Asian Linguistics*, 2: 167–211.
Kameyama, M. (1984), 'Subjective/Logophoric Bound Anaphor Zibun', in J. Drogo *et al.* (eds.), *Proceedings of the Chicago Linguistics Society*, 20, 228–38, Chicago Linguistics Society, Chicago.
——(1985), 'Zero Anaphora: The Case of Japanese', Ph.D. thesis, Stanford University.

Katada, F. (1991), 'The LF Representation of Anaphors', *Linguistic Inquiry*, 22(2): 287–313.

Kiss, K. (1981), 'On the Japanese "Double Subject" Construction', *The Linguistic Review*, 1: 155–70.

Kratzer, A. (1989), 'Stage-Level and Individual-Level Predicates', Ms., University of Massachusetts, Amherst.

——(1995), 'Stage Level and Individual Level Predicates', in G. Carlson and F. Pelletier (eds.), *The Generic Book*, University of Chicago Press, Chicago, 125–75.

Kuno, S. (1972), 'Pronominalization, Reflexivization, and Direct Discourse', *Linguistic Inquiry*, 3(2): 161–95.

——(1973), *The Structure of the Japanese Language*, MIT Press, Cambridge, Mass.

——(1978), 'Theoretical Perspectives on Japanese Linguistics', in J. Hinds and I. Howard (eds.), *Problems in Japanese Syntax and Semantics*, Kaitakusha, Tokyo.

——and Kaburaki, E. (1977), 'Empathy and Syntax', *Linguistic Inquiry*, 8(4): 627–72.

Kurata, K. (1986), 'Asymmetries in Japanese', Ms., University of Massachusetts, Amherst.

Kuroda, S.-Y. (1986), 'Movement of Noun Phrases in Japanese', in T. Imai and M. Saito (eds.), *Issues in Japanese Linguistics*, Foris, Dordrecht, 229–72.

Nahir, S. (1955), *Iqarey Torat Hamishpat*, Reali, Haifa.

Ornan, U. (1979), *Hamishpat Hapashut*, Akademon, Jerusalem.

Peretz, Y. (1961), *Taxbir Halashon Haivrit*, Massada, Tel Aviv.

Rizzi, L. (1986), 'Null Objects in Italian and the Theory of *pro*', *Linguistic Inquiry*, 17(3): 501–57.

Rosén, H. B. (1977), *Contemporary Hebrew*, Mouton, The Hague.

Saito, M. (1982), 'Case Marking in Japanese: A Preliminary Study', Ms., MIT.

Sakai, H. (1994), 'Complex NP Constraint and Case-Conversions in Japanese', in M. Nakamura (ed.), *Current Topics in English and Japanese*, Hituzi Syobo, Tokyo, 179–203.

Sells, P. (1987), 'Aspects of Logophoricity', *Linguistic Inquiry*, 18(3): 445–79.

Ura, H. (1994), 'Varieties of Raising and the Feature-Based Bare Phrase Structure Theory', *MIT Occasional Papers in Linguistics*, 7, MIT, Cambridge, Mass. (distributed by *MIT Working Papers in Linguistics*).

——(1996), 'Multiple Feature-Checking: A Theory of Grammatical Function Splitting', Ph.D. thesis, MIT.

PART II
Specifiers, Movement, and Feature Checking

5

EPP without Spec, IP

ARTEMIS ALEXIADOU
and ELENA ANAGNOSTOPOULOU

I. INTRODUCTION

In Chomsky (1995), it is assumed that checking of strong nominal features of a non-substantive category takes place in a Spec–head configuration. In this system it is actually the presence of such a strong feature that forces the structural realization of the specifier of a given head. A case in point is the checking of the *Extended Projection Principle* (EPP) feature. The EPP is defined in Chomsky (1995) as a D-feature on I which, when strong, forces the licensing of [Spec, IP][1] by either *movement* or *merging* of an XP. In this chapter, we show that the uniqueness and obligatoriness of [Spec, IP] as an overt subject position that characterizes languages like English does not hold cross-linguistically. We further demonstrate that the presence of a specifier for the checking of the EPP is not necessary and can be dispensed with.

Specifically, we examine SVO/VS(O) alternations across languages, focusing on null-subject languages (NSLs) such as Greek, Spanish, and Catalan[2] and non-NSLs such as English and Icelandic. We present evidence that SVO orders in the former group, as opposed to the latter, are not a result of subject movement to [Spec, IP], and that inverted orders do not involve an expletive merged in [Spec, IP]. We propose that, although the above holds, NSLs do have a strong EPP feature which is checked in another way. We argue that the key factor in differentiating NSLs from non-NSLs is a parameterization of EPP checking related to the (non-)availability of [Spec, IP]: while non-NSLs move or merge an XP to check the EPP feature and thus always project [Spec, IP], NSLs never project [Spec, IP] but use an alternative mode of EPP checking, namely a head-adjunction configuration, which is the result of verb movement to I°.

We would like to thank David Adger, Viviane Deprez, Eric Haeberli, Teun Hoekstra, Henk van Riemsdijk, Ian Roberts, George Tsoulas, and two anonymous reviewers for comments and discussion. Parts of the material presented here are also included in Alexiadou and Anagnostopoulou (1998).

[1] By [Spec, IP] we refer to [Spec, AgrSP].

[2] In our discussion we leave Italian aside, as it presents further complications which we hope to address in future work.

According to our proposal, EPP relates to checking of a nominal feature in AGR, and NSLs satisfy the EPP via V raising, as their verbal agreement morphology includes the nominal feature required (cf. Taraldsen 1978). Thus, there seems to be no one-to-one correspondence between EPP and the presence of [Spec, IP]. Viewed this way, the formal features and requirements of I are very close to those of the functional category C, as described in Chomsky (1995: 289 ff.).

The chapter is organized as follows: in Section 2, we present the definitions from Chomsky (1995) that we adopt throughout. In Section 3, we examine word order alternations in the languages under consideration. In Section 4, we present our arguments that NSLs lack [Spec, IP] by demonstrating that in this language group, SVO orders do not involve subject movement and VS(O) orders lack expletives. In section 5, we outline our proposal. Section 6 concludes the chapter.

2. SVO AND EXPL-VS(O) ORDERS IN CHOMSKY (1995)

In Chomsky (1995), word-order alternations like the ones presented in (1) and (2) below are taken to be the result of the two ways available in the framework to check the EPP feature. Recall that this strong feature can be checked by either merging an expletive or by moving the subject NP to IP. The former is illustrated in (1*a*) and (2*a*), while the latter is shown in (1*b*) and (2*b*).

(1) (*a*)   There arrived a man   (English)

    (*b*)   A man arrived

(2) (*a*)   Það   lasu   einhverjir stúdentar bókina   (Icelandic)
        there read   some   students   book-the
        'Some students read the book.'

    (*b*)   Einhverjir stúdentar lasu bókina
        some   students   read book-the
        'Some students read the book.'

In this system, SVO orders are derived from a numeration without an expletive. Expletive constructions, on the other hand, are derived from a numeration with an expletive. In that case, *Expletive Merge* is less costly than overt movement of the subject. Adopting Chomsky's (1995) definition of the *reference set*, the two derivations, the one with the expletive and the one without, cannot be compared, since in evaluating derivations for economy only alternatives with the same numeration can be considered.

Given what is said above, the projection of [Spec, IP] is the immediate reflex of overt EPP checking by either Merge or Move forced by the presence of a strong feature. Under this reasoning, if a language is shown to lack Move/ Merge XP, then the language will qualify as a 'no/weak EPP = no [Spec, IP]' language. If a language lacks these options, then no strong feature in I is present, and as a result [Spec, IP] is not projected in this language. Moreover, SV(O) orders involving A-movement to [Spec, IP] will always be ruled out as *Procrastinate* violations, since, lacking an expletive, VS(O)/SV(O) orders in this language would have the same numeration, and the most economical derivation would be preferred, namely the one without movement.

3. WORD-ORDER ALTERNATIONS IN NULL-SUBJECT LANGUAGES

Given the treatment of (1) and (2) presented above, the question that immediately arises is whether SVO/VSO orders in NSLs, like the ones exemplified in (3a, b) for Greek and (3c, d) for Spanish, can be treated on a par.

(3) (a) O Aleksandros   filise   ti   Roksani
         the-Alexander-NOM kissed the-Roxane-ACC
         'Alexander kissed Roxane.'

    (b) filise   o Aleksandros   ti   Roksani
         kissed the-Alexander-NOM the-Roxane-ACC

    (c) Juan leyo el   libro
         Juan read the book
         'Juan read the book.'

    (d) leyo Juan el   libro
         read Juan the book

Before turning to a specific analysis of these alternations, let us look more closely at some of their properties. We illustrate these properties for Greek, assuming that they hold for the other NSLs as well (cf. Dobrovie-Sorin 1987 for Romanian; Zubizarreta 1992 for Spanish, among others).

A first characteristic of this alternation is that it is not restricted to root clauses, but also occurs in non-root contexts (and in non-CP-recursion contexts, cf. Iatridou and Kroch 1992, among others). Example (4a), an example with a complex NP, shows that the subject can both precede and follow the verb; (4b) illustrates the same point with an adjunct *if*-clause.

(4) (a) i   idisi oti (o Paris)   episkeftike (o Paris)
         the news   that the-Paris-NOM visited   the-Paris-NOM
         tin Athina   (complex NP)
         the-Athena-ACC
         'The news that Paris visited Athena'

    (b) an (o Paris)   episkefti (o Paris)   tin Athina   (*if*-clause)
         if the-Paris-NOM visits   the-Paris-NOM the-Athena-ACC
         'If Paris visits Athena . . .'

Moreover, postverbal subjects occur with all eventive predicates (both transitives and intransitives) as shown in the examples in (5).

(5) (*a*) efige   o Kostas   (unaccusative)
           left-3s the-Kostas-NOM
           'Kostas left.'

    (*b*) epekse   o Petros   (unergative)
           played-3s the-Peter-NOM
           'Peter played.'

    (*c*) ektise i Nana   to spiti   (accomplishment)
           built the-Nana-NOM the-house-ACC
           'Nana built the house.'

    (*d*) kerdise i Niki   ton agona   (achievement)
           won   the-Niki-NOM the-race-ACC
           'Niki won the race.'

    (*e*) egrafe   i Anastasia   to grama   olo to proi   (process)
           wrote-IMP the-Anastasia-NOM the-letter-ACC all the morning
           'Anastasia was writing the letter the whole morning.'

In English, as is well known, subject-inverted constructions display an intransitivity constraint (cf. Hoekstra and Mulder 1990; Levin and Rappaport 1995, among others).

Furthermore, VS orders in Greek do not display any Definiteness Restriction (DR) effects, unlike their counterparts in English, Icelandic, Dutch, or French. The Greek example (6*a*) with a strong, universally quantified NP in postverbal position, is grammatical, while the English example (6*b*) is not.

(6) (*a*) irthe   kathe pedi
           arrived every child
           'Every child arrived.'

    (*b*) *There arrived every child

Finally, in VSO orders the subject is VP-internal, unlike Icelandic transitive expletive constructions (cf. Jonas and Bobaljik 1993) and Irish VSO orders (cf. Carnie 1993; McCloskey 1996*a*, *b*). Evidence for this comes from a combination of adverbial and participial placement facts in periphrastic constructions (cf. Alexiadou 1994). As illustrated in (7*a*), the order of constituents in Greek is auxiliary, aspectual adverb, participle, light manner adverb, and subject. In Alexiadou (1994), the relative order of the light manner adverb, which marks (at least) the left edge of the VP, and the participle is taken as evidence that the participle has moved outside the VP domain. The subject in Greek follows both the light manner adverb and the participle. From this we can conclude that the subject occupies its VP-internal position. Example (7*b*), where the subject intervenes between the auxiliary and the participle, is ungrammatical. Note that there is no strict adjacency requirement between the participle and the auxiliary, since aspectual adverbs can intervene.

(7) (a) an ehi idi   diavasi kala o   Petros   to   mathima
      if   has   already   read   well   the-Peter-NOM   the   lesson-ACC
      'If Peter has already read the lesson well . . .'

(b) *an ehi idi o Petros diavasi kala

On the other hand, in Icelandic (cf. (8)) the participle follows the manner adverb. That the participle does not move in Icelandic has been argued for by a number of people (cf. Holmberg 1986, among others). Yet the subject precedes both the manner adverb and the participle and is therefore VP-external.

(8)   Það   hefur   sennilega   einhver   alveg   lokið
        there   has   probably   someone   completely   finished
        verkefninu
        the assignment
        'Someone has probably completely finished the assignment.'

A similar argument concerning the placement of the subject relative to both the participle and certain adverbs has also been made for Irish (cf. (9) from Carnie 1995: 118).

(9)   Tá mé tar   éis   an teach a^L thógáil
       be I   after   the house   build
       'I have just built the house.'

In inverted orders, aspectual adverbs and manner adverbs obligatorily precede subjects in Greek, as the contrast between (10b) and (10a) shows.

(10) (a) an diavaze sinithos kala o   Janis
       if   read   usually   well   the-John-NOM
       'If John usually read well . . .'

(b) *an diavaze o   Janis   sinithos kala
      if   read   the-John-NOM   usually   well

More generally, VS sequences in VSO orders may be interrupted by adverbials in Greek, unlike in Irish (cf. McCloskey 1996a, the source of (11a)). As shown in (11a), adverbs cannot intervene between the verb and the postverbal subject in Irish, while this is possible in Greek (cf. (11b)). This contrast indicates that subjects are VP-external in Irish, but not in Greek (see also Rouveret 1994 for similar arguments concerning VP-external subjects in Welsh VSO clauses).[3]

---

[3] Benmamoun (Ch. 6, this volume) argues that in Arabic VSO orders, subjects are also VP-external. Thus there seems to be a split among VSO languages: (i) the VSO group of the Irish/ Arabic type, where subjects occupy [Spec, TP], and (ii) the VSO group of the Greek type, where subjects are VP-internal.

(11) (a) deireann (*i gcónaí) siad (i gcónaí) paidir   roimh am luí
         say   always they always   a prayer before time lie
         'They always say a prayer before bed-time.'

   (b) an pandreftike ktes   i   Maria   ton Petro
       if married   yesterday the-Mary-NOM the-Peter-ACC
       'If yesterday Mary married Peter . . .'

The conclusions we can draw from the discussion so far are the following:
(i) VSO orders cannot be analysed as involving I-to-C movement, since there
is an absence of root- vs. non-root-clause asymmetries (see also McCloskey
1996*b* for a similar conclusion concerning Irish VSO orders); and (ii) the subject in VSO orders is VP-internal, and thus the N features of I must be weak
in Greek and Spanish.

The above facts can be captured if we assume a phrase structure such as the
one given in (12), where * stands for potential subject landing-sites. The participle moves to Asp^0, the aspectual adverb occupies [Spec, AspP], the auxiliary
is inserted in T^0 and subsequently moves to $AgrS^0$. The subject remains in its
VP-internal position.[4]

(12)

Given that subjects in inverted orders are VP-internal, the question that arises
is what occupies [Spec, IP]. If VS(O) orders in NSLs involved a pro_{expl} in [Spec,
IP] (cf. Rizzi 1982), this would make Greek and Spanish qualify as strong EPP
languages, under the assumptions presented in Section 2. In other words, in

---

[4] See also Varlokosta *et al.* (1996), who argue for a similar structural representation and for
verb raising to Asp^0 on the basis of acquisition evidence.

these languages [Spec, IP] would be always licensed, either by merging an expletive or by A-moving the subject NP. If this analysis were correct, then Greek and English/Icelandic subjects would behave alike, as their preverbal position would be the result of A-fronting in both language groups.

If, however, VS(O) orders in NSLs did not involve an expletive *pro*, things would be different. In principle, Greek and Spanish would qualify as 'no/weak EPP = no [Spec, IP]' languages, and SVO orders would be an instance of Clitic Left Dislocation (CLLD). Given the reasoning presented in Section 2, SV(O) orders as the result of subject A-movement to [Spec, IP] will always be ruled out as Procrastinate violations. If this were correct, then Greek and English/Icelandic subjects would be expected to behave differently.

Here, we argue that [Spec, IP] as a structural position is not licensed in NSLs. In order for [Spec, IP] not to be licensed, two things need to be shown: first, that in SVO orders the subject is CLLDed, and secondly, that VSO orders lack an expletive. Note that it does not directly follow from the CLLD nature of the preverbal subject that [Spec, IP] is absent, since *pro* could always be argued to be there. It does, however, follow from the lack of an expletive that [Spec, IP] is absent, under the assumption that specifier positions are present in the structure only when an XP is merged to the maximal projection.

4. [SPEC, IP] IS NOT PROJECTED IN NULL-SUBJECT LANGUAGES

4.1. *Preverbal subjects have A'-properties*

In this section we review the arguments that preverbal subjects are CLLDed.[5] Once again, we demonstrate these properties for Greek, but we assume that they hold for Spanish and Romanian as well (see Barbosa 1994 for Romance in general).

It has been argued that SVO in Greek involves V raising to AgrS (cf. Rivero 1994, among others). SVO does not involve a Spec–head configuration: as we see in (13*a*), a number of adverbs intervene between the preverbal subject and the verb, while (13*b*) shows that adverbs cannot intervene between the subject and the auxiliary in English.

(13) (*a*)   O   Janis   xtes   meta apo   poles prospathies sinandise
       the-John-NOM yesterday after from many efforts   met
       ti   Maria
       the-Mary-ACC
       'John finally met Mary yesterday.'

(*b*)   *John after many efforts has met Mary

---

[5] See also Philippaki-Warburton (1985), Tsimpli (1990), Drachman and Klidi (1992), Anagnostopoulou (1994), Horrocks (1994), Alexiadou (1995), Alexiadou and Anagnostopoulou (1998), among others, for variants of this proposal.

As is clear from the above facts, Greek permits multiple dislocations. Furthermore, subjects in Greek can precede complementizers and *if*-clauses, as shown in (14*a*), while this is not possible in English, as shown in (14*b*).

(14) (*a*) epidi   o Janis   an erthi i Maria   tha figi
        because the-John-NOM if comes the-Mary-NOM-FUT leave
        'Because if Mary comes, John will leave.'

   (*b*) *because John if Mary comes will leave

Another type of evidence for the CLLD nature of the preverbal subject comes from interpretational effects involving QPs and indefinites (cf. Philippaki-Warburton 1985 for Greek; Sola 1992 for Catalan; and Barbosa 1994 for Romance). The preverbal subject has strong (partitive/specific) interpretation in (15*a*), but it has weak, existential interpretation in (15*b*), where it is in postverbal position. This is not the case in English, where preverbal QPs are ambiguous. Moreover, the subject in (15*a*) has a similar interpretation to the CLLDed object in (15*c*).

(15) (*a*) Enas heretise ti Maria
        one greeted the-Mary-ACC
        'A certain person/one of the people greeted Mary.'

   (*b*) heretise enas ti Maria
        greeted one the-Mary-ACC
        'Someone greeted Mary.'

   (*c*) ?Enan   ton   heretise i Maria
        one-ACC cl-ACC greeted the-Mary-NOM
        'Mary greeted one of the people.'

A similar point can be made on the basis of relative scope of indefinites and quantificational phrases (cf. (16)). The indefinite 'some student' in preverbal position in (16*a*) necessarily has wide scope over the universally quantified NP in object position, while it can have narrow scope in postverbal position (cf. (16*b*)). Once again, the subject in (14*a*) behaves like the CLLDed object in (16*c*).

(16) (*a*) kapjos fititis   arhiothetise kathe arthro
        some   student-NOM filed   every article

   (*b*) arhiothetise kapjos fititis kathe arthro

   (*c*) kapjo pedi   to   eksetase kathe kathigitis
        some child-ACC cl-ACC examined every professor-NOM

A potential objection to the proposal that in SVO orders the subject is CLLDed comes from the observation that indefinites and QPs appear in this position. Assuming that CLLD involves topichood, and under the standard assumption that indefinites and QPs are not tolerated as topics, we would not expect them to appear in preverbal position. However, note that quantifiers and indefinites are permitted in Greek in positions clearly involving CLLD, as shown in (17), where the indefinite subject 'someone' precedes the CLLDed object 'Peter'. Thus, Greek CLLDed subjects have some of the properties of Japanese and Hebrew 'Broad Subjects' (see Doron and Heycock, Chapter 4, this volume).

(17) Kapjos   ton Petro   ton   sinelave
      someone-NOM the-Peter-ACC cl-ACC arrested-3SG
      'Someone arrested Peter.'

Another piece of evidence pointing in the same direction as the previous examples comes from the facts of relative clause extraposition. As observed by Cinque (1983) (see Barbosa 1994 and Kayne 1994 for more recent discussions), relative clauses do not undergo extraposition in NSLs, as opposed to English (cf. (18a) vs. (19)). Extraposition, as is known, is blocked when the 'head' of the relative clause is a definite NP (cf. (18b)).

(18) (a) A man came that wanted to talk to you
     (b) *The man came that wanted to talk to you

(19) *Enas andras irthe pu ithele na su milisi
       a   man   came that wanted SUBJ you-GEN talk-2SG

These facts can be accounted for in terms of the *Specificity Constraint* of Fiengo and Higginbotham (1981). Preverbal indefinites in NSLs are, as we saw, specific, and extraposition is expected to be ungrammatical.

A further argument in favour of the CLLDed nature of the preverbal subject comes from a reinterpretation of 'Montalbetti's facts' given in (20). Montalbetti (1984) observed that overt personal pronouns in NSLs cannot be construed as bound variables, as shown in the Catalan example (20a). However, Sola (1992) and Barbosa (1994) point out that bound-variable construals with overt pronouns are possible when the pronouns appear in postverbal position, as in (20b).

(20) (a) *Tots els estudiants$_i$ es pensen que ells$_i$ aprovaran
            all the students   think   that they will-pass
            *'All the students$_i$ think that they$_i$ will pass.'
     (b) tots els jugadors$_i$ estan convencus que guanyaran ells$_i$
            all the players   are   persuaded that will-win   they
            'All the players$_i$ are persuaded that they$_i$ are the ones who will win.'

Sola (1992) and Barbosa (1994) account for these facts by assuming that only postverbal subjects occupy an A-position, and are thus able to be construed as bound variables. The same point cannot be made for Greek, since Greek lacks personal pronouns and makes use instead of demonstratives, which have different binding possibilities.

A final argument in favour of the CLLDed nature of the preverbal subject

comes from its interference with *wh*-movement in 'triggered' inversion constructions (cf. Torrego 1984; Canac-Marquis 1991; Drachman and Klidi 1992;
Anagnostopoulou 1994; Horrocks 1994):

(21) (*a*) Pjon   (*o Petros)   ide   (o Petros)?
       whom   the-Peter-NOM saw   the-Peter-NOM
       'Who did Peter see?'

   (*b*) Pote (o laos)   apofasise (o laos)   na   andidrasi?
       when the-people-NOM decided   the-people-NOM SUBJ react
       'When did the people decide to react?'

   (*c*) Pjon apo tus filus   tu (o Petros)   agapai (o Petros)
       whom from the friends his the-Peter-NOM loves the-Peter-NOM
       perisotero?
       more
       'Which one of his friends does Peter like most?'

(22) (*a*) *Pjos ton Petro   ton   ide?
       who the-Peter-ACC cl-ACC saw
       'Who saw Peter?'

   (*b*) Pote tin tenia   tin   provalan   ja proti fora?
       when the-movie-ACC cl-ACC showed-3PL for first time
       'When did they show the movie for the first time?'

   (*c*) Pjos apo tus fitites   tin askisi   tin   elise
       who from the students the-exercise-ACC cl-ACC solved-3SG
       amesos?
       immediately?
       'Which one of the students solved the exercise immediately?'

As (21) and (22) show, subjects and CLLDed objects are not allowed to inter-
fere between the *wh*-phrase and the verb when the fronted element is a non-D-
linked argument. Torrego (1984) and Canac-Marquis (1991) analyse this as a
subjacency effect, which Anagnostopoulou (1994) attributes to the status of
preverbal subjects as LDs.

From the above discussion, we conclude that SVO orders involve CLLD.
Thus, SVO orders are not the result of the Move XP option to check the EPP
feature. In the next section we turn to VSO orders.

4.2. *VSO orders do not involve an expletive*

According to Rizzi (1982) and related literature, inverted (VOS) constructions
involve an expletive *pro*. Chomsky (1995) adopts this analysis. Let us see
whether there is independent evidence for assuming that VSO orders do (not)
involve Expletive Merge. Since we never see the expletive in NSLs, the analysis
of VSO orders is not transparent. A potential argument for the presence of *pro*
in VSO structures might be the occurrence of Definiteness Restriction (DR)

effects. As is well known (cf. (23)), DR effects show up with *there*-type expletives and *il*-type expletives.

(23) (*a*) There arrived a man/*the man/*every man (English)

(*b*) il est arrive   un homme/*l'homme (French)
it is arrived a   man   /*the man

(*c*) er heeft iemand /*Jan een huis gebouwd (Dutch)
there has someone/*Jan a   house built

However, it has been observed (cf. Rizzi 1980; Burzio 1981; Chomsky 1981; Jaeggli 1982; Safir 1985; and see (24)), contra Belletti (1988), that DR effects in unaccusative constructions are systematically absent in NSLs. As (24) shows, in Greek the postverbal subject can be an indefinite, a proper name, or a strong, universally quantified NP.

(24) eftase ena pedi   /o Jorgos   /kathe filos mu
arrived a   child-NOM/the-George-NOM/every friend mine
'A child/John/every friend of mine arrived.'

Moreover, in transitive constructions, DR effects are absent in Greek (cf. (25*a*)), while they are present in Icelandic (cf. (25*b*)):

(25) (*a*) diavase ena pedi /kathe pedi to vivlio
read-3s a   child/every child the-book-ACC
'A/every child read the book.'

(*b*) Það lasu einhverjir stúdentar bókina
there read some   students the book
'Some students read the book.'

We take the non-universality of DR effects in unaccusative (and some unergative and transitive) constructions as evidence that DR effects are syntactically triggered in these contexts (unlike in existential and 'donkey anaphors' contexts). For this reason, we will adopt, for these constructions, Chomsky's (1995) analysis of the DR effects. More specifically, we will assume that *there* is a Determiner head which takes an NP complement, hence the DR effects (cf. Chomsky 1995; Frampton 1995—contra Hoekstra and Mulder 1990; Moro 1997, among others). On the basis of this reasoning, we can conclude that the lack of DR effects is an argument that there is no expletive in VS(O) orders in NSLs.

Of course, it could be claimed that the lack of DR effects is related to the nature of the expletive, overt vs. covert. English and Icelandic have overt expletives which trigger DR effects, while Greek and Spanish have covert expletives which do not trigger DR effects. However, the null hypothesis is that there should be no difference between overt and covert expletives, and that if there is one, this should be a PF-related difference. Moreover, there are languages that do not show DR effects with overt expletives (Arabic, cf. (26) from

Huybregts 1996) and languages that show DR effects with covert expletives (expletive-drop in Germanic, cf. (27)).

(26)   inna-hu fatah-a   l-'awlaad-u l-baab-a
        that-cl PERF.open-3SG.M the boys   the door

(27) (a) *um nottina   hafði [e] sokkið baturinn
        in   the night had   sunk   the boat
    (b) Um nottina   hafðu [e] sokkið nokkrir batar
        in   the night have   sunk   several boats

(cf. Sigurðsson 1989: 286)

Naturally, it is possible to postulate several types of expletive, as is the case in English (*it* vs. *there*). The question is whether it is necessary to analyse VS(O) as constructions with an expletive. As is clear from the discussion so far, there are arguments not to. Note that McCloskey (1996*a*) has reached a similar conclusion for Irish, taking the lack of DR effects (cf. (11*a*) above) to indicate that there is no expletive in the language.

Summarizing, in the previous sections we have shown (i) that SVO involves CLLD and (ii) that VSO orders lack an expletive. That SVO involves LD does not necessarily imply that VSO lacks an expletive, since one can always assume that an expletive is present. That VSO orders lack an expletive implies that SVO orders involve CLLD, since the lack of an expletive means that the language lacks [Spec, IP], and so it would qualify as a no-EPP language. As a result, SVO orders cannot be analysed as involving EPP-driven movement.

5. A PROPOSAL: PRONOMINAL AGREEMENT AND EPP

From the discussion so far, the immediate conclusion would be that, given that NSLs lack [Spec, IP], a reflex of the overt checking of the EPP, they must be no/weak-EPP languages. Such a conclusion is reached, for instance, by McCloskey (1996*a*) for Irish. However, here we would like to pursue an alternative, namely that NSLs are strong EPP languages where the EPP feature is not checked by Move/Merge XP but rather by V movement (see also Alexiadou and Anagnostopoulou, 1998).

The basic consideration is the following: if the EPP feature in I is strong, it must be eliminated when I is introduced into the derivation by insertion of a matching feature in its checking domain, before I is embedded in any distinct configuration. The matching feature may enter the checking domain of I by either Merge or Move, by substitution or adjunction. Here we explore the adjunction option.

Our proposal is couched in the basic intuition in the GB literature about NSLs, which is that they have (pro-)nominal agreement (cf. Taraldsen 1978; Chomsky 1981; Rizzi 1982; Safir 1985, among others). Capitalizing on this, we propose that verbal agreement morphology in NSLs includes a nominal element ([+D, +interpretable phi-features, potentially +Case]). In other words, we propose that the verbal agreement affixes in the Greek verbal paradigm in (28*b*) play exactly the same role as the pronouns do in the English paradigm in (28*a*).[6] Thus, V raising to AgrS° suffices to erase the EPP feature (see Alexiadou and Anagnostopoulou, 1998 for further elaboration).

(28) (*a*) I love   (*b*) agap*o*
           you love   agap*as*
           he loves   agap*a*
           we love   agap*ame*
           you love   agap*ate*
           they love   agap*ane*

Under our proposal, EPP checking is reduced to AGR checking in the sense of [nominal] feature checking. *Pro*-drop languages are the only ones that have the verbal agreement properties that permit this.

Under our view, verb movement is sufficient to check the EPP feature; moreover, it is less costly owing to its formal similarity to covert feature movement. Specifically, verb movement to AgrS° gives a head-adjunction structure, which is not strictly to the root; as such, it does not extend the phrase marker. Hence, it should be preferred for reasons of 'Economy of Projection'.[7] Since the checking relation is established in a head–head configuration, the projection of a specifier, which extends the phrase marker, is not necessary (see Alexiadou and Anagnostopoulou, 1998 for further discussion).[8]

This proposal makes an attempt to link the (non-)availability of [Spec, IP] to the syntactic and morphological properties of the languages in question. However, it differs from other similar proposals in the literature, for instance Ouhalla (1994). Ouhalla argues that the EPP is related to the relative richness/impoverishment of agreement morphology. English-type languages insert an overt expletive in subject positions not filled with a noun phrase argument to satisfy the EPP. NSLs do not have to insert an expletive because the features of AgrS are 'identified' in terms of agreement morphology. Under our proposal, the languages that are able to erase the EPP feature via V movement are not only those that have visibly rich agreement. Celtic and Arabic also behave similarly to Greek and Spanish, although these languages exhibit impoverished agreement in their VSO orders. What is important for our account is the syntactic behaviour of the subjects in the languages under discussion, and whether

---

[6] Cf. Philippaki-Warburton (1987, 1989), who has proposed that subjects in Greek are included in the morphology of the verb.

[7] Here we use the term differently from Speas (1994).

[8] The checking of the EPP by movement of a head rather than a noun phrase is also argued for independently by Svenonius (1996) for verb–particle constructions. Pollock (1996) also makes a similar proposal. He proposes that in Italian, verb movement suffices to check the EPP feature. However, in Pollock's system the verb movement is triggered by the non-interpretable Case feature of the nominal agreement morphology. Thus, EPP checking is parasitic on Case checking.

the languages that have VSO orders also permit a *pro*-drop structure. And, as a matter of fact, all of these languages do so.[9]

The implications of our proposal can be summarized as follows: EPP is universally strong, since it is a formal property of sentences. EPP must be seen as a formal property related to the interfaces (preferably the PF part of the grammar, see Alexiadou and Anagnostopoulou, 1998), given that in Chomsky (1995) AGR is present only when strong (i.e. relevant for one of the two interfaces).[10] What is parameterized is the mode of EPP checking, namely projection of a specifier vs. head adjunction. Moreover, the need to check the strong D-feature of AgrS is the trigger for V raising in NSLs.[11]

6. CONCLUSION

In this chapter we have examined the relation between the EPP and the (non-) availability of [Spec, IP]. We have shown that NSLs differ from non-NSLs in that they lack [Spec, IP]; thus, the obligatoriness of [Spec, IP] for the EPP requirement does not hold across all languages. We have proposed that, although [Spec, IP] is not universally present, EPP is universally strong. Crucially, we have outlined a parameterization of EPP checking: projection of [Spec, IP], as a result of Move/Merge XP, vs. head adjunction, as a result of X^0 (verb) movement, suggesting that NSLs opt for the latter. We have proposed that it is the pronominal character of verbal agreement in this language group that permits checking of the EPP feature in $AgrS^0$ via verb movement.

What the proposed parameter actually does, apart from presenting two possible ways in which EPP is checked, is to regulate the presence vs. absence of [Spec, AgrSP] and correlate this to the presence vs. absence of DR effects. In other words, it identifies which languages have an active [Spec, AgrSP]. These also exhibit DR effects. The ones that lack [Spec, AgrSP] also lack DR effects. As pointed out in Alexiadou and Anagnostopoulou (1998), this parameter interacts with the [Spec, TP] parameter (cf. Carnie 1993; Jonas and Bobaljik 1993) in an interesting way, regulating word-order variation in the IP domain cross-linguistically.

The [Spec, TP] parameter identifies the languages in which subjects occupy

---

[9] Note that non-finite clauses in Irish and in Welsh exhibit SOV and SVO orders, respectively. However, it is not clear to us whether these constructions are indeed of a verbal nature. The issue awaits further research.

[10] Note that, in principle, we could follow Chomsky in dispensing with the category AGR altogether, and suggest that V raising to T erases the EPP feature. However, if T were the relevant category, then no interesting parallels concerning the various types of VSO languages could be drawn (see Sect. 6 and Alexiadou and Anagnostopoulou, 1998 for further discussion).

[11] While our proposal can potentially explain why it is the case that NSLs are also verb-raising languages, it says nothing about the triggers for verb raising in non-NSLs such as French (see Alexiadou and Anagnostopoulou, 1998 for further discussion).

[Spec, TP], and contrasts them with those in which subjects never appear in this position. As Jonas and Bobaljik (1993) argue, the following descriptive generalization holds: subject-inverted orders with transitive predicates and object shift can only exist in languages which license [Spec, TP] as an intermediate landing-site for the subject. Thus, Icelandic licenses [Spec, TP] and permits transitive expletive constructions, while English does not license [Spec, TP] and shows an intransitivity constraint on inverted orders. Celtic and Arabic have also been argued to be similar to Icelandic with respect to the [Spec, TP] parameter.

Combining these two parameters, we are led to four combinations, illustrated in (29), where [+/–] refer to presence/absence of [Spec, AgrSP] and [Spec, TP], respectively.

(29)	Spec, AgrSP	Spec, TP
(*a*)	+	–
(*b*)	+	+
(*c*)	–	–
(*d*)	–	+

Languages that instantiate the combinations in (29) are: (*a*) English; (*b*) Icelandic; (*c*) Greek; and (*d*) Celtic/Arabic. The properties associated with these languages are correctly predicted to follow from the combination of the two parameters: language type (*a*), which has an active [Spec, AgrSP] but not an active [Spec, TP], has (i) ECs with intransitivity and VP-internal subjects and (ii) DR effects. Language type (*b*), which has both specifiers active, has (i) TECs with external subjects and (ii) DR effects. Language type (*c*), in which both specifiers are not active, has (i) VSO with internal subjects and (ii) no DR effects. Language type (*d*), in which only [Spec, TP] is active, has (i) VSO with external subjects (see footnote 3) and (ii) no DR effects.

REFERENCES

Alexiadou, A. (1994), 'Issues in the Syntax of Adverbs', Ph.D. dissertation, University of Potsdam.
——(1995), 'Word Order Alternations in Modern Greek', paper presented at the 5th CGG in La Coruña.
——and Anagnostopoulou, E. (1998), 'Parameterizing Agr: Word Order, Verb-Movement and EPP-Checking', *Natural Language and Linguistic Theory*, 16.3.
Anagnostopoulou, E. (1994), 'Clitic Dependencies in Modern Greek', Ph.D. dissertation, University of Salzburg.
Barbosa, P. (1994), 'A New Look at the Null Subject Parameter', paper presented at CONSOLE III, Venice.
Belletti, A. (1988), 'The Case of Unaccusatives', *Linguistic Inquiry*, 19: 1–34.

Burzio, L. (1981), 'Intransitive Verbs and Italian Auxiliaries', Ph.D. dissertation, MIT.

Canac-Marquis, R. (1991), 'On the Obligatory Character of Inversion in Spanish', in D. Bates (ed.), *Proceedings of West Coast Conference on Formal Linguistics*, 10: 309–18.

Carnie, A. (1993), 'Nominal Predicates and Absolutive Case Marking in Irish', *MIT Working Papers*, 19: 131–74.

——(1995), 'Non-Verbal Predication and Head-Movement', Ph.D. dissertation, MIT.

Chomsky, N. (1981), *Lectures on Government and Binding*, Foris, Dordrecht.

——(1995), *The Minimalist Program*, MIT Press, Cambridge, Mass.

Cinque, G. (1983), 'On the Theory of Relative Clauses and Markedness', *The Linguistic Review*, 1: 247–94.

Dobrovie-Sorin, C. (1987), 'Syntaxe du roumain', Thèse de Doctorat d'Etat, Université de Paris VII.

Drachman, G., and Klidi, S. (1992), 'The Proper Treatment of Adverbial Questions in Greek: The Extended Minimal Structure Hypothesis', *Studies in Greek Linguistics*, 13: 371–90.

Fiengo, R., and Higginbotham, J. (1981), 'Opacity in NP', *Linguistic Analysis*, 7: 395–421.

Frampton, J. (1995), 'Expletive Insertion', paper presented at the Role Economy Principles in Linguistic Theory Workshop in Berlin, 9–12 February.

Hoekstra, T., and Mulder, R. (1990), 'Unergatives as Copular Verbs: Locational and Existential Predication', *The Linguistic Review*, 7: 1–79.

Holmberg, A. (1986), 'Word Order and Syntactic Features in the Scandinavian Languages and English', Ph.D. dissertation, University of Stockholm.

Horrocks, G. (1994), 'Subjects and Configurationality', *Journal of Linguistics*, 30: 81–109.

Huybregts, R. (1996), 'Minimalism, Typology and Language Universals', paper presented at TIN 96, Utrecht.

Iatridou, S., and Kroch, A. (1992), 'On the Licensing of CP-Recursion and its Relevance to the Germanic Verb-Second Phenomena', *Working Papers in Scandinavian Syntax*, 50: 1–24.

Jaeggli, O. (1982), *Topics in Romance Syntax*, Foris, Dordrecht.

Jonas, D., and Bobaljik, J. (1993), 'Specs for Subjects', *MIT Working Papers*, 18: 59–98.

Kayne, R. (1994), *The Antisymmetry of Syntax*, MIT Press, Cambridge, Mass.

Levin, B., and Rappaport, M. (1995), *Unaccusativity: At the Syntax–Lexical Semantics Interface*, MIT Press, Cambridge, Mass.

McCloskey, J. (1996a), 'Subjects and Subject Positions in Irish', in B. Borsley and I. Roberts (eds.), *The Syntax of the Celtic Languages*, Cambridge University Press, Cambridge, 241–83.

——(1996b), 'On the Scope of Verb Movement in Irish', *Natural Language and Linguistic Theory*, 14: 47–104.

Montalbetti, M. (1984), 'After Binding: On the Interpretation of Pronouns', Ph.D. dissertation, MIT.

Moro, A. (1997), *The Raising of Predicates: Predicative Noun Phrases and the Theory of Clause Structure*, Cambridge University Press, Cambridge.

Ouhalla, J. (1994), 'The Syntactic Representation of Arguments', Ms., Max Planck Berlin.

Philippaki-Warburton, I. (1985), 'Word Order in Modern Greek', *Transactions of the Philological Society*, 2: 113–43.

——(1987), 'The Theory of Empty Categories and the Pro-Drop Parameter in Modern Greek', *Journal of Linguistics*, 23: 289–318.

——(1989), 'Subjects in English and in Greek', Ms., University of Reading.

Pollock, J.-Y. (1996), 'Eléments de syntaxe du verbe dans les langues germaniques et romanes', Ms., University of Amiens.

Rivero, M.-L. (1994), 'Verb Movement and the Structure of IP in the Languages of the Balkans', *Natural Language and Linguistic Theory*, 12: 63–120.

Rizzi, L. (1980), 'Negation, *Wh*-Movement and the Null Subject Parameter', paper read at the 5th GLOW Colloquium.

——(1982), *Issues in Italian Syntax*, Foris, Dordrecht.

Rouveret, A. (1994), *Syntaxe du gallois*, CNRS Editions, Paris.

Safir, K. (1985), *Syntactic Chains*, Cambridge University Press, Cambridge.

Sigurðsson, H. A. (1989), 'Verbal Syntax and Case in Icelandic: A Comparative GB Approach', Ph.D. dissertation, University of Lund.

Sola, J. (1992), 'Agreement and Subjects', Ph.D. dissertation, Universitat Autonoma de Barcelona.

Speas, M. (1994), 'Null Arguments in a Theory of Economy of Projection', University of Massachusetts Occasional Papers 17: 179–208, GLSA: University of Massachusetts, Amherst.

Svenonius, P. (1996), 'The Verb–Particle Alternation in the Scandinavian Languages', Ms., University of Tromsø.

Taraldsen, K. (1978), 'On the NIC, Vacuous Application and the That-Trace Filter', Ms., MIT.

Torrego, E. (1984), 'On Inversion in Spanish and Some of Its Effects', *Linguistic Inquiry*, 15: 103–30.

Tsimpli, I.-M. (1990), 'The Clause Structure and Word Order of Modern Greek', *UCL Working Papers in Linguistics*, 2: 226–55.

Varlokosta, S., Vainikka, A., and Rohrbacher, B. (1996), 'Functional Projections, Markedness and "Root Infinitives" in Early Child Greek', paper presented at the GLOW Workshop on Current Trends in Modern Greek Syntax.

Zubizarreta, M.-L. (1992), 'Word Order in Spanish and the Nature of Nominative Case', Ms., University of Southern California.

6

Spec–Head Agreement and
Overt Case in Arabic

ELABBAS BENMAMOUN

1. INTRODUCTION

In pre-Minimalist analyses of nominative and accusative Case in languages
such as English, the standard assumption was that nominative Case is assigned
in a Spec–head relation with I and accusative Case in a government configuration. Chomsky (1995), on the other hand, proposes a Minimalist theory of
Structural Case that requires that it be checked exclusively in a Spec–head configuration. However, while the Spec–head requirement dispenses with government and the disjunction it introduces into the configurational requirements
on structural Case, this theory introduces another disjunction with respect to
the point in the derivation where the Case features are checked (by or after
Spellout, essentially overtly or covertly).[1] Moreover, this theory departs from
the original insight of Vergnaud (1982) that Case interfaces primarily with PF.
In this chapter, I shall argue for (1), which maintains both Chomsky's Minimalist proposal that Case is checked exclusively in a Spec–head configuration
and Vergnaud's insight that the Case module interfaces with PF. To do that I
shall reanalyse Arabic data that on the surface seems to support the theory that
Case can be checked after Spellout. I shall attempt to show that at an overt
point in the derivation the two elements involved in Case checking are in a
Spec–head configuration suitable for Case checking.

(1)   Structural Case is checked overtly in a Spec–head configuration.

With respect to Standard Arabic (SA) (2) and Moroccan Arabic (MA) (3),
the challenge to (1) comes primarily from postverbal subjects (2a and 3a) and
genitive NPs (2b and 3b) which follow the elements that check their Case.[2]

(2) (a)   žaaʔa l-kaatib-u   (SA)
           came   the-writer-NOM
           'The writer came.'

---

[1] Chomsky (1995: ch. 4) proposes that Case checking at LF might involve feature adjunction;
the assumption being that overt movement of categories is driven by PF requirements.
[2] Objects can be argued to check their Case overtly in a Spec–head configuration within the VP
shell as argued in Koizumi (1993) and Lasnik (1995).

(b)   žaaʔa kaatib-u   l-maqaal-i
       came writer-NOM the-article-GEN
       'The author of the article came.'

(3) (a)   ža   l-wəld   (MA)
           came the-boy
           'The boy came.'

(b)   qrit ktab l-wəld
               (I) read book the-boy
               'I read the boy's book.'

If the postverbal subjects and genitive NPs are within the lexical projection (in the Spec of the VP and NP, respectively) the only assumption that is consistent with the Minimalist theory of Case is that these NPs raise at LF to check their Case. However, there is strong evidence that this assumption is not correct. I will start first with postverbal subjects.

2. POSTVERBAL SUBJECTS

The standard analyses for sentences with the VSO order (Mohammad 1989; Benmamoun 1992; Fassi Fehri 1993) assume that the verb is in I and the subject is in the Spec of VP:

(4)

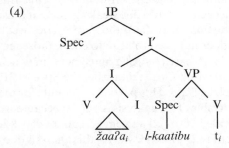

Moreover, since in Arabic SVO order is also available (5), these analyses assume that in these instances the subject moves overtly to the Spec of IP.[3]

(5) (a)   l-kaatib-u   žaaʔa   (SA)
           the-writer-NOM came
           'The writer came.'

(b)   l-wəld   ža   (MA)
       the-boy came
       'The boy came.'

Since nominative Case must be checked with the head of IP, in the VSO order the checking relation must take place in the covert component given that

---

[3] See Doron and Heycock (Ch. 4, this volume) for arguments that the preverbal NP is a real subject.

government as a legitimate configuration for checking Case is dispensed with. By contrast, in the SVO order this checking relation obtains overtly.[4]

One potential argument that the postverbal subject is in the Spec of VP comes from the well-known agreement asymmetries that characterize the VSO and SVO orders in Standard Arabic. When the subject follows the verb, it agrees with it in person and gender (partial agreement). But when the subject precedes the verb, agreement is in person, gender, and number (full agreement):

(6) (a)   ʔakal-*at* T-Taalibaat-u   (SA)
          ate-3FS   the-students.FP-NOM
          'The women students ate.'

   (b)   *ʔakal-*na* T-Taalibaat-u
          ate-3FP   the-student.FP-NOM

(7) (a)   T-Taalibaat-u   ʔakal-*na*
          the-student.FP-NOM ate-3FP
          'The woman student ate.'

   (b)   *T-Taalibaat-u   ʔakal-*at*
          the-student.FP-NOM ate-3FS

Suppose that agreement must be checked in a Spec–head configuration (Sportiche 1990). Suppose further that partial agreement is weak and full agreement is strong (Roberts and Shlonsky 1996). In Minimalist terms, this entails that full agreement must be checked overtly while weak agreement must be checked covertly (owing to Procrastinate). In (6a), the verb carries weak agreement and therefore the subject does not need to raise to check those fea-· tures overtly. By contrast, in (7a) the verb carries strong agreement, in which case the subject must raise overtly and check those features in the Spec of IP, a configuration where it can also check its Case. This partially accounts for the agreement asymmetries in Standard Arabic. This analysis is partial because we still need to explain why a verb generated with full agreement cannot check it in the Spec of VP prior to its movement to I.[5] In other words, this analysis does not fully account for why (6b) is ill formed. This is where the idea that the postverbal subject is in the Spec of VP comes in. Being in the Spec of VP, the subject cannot check the agreement features because those features, according to Chomsky (1995), must be checked in a functional projection and not in the thematic shell. Given this crucial assumption, (6b) receives a straightforward analysis. Since the subject in (6b) is in the Spec of VP it could not check the strong agreement features on the verb prior to the movement of the latter to I. Therefore, the only alternative to checking nominative Case overtly under government is LF movement of the postverbal subject to the Spec of IP.

---

[4] In pre-Minimalist terms, VSO involves Case under government and SVO involves Case under Spec–head agreement (Koopman and Sportiche 1991).

[5] I am assuming with Chomsky (1995) that agreement does not correspond to an autonomous syntactic projection (see Benmamoun 1993a for arguments from Arabic).

However, there are strong arguments that show that the postverbal subject must be outside the VP overtly.[6]

The first argument comes from the distribution of sentential negation in the context of copular constructions. Sentential negation in Moroccan Arabic consists of two morphemes, the proclitic *ma* and the enclitic *š*. When there is a verb in the sentence, *ma* occurs as a prefix and *š* as a suffix:

(8)   Omar ma-qra-š   lə-ktab   (MA)
        Omar NEG-read-NEG the-book
        'Omar did not read the book.'

In Benmamoun (1992, 1997*a*) *ma* is posited as head of the negative projection located between TP and VP. *Š*, by contrast, is analysed as an adjunct to the VP. Verb movement to T proceeds through the negative projection (to circumvent relativized minimality, Benmamoun 1992).

(9)

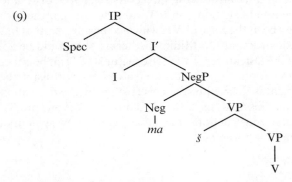

In copular sentences with present tense interpretation, the so-called verbless sentences, *ma* merges with *š*:

(10) (*a*) Omar ma-ši   f-d-dar   (MA)
            Omar NEG-NEG   in-the-house
            'Omar is not in the house.'

     (*b*) Omar ma-ši   kaddab
            Omar NEG-NEG   liar
            'Omar is not a liar.'

     (*c*) Omar ma-ši   mriD
            Omar NEG-NEG   sick
            'Omar is not sick.'

This merger is not possible when there is a verb in the sentence:

(11) (*a*) *Omar ma-ši   qra lə-ktab   (MA)
            Omar NEG-NEG   read the-book

---

[6] McCloskey (1996) and Shlonsky (1997) also argue that the postverbal subject in Irish and Hebrew, respectively, must be out of the VP.

(*b*) *Omar qra ma-ši lə-ktab
    Omar read NEG-NEG the-book

Example (11*a*) is ruled out because verb movement to T has not taken place. On the other hand, (11*b*) is ill formed because the movement of the verb to I violates relativized minimality. Now consider the distribution of the subject. In sentences with a verbal head, the subject can either follow or precede the verb:

(12) (*a*) Omar ma-qra-š lə-ktab   (MA)
        Omar NEG-read-NEG the-book
        'Omar did not read the book.'

    (*b*) ma-qra-š Omar lə-ktab
        NEG-read-NEG Omar the-book
        'Omar did not read the book.'

Example (12*a*) follows straightforwardly if the subject is in the Spec of IP and the verb together with sentential negation is in I. Turning to (12*b*), if the verb is in I then the subject must be in the Spec of VP, which is the analysis that has been provided for these constructions. In Minimalist terms, that could be accounted for by saying that the D-features or the Case features of I can be either weak or strong. If they are strong, movement is obligatory. By contrast if the features are weak, movement is delayed to the covert stage of the derivation (by Procrastinate). However, this analysis of the VSO order makes one prediction, namely that in copular constructions, the subject can follow sentential negation. This prediction is not borne out:

(13) (*a*) *ma-ši Omar mriD   (MA)
        NEG-NEG Omar sick

    (*b*) Omar ma-ši mriD
        Omar NEG-NEG sick
        'Omar is not sick.'

Consider the derivation of (13). At the point in the derivation when I merges with NegP, the representation is as in (14).

(14)

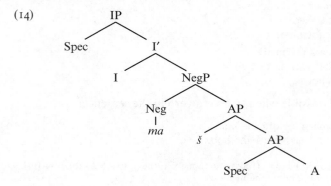

The NP *Omar* is generated in the Spec of the lexical projection where it gets its thematic role, namely AP. Assuming that movement to the Spec of IP is optional, the subject can stay in the Spec of AP.[7] Since there is no head movement, *ma* merges with *š*.

The above problem does not arise if we give up the idea that the VSO order always entails that the subject is in the Spec of the lexical projection where it gets its thematic role. Suppose that the subject must move to the Spec of I to check its Case overtly in a Spec–head configuration in conformity with the principle in (1). Then, (13) is ruled out because the subject has not moved overtly to the Spec of IP. If this is correct, the VSO order must involve verb movement beyond IP (Aoun *et al.* 1994).

The second piece of evidence that the VSO order does not always entail that the subject is in the specifier of the lexical projection comes from existential constructions in Standard Arabic. Like the situation in English, the Arabic existential construction involves the locative *pro*-form *there* and an indefinite NP marked with nominative Case.[8]

(15)   hunaaka Taalib-un   fii l-ḥadiiqati   (SA)
        there   student-NOM in the-garden
        'There is a student in the garden.'

Now consider the above sentence with an overt auxiliary:

(16)   kaana hunaaka Taalib-un   fii l-ḥadiiqati   (SA)
        was   there   student-NOM in the-garden
        'There was a student in the garden.'

(17)   *hunaaka kaana Taalib-un   fii l-ḥadiiqati   (SA)
        there   was   student-NOM in the-garden

---

[7] I will assume with Benmamoun (1992) and Fassi Fehri (1993) that there is a temporal projection in copular constructions (see also Déchaine 1993).

[8] This suggests that maybe in English as well the indefinite is nominative rather than partitive. Notice that the lexical NP is in the Spec of the lexical projection. I will assume that the expletive itself could be a spellout of the overtly moved N-features of the NP. Chomsky (1995) and Hornstein (1996), by contrast, propose that the NP moves and adjoins to the expletive (to check Case). The main reason for movement as far as Hornstein (1996) is concerned is the fact that the relation between the expletive and the associate is subject to the restrictions on A-movement. However, there are no discernible LF effects from this putative LF raising (see Hornstein's arguments against Chomsky's evidence from binding theory for raising the features of the associate covertly). In fact, as far as scope and polarity licensing are concerned, the associate is interpreted in its surface position (Brody 1995; Hornstein 1996). This motivates Hornstein to propose that the associate reconstructs to its surface position. All these facts follow if we assume that the expletive is a spellout of an overtly moved N-feature of the NP in situ (i.e. *there*-insertion is akin to *do*-support in the context of verb movement; it is inserted to support/spell out a stranded feature). The fact that no binding effects result from this movement is due to the fact that the overt movement does not move interpretable features. The relation between the expletive and the NP displays properties of A-movement because it involves movement from one A-position to another A-position.

In (16) the expletive must follow the auxiliary verb. That sentence receives a straightforward analysis if we assume that the expletive is in the Spec of IP and the lexical NP is in the Spec of the lexical projection. This shows clearly that the VSO order does not necessarily entail that the subject is within the thematic projection. The expletive, not being an argument, cannot be generated in the Spec of the lexical projection. The VSO order exhibited in (16) does, however, show that the verb is in a position higher than IP. I will assume that this is a focus projection[9] (Ouhalla 1992):[10]

(18)

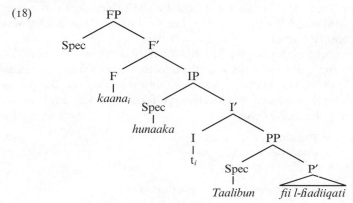

If the above remarks are on the right track, then we need to find an alternative account for partial agreement in Standard Arabic. In particular, if the postverbal subject is indeed in the Spec of IP overtly, where it checks its Case, we have to explain why (6b) is ill formed.

In Benmamoun (1996, 1997b), an alternative explanation of the agreement asymmetries in Standard Arabic is given. It is proposed that the agreement asymmetry in question is essentially a matter of how the number feature on the verb is spelled out in PF. The verb is generated with the full set of agreement features, which are checked overtly in a Spec–head configuration with the NP subject. In PF, the number feature can be spelled out either by an affix, which is the case when the subject precedes the verb (SV order), or by merger between the verb and the subject, which is the case when the subject follows the verb (VS order):

---

[9] The fact that the expletive cannot occur in the preverbal position suggests that in the SVO order the subject is in the Spec of FP. That is, the movement of the subject to FP is optional but that of the verb is not. Expletives cannot move to the Spec of FP since they are inserted in the Spec of IP to check Case and the EPP features only. This analysis could also shed some light on the well-known restriction in Arabic on the distribution of non-specific indefinites (Ayoub 1981). The latter are not allowed in the preverbal position. Since we are arguing that Case must be checked overtly, this implies that non-specific indefinites are banned from the Spec of FP and not the Spec of TP (see Bobaljik and Jonas 1996 for the same argument based on Icelandic).

[10] For other functional projections between IP and CP see Rizzi (1995). For Arabic in particular, see Shlonsky (1996).

(19)   *Number agreement spellout in PF*

        SA
        V [α number]
    V   Affix[α number]/NP[α number]

Since number is an intrinsic feature of the subject, the merger of the latter with the verb in PF amounts to spelling out the number feature. This in turn makes spelling out the number feature by an affix redundant.[11] This analysis predicts that in dialects where this merger does not take place, we should expect full agreement with the postverbal subject. This is indeed the case in Moroccan Arabic:

(20) (a) kla-w lə-wlad   (MA)
          ate-3P the-children
          'The children ate.'

     (b) lə-wlad   kla-w
          the-children ate-3P
          'The children ate.'

     (c) *kla   lə-wlad
          ate-3S the-children

If this analysis is on the right track, we can maintain the principle in (1) as far as nominative Case in Arabic is concerned. The postverbal subject is at least in the Spec of IP, where it checks Case and agreement overtly.

One of the advantages of the above analysis is that it explains some puzzling facts in Standard Arabic. The first set of facts concerns null pronominals. Consider the agreement patterns when the subject occurs between an auxiliary verb and the main verb:

(21) (a) kaan-*at*   T-Taalibaat-u   *ya-ʔkul-na*   (SA)
          be.PAST.3FS the-students.FP-NOM 3-eat-FP
          'The students were eating.'

     (b) T-Taalibaat-u   kun-*na*   *ya-ʔkul-na*
          the-students.FP-NOM be.PAST.3FP 3-eat-FP
          'The students were eating.'

As expected, the main verb carries full agreement and the auxiliary verb partial agreement. Interestingly, when the subject is a null pronominal, both verbs must carry full agreement:

(22) (a) kun-*na*   *ya-ʔkul-na*   (SA)
          be.PAST.3FP 3-eat-FP
          'They were eating.'

---

[11] See Benmamoun (1996) for arguments that this merger takes place in PF rather than in the syntax or the lexicon.

(*b*) *kaan-at   ya-ʔkul-na
be.PAST.3FS 3-eat.FP

Notice that these facts cannot be explained away by resorting to the identification condition on null pronominals; the reason being that the main verb carries all the features necessary to license the null pronominal. Under an analysis that takes full agreement as an indication that the subject is in the Spec of IP overtly, the only viable analysis is to assume that null pronominals must check their Case overtly. In Minimalist terms, this could be implemented by assuming that the Case features on null pronominals are strong but those on lexical NPs can be either weak or strong. However, it is not clear what makes the Case features on null pronominals strong.

This problem does not arise once we assume that both lexical NPs and null pronominals check their Case and agreement overtly. The difference between them resides in how the features are spelled out on the verb. In the case of lexical NPs, they can be spelled out by merger between the verb and the lexical NP. In the case of null pronominals, on the other hand, they can only be spelled out by an affix. They cannot be spelled out by merger because null pronominals do not have a phonological matrix that will allow them to participate in PF merger.

The second set of puzzling facts comes from agreement in the context of variables. In these contexts, extraction of the subject seems to require full agreement:

(23) (*a*)   raʔaytu T-Tullaba   l-ladiina nažaħ*uu*   (SA)
      (I) saw   the-students who   succeeded.3MP
      'I saw the students who passed.'

   (*b*) *   raʔaytu T-Tullaba   l-ladiina na žaħ*a*
      (I) saw   the-students who   succeeded.3MS

Again, rather than resorting to some *ad hoc* analysis that stipulates that variables must check their Case overtly, the fact that full agreement is obligatory when the subject is a trace follows automatically from the assumption that Case and agreement are checked overtly. When the subject is a trace, agreement must be spelled out by an affix given that the alternative, namely merger, is not possible since the trace, like the null pronominal, does not have a phonological matrix.

To sum up, there are strong arguments that show that the postverbal subject is at least in the Spec of IP overtly, where it can check Case and agreement as required by (1).[12] The partial agreement facts do not show that the subject is in the Spec of VP on the surface, they just illustrate another strategy of spelling out number agreement features in PF.

---

[12] See also Alexiadou and Anagnostopoulou (Ch. 5, this volume) for arguments that the EPP features are checked overtly.

3. GENITIVE CASE

In this section, I consider another instance of a genitive NP that follows the head that checks its Case and suggest that here too genitive Case is checked in a Spec–head configuration overtly as required by (1).

The main argument comes from genitive NPs in the context of quantifiers such as *kull* (all) in Standard Arabic. Constructions headed by this quantifier display the standard properties of the construct state in Arabic (Fassi Fehri 1982; Benmamoun 1993*b*).[13] The head Q carries the Case assigned to the whole projection, while the NP following Q is assigned genitive Case. Compare (24) and (25).

(24)   ra?aytu *kull-a*   T-Tullaab-i   (SA)
         (I) saw   all-ACC the-students-GEN
         'I saw all the students.'

(25)   ra?aytu muʕallim-a l-walad-i   (SA)
         (I) saw   teacher-ACC the-boy-GEN
         'I saw the boy's teacher.'

In (24), *kull* carries accusative Case and the NP following it carries genitive Case. Similarly, in (25) *muʕallim* carries accusative Case and the NP following it carries genitive Case. Notice that the fact that the NP has genitive Case in the context of Q shows that this Case is not inherent since there is no thematic relation between the quantifier and the lexical NP. Fassi Fehri (1993) and Siloni (1994) also show that genitive Case must be structural since it can be assigned in ECM contexts, as the following example from Fassi Fehri (1993: 220) illustrates:

(26)   ðann-u   r-ražuli   ðakiyy-an xaTa?un   (SA)
       believing-NOM the-man-GEN clever-ACC error-NOM
       'Believing that the man is clever is an error.'

Returning to QPs and adopting the essential insight of Ritter (1991) and Siloni (1994), I will assume that there are two functional projections above the lexical projection in the construct state. Departing slightly from their analysis, I will assume that the first projection above the lexical projection is a DP and the projection above DP is the equivalent of the FP projection in sentences.[14]

The genitive is generated in the Spec of NP and then moves to the Spec of

---

[13] Some of the main properties of the construct state are: (i) nothing can intervene between the members of the construct state (CS)—thus, adjectives must follow all members of the CS; (ii) the CS complex constitutes a single prosodic unit; and (iii) only the last member of the CS can carry the marker of definiteness (see Borer 1994).

[14] Ritter (1991) argues that the highest projection is DP and the intermediate projection is NumP (number phrase). Siloni (1994) also takes the highest XP to be DP, but takes the intermediate XP to be AgrP. What is important for the present concern is their insight that there are two functional positions that attract the head noun in the construct state.

DP, where it checks genitive Case.[15] The head of NP moves to D and then to F. This derives the order where the head noun precedes the genitive NP.

(27)

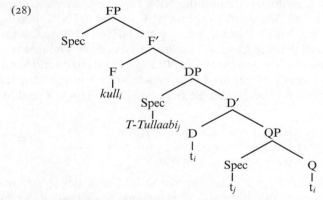

Since the phrase headed by *kull* displays the standard properties of the construct state, it has the representation in (28) (for more detailed discussion of this construction in Arabic, see Benmamoun 1993*b*).

(28)   FP
        /   \
     Spec   F'
            /   \
          F   DP
          | /   \
        kull_i Spec   D'
              | /   \
         T-Tullaabi_j D   QP
                      | /   \
                    t_i Spec   Q
                          | |
                        t_j   *t_i*

Q is generated as head of the QP projection complement of D. Like nouns, Q moves to the head of DP and the head of FP. This movement derives the order where Q precedes the genitive (Benmamoun 1993*b*). That Q is in Spec–head relation with the genitive is confirmed by some intriguing agreement facts discussed in Benmamoun (1993*b*). When the genitive is a null pronominal, both Q and the lexical noun head must carry agreement.[16] This is illustrated in (29).[17]

---

[15] The underlying assumption is that genitive Case and agreement are checked in the Spec of DP. That DP is implicated in genitive Case is not controversial.

[16] I am assuming that clitics are agreement markers and not incorporated pronouns. For evidence to that effect see Aoun (1993), Benmamoun (1993*b*), Shlonsky (1997), and Aoun and Benmamoun (1998).

[17] The same facts obtain with objects and complements of PPs (see Benmamoun 1993*b* for details):

(29) (a) daxala   ʕamm-u-hum   kull-i-him   (SA)
         entered.3MS uncle-NOM-3MP all-GEN-3MP
         'The uncle of them all came in.'

    (b) *daxala   ʕamm-u   kull-i-him
         entered.3MS uncle-NOM all-GEN-3MP

One possible analysis is that agreement is due to the identification requirement on *pro*; Q must carry the necessary agreement features to identify *pro*. However, the identification condition on *pro* cannot explain the agreement on the head noun in (29a), since agreement on one head should be sufficient to identify *pro*. On the other hand, if we assume that Case must be checked overtly in a Spec–head configuration, the fact that the head noun carries agreement follows. Recall that Q carries agreement features owing to its Spec–head relation with the genitive NP in the Spec of DP. Now, notice that in (29a), illustrated in (30), the FP containing the QP is itself a genitive in the Spec of the NP headed by *ʕamm*. Since genitive Case must be checked overtly, the FP containing the QP raises to the Spec of the DP headed by *ʕamm* and enters into a Spec–head relation with it. This explains why *ʕamm*, like Q, carries overt agreement features.

(30)

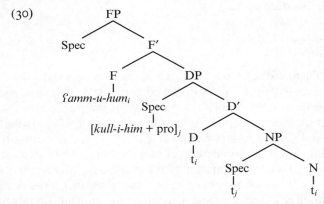

If this analysis is correct, it provides strong support for the theory that genitive Case is checked overtly in a Spec–head configuration, as required by the principle in (1).

(i) (a)   raʔaytu-*hum* kull-a-*hum*   (SA)
           (I) saw-3MP   all-ACC-3MP
           'I saw them all.'
    (b)   *   raʔaytu kull-a-*hum*
             (I) saw   all-ACC-3MP
(ii) (a)   kuntu mʕa-hum kull-i-him
           was.1S with-3MP all-GEN-3MP
           'I was with all of them.'
    (b)   *kuntu maʕa kull-i-him
           was.1S with all-GEN-3MP

However, one problem remains. We have argued that in (31) the lexical genitive NP and Q are in a Spec–head relation:

(31)   kull-u   T-Tullaab-i   (SA)
             all-NOM the-students-GEN
             'All the students'

Since the quantifier *kull* and the genitive *T-Tullaab* are in a Spec–head relation, we expect Q to carry the agreement clitic as it does when the genitive is a pronominal. However, this prediction is not borne out:

(32)   *kull-u-hum T-Tullaab-i   (SA)
             all-NOM-3MP the-students-GEN

In fact, this is a general problem regarding genitives in the construct state which parallels the situation with subject agreement in the VS order in Standard Arabic. Though the genitive and the head noun are in a Spec–head relation, the expected agreement clitic does not surface when the genitive is a lexical NP:

(33) (*a*) ʕammm-u T-Tullaab-i   (SA)
             uncle-NOM the-students-GEN
             'The students' uncle'

     (*b*) *ʕammm-u-hum T-Tullaab-i
             uncle-NOM-3MP the-students-GEN

To deal with this problem, we need to look closely at the construct state. Borer (1988) shows convincingly that members of the construct state form a single prosodic unit, as is evident from the fact that they behave metrically as single words. She accounts for this by proposing that the members of the construct state combine morphologically. In Benmamoun (1996), several arguments are given to show that this merger of the members of the construct state takes place post-syntactically (in PF). Given PF merger of the members of the construct state, the question of why the agreement clitic does not show up on the head noun follows automatically. The agreement features on the head noun are spelled out by merger with the genitive NP.[18] By contrast, when the genitive is

---

[18] The only instance where there seems to be some agreement spelled out is with the quantifier *ʔayy* (any, which). Like *kull* (all), this quantifier displays all the properties of the construct state in that the NP following it carries genitive Case and it carries the Case that is assigned to the whole projection:

(i)   lam   ʔaqraʔ ʔayy-a   kitaab-in
       NEG.PAST read   any-ACC book-GEN
       'I didn't read any book.'

(ii)   ʔayy-u   Taalib-in   žaaʔa
        which-NOM student-GEN came
        'Which student came?'

However, unlike *kull*, *ʔayy* can carry gender agreement:

a null pronominal agreement must be spelled out by the agreement clitic. Thus, the complementary distribution between agreement clitics and overt genitives is a question of how agreement is spelled out in PF. This mirrors the situation that obtains in the context of number agreement with postverbal subjects.

4. CONCLUSION

In this chapter, I have argued that structural nominative and genitive Cases in Arabic are checked overtly in a Spec–head configuration.[19] I have shown that the main argument for LF nominative Case checking, namely that the subject in VSO orders is in the Spec of VP, cannot be maintained in the face of evidence that the subject is outside VP overtly. The evidence for LF Case checking based on lack of number agreement in VSO orders in Standard Arabic was given an alternative explanation that relies on the mechanisms available to this language to spell out the checked agreement features. Then, I argued, on the basis of agreement facts in the context of the QP headed by *kull*, that genitive Case is also checked in a Spec–head configuration overtly. While many issues remain open such as the relation between abstract Case and morphological Case and the PF dimension of the former, this analysis has the advantage of dispensing with the disjunction with respect to the configurations required for Case checking/assignment inherent in the GB and Minimalist systems. It is also consistent with the long-standing assumption that the Case module interfaces with PF.

(iii)   ?ayyat-u   fataat-in   žaa?at
        which-NOM girl-GEN   came
        'Which girl came?'

This seems to parallel the situation with postverbal subjects, where the verb carries gender and person agreement but not number.

[19] If the proposal that structural Case is universally checked overtly in a Spec–head configuration turns out to be correct, one might argue that this amounts to reintroducing S-structure as a significant level of representation, since the requirement in (1) will be exclusive to overt derivations. However, this conclusion does not necessarily follow, since we are assuming that Case interfaces with PF, which means that there must be a PF reason for overt Case checking. The problem of reintroducing S-structure does arise if there is a syntactic process that universally takes place overtly but is not driven by PF requirements. Incidentally, notice that the analysis in the text avoids the conceptual problem of having structural Case features, which are apparently non-interpretable in the sense of Chomsky (1995), drive movement at a level that is mainly concerned with interpretable features.

REFERENCES

Aoun, J. (1978), 'Structure interne du syntagme nominal en arabe: l'ʔidafa', *Analyses et Theorie*, 1: 1–40, University of Paris VIII.

——(1993), 'Representation and Interpretation of Doubled Arguments', paper presented at the Arabic Linguistic Symposium, University of Texas at Austin.

——and Benmamoun, E. (1998), 'Minimality, Reconstruction, and PF Movement', *Linguistic Inquiry*.

————and Sportiche, D. (1994), 'Agreement and Conjunction in Some Varieties of Arabic', *Linguistic Inquiry*, 25: 195–220.

Ayoub, G. (1981), 'Structure de la phrase en arabe standard', Doctoral thesis, Université de Paris VII.

Benmamoun, E. (1992), 'Functional and Inflectional Morphology: Problems of Projection, Representation and Derivation', Doctoral dissertation, USC, Los Angeles, Calif.

——(1993*a*), 'Agreement and the Agreement Projection in Arabic', *Studies in Linguistic Sciences*, 23(1): 61–71, University of Illinois at Urbana-Champaign.

——(1993*b*), 'Null Pronominals in the Context of NPs and QPs', in J. Mead (ed.), *Proceedings of WCCFL 11*, 32–43, Center for the Study of Language and Information, Stanford, Calif.

——(1996), 'Agreement Asymmetries and the PF Interface', *SOAS Working Papers in Linguistics*, 6: 106–28.

——(1997*a*), 'Licensing of Negative Polarity in Moroccan Arabic', *Natural Language and Linguistic Theory*, 15: 263–87.

——(1997*b*), 'Agreement in Arabic and the PF Interface', *Proceedings of WCCFL XV*, 33–47, Center for the Study of Language and Information, Stanford, Calif.

Bobaljik, J., and Jonas, D. (1996), 'Subject Positions and the Roles of TP', *Linguistic Inquiry*, 27: 195–236.

Borer, H. (1988), 'On the Morphological Parallelism between Compounds and Constructs', in G. Booij and J. van Marle (eds.), *Morphology Yearbook*, 1: 45–65.

——(1994), 'Deconstructing the Construct', Ms., University of Massachusetts, Amherst.

Brody, M. (1995), *Lexico-Logical Form: A Radically Minimalist Theory*, MIT Press, Cambridge, Mass.

Chomsky, N. (1995), *The Minimalist Program*, MIT Press, Cambridge, Mass.

Déchaine, R.-M. (1993), 'Predicates across Categories', Ph.D. thesis, University of Massachusetts, Amherst.

Di Sciullo, A.-M., and Tremblay, M. (1996), 'Configurations et interprétation: les morphèmes de negation', *Recherches Linguistiques de Vincennes*, 25: 27–52.

Fassi Fehri, A. (1982), *La Linguistique arabe: forme et interprétation*, Publications de La Faculté des Lettres de Rabat, Morocco.

——(1993), *Issues in the Structure of Arabic Clauses and Words*, Kluwer, Dordrecht.

Hirschbühler, P., and Labelle, M. (1994), 'Changes in Verb Position in French Negative Infinitival Clauses', *Language Variation and Change*, 6: 149–78.

Hornstein, N. (1996), 'Existentials, A-Chains and Reconstruction', Ms., University of Maryland, College Park.

Koizumi, M. (1993), 'Object and the Split VP Hypothesis', *MIT Working Papers in Linguistics*, 18: 99–148.

Koopman, H., and Sportiche, D. (1991), 'The Position of Subjects', *Lingua*, 85: 211–58 (special issue, ed. James McCloskey).

Lasnik, H. (1993), 'Lectures in Minimalist Syntax', *University of Connecticut Occasional Papers in Linguistics*, 1.

——(1995), 'A Note on Pseudogapping', Ms., University of Connecticut.

McCloskey, J. (1996), 'Subjects and Subject Positions in Irish', in R. Borsley and I. Roberts (eds.), *The Syntax of the Celtic Languages*, Cambridge University Press, Cambridge, 241–83.

Mohammad, M. (1989), 'The Sentence Structure of Arabic', Doctoral dissertation, USC, Los Angeles, Calif.

Ouhalla, J. (1992), 'Focus in Standard Arabic', *Linguistics in Potsdam*, 1: 65–92.

Ritter, E. (1991), 'Two Functional Categories in Noun Phrases: Evidence from Modern Hebrew', *Syntax and Semantics*, 25: 37–62.

Rizzi, L. (1995), 'The Fine Structure of the Left Periphery', Ms., University of Geneva.

Roberts, I., and Shlonsky, U. (1996), 'Pronominal Enclisis in VSO Languages', in R. Borsley and I. Roberts (eds.), *The Syntax of the Celtic Languages*, Cambridge University Press, Cambridge, 171–99.

Shlonsky, U. (1996), 'Remarks on the Complementizer Layer of Standard Arabic', Ms., University of Geneva.

——(1997), *Clause Structure and Word Order in Arabic and Hebrew*, Oxford University Press, New York.

Siloni, T. (1994), *Hebrew Noun Phrases*, Doctoral dissertation, Université de Genève.

Sportiche, D. (1990), 'Movement, Agreement and Case', Ms., UCLA.

Vergnaud, J.-R. (1982), 'Dépendances et niveaux de representation en syntax', Thèse de Doctorat d'Etat, Université de Paris VII.

7
Adjectival Modifiers and the Specifier–Adjunct Distinction

NIGEL DUFFIELD

I. INTRODUCTION

It has recently been proposed that the categorial distinction between specifiers and adjuncts is unnecessary and that reference to specifiers as unique, distinguished positions should be eliminated from grammatical descriptions (see e.g. Kayne 1994; Chomsky 1995a, b).[1] Whatever the conceptual attractions of this move, it is obviously important that this should not involve any significant loss of empirical coverage. In this chapter, I will suggest that the cost of retaining reference to specifiers as distinguished positions is compensated for by the possibility of a restrictive treatment of certain parametric differences across typologically related languages.

Empirical motivation for this proposal comes from certain contrasts in the structure and distribution of attributive adjective phrases in Maltese (Arabic) and Modern Irish. Attributive adjectives are of interest by virtue of the fact that they are always optional elements. A standard assumption about such modifiers within the Principles and Parameters framework has been that their position in phrase structure is relatively fixed, specifically, that they do not undergo syntactic movement. Just as the fixed position of negation and VP adverbs has been taken as evidence of verb movement (see Pollock 1989; Wexler

This is the revised version of a talk presented to the Specifiers Conference. I am grateful to members of that audience, as well as to David Adger, Elizabeth Cowper, Ayumi Matsuo, Lisa Travis, and two anonymous reviewers for their comments and suggestions. Special thanks go to Mark Baker for his insightful and constructive criticism. Naturally, I am solely responsible for all remaining weaknesses and errors.

[1] Chomsky (1995a: 402) suggests that the distinction between substitution and adjunction should be maintained, which at first glance appears similar to the present argument. However, this is rather different from the present claim, in that it distinguishes two instances of the Minimalist transformation Move. By contrast, we are concerned here with the Minimalist operations Select and Merge, that is, with what was formerly termed 'base-generation'. Chomsky (1995a) does not deal directly with adjectival modifiers; however, his treatment of VP adverbs (pp. 420 ff.) implies that Merge applies *uniformly* to all non-complement XPs, even though they may subsequently be distinguished by Move.

1994, amongst others), so the putatively fixed position of attributive adjectives has been diagnostic of the movement of other nominal elements, the head noun in particular (see Cinque 1993, amongst others). In Minimalist terms, the fixed position of such phrases is attributed to their lack of formal features: following selection and merger, these elements have no need to move to check features; thus, by economy, movement is prohibited.[2]

In light of this, if systematic differences are observed in the structure and distribution of adjective phrases across languages, then these should be explained by some theoretical distinction or mechanism other than syntactic movement. In this chapter, I will present evidence to show that Semitic and Celtic adjective phrases exhibit quite distinct characteristics; most generally, the observation is that APs in Semitic display much greater freedom of attachment than their Celtic counterparts. I will then consider a number of ways of addressing these facts, arguing that, of the analytic options currently available, the most satisfactory approach is in terms of a parametric distinction between adjectives as specifiers and adjectives as adjuncts. I have in mind a parameter of the kind in (1).

(1) With respect to some head H, a modifying XP is
     (i) a specifier or
     (ii) an adjunct.

Slightly more technically, though still informally, let us define a specifier position as a distinguished, usually peripheral, phrasal position uniquely related to some subjacent head H through agreement, predication, or (indirectly through) selection. By this definition, an adjunct is taken to be any (non-complement) XP that does not meet these uniqueness conditions.[3] If X-bar theory (see e.g. Chomsky 1986) is adopted, it follows that phrasal modifiers that are also specifiers must host their own phrasal projections, where the modifiee appears as the complement of the head of this projection (cf. Abney 1987; Cinque 1993). This follows from the assumption that the specifiers of other projections must be occupied by other elements: specifiers of *lexical* categories will only be projected if they host thematically related XPs—by the Internal

---

[2] Carnie and Harley (1994) make the claim that predicate adjectives in Irish do have formal features; however, they make no similar claims regarding attributive adjectival modifiers.

[3] For Stowell (1981), the peripherality of the specifier position is a stipulated configurational property: it is just that position which is immediately dominated by the maximal projection of a head. If, as is commonly assumed, adjunction is to YP—rather than, say, to Y′—then clearly many cases of apparent non-peripherality will be observed. In a theory which retains the use of category labels, Stowell's stipulation of peripherality can be redefined in terms of segments. Under a strictly binary treatment of adjunct modification, such as that of Larson (1988), however, this peripherality condition, and indeed the specifier–adjunct distinction more generally, cannot be captured structurally (although it may be reconstructable in certain instances in terms of theta-theory. The present claim appears to be incompatible with Larson's approach.

Subject Hypothesis—while specifiers of *functional* categories will be either absent or occupied by abstract operators of one kind or another (Tense operators, Negative operators, etc.). Adjunct XP modifiers, on the other hand, will attach directly to the maximal projection of the head they modify, and will be 'inert' with respect to syntactic processes, such as A-movement and binding.[4] This contrast is illustrated in (2).

(2) (a)   *AP as specifier*   (b)   *AP as adjunct*

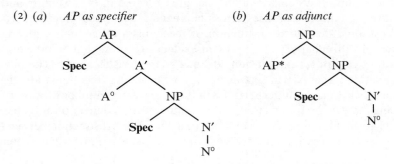

Notice that there is an ambiguity in (2a) with respect to the position of the attributive adjective itself: in principle, either it could be projected as the head of the AP with a phonetically empty Spec position, or it might be projected in its own (non-branching) Spec with a phonetically empty head. This structural ambiguity is comparable to that exhibited by negative elements cross-linguistically (cf. Pollock 1989; Rizzi 1990; Zanuttini 1990; Belletti 1994). If we adopt the former—a priori more plausible—construal, namely that attributive adjectives occupy the head of their own projection in (2a), then the claim that some adjectives are specifiers, whereas others are adjuncts with respect to a head H, might be better understood as the claim that APs vary according to whether they function as 'integrated' projections selecting NP complements or whether they modify through adjunction (2b). While I will ultimately adopt this more indirect notion of AP as specifier, there is at least one theoretical reason for preferring the alternative construal, namely where the attributive adjective occupies [Spec, AP], and where the head (A°) is empty: if there is evidence that head nouns raise overtly to some functional projection above AP, then standard assumptions regarding head movement would require that in (2a) A° should be empty to avoid Minimality violations (Rizzi 1990; Cinque 1993, forthcoming). As we shall see directly, there is some empirical support for N° raising in the languages under investigation here; hence, the more obvious, though less likely, construal of APs as specifiers may turn out to be correct after all.

---

[4] For some discussion of the conditions on adverbial adjunction, see Travis (1988), also Chomsky (1995b) as well as the remarks below.

2. ADJECTIVE PHRASES IN CELTIC AND SEMITIC

The data considered here illustrate differences between Modern Irish on the one hand, and Modern Hebrew and Maltese Arabic on the other, with respect to the placement and ordering of attributive adjective phrases within the noun phrase. For what follows, I will assume the articulated DP analysis in (3), which is argued for in some detail in Duffield (1995, 1996).[5]

(3)

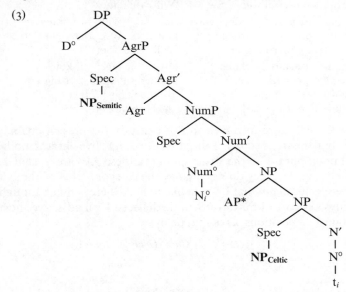

The most relevant feature of this analysis is the generalized raising of the head noun to the functional category NumP (see also Ritter 1991, 1993). The principal parametric difference between Semitic and Celtic concerns the presence or absence of overt possessor subject raising in complex noun phrases of the type known as construct state nominals: in Semitic, this movement is claimed to take place in the overt syntax; in Celtic, movement takes place at LF (see (3) above).[6]

Empirical support for the analysis in (3) comes from a variety of sources, including adjective placement. The main point to notice about the data in (4)— here, the comparison is between Irish and Maltese—is that whereas adjective phrases modifying the head noun invariably follow the possessor noun phrase

---

[5] This analysis is an extension of earlier work by Mohammad (1987), Ritter (1987, 1993), and Lyons (1992); cf. also Borer (1995) for an alternative approach.

[6] Alternatively, following Chomsky (1995b), it may be that in the case of Irish only the relevant features are attracted at LF. The evidence presented here does not arbitrate between these two approaches. For a somewhat different interpretation of Case checking in Semitic, see Benmamoun (Ch. 6, this volume).

in Semitic, giving rise to potential ambiguity where both nouns agree in gender (4c), the corresponding Irish structures place the adjective phrase between the head noun and the possessor NP, and hence do not permit any ambiguity of modification.[7]

(4)   *Modern Irish*   *Maltese*

(a)   guth   láidir   an   tsagairt   *sieq   l-leminij-a   Willi
      voice   strong   DET   priest-GEN   foot-F.SG. DET-right-F.SG. W.
      'the priest's powerful voice'   'Will's right foot'

(b)   guth   an   tsagairt   láidir   sieq   Willi   l-leminij-a
      voice   DET   priest-GEN strong   foot-F.SG. W.   DET-right-F.SG.
      *'the priest's powerful voice'   'Will's right foot'

(c)   teach   an   tsagairt   chiúin   ħu   ir-raġel   il-kbir
      house   DET   priest-GEN quiet-GEN   brother   DET man   DET-big
      'the quiet priest's house'/   'the man's big brother'/
      *'the priest's quiet house'   'the big man's brother'

Although I will have cause to return to this analysis, the present chapter focuses on the X-bar-theoretic status of the attributive adjective phrases modifying the lexical noun phrase. In the structure in (3), these APs are treated as traditional adjuncts, in that they do not change the category label of the NP they modify. The specific claim that I would like to make here is that although this adjunct analysis is correct for most Semitic dialects, Irish adjectives host their own distinguished positions, as in (5a) below.

(5) (a)   *Irish*   (b)   *Hebrew/Maltese*

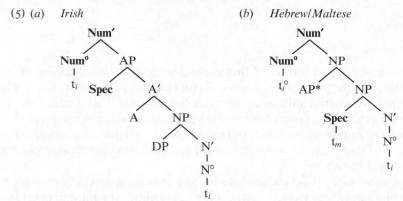

---

[7] Note that a fixed 'nested order' is required where different NPs are modified (data from Borer, personal communication, cited in Baker, forthcoming). This ordering constraint again follows directly from the analysis in (3): the AP modifying the genitive possessor NP is carried with it to the higher [Spec, Agr'] position:

(i)   [tmunat   [ha-more   ha-ca'ir   ] ha-marshima   ]
       picture(F)   DET-teacher(M) DET-young(M) DET-impressive(F)
       'the impressive picture of the young teacher'

(ii)   *tmunat   ha-more   ha-marshima   ha-ca'ir

The data introduced in the following sections offer some empirical support for this parametric distinction. In general terms, what these data will show is that adjective phrases in Semitic display a considerable freedom of attachment by comparison with APs in Irish, whose distribution is tightly constrained: in certain contexts, Maltese appears to allow both Celtic and Semitic options. The argument presented here depends on cumulative evidence: although no single contrast constitutes a clinching argument for the specifier–adjunct distinction, the claim will be that these effects taken together support the idea of a truly parametric contrast between APs as integrated projections and APs as adjuncts.

2.1. *Serialization effects*

Intuitively, one of the defining characteristics of integrated projections is their fixed position with respect to other lexical or functional categories (see also footnote 3 above). This fixedness contrasts with other XP modifiers that have a freer distribution *vis-à-vis* some particular phrasal head. Sentential adverbs are often presented as the typical adjuncts, just in virtue of their apparent 'transportability' (Keyser 1968). The distinction has become somewhat more subtle, particularly in light of a theory like Kayne's, which admits at most one adjunct per maximal projection (cf. Cann, Chapter 2, this volume). Nevertheless, it seems reasonable to take 'fixed position' as diagnostic of integrated projections, particularly if there is some interesting cross-linguistic variation for the same class of modifiers.

I will begin, then, with a phenomenon that has recently assumed some theoretical significance, namely that of ordering restrictions among adjective phrases (see Crisma 1990; Sproat and Shih 1991; Cinque 1993). Crisma (1990) and Sproat and Shih (1991) observe that certain languages impose a hierarchy of attributive adjective placement, such that different semantic classes of adjective (adjectives of size, shape, colour, and so forth) appear closer to the head they modify than others. The hierarchy proposed in Cinque (1993)—adopted from Crisma (1990)—is reproduced in (6*a*) and is illustrated by the Italian, French, and German examples in (6*b–d*), respectively.

(6) (*a*) possessive < cardinal < ordinal < quality < size < shape < colour < nationality < N

  (*b*) i   suoi due altri bei grandi *quadri$_i$* tondi grigi *t$_i$*
     the his two other nice big   pictures round grey
     'his two other nice big round grey pictures'

  (*c*) mes trois beaux   grands *fauteuils$_i$* rouges *t$_i$*
     my three beautiful big   armchairs red
     'my three beautiful red chairs'

(*d*)   ihre drei   außergewöhnliche dreieckige rote französische Bücher
       her three extraordinary   triangular red French   books
       'her three extraordinary triangular red French books'

Notice that in the Romance examples it must be assumed that partial N^0 raising has taken place in order to maintain the generalization about adjective order; otherwise, for example, Italian colour adjectives would be further away from their head noun than adjectives denoting shape, the reversal of the German pattern. If, on the other hand, the surface distributional differences are due to N^0 movement from a right-peripheral position, then the hierarchy can be maintained, since it will be the N^0-trace, rather than the surface position of the head noun, that will count as the orientation point.

Sproat and Shih (1991) extend this proposal to Irish. On the basis of the distributions illustrated in (7), they argue that the derivation of Irish noun phrases must also involve N^0 raising, given that the observed order of adjectival modifiers once again shows orientation to a rightward head position. In Rouveret (1994), a similar claim is made for Modern Welsh.

(7) (*a*)   cl*a*bhsúr a   n-ochtú hóstán$_i$ mór daorluachach t_i
         closure 3PL. eighth hotel big expensive
         'the closure of their eighth big expensive hotel'   (N < size < quality < t)

   (*a'*) ??clabhsúr a n-ochtú hóstán$_i$ daorluachach mór t_i

   (*b*)   fear$_i$ mór cnámhnach láidir t_i a   bhí ann
         man big bony   strong   PTC was in-it
         'He was a big stocky strong man.'   (N < size < quality < t)

   (*b'*) ??fear$_i$ cnámhnach mór láidir t_i a bhí ann

   (*c*)   liathróid$_i$ bheag bhuí t_i
         ball   small yellow
         'a small yellow ball'   (N < size < colour < t)

   (*c'*) ??liathróid$_i$ bhuí bheag t_i

As Cinque (1993) notes, the fact that adjectives display these serialization effects in many language constitutes prima-facie evidence that they are generated in integrated specifier position, rather than as adjuncts. In light of this, it is interesting to observe that adjective order in Semitic appears to be much freer than in Celtic. The Modern Hebrew data in (8), taken from Glinert (1989), show adjectives of size and colour (8*a*, *b*), and quality and nationality (8*c*, *d*), appearing in either order with respect to the head noun.[8]

---

[8] This freedom of ordering is generally confirmed by a number of native speakers: I am most grateful to Asya Pereltsvaig for her informal survey. Interestingly, those speakers who have a clear preference generally prefer the surface order in which colour adjectives precede size adjectives— i.e. the opposite of the Indo-European ranking. This would follow from the present proposal: as adjuncts, Semitic APs cannot be interpreted configurationally; therefore, they must be interpreted linearly with respect to the surface position of the head noun instead. (One speaker consulted reported a difference in intersectivity: N < colour < size must be interpreted non-intersectively,

(8) (*a*) ha ke'lev ha-gadol ha-lavan
          the-dog   the-large the-white
          'the large *white* dog'

    (*b*) ha ke'lev ha-lavan ha-gadol
          the-dog   the-white the-large
          'the *large* white dog'

    (*c*) ha-hatsa'a   ha-hadasha ha-mitsrit
          DET-proposal DET-new   DET-Egyptian
          'the new *Egyptian* proposal'

    (*d*) ha-hatsa'a   ha-mitsrit   ha-hadasha
          DET-proposal DET-Egyptian DET-new
          'the *new* Egyptian proposal'

It is of course possible to reverse the order of modifiers even in English: beside the *new Irish novel*, we have the *Irish new novel*, but in addition to the obligatory intonational differences involved, this reversal in ordering produces a difference in interpretation: *Irish* now modifies *new novels*, rather than *novels* in general. In other words, the reversal of modifiers induces 'non-intersectivity' in the sense of Siegel (1980).[9] Glinert (1989) implies that change in adjective order does not result in differences of scope in Hebrew, while Gil (1987) claims the same is true of Japanese, though this seems much more doubtful (cf. Löbel 1990).

This is not to say that there is no unmarked order in Semitic, but alternations for stylistic purposes would appear to be much freer in these languages. If we equate rigid serialization with specifier status and take freedom of attachment without change of interpretation as diagnostic of adjuncts, this contrast provides prima-facie evidence for retaining the specifier–adjunct distinction.

2.2. *Interaction with demonstratives and contrastive particles*

Just as adjective phrases in Irish have a fixed distribution according to semantic subtype, so too their distribution *vis-à-vis* demonstrative and emphatic elements is strictly determined. In possessive constructions, such as those in (9) below, APs must be placed to the left of demonstrative and contrastive elements in Irish. In Semitic, on the other hand, adjective phrases may appear

whereas N < size < colour receives an intersective interpretation. This question clearly requires further research before conclusions can be drawn: however, it does not affect the main point at issue here, namely that adjective order is freer in Semitic.)

  [9] One way of analysing this effect would be to suppose that deviations from canonical ordering in a language with specifier APs are only achieved by 'compounding' the non-canonical adjective: in the case at hand 'Irish' would remain in its specifier position, while the only available position for 'new' would be immediately under N^0 as the first part of a compound $[_{AP}$ Irish] $[_{NP} [_{N'}$ [new-novel]]]. This would induce non-intersectivity, since now the adjective *Irish* can only see the compound noun *new-novels*: *novels* and *Irish* cannot be evaluated independently of *new*. See also Section 2.6 below.

either to the left or to the right of such elements, as shown by the examples in
(10), once again from Glinert (1989).

(9) (*a*) an   rud   mór sin
    DET thing big DEM
    'that big thing'

(*b*) *an   rud   sin   mór
    DET thing DEM big
    'that big thing'

(10) (*a*) ha-toHnit   ha-Hadasha ha-zot
     DET-program DET-new   DET-DEM
     'this new program'

(*b*) ha-toHnit   ha-zot   ha-Hadasha
     DET-program DET-DEM DET-new
     'this new program'

The Irish examples in (11*a–d*) show that a similar constraint with respect
to adjective placement obtains with postnominal contrastive particles such as
-sean/sa. Here, direct comparison is impossible since these possessive constructions are a subset of construct state nominals, and Semitic languages do not
permit demonstratives in CSNs.

(11) (*a*) a   mhac [cróga agus éirimiúil]-sean
     3RD.SG.M. son   brave and intelligent -CONTR.
     '*his* brave and intelligent son'

(*b*) *a mhac-sean [cróga agus éirimiúil]

(*c*) ár   d*r*igh beag deas compordach-na
    our house little nice comfortable-EMPH
    '*our* nice little comfortable house'

(*d*) *ár d*r*igh-na beag deas compordach

(*e*)

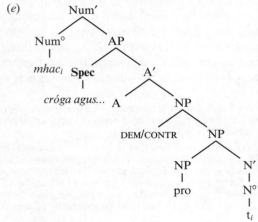

The main point here, however, is that the interpretation and distribution of demonstrative and contrastive elements *vis-à-vis* APs can be directly accounted for on an analysis such as that in (11e), in which contrastive particles in Irish are adjoined to NP with adjectives hosting their own specifier positions (cf. Duffield 1995). This requires, however, that specifiers should be formally distinguishable from adjuncts.

2.3. *Obligatory vs. optional determiners in Maltese*

Consider next two facts about Maltese that again provide support for the specifier–adjunct distinction. From a typological perspective, Maltese presents a rather mixed grammar, in that Italian dialects (Sicilian in particular) have had a powerful influence on the development of the language, such that Maltese grammarians routinely distinguish between Semitic and Romance Maltese (see e.g. Aquilina 1959).

It is commonly noted that attributive adjectives in Semitic must agree in definiteness with the head noun, and that they are always accompanied by their own determiner, if the head noun is definite. In Maltese, however, this is not quite true, as is discussed by Fabri (1993), from whom the following data and judgements are taken. Although it is the case that attributive adjectives must not have a determiner where the head noun is indefinite (12a), the converse does not hold: definite nouns may optionally co-occur with 'bare' attributive adjectives, as in (12b).

(12) (a) *bozza   l-ħamra
          pear   DET-red
          'a red pear'

   (b) l-bozza   (l-)ħamra
        DET-pear (DET)-red
        'the red pear'

Interestingly, though, this optionality is constrained: where two or more attributive adjectives modify the head noun, one of which is 'undetermined', the determined AP must be the rightward one, as shown by the contrast between (13b) and (13c) below. One way of accounting for this constraint would be to suggest that Maltese allows both options: adjectives may be either specifiers or adjuncts: where they are projected as specifiers, they need not be independently determined (cf. Fabri 1993: 55), but given where specifier APs are projected, they must appear closer to the nominal head, following N° raising to Num°.

(13) (a) il-bozza   l-ħamra   l-ġdida
          DET-pear   DET-red   DET-new
          'the new red pear'

(b) ?il-bozza   ħamra   l-ġdida
    DET-pear   red   DET-new
    'the new red pear'

(c) *il-bozza   l-ħamra   ġdida
    DET-pear   DET-red   new
    'the new red pear'

(d) ??il-bozza   ħamra   ġdida
    DET-pear   red   new
    'the new red pear'

In this case, the ordering constraint on the two types of AP would follow from the representation in (14), in which adjuncts are adjoined directly to the lexical NP, and thus appear furthest away from the nominal head, following overt N° movement to Num°.

(14) (a)

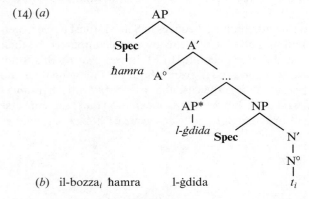

(b) il-bozza$_i$ ħamra   l-ġdida t_i

This treatment would also go some way towards explaining the contrast in grammaticality between (12b) and (13d), which shows that whereas single attributive adjectives need not be marked by a determiner in definite contexts, this is clearly disfavoured where more than one adjective is involved. This would follow if Maltese had developed one default AP specifier position to accommodate 'bare' adjectives, but had not yet incorporated the generalized (and serialized) AP specifier system of Romance, as argued for in Crisma (1990) and Cinque (1993).

A reviewer of this chapter questioned why it should necessarily be the case that adjuncts are specified as agreeing in definiteness with the modifiee but that specifiers are not; in other words, why the presence of definiteness agreement forces a difference of categorization and, hence, a difference in distribution. In fact, it does not seem to be the case that 'semantic' agreement in definiteness, or indeed that syntactic Agreement *in general* is the relevant distinction here. Rather, the distinction appears to be a strictly morphosyntactic one: adjunct modifiers may host their own determiners, specifiers may not. Why this should be so is, admittedly, less than obvious; one (highly tentative) suggestion runs as follows.

Suppose one were to take the presence of determiners as indicative of the presence of D-features, such that agreeing adjectival modifiers are actually DPs rather than APs. In this case, then, in Minimalist terms, the fact that 'determined APs' must be adjuncts could be made to follow from conditions on the operation Merge. Chomsky (1995*b*: 246) claims that Merge requires asymmetry between the two candidates undergoing merger; therefore, it should not be possible to merge two elements containing the same formal features. From this it would follow that if a modifying adjective phrase contained D+ features, it would perforce be projected as an adjunct.[10]

2.4. *Prenominal APs*

Further evidence for the adjunct status of APs in Maltese comes from the fact that in construct state nominals, APs may even precede the head noun (15), something which is quite impossible in Irish.

(15) (*a*) is-sabiħa   omm   Pawlu
            DET-beautiful mother Paul
            'Paul's beautiful mother'

    (*b*) ix-xiħ   missier Karla
            DET-old father K.
            'Karla's old father'

It should be noted that these APs are still claimed to be functioning attributively, rather than predicatively: that is, the prenominal AP is still an NP modifier, rather than an independent predicate. Fabri (1993), working within a rather different framework, explicitly analyses the APs in these constructions as adjunct topics, related to other types of topic construction. It is important to stress, however, that these do not show the type of intonation pattern associ-

---

[10] This preliminary sketch depends on two assumptions: first, that Merge *is* necessarily asymmetric; secondly, that some additional mechanism is available for checking the D-features of the 'unmerged' AP. With respect to the first question, it might seem that this type of modification should be the prime candidate for the type of merger that is explicitly excluded by Chomsky (1995*b*)—i.e. the union of the two elements α and β, since α and β should not differ in value with respect to the relevant formal features. Yet, the very fact that just these adjuncts are not distributionally restricted with respect to their modifiee suggests that this type of merger is excluded, despite its apparent plausibility.

Regarding the second question of how the D-features of the unmerged constituent are checked, or, in other words, of what mechanism is responsible for attributive adjective agreement in Maltese and Hebrew, I have currently no clear proposal to offer: presumably, it should be treated by whatever mechanism handles other instances of secondary predication, including (non-) restrictive relative clauses (cf. Higginbotham 1985). This handwaving is certainly unfortunate: however, a satisfactory analysis of secondary predication is (equally certainly) beyond the scope of the current chapter.

ated with typical dislocation constructions: in other words, these seem to behave as though they are base-generated prenominally.

Once again, whatever framework is adopted, some means is required of distinguishing the 'fixed' nature of adjectival modifiers in Irish from the rather
'freer' nature of their counterparts in Maltese. The specifier–adjunct distinction appears to capture this contrast appropriately.

2.5. *APs in free genitive constructions*

It is not only in construct state constructions that APs behave differently in
Irish and Maltese. In both Semitic and Celtic, possessor–possessed relationships can also be expressed through periphrastic prepositional constructions,
the so-called free state or free genitive constructions (cf. Ritter 1991, amongst
others). Once again, in Maltese free genitive constructions, adjective phrases
modifying the head noun show a surprising freedom of attachment: they may
optionally appear to the right of the prepositional phrase—as in (16b)—
something which is quite impossible in Irish, or even in Hebrew.[11]

(16) (a) ir-rot-a   l-ġdid-a   [ta' Pawlu]   (Maltese)
          the-bicycle-F.SG. the-new-F.SG. ta' Paul
          'Paul's new bicycle'

    (b)   ir-rot-a   [ta' Pawlu] l-ġdid-a
          the-bicycle-F.SG. ta' Paul   the-new-F.SG.
          'Paul's new bicycle'

(17) (a) an   mac mór sin [aige   ]   (Irish)
          DET son big DEM ag+3SG.M
          'that big son of his'

    (b)   *an   mac sin [aige   ] mór
          DET son DEM ag+3SG.M big
          'that big son of his'

(18) (a) ha-bayit   ha-gadol shel ha-mora   (Hebrew)
          DET-house DET-big   shel DET-teacher
          'the teacher's big house'

    (b)   *ha-bayit   shel ha-mora   ha-gadol
          DET-house shel DET-teacher DET-big
          'the teacher's big house'

It is possible to derive the Maltese alternation by assuming that the prepositional phrase as well as the adjective phrase—both of which are semantically
optional modifiers of the head noun in this context—are freely adjoined to the
lexical NP; that is, that they are both adjuncts:

[11] Maltese employs free genitive constructions more widely than do the other Semitic languages,
since the construct state in Maltese is generally restricted to noun phrases headed by 'inalienable'
nouns, specifically, to nouns denoting body or kinship relations (see Fabri 1993 for detailed discussion).

(19)

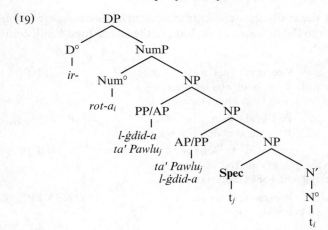

Such an assumption could then account for the fact that this optionality disappears in free genitive constructions headed by derived nominals, where the prepositional phrase contains an argument: in these cases, such as (20*a*), one assumes that the PP is in the specifier position of N′ (see Ritter 1991).

(20) (*a*) l-iskoperta   importanti ta' l-Amerika   (Maltese)
         DET-discovery important ta DET-America
         'the important discovery of America'

   (*b*) *l-iskoperta   ta' l-Amerika   importanti
         DET discovery   ta DET-America important
         'the important discovery of America'

   (*c*)

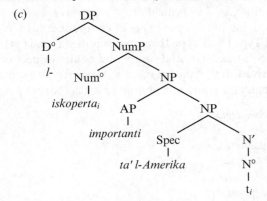

Incidentally, the fact that this movement is thematically constrained, that these PPs are restricted in their distribution to when theta-marked, once again supports the specifier–adjunct distinction. A similar contrast is observed in Dutch. Hoekstra (Chapter 9, this volume) points out that whereas *adjunct* PPs may appear on either side of a verbal head—here, the standard (non-Kaynian)

analysis has it that these adjuncts are 'extraposed' rightwards—*complement* PPs can only appear in their canonical position to the left of their head; compare (21*b*) and (21*d*):

(21) (*a*) dat Jan met Piet over het weer praat (PP PP V)
        that J. with P. about the weather talks
        'that John talks with Peter about the weather'

(*b*) dat Jan met Piet praat over het weer (PP V PP$_{adjunct}$)
        that J. with P. talks about the weather

(*c*) dat Jan de boeken in de kast zet (NP PP V)
        that J. the books in the box puts
        'that John puts the books in the box'

(*d*) *dat Jan de boeken zet in de kast (*NP V PP$_{compl}$)
        that J. the books puts in the box

Both sets of facts, in (20) and (21), are covered by the generalization that arguments, unlike adjuncts, cannot scramble out of specifier positions. Once again, however, it appears possible to state this generalization only if specifiers and adjuncts are formally distinguished from one another.

2.6. *Adjectives in Irish compounds*

The final set of contrasts to be presented in support of the specifier–adjunct distinction is observed in adjective–noun compounds of the type given in (24) below. Since compounding is standardly considered the epitome of a lexical, rather than a syntactic, process, it might seem odd to adduce such data in support of a syntactic distinction. In Duffield (1997), however, I offer some evidence in support of the claim that all *other* types of compounding in Irish— those that are here termed Type I and Type II compounds in (22) and (23), and which Borer (1988) labels construct state and compound nouns, respectively— are in fact syntactically derived, in that they make crucial reference to syntactic information for their interpretation and morphophonological form.

(22)   *Type I (N–DP) compounds*
(*a*) (*an) bean an ti
      DET woman the house-GEN
      'the woman of the house'

(*b*) (*an) Hata an tSagairt
      DET hat the priest-GEN
      'the sea-anemone' ('priest's hat')

(23)   *Type II (N–N$_{GEN}$) compounds*
(*a*) an mac (*na) léinn
      DET son DET learning-GEN
      'the student' (m. or fem.)

(b) an mac (*na) tíre
DET son   DET country-GEN
'the wolf'

Granting this controversial assumption, the contrast between the Irish forms in (24) and their Semitic counterparts in (25) now becomes theoretically relevant. The most obvious difference between the two data-sets is the contrast in headedness of compounds containing adjectives: adjectival compounds in Irish are right-headed, whereas they appear to be left-headed in Hebrew.[12] The Irish order is particularly striking, since this is the only environment where attributive adjectives appear prenominally.

(24) (a) an nua[-]fhocal   (b) an beag[-]uchtach   (Irish)
       DET new-word   DET little courage
       'neologism'   'lack of courage'

      (c) mion[-]bhradái   (d) an garbh-bhéal
          small thief   DET rough mouth
          'petty thief'   'coarse speech'

(25) (a) ha-Haydak   (b) ha-dag ha-ma'lu'ach   (Semitic)
       DET-life-thin   fish   salty
       'the microbe'   'herring'

      (c) ha-shaná-tova   (d) ha-yéled-ha-tov
          DET-year-new   DET-boy-good
          'the New Year card'   'goody-goody'

If we grant the assumption that compounding is a syntactic process in Celtic and Semitic, how might we obtain this cross-linguistic contrast? Here again, the specifier–adjunct distinction offers a possible solution. Consider once more the trees in (5) above, repeated here as (26) for convenience.

(26) (a) *Irish*   (b) *Hebrew/Maltese*

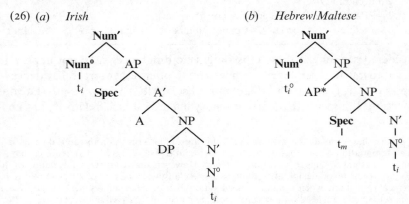

---

[12] This assumes that the somewhat limited data presented in Glinert (1989) are representative of Semitic adjectival compounds.

Now let us assume, contrary to the analysis in Section 2.1, that Irish adjectives project as the heads of their projections, rather than being projected within the Spec position of their functional projection.[13] Whether we assume the same for Semitic is irrelevant at this point, so long as we retain the distinction between Irish APs as 'integrated functional projections' and Semitic APs as adjuncts. Suppose now that Irish A–N order is obtained by lowering the A° head down to the adjacent N° prior to N raising into Num° (for number checking). This type of lowering will be possible in Irish since the functional head A° selects its NP complement. In Semitic, by contrast, lowering will be blocked, under the standardly-accepted assumption that it is impossible to incorporate from adjuncts: Semitic N° heads must then raise directly to Num°, skipping the adjoined adjective position, deriving left-headed compounds. Once again, to the extent that such an analysis is plausible, it is only technically possible as long as a distinction is maintained between specifiers (as integrated projections) on the one hand, and adjuncts on the other.[14]

3. CONCLUSION

In conclusion, distributional evidence has been presented from Celtic and Semitic languages in support of a theoretical distinction whose usefulness has recently been challenged. The cross-linguistic contrasts discussed here are summarized in (27).

(27)

	Irish	Maltese	Hebrew
Fixed adjective order *vis-à-vis* other APs?	✓	✗	✗
Fixed adjective order *vis-à-vis* demonstratives?	✓	n/a	✗
Determiner-less APs in definite contexts?	✓	(✓)	✗
Prenominal D-APs?	✗	✓	?
N–PP–AP order in 'free genitive construction'?	✗	✓	✓
Headedness of Type III N–A compounds?	Right	—	Left

Considered separately, these cross-linguistic differences may not appear to amount to much; taken together, they seem to offer rather forceful evidence in support of a truly parametric distinction. The question is how best to state this distinction. It appears that current theory makes available relatively few ana-

---

[13] Notice that we made this assumption, following Cinque (1993), on theoretical grounds: a literal interpretation of the Head Movement Constraint (HMC) (Travis 1984), requires that A° be empty so as not to impede N° raising to Num°. However, such a literal interpretation of the HMC now seems theoretically rather dubious: more plausible is the idea of a Relativized Head Movement Constraint, where economy considerations block movement to some head position, if there is a closer relevant head with the same checking potential. If this is the correct interpretation, there is no reason not to project attributive adjectives as heads of their own projection; they should be invisible to N° raising.

[14] I am again extremely grateful to Mark Baker for discussion of this point.

lytic options for distinguishing among non-argument modifiers. As well as I can determine, the options are the following:

(28) (i)   APs as specifiers (integrated projections) vs. APs as adjuncts
(ii) Adjectives as heads vs. adjectives as maximal projections
(iii) APs as heads of AP vs. APs as specifiers of AP

Of these, (28.i) is the current proposal. The distinction in (28.ii) is reminiscent of the treatment of adverbs proposed in Travis (1988), whereby certain adverbs are treated as heads adjoining directly to other heads, whereas others function as maximal projections, adjoining to other maximal projections. Although it might indeed be possible to account for several of the contrasts observed in this chapter by taking Travis's proposal plus some ancillary assumptions, it seems as if it is the ancillary assumptions, rather than the original proposal, that would carry the explanatory burden. For instance, it is unclear why it should be possible to attach an AP to the right of the PP in the Maltese free genitives in (16), or why this attachment should be blocked in (19). Moreover, characterizing the distinction in terms of (28.ii) receives considerably less empirical support here than in Travis's original proposal. In Travis (1988), the principal reason for treating a particular adjective type as head or maximal projection was the (in)ability of the adjective in question to take its own complement: cf. '*the proud of his achievements student*'. Yet this does not correctly distinguish Celtic from Semitic adjectives; adjectives in both languages appear equally able to take complements in contexts other than possessor noun phrases, and show identical restrictions with respect to complement taking in construct state contexts. In short, there is no internal structural evidence for a 'head vs. phrase' approach to this problem; even if one were to adopt such an approach, most of the distributional effects reported here would remain unaccounted for, without additional assumptions.

Finally, the analytic option in (28.iii) appears subject to the same criticism as in the case just discussed: in the absence of some additional principle driving optional movement of either heads or specifiers of AP to higher positions, there is no reason why adjectives should display different distributions in the two language families. (The key word here is optional. If it were the case that adjectives in Semitic and Celtic systematically appeared in different positions, one might be justified in postulating specifier or head movement to account for this. However, in most instances, adjectives have the same distribution; the contrast here is between fixedness and relative freedom of positioning. It is not clear how a distinction between specifiers and heads could capture this optionality in any principled fashion (although it will always be possible to state these effects individually in terms of *ad hoc* conditions of feature strength).)

In summary, the evidence presented provides some prima-facie motivation for retaining a particular theoretical distinction, that between specifiers and adjuncts. The claim here is not that this distinction should be maintained at all costs; ideally, one should work for the simplest possible theory that handles the relevant data. The intention of this chapter is simply to draw attention to what should be 'relevant data', so that facts are not lost sight of in the process of 'paring down' grammatical explanations.

REFERENCES

Abney, S. (1987), 'The English Noun-Phrase in its Sentential Aspect', Ph.D. dissertation, MIT.

Aquilina, J. (1959), *The Structure of Maltese: A Study in Mixed Grammar and Vocabulary*, The Royal University of Malta, Valetta.

Baker, M. (forthcoming), 'Comments on the Paper by Sadock', in S. Lapointe, B. Brentari, and P. Farrell (eds.), *Morphology and Its Relation to Phonology and Syntax*, CSLI Publications, Stanford, Calif., 188–212.

Belletti, A. (1994), 'Verb-Movement: Evidence from Italian', in D. Lightfoot and N. Hornstein (eds.), *Verb Movement*, Cambridge University Press, Cambridge, 19–40.

Borer, H. (1988), 'On the Morphological Parallelism between Compounds and Constructs', *Yearbook of Morphology*, 1: 45–66.

——(1995), 'Deconstructing the Construct', Ms., University of Massachusetts, Amherst.

Carnie, A., and Harley, H. (1994), 'Predicate Raising and the Irish Copula', Ms., MIT.

Chomsky, N. (1986), *Knowledge of Language: Its Nature, Origin and Use*, Praeger, New York.

——(1995a), 'Bare Phrase Structure', in G. Webelhuth (ed.), *Government and Binding Theory and the Minimalist Program*, Blackwell, Oxford, 383–439.

——(1995b), *The Minimalist Program*, MIT Press, Cambridge, Mass.

Cinque, G. (1993), 'On the Evidence for Partial N-Movement in the Romance DP', Ms., University of Venice.

——(forthcoming), *Adverbs and Functional Heads: A Crosslinguistic Perspective*, Oxford University Press, New York.

Crisma, P. (1990), 'Functional Categories inside the Noun Phrase: A Study on the Distribution of Nominal Modifiers', Tesi di Lauria, University of Venice.

Duffield, N. (1995), *Particles and Projections in Irish Syntax*, Kluwer, Boston/Dordrecht.

——(1996), 'On Structural Invariance and Lexical Diversity in VSO Languages: Arguments from Irish Noun-Phrases', in R. Borsley and I. Roberts (eds.), *The Syntax of the Celtic Languages*, Cambridge University Press, Cambridge, 314–40.

——(1997), 'Irish Noun Compounds: A Study in Concatenation and Merger', Ms., McGill University.

Fabri, R. (1993), *Kongruenz und die Grammatik des Maltesischen*, Max Niemeyer Verlag, Tübingen.

Gil, D. (1987), 'Definiteness, Noun-Phrase Configurationality, and the Count–Mass Distinction', in A. ter Meulen (ed.), *The Representation of (In)definiteness*, MIT Press, Cambridge, Mass., 254–69.

Glinert, L. (1989), *The Grammar of Modern Hebrew*, Cambridge University Press, Cambridge.

Higginbotham, J. (1985), 'On Semantics', *Linguistic Inquiry*, 16: 547–93.

Kayne, R. (1994), *The Antisymmetry of Syntax*, MIT Press, Cambridge, Mass.

Keyser, S. J. (1968), 'Review of Sven Jacobson: Adverbial Position in English', *Language*, 44: 367–74.

Larson, R. (1988), 'On the Double Object Construction', *Linguistic Inquiry*, 19: 335–91.

Löbel, E. (1990), 'Typologische Aspekte funktionaler Kategorien in der Nominalphrase', *Zeitschrift für Sprachwissenschaft*, 9: 135–69.

Lyons, C. (1992), 'The Construct: VSO "Genitive" Structures', Ms., University of Salford.

Mohammad, M. (1987), 'On the Parallelism between IP and DP', in H. Borer (ed.), *Proceedings of WCCFL 7*, Stanford Linguistics Association, Stanford, Calif., 241–54.

Pollock, J.-Y. (1989), 'Verb Movement, UG and the Structure of IP', *Linguistic Inquiry*, 20: 365–424.

Ritter, E. (1987), 'NSO Noun Phrases in a VSO Language', in J. McDonough and B. Plunkett (eds.), *Proceedings of NELS 17*, GLSA, University of Massachusetts, Amherst, 521–37.

——(1991), 'Two Functional Categories in Noun-Phrases: Evidence from Modern Hebrew', in S. Rothstein (ed.), *Perspectives on Phrase-Structure*, Academic Press, New York.

——(1993), 'Cross-Linguistic Evidence for Number Phrase', Ms., University of Calgary.

Rizzi, L. (1990), *Relativized Minimality*, MIT Press, Cambridge, Mass.

Rouveret, A. (1994), *Syntaxe du gallois*, CNRS Éditions, Paris.

Siegel, M. (1980), *Capturing the Adjective*, Garland Press, New York.

Sproat, R., and Shih, C. (1991), 'The Crosslinguistic Distribution of Adjective Ordering Restrictions', in C. Georgopoulos and R. Ishihara (eds.), *Interdisciplinary Approaches to Language: Essays in Honor of S.-Y. Kuroda*, Kluwer, Dordrecht, 565–95.

Stowell, T. (1981), 'Origins of Phrase Structure', Ph.D. dissertation, MIT.

Travis, L. (1984), 'Parameters and Effects of Word Order Variation', Ph.D. dissertation, MIT.

——(1988), 'The Syntax of Adverbs', *McGill Working Papers in Linguistics* (special issue on comparative Germanic syntax), 280–310.

Wexler, K. (1994), 'Optional Infinitives, Head Movement and the Economy of Derivations', in D. Lightfoot and N. Hornstein (eds.), *Verb Movement*, Cambridge University Press, Cambridge, 305–50.

Zanuttini, R. (1990), 'Two Types of Negative Markers', in J. Carter *et al.* (eds.), *Proceedings of NELS 20*, GLSA, University of Massachusetts, Amherst, 517–30.

8

The Additional-*wh* Effect and Multiple *Wh*-Fronting

GÜNTHER GREWENDORF

I. INTRODUCTION

This chapter suggests an analysis of Saito's (1994*b*) additional-*wh* effect which is based on a new account of multiple *wh*-in-situ. It will be shown that Japanese is an LF-type 'multiple fronting language' displaying properties analogous to languages such as Bulgarian and Romanian, which are 'overt' multiple fronting languages. For the latter, a new analysis in terms of formation of a *wh*-cluster is proposed. In Section 2 of this chapter, I point out some differences between scrambling in German and scrambling in Japanese (extensively discussed in Grewendorf and Sabel 1996) that will turn out to be crucial for my analysis of the additional-*wh* effect (Saito 1994*b*). The relevant generalizations describing the additional-*wh* effect along with the constraints it is subject to are outlined in Section 3. In Section 4, I suggest an account of the additional-*wh* effect crucially based on an analysis of Japanese scrambling, according to which the particular properties of Japanese scrambling are attributed to the presence of multiple specifiers in the Japanese agreement system. This account is in turn based on a new theory of multiple *wh*-fronting languages. I will first argue that multiple *wh*-fronting, as can be observed in languages such as Bulgarian and Romanian, does not constitute a series of operations all of which move a *wh*-element to the CP-Spec position; I will instead suggest that prior to *wh*-movement to CP-Spec, *wh*-phrases form a complex *wh*-element by an adjunction process, so that only a single *complex wh*-element moves to the CP specifier position in multiple *wh*-fronting languages. Following an idea in Cheng (1991), this property of multiple *wh*-fronting languages will be attributed to specific lexical properties of the *wh*-words themselves. It will be argued in Section 5 that Japanese represents a language with covert multiple *wh*-fronting and that the account of multiple *wh*-fronting developed in Section 4 applies to

This chapter is largely based on joint work with Joachim Sabel, whose contribution I would like to acknowledge. Furthermore, I wish to thank Andrew Simpson and Jochen Zeller for helpful discussion and two anonymous reviewers for their valuable comments. The chapter derives from a project on economy principles supported by DFG grant no. GR 559/5-1.

both overt and covert multiple *wh*-fronting languages. Finally, the assumption that Japanese is a covert multiple *wh*-fronting language in the suggested sense makes it possible to derive an analysis of the additional-*wh* effect which, unlike the account suggested in Watanabe (1992), enables us to explain the constraints this effect is subject to.

2. A-/A'-PROPERTIES OF SCRAMBLING AND LAYERED SPECIFIERS

Let us first turn to some basic generalizations on scrambling in German and Japanese. As is well known, Japanese but not German allows scrambling out of finite clauses:

(1)   [$_{IP}$ sono hon-o$_i$ [$_{IP}$ John-ga [$_{VP}$ Bill-ni [$_{CP}$ Mary-ga t_i motteiru to]
        that book-ACC   J.-NOM   B.-DAT   M.-NOM   have   C°
      itta]]] (koto)
      said   fact
      'That book, John said to Bill that Mary has'   (Saito 1994*b*)

(2) (*a*)   *daß [$_{IP}$ dieses Buch$_i$ [$_{IP}$ Hans [$_{VP}$ dem Studenten   gesagt hat
          that that book-ACC   H.-NOM   the student-DAT said   has
        [$_{CP}$ daß Maria t_i besitzt]]]]
          that M.-NOM   owns

   (*b*)   daß Hans   Peter   gesagt hat [$_{CP}$ daß [$_{IP}$ dieses Buch$_i$ [$_{IP}$ Maria
        that H.-NOM P.-DAT said   has   that   that book-ACC   M.-NOM
        t_i besitzt]]]
        owns

In (1), the direct object *sono hon-o* of the finite embedded declarative clause has been scrambled to a position in front of the matrix clause. Saito (1992) has established that only objects, and not subjects or adjuncts, allow long scrambling out of finite clauses in Japanese. Furthermore, Saito (1992) has convincingly shown that Japanese scrambling out of finite clauses is adjunction to IP. As can be seen from the examples in (2), German does not allow scrambling out of finite clauses.

It has been argued in the literature (Saito 1992, 1994*b*) that long scrambling constitutes an instance of A'-movement, while clause-internal scrambling may be both A- and A'-movement in Japanese as well as in German (Webelhuth 1989). The crucial tests that have traditionally been used to establish this claim include reconstructability connected with anaphor binding and weak crossover effects. However, as shown in Grewendorf and Sabel (1996), these tests for various reasons in fact do not provide conclusive evidence for such a claim. In order to determine whether scrambling should be taken to be A- or A'-movement, Grewendorf and Sabel (1996) took as a critical diagnostic the well-known observation that although elements moved to an A-position *may* act as antecedents for an anaphor, A'-moved elements may *not*. Applying this test to Japanese and German, we can observe that a short-scrambled element may function as an antecedent of an anaphor in Japanese but not in German:

(3) (*a*)   ?*[[Otagai$_i$-no   sensei]-ga   [karera-o hihansita]] (koto)
        each other-GEN teacher-NOM they-ACC criticized   fact
        'Each other's teacher criticized them'

   (*b*)   ?[*Karera-o$_i$* [[otagai$_i$-no   sensei]-ga   [*t* hihansita]]] (koto)
        they-ACC   each other-GEN teacher-NOM   criticized   fact
        'Them$_i$, each other's$_i$ teachers criticized'   (Saito 1994*b*)

   (*c*)   *weil *den Studenten$_i$*   [die Lehrer   von sich$_i$]   zweifellos
        since the student-ACC [the teachers of   himself]-NOM undoubtedly
        t in guter Erinnerung behalten haben
        in good memory   kept   have

In (3*a*), the anaphor contained in the subject is unbound and the sentence is ungrammatical. In (3*b*), this anaphor is bound by the direct object *karera-o*, which has undergone short scrambling to the front of the clause. In contrast, the anaphor contained in the subject of the German clause (3*c*) cannot be rescued by analogous scrambling of its antecedent. We can therefore conclude that short scrambling behaves like A-movement in Japanese but not in German. Considering scrambling out of a control infinitive, we arrive at the same conclusion as in the case of short scrambling: scrambling out of a control infinitive likewise behaves like A-movement in Japanese, since the scrambled element can function as the antecedent of an anaphor (see Saito 1994*b* for relevant examples).

A different picture emerges in the case of long scrambling out of a finite clause. As can be seen from the example in (4), unlike short-scrambled elements, an element that has undergone scrambling out of a finite clause cannot function as the antecedent of an anaphor.

(4)   *[karera-o$_i$ [[otagai$_i$-no   sensei]-ga   [Hanako-ga *t$_i$* hihansita to]
        they-ACC   each other-GEN teacher-NOM H.-NOM   criticized C
        itta]] (koto)
        said fact
        'Them each other's teachers said that Hanako criticized'   (Saito 1994*b*)

The conclusion to be drawn from this observation is that scrambling out of finite clauses is A'-movement.

To account for the properties of scrambling in Japanese, Grewendorf and Sabel (1996) combine an analysis of Japanese phrase structure in which the agreement system allows for multiple specifiers with a proposal that scrambling is a feature-mediated process driven by a 'scrambling' feature Σ that is optionally realized with Agr heads.[1] It is a consequence of this analysis that a scrambling feature located in an Agr head can be checked by moving an appropriate phrase into the outer Spec position of AgrP. Unlike Japanese, the German agreement system, however, does not permit multiple specifiers (see Grewendorf and Sabel 1996). Consequently, a scrambling feature borne by an Agr head can only be checked by adjoining an appropriate phrase to AgrP. The basic idea of this analysis is depicted in (5).

(5) (a) *Japanese*   (b) *German*

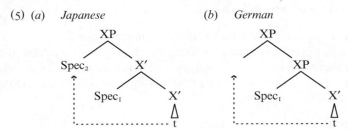

As (5*a*) shows, scrambling in Japanese is analysed as substitution into Spec$_2$ of AgrP, which is movement to a (narrowly) L-related position, and movement to an L-related position is by definition A-movement (Chomsky 1993). This analysis then provides an account of the binding properties found in (3*b*).

The diagram in (5*b*) represents the German case. Since German lacks multiple specifiers, scrambling can only take the form of adjunction, which is movement to a broadly L-related position. Since movement to broadly L-related and non-L-related positions is A'-movement by definition (Chomsky 1993), we then have a straightforward account of the particular binding-theoretic properties of sentences such as (3*c*).[2]

As already mentioned, Saito (1992, 1994*b*) has provided convincing evidence that Japanese scrambling out of finite clauses is adjunction to IP, and hence may not target a specifier position (an articulated account of why this is so is offered in Grewendorf and Sabel 1996). Scrambling out of a finite clause in Japanese is, therefore, necessarily realized as an instance of the structure in (5*b*), which accounts for the lack of anaphor licensing found in (4).

Having shown that Japanese clause-internal scrambling as well as scrambling out of a control infinitive behaves like A-movement, while scrambling out of a finite clause shows the properties of A'-movement, let us now turn to the properties of the so-called additional-*wh* effect.

---

[1] The suggestion that there exist multiple A-specifiers in Japanese is supported by a variety of evidence, e.g. the clear occurrence of multiple subjects discussed at length in Ch. 4 of this volume by Doron and Heycock and the possibility of 'superraising' as analysed in Ura (1994, 1996). For further evidence see Grewendorf and Sabel (1996).

[2] Note that throughout the remainder of this chapter, the term 'L-related position' is used to refer to narrowly L-related positions.

3. THE ADDITIONAL-*WH* EFFECT

It has been observed (Watanabe 1992; Saito 1994*a*) that *wh*-questions in Japanese in which a *wh*-adjunct such as *naze* precedes a *wh*-object, as in (6), are fully unacceptable.

(6)　　*John-ga naze nani-o　　katta　no
　　　　J.-NOM　why　what-ACC bought Q

Interestingly, a configuration in which the *wh*-adjunct *naze* precedes the *wh*-object *nani-o* is, however, grammatical when a third *wh*-phrase is added in a position higher than the *wh*-adjunct, as shown in (7*b*); (6) can also alternatively be rendered grammatical via scrambling of the *wh*-object to a position in front of the *wh*-adjunct, as shown in (7*a*).

(7) (*a*)　John-ga *nani-o*　　naze *t* katta　no
　　　　　J.-NOM　what-ACC why　　bought Q

　　(*b*)　Dare-ga　naze nani-o　　katta　no
　　　　　who-NOM why what-ACC bought Q

The fact that an ungrammatical configuration such as (6) can thus be 'rescued' by the addition of a higher *wh*-phrase as in (7*b*) has been referred to as the 'additional-*wh* effect' (Saito 1994*a*).

Some sort of additional-*wh* effect may in fact also be observed in English, in sentences constituting potential superiority violations, viz. the contrast between (8*a*) and (8*b*) below. The crucial difference between Japanese and English is that in English, the rescuing effect is achieved by adding a *wh*-phrase in a position that is *lower* than the other *wh*-phrases.

(8) (*a*)　　* *What books* did you persuade who to give *t* to Peter?
　　(*b*)　　*What books* did you persuade who to give *t* to whom?

This difference between English and Japanese has led Watanabe (1992) to speak of an 'antisuperiority effect' in Japanese, suggesting that the ungrammaticality of (6) is basically due to a ban on extracting the *highest wh*-phrase in any multiple-*wh*-string in Japanese *first*, while in English, the *lowest wh*-phrase may not be extracted first. Watanabe (1992) accounts for the antisuperiority effect in Japanese in terms of his *Principle of Relation Preservation*, according to which a relation established at a certain point in the derivation must be maintained throughout. To apply the Principle of Relation Preservation to the analysis of (6) and (7), one has to recall Watanabe's proposal that Japanese has movement of a 'pure' *wh*-operator occurring at S-structure. At LF, the lexical *wh*-element from which the empty operator originates has to adjoin to the operator in CP-Spec, followed by the adjunction of other *wh*-phrases. The ungrammaticality of (6) can then be accounted for along the following lines: to ensure antecedent government of the trace of the *wh*-adjunct, (the empty operator of) *naze* has to be moved first, as depicted in (9). Then, however, as shown again in (9), the *wh*-object *nani-o*, which adjoins to the *wh*-adjunct in CP-Spec, would c-command the *wh*-adjunct at LF (given Watanabe's specific notion of 'c-command'), and would so fail to meet the Principle of Relation Preservation, since at S-structure the *wh*-adjunct c-commands the *wh*-object.

(9)

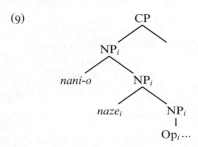

For reasons of antecedent government, the CP-Spec configuration depicted in (9) has to be assumed for the LF of (7*a*) as well. But in this case, the Principle of Relation Preservation is fulfilled, since at S-structure the *wh*-object c-commands the *wh*-adjunct. As far as the additional-*wh* effect in (7*b*) is concerned, Watanabe assumes that the Principle of Relation Preservation is satisfied as long as the LF configuration in CP-Spec preserves the S-structural relation of the *wh*-phrase which is extracted first with at least one other *wh*-phrase. In the case of (7*b*), it is the relation between the *wh*-adjunct *naze* and the added *wh*-subject *dare-ga* which ensures that the Principle of Relation Preservation is fulfilled (i.e. *dare-ga* c-commands *naze* at S-structure and will also do so at LF after raising).

Even though Watanabe's account seems to provide an adequate analysis of the data in (6) and (7), it faces serious problems in view of the fact that the additional-*wh* effect is subject to several constraints which are pointed out by Saito (1994*a*). As Saito has shown, Watanabe's analysis fails to account for two clause-boundedness restrictions which constrain the operation of the additional-*wh* strategy. The first one concerns the addition of a higher *wh*-phrase which has been scrambled out of a finite clause. The examples in (10) show familiar '*naze*-rescuing' by scrambling a *wh*-phrase (the indirect object *dare-ni*) to a position in front of the offending *wh*-adjunct.

(10) (*a*) *naze dare-ga   Mary-ni [CP John-ga sono hon-o   katta   to]
          why who-NOM   M.-DAT   J.-NOM   that book-ACC bought C
          itta   no
          said Q
          'Q who told Mary [that John bought that book] why'   (Saito 1994*a*)

(*b*) dare-ni$_i$ naze dare-ga t_i [$_{CP}$ John-ga sono hon-o   katta   to]
who-DAT why who-NOM   J.-NOM   that book-ACC bought C
itta no
said Q

As shown by the examples in (11), the additional-*wh* strategy fails if the added *wh*-phrase has been scrambled out of a *finite* clause.

(11) (*a*) *naze dare-ga   Mary-ni [$_{CP}$ John-ga sono hon-o   katta   to]
why who-NOM M.-DAT   J.-NOM   that book-ACC bought C
itta no
said Q
'Q who told Mary [that John bought that book] why'

(*b*) ?*nani-o$_i$ naze dare-ga   Mary-ni [$_{CP}$ John-ga t_i katta   to]
what-ACC why who-NOM M.-DAT   J.-NOM   bought C
itta no
said Q
'Q who told Mary [that John bought what] why'   (Saito 1994*a*)

As can easily be seen, (11*b*) fulfils the Principle of Relation Preservation: the *wh*-adjunct *naze* (its empty operator) has to move first to CP-Spec for reasons of antecedent government. But then, LF adjunction of *nani-o* to the *wh*-adjunct in CP-Spec preserves the relation that exists at S-structure, where the long-scrambled *nani-o* c-commands the *wh*-adjunct.

According to a second clause-boundedness restriction noted in Saito (1994*b*), the additional-*wh* effect fails to be operative if the added higher *wh*-phrase is base-generated in a clause other than that containing the *wh*-phrase to be rescued. This restriction is illustrated in (12*c*), where the *wh*-adjunct to be rescued is located in the embedded clause and the added *wh*-phrase is the matrix subject. Example (12*b*) shows that the ungrammatical configuration in the embedded clause can be rescued, however, if the added *wh*-phrase is made the subject of this clause.

(12) (*a*) *Mary-ga [$_{CP}$ John-ga naze nani-o   katta   to] omotteiru no
M.-NOM   J.-NOM   why what-ACC bought C think   Q
'Q Mary thinks [that John bought what why]'

(*b*) Mary-ga [$_{CP}$ dare-ga   naze nani-o   katta   to] omotteiru no
M.-NOM   who-NOM why what-ACC bought C think   Q
'Q Mary thinks [that who bought what why]'

(*c*) ?*dare-ga   [$_{CP}$ John-ga naze nani-o   katta   to] omotteiru no
who-NOM   J.-NOM   why what-ACC bought C think   Q
'Q who thinks [that John bought what why]'

In (12*b*) as well as in (12*c*), the *wh*-adjunct has to move first to CP-Spec, with the *wh*-subject LF-adjoining to it in either case. Consequently, the Principle of Relation Preservation makes the wrong prediction for (12*c*), since it is fulfilled here as well.

An observation made by Maki (1994) raises a further problem for Watanabe's analysis. Maki notes that the *wh*-island effect is remedied in Japanese by an additional *wh*-phrase in the higher clause:

(13) (*a*) ??[John-ga [Mary-ga nani-o   katta   kadooka] oboeteiru ka] osiete
                   J.-NOM   M.-NOM   what-ACC bought whether remember Q   tell
            kudasai
            please
            'Please tell me [Q John remembers [whether Mary bought what]]'

   (*b*) [dare-ga   [Mary-ga nani-o   katta   kadooka] oboeteiru ka] osiete
            who-NOM   M.-NOM   what-ACC bought whether remember Q   tell
            kudasai
            please
            'Please tell me [who remembers [whether Mary bought what]]'

(Maki 1994)

Owing to the *wh*-island created by *kadooka* (whether), (13*a*) can be considered an instance of a subjacency violation in Watanabe's theory. As for (13*b*), the Principle of Relation Preservation ('antisuperiority') would require the (empty operator of the) embedded *wh*-phrase to be extracted first in this case so that we would expect (13*b*) to violate subjacency in exactly the same way as (13*a*). Again, we can observe that Watanabe's account makes the wrong prediction. Hence, an alternative analysis should be found which avoids the problems associated with the Principle of Relation Preservation.

4. JAPANESE AS A MULTIPLE *WH*-FRONTING LANGUAGE

In what follows, I shall develop an analysis of the additional-*wh* effect that does not rely on the idea of relation preservation. I will rather proceed from Saito's (1994*a*) idea that *naze*-rescuing in examples like (10*b*) is achieved by adjunction of the *wh*-adjunct to the scrambled *wh*-argument *dare-ni*. Saito (1994*a*) (see also Saito and Fukui 1996) motivates this movement of the *wh*-adjunct by suggesting that there exist different licensing requirements on *wh*-arguments and *wh*-adjuncts: whereas the former may essentially be licensed via unselective binding, it is proposed that a *wh*-adjunct may only be licensed through Spec–head agreement with a [+wh] head, this being potentially achieved either when the *wh*-adjunct occurs in CP-Spec or when it is adjoined to an independently licensed *wh*-phrase.

I want to extend Saito's idea and argue that at stake here is a fundamental property of *wh*-movement which can affect *wh*-phrases in general and determine typological properties of languages depending on whether it is operative, if at all, in the overt or covert syntax. I will assume that owing to morphological properties of *wh*-words, *wh*-phrases may establish an internal operator position which is able to 'attract' *wh*-elements in multiple *wh*-constructions. In terms of the Checking Theory, we could also say that when endowed with this option, *wh*-phrases can function as 'checkers' of a *wh*-feature. For reasons that will become clear later, I want to restrict this option to *wh*-arguments. The basic idea of this suggestion is stated in (14).

(14)   Wh-*Cluster Hypothesis*
        A *wh*-element acts as a checker for other *wh*-elements (*wh*-arguments as well as *wh*-adjuncts).

Let us now turn to the question of what the morphological properties of *wh*-elements are that are responsible for this lexically determined property of *wh*-phrases. In order to answer this question, I would like to make use of a generalization suggested in Cheng (1991) according to which *wh*-words may be interpreted as indefinite NPs in multiple *wh*-fronting languages if a particular affix is added. Cheng concludes from this observation that in multiple *wh*-fronting languages, the *wh*-words themselves are similar to indefinite NPs in that they do not have any inherent quantificational force. Just as the interpretation of indefinite NPs as either existential NPs or universally quantified elements is determined by other elements with inherent quantificational force (e.g. adverbs of quantification), the interpretation of *wh*-words in multiple fronting languages as interrogative or existential is taken to be determined by certain affixes. Proposing that the overt affix which results in the *existential* reading of a *wh*-word may be treated as a determiner, Cheng then argues that the *interrogative* force of *wh*-words in *wh*-questions of multiple *wh*-fronting languages is determined by a *null* determiner, and that an interrogative *wh*-word consequently has a DP structure as shown in (15).

(15)

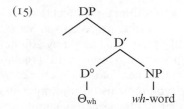

Multiple *wh*-fronting is then attributed to a licensing requirement—the DP head $[_D \Theta_{[+wh]}]$ which contributes the interrogative force to the *wh*-word is conceived of as being similar in certain ways to the empty pronominal *pro*, so that like *pro* it must be licensed (i.e. identified and governed), here by occurring in a Spec–head relationship with a [+wh] C°.

In what follows, I want to adopt Cheng's basic idea but reinterpret the licensing requirement for the $[_D \Theta_{[+wh]}]$ head in terms of the Checking Theory, along the following lines: the *wh*-feature in a $[_D \Theta_{[+wh]}]$ head must be checked, and *wh*-phrases themselves can act as checkers in these languages, since owing to the particular property of their DP heads, they establish an internal operator position in much the same way as in the case of a $C_{[+wh]}$ head. However, unlike the operator position established by the latter, the operator position created by a $[_D \Theta_{[+wh]}]$ head must be an adjunction position, since the specifier position of DP is a Case position and as such cannot function as an operator position.

Let us now consider how such ideas concerning the lexically determined internal structure of *wh*-phrases can be applied to an account of overt *wh*-fronting as is found in languages such as Bulgarian and Romanian.[3] In these languages, all *wh*-words undergo overt fronting in multiple *wh*-questions, as can be seen from the Bulgarian example in (16).

(16)   Koj₁ kakvo₂ na kogo₃ t_1 e   dal t_2 t_3?
        who what to whom   has given
        'Who gave what to whom?'   (Rudin 1988)

If we assume that the *wh*-feature of the $[_D \Theta_{[+wh]}]$ head of Bulgarian *wh*-phrases must be checked and that *wh*-phrases can act as checkers because they supply an operator position, we can derive (16) by first (right-)adjoining the indirect object *na kogo* to the direct object *kakvo*, where the *wh*-feature of the indirect object is checked by the *wh*-object *kakvo*. Then the *wh*-cluster so formed (right-)adjoins to the *wh*-subject, where the *wh*-feature of the *wh*-object is checked by the *wh*-subject, and finally the entire *wh*-complex moves to CP-Spec, where the *wh*-feature of the subject is checked by $C_{[+wh]}$.

This derivation, in which *wh*-phrases form a *wh*-cluster before moving to CP-Spec rather than moving there one by one, not only strictly obeys the Doubly Filled COMP Filter, but also avoids a serious ECP problem that arises for the traditional approach when certain ordering facts are taken into account. As pointed out by Rudin (1985, 1988), the unmarked order of the fronted *wh*-phrases in Bulgarian is: (i) *wh*-subject precedes *wh*-object; (ii) *wh*-argument precedes *wh*-adjunct.[4] Rudin (1988) argues that multiple *wh*-fronting consists of moving one *wh*-phrase to CP-Spec and right-adjoining others to the *wh*-phrase in CP-Spec. Based on her particular version of the ECP,[5] she in this way accounts for the fact that the trace of the subject in (16) is properly bound. However, she faces the dilemma that a *wh*-adjunct has to be right-adjoined to a *wh*-subject, which implies that the adjunct trace does not fulfil the ECP. This problem does not arise if we assume that prior to *wh*-movement to CP-Spec, the *wh*-adjunct adjoins to the *wh*-subject for the checking reasons mentioned

---

[3] See also Simpson (Ch. 12, this volume) for a different treatment of multiple *wh*-fronting languages.

[4] As emphasized in Comorovski (1989), the order of fronted *wh*-phrases in Bulgarian as well as in Romanian is also determined by D-linking and clitic doubling. In the present context, I want to neglect these interfering factors and focus exclusively on some sort of 'unmarked reading' of fronted *wh*-phrases.

[5] Rudin (1988) assumes a conjunctive version of the ECP with one part stated in terms of an A′-binding approach along the lines of Aoun (1986).

above, since from the position adjoined to the *wh*-argument, the adjunct trace may be properly bound.

I will now turn to considering how and to what extent these ideas about overt multiple *wh*-fronting languages may be applied to an analysis of languages such as Japanese which do not show overt *wh*-movement to CP-Spec at all.[6]

As can be seen from the examples in (17) taken from Cheng (1991), in languages such as Japanese,[7] Mandarin Chinese, and Korean, *wh*-words can be used as indefinites even without any overt morphological alternations.

(17) (*a*) *Mandarin Chinese*   (*b*) *Japanese*
        shei   who anyone   *dare*   who someone
        sheme what anything   *nani*   what something

Cheng (1991) concludes from this observation that, as is the case in Bulgarian and Romanian, *wh*-words in these languages do not have inherent quantificational force (for a similar conclusion, see Aoun and Li 1993; Ouhalla 1996). Even though this conclusion may be taken to imply that in these languages, too, *wh*-phrases contain a null determiner $[_D \; \Theta_{[+wh]}]$ in need of licensing via raising to a [+wh] C°, Cheng in fact assumes that such *wh*-elements are simply licensed in their in situ positions. Here I wish to draw the opposite conclusion. In other words, I assume that *wh*-phrases in languages such as Japanese have the structure in (15), which was assumed for *wh*-phrases in Bulgarian, so that in these languages, too, *wh*-phrases establish an operator position and are subject to the same kind of checking mechanism that was assumed for overt multiple *wh*-fronting languages. That is, in languages such as Japanese, multiple *wh*-in-situ elements will indeed be forced to undergo some kind of raising for licensing purposes; however, such *wh*-phrases do not raise individually to CP-Spec but rather covertly form *wh*-clusters prior to *wh*-movement to CP-Spec in a way entirely analogous to languages such as Bulgarian.[8] The crucial difference between overt and covert multiple *wh*-fronting languages lies in the fact that in the former, the *wh*-feature in C° as well as in D° is strong, while in the latter, it is weak in both heads.

There is ample independent evidence that *wh*-cluster formation as hypothesized in (14) applies in the covert syntax in Japanese: it is well known that in this language, complex NPs and adjuncts are islands for LF extraction of *wh*-adjuncts.

---

[6] Takahashi (1993) argues that Japanese has overt *wh*-movement to the CP-Spec position. For problems with this analysis, see Grewendorf and Sabel (1996), Nishiyama *et al.* (1996).

[7] As mentioned in Cheng (1991: fn. 14), *dare* and *nani* need to be attached to *-ka* in order to have an indefinite NP reading. However, Cheng notes that Nishigauchi (1990) provides convincing arguments that this is not a morphological derivation.

[8] Here I am assuming (unlike Chomsky 1995) that whole categories and not just features may be subject to LF movement. The analysis proposed here could, however, arguably be reinterpreted in terms of a more articulated feature-based approach.

(18) (*a*) *John-wa [$_{NP}$ [$_{IP}$ sono hon-o   naze katta] hito]-o   sagasiteru
       J.-TOP   that book-ACC why bought person-ACC looking-for
       no
       Q
       'Q John is looking for [the person [that bought that book why]]'

     (*b*) *John-wa [$_{PP}$ [$_{IP}$ Mary-ga sono hon-o   naze katta] kara]
       J.-TOP   M.-NOM that book-ACC why bought since
       okoterru no
       angry   Q
       'Q John is angry [because Mary bought that book why]'   (Saito 1994*a*)

However, it has been observed (Saito 1994*a*) that these sentences considerably improve if a *wh*-argument is added within the island in a position higher than the *wh*-adjunct, as in (19*a*, *b*).

(19) (*a*) ??John-wa [$_{NP}$ [$_{IP}$ nani-o   naze katta] hito]-o   sagasiteru   no
       J.-TOP   what-ACC why bought person-ACC looking-for Q
       'Q John is looking for [the person [that bought what why]]'

     (*b*) ?John-wa [$_{PP}$ [$_{IP}$ Mary-ga nani-o   naze katta] kara] okotteru no
       J.-TOP   M.-NOM what-ACC why bought since angry   Q
       'Q John is angry [because Mary bought what why]'   (Saito 1994*a*)

If the *wh*-phrases in (19) are raised out of the island one by one, we would expect extraction of the *wh*-adjunct in (19) to create the same sort of ungrammaticality as in the case of (18). We can therefore take the relative acceptability of the sentences in (19) to indicate that the *wh*-phrases in (19) do not leave the island one by one. Given that complex NPs and adjuncts are not islands for LF extraction of *wh*-arguments, we can rather account for the improved status of (19) by assuming that the *wh*-adjunct in (19*a*, *b*) adjoins to the *wh*-argument, and that it is in fact the *wh*-cluster so formed that undergoes LF extraction from the island.

I have already mentioned that the *Wh*-Cluster Hypothesis (14) is restricted to *wh*-arguments in the sense that only *wh*-arguments establish an internal operator position. This restriction is stated in (20).

(20)   *Constraint on* wh-*cluster formation*
       Adjunction to a *wh*-element is only possible if this element occupies an L-related position.

It is a consequence of this constraint that there can be no adjunction of *wh*-phrases to adjoined *wh*-elements, to *wh*-adjuncts, and to *wh*-elements in CP-Spec. To provide independent evidence for (20), let us consider these consequences in turn.

Saito and Fukui (1996) have independently argued that adjunction to an adjoined category is disallowed, since the resulting configuration would violate a condition on the uniqueness of the adjunction site. If adjunction is defined in terms of absence of domination and exclusion, adjunction to an adjoined category would imply an indeterminacy of the adjunction site in the sense that adjoining Z^{max} to an X^{max} which is itself adjoined to Y^{max} would come down to adjoining Z^{max} simultaneously to X^{max} and Y^{max}.[9]

Turning to the prohibition against adjoining a *wh*-element to a *wh*-adjunct, it should be recalled that the claim that *wh*-phrases establish an internal operator position is crucially associated with the configuration represented in (15) (i.e. $[_{DP} [_{D'} [_{D^o} \Theta_{[+wh]}] NP]]$), and in such a structure only *nominal wh*-words can occur as the complement of a null determiner $[_D \Theta_{[+wh]}]$. Given that adjuncts like *naze* (why) do not have any nominal properties, we can conclude that they do not occur in such structures and hence do not project any internal operator position. Finally, the consequence that there is no adjunction to elements in CP-Spec may derive conceptual plausibility from the traditional idea of the Doubly Filled COMP Filter.

In the following and final sections, I want to show that given the generalizations on Japanese scrambling stated in Section 2, the theory of covert multiple *wh*-fronting developed in the present section provides us with a new account of the additional-*wh* effect which also accommodates the clause-boundedness constraints that created empirical problems for Watanabe's analysis.

5. MULTIPLE A-SPECIFIERS AND *WH*-CLUSTER FORMATION

The additional-*wh* effect was illustrated in Section 3 by the contrast between (6) and (7). The theory developed in Section 4 provides us with a simple account of the ungrammaticality of (6) which does not employ the Principle of Relation Preservation. We have seen that the *wh*-feature of the *wh*-object *nani-o* needs to be checked, since it is a D-feature in the sense of representation (15), but checking cannot take place by adjoining the *wh*-object to the *wh*-adjunct *naze*, since the constraint on *wh*-cluster formation expressed in (20) only allows adjunction to *wh*-elements in L-related positions. On the other hand, the *wh*-feature of *nani-o* cannot be checked by $C_{[wh]}$ either, since crossing *naze* is disallowed by the Minimal Link Condition. Finally, the adjunct *naze* cannot move first to CP-Spec with *nani-o* adjoining there, since this move is likewise forbidden by constraint (20). We can conclude, then, that there is no possibility for the *wh*-object *nani-o* to get its *wh*-feature checked, hence the structure crashes.

Turning to (7a), one should recall (from Section 2) that short scrambling in Japanese is A-movement to a specifier position. Consequently, the short-scrambled *wh*-object *nani-o* occupies a position to which constraint (20) *does* allow adjunction of the *wh*-adjunct *naze* in order to get its *wh*-feature checked.

---

[9] To avoid problems in the case of head adjunction, Saito and Fukui (1996) point out that their condition applies only to operations rather than to representations.

The *wh*-cluster so formed moves to CP-Spec to check the *wh*-feature of *nani-o* against $C_{[wh]}$. Thus, (7*a*) is correctly predicted to be grammatical.

Finally, the situation with (7*b*) is analogous to that of (7*a*). The added *wh*-argument *dare-ga* occupies an L-related position and can thus attract the *wh*-adjunct. Notice that subsequently the *wh*-object also has to adjoin to the *wh*-subject to check its *wh*-feature. This implies that *wh*-phrases in Japanese must, in principle, be able to check more than once. This, however, does not create a problem for our analysis; it might be that some parameterized property similar to that suggested by Chomsky (1995) to allow for multiple subjects in Icelandic is involved here, or we might equally appeal to another idea of Chomsky's Checking Theory according to which interpretable features are not erased after checking.

Let us now consider how our analysis fares with the two clause-boundedness constraints that the additional-*wh* effect is subject to. According to the first constraint, the additional-*wh* 'rescuing' effect is neutralized if the addition of a higher *wh*-phrase is the result of long scrambling. The relevant examples were given in (10) and (11).

As for (10*a*), the *Wh*-Cluster Hypothesis requires that a complex *wh*-phrase be formed. But as in the case of (6), *dare-ga* can neither check its *wh*-feature by adjoining to the *wh*-adjunct because of constraint (20) nor move to CP-Spec because of the Minimal Link Condition. In (10*b*), the addition of the higher *wh*-phrase *dare-ni* is the consequence of short scrambling, which, as per Section 2, is movement to an L-related position. The *wh*-adjunct *naze* is therefore allowed to adjoin to the added *wh*-phrase, as is the *wh*-subject *dare-ga*.

Turning to (11*b*), which illustrates the first clause-boundedness constraint, we again have to recall a generalization on Japanese scrambling arrived at in Section 2, namely that long scrambling in Japanese is adjunction to IP. Given this result, we can easily explain why neither the *wh*-adjunct *naze* nor the *wh*-subject *dare-ga* is allowed to adjoin to the long-scrambled *wh*-phrase. Since adjunction constitutes an instance of A′-movement, the long-scrambled *wh*-phrase in (11*b*) does not occupy an L-related position and is thus prevented by constraint (20) from acting as a target for *wh*-adjunction. Since, owing to the Minimal Link Condition, neither of the other *wh*-phrases is allowed to cross the long-scrambled *nani-o* and check its *wh*-feature against $C_{[wh]}$, the ungrammaticality of (11*b*) can be attributed to the fact that the *wh*-features of *naze* and *dare-ga* remain unchecked throughout the LF derivation.

This account of the first clause-boundedness constraint allows us to make an interesting prediction regarding additional-*wh* effects in cases where the addition of a *wh*-phrase is the result of long scrambling out of a control infinitive. We have seen in Section 2 that long scrambling out of a control infinitive behaves like A-movement in Japanese. This amounts to saying that a *wh*-phrase which has been scrambled out of a control infinitive occupies an L-related position. We can therefore predict that, unlike the long-scrambled *wh*-phrase in (11*b*), a *wh*-phrase scrambled out of a control infinitive does in fact trigger the additional-*wh* effect and rescue a configuration of *wh*-phrases which would otherwise be ungrammatical. This prediction is actually borne out, as can be seen from the grammaticality of example (21).

(21)   Nani-o$_i$ naze dare-ga   Michael-ni [PRO t_i utau yoo(ni)] itta   no
        what-ACC why who-NOM M.-DAT   sing   told Q
        'What, why who told Michael to sing'   (Nemoto 1993)

Since the long-scrambled *wh*-object in (21) occupies an L-related position, the *wh*-adjunct as well as the *wh*-subject can adjoin to it to check their *wh*-features, and the cluster so formed can move to CP-Spec to check the *wh*-feature of the *wh*-object.

Let us finally turn to the second clause-boundedness constraint, which is illustrated by (12). We have to answer the question of why it is that the added *wh*-subject *dare-ga* rescues an ungrammatical configuration of *wh*-phrases when it is a clause-mate as in (12*b*), but fails to rescue this configuration when it is located in a higher clause as in (12*c*). In terms of our theory, this question can be put as follows: why is it that the *wh*-adjunct (along with the *wh*-object) is allowed to adjoin to the *wh*-subject in (12*b*) but not in (12*c*)? In answering this question, one must bear in mind that long extraction of adjuncts is commonly taken to occur via successive cyclic movement through intermediate scope positions, unlike long extraction of (referential) arguments, which need not proceed through intermediate positions (see Rizzi 1990; Grewendorf and Sabel 1994). In order to be able to leave the embedded clause in (12*c*), the *wh*-adjunct is thus first forced to move to the embedded CP-Spec position. However, it has been variously argued by Hoekstra and Bennis (1989), Müller and Sternefeld (1993), and Grewendorf and Sabel (1994) that an element which has been moved to CP-Spec is not allowed to undergo any subsequent adjunction operation thereafter. Consequently, the *wh*-adjunct *naze*, once moved to a lower CP-Spec, cannot then raise to adjoin to a higher *wh*-phrase for checking. On the other hand, the constraint on the *Wh*-Cluster Hypothesis also prevents the *wh*-adjunct from moving from COMP to COMP, since in this case, the other *wh*-phrases would not be allowed to check their *wh*-features by undergoing LF adjunction to the *wh*-adjunct in the [+wh] Comp (see (20)).[10]

Final additional support for the theory presented in this chapter is provided by the fact that it also offers an explanation for Maki's (1994) observation that a *wh*-island violation can be neutralized by adding a *wh*-phrase in the matrix clause. This observation, which constituted a serious counterexample to

---

[10]   A reviewer points out that an interesting question would be whether the additional-*wh* effect can be detected in languages with overt multiple *wh*-fronting. Relevant evidence for this might be found in the ordering restrictions on sequences of multiply fronted *wh*-phrases. The analysis here would predict that an unacceptable sequence of two *wh*-adjuncts should be rescued by a preceding *wh*-argument. Initial investigation seems to indicate that this prediction is indeed correct.

Watanabe's Principle of Relation Preservation, was illustrated by the examples in (13). If (13a) is in fact a subjacency violation, we will have to assume that subjacency applies to covert movement. Then, however, our theory provides us with a simple account for the fact that there is no subjacency violation in the case of (13b). If the ungrammaticality of (13a) is due to the fact that the embedded *wh*-phrase crosses two IP nodes, our theory entails that in (13b) the embedded *wh*-argument has to adjoin to the *wh*-phrase in the matrix clause, thereby crossing only one IP node, and that the cluster formed by this operation then undergoes movement to the *wh*-operator position of the matrix clause.

6. CONCLUDING REMARKS

In this chapter, I have shown that the analysis of multiple *wh*-fronting suggested in Section 4 reveals interesting similarities between languages with overt multiple *wh*-fronting and languages with multiple *wh*-in-situ. Furthermore, it has been demonstrated that this analysis provides us with a new account of several order restrictions which multiple *wh*-in-situ constructions in Japanese are subject to. Moreover, a new explanation has been offered for the so-called additional-*wh* effect and its constraints. The explanation of the latter was crucially based on an analysis of Japanese scrambling that attributed the A-properties of this operation to the presence of multiple specifiers in the Japanese agreement system. Should this explanation be on the right track, it provides independent evidence for the existence of multiple A-specifiers in Japanese.

REFERENCES

Aoun, J. (1986), *Generalized Binding*, Foris, Dordrecht.

——and Li, Y. A. (1993), *Syntax of Scope*, MIT Press, Cambridge, Mass.

Cheng, L. (1991), 'On the Typology of Wh-Questions', Ph.D. thesis, MIT.

Chomsky, N. (1993), 'A Minimalist Program for Linguistic Theory', in K. Hale and J. K. Keyser (eds.), *The View from Building 20*, MIT Press, Cambridge, Mass., 1–52.

——(1995), *The Minimalist Program*, MIT Press, Cambridge, Mass.

Comorovski, I. (1989), 'Discourse and the Syntax of Multiple Constituent Questions', Ph.D. thesis, Cornell University.

Grewendorf, G., and Sabel, J. (1994), 'Long Scrambling and Incorporation', *Linguistic Inquiry*, 25: 263–308.

————(1996), *Multiple Specifiers and the Theory of Adjunction: On Scrambling in German and Japanese*, Sprachwissenschaft in Frankfurt, 16.

Hoekstra, T., and Bennis, H. (1989), 'A Representational Theory of Empty Categories', in H. Bennis and A. v. Kemenade (eds.), *Linguistics in the Netherlands 1989*, Foris, Dordrecht, 91–9.

Maki, H. (1994), 'Anti-Anti-Superiority', *Proceedings of the Eastern States Conference on Linguistics—ESCOL*, 11: 199–209.

Müller, G., and Sternefeld, W. (1993), 'Improper Movement and Unambiguous Binding', *Linguistic Inquiry*, 24: 461–507.

Nemoto, N. (1993), 'Chains and Case Positions: A Study from Scrambling in Japanese', Ph.D. thesis, University of Connecticut.

Nishigauchi, T. (1990), *Quantification in the Theory of Grammar*, Kluwer, Dordrecht.

Nishiyama, N., Whitman, J., and Yi, E.-Y. (1996), 'Syntactic Movement of Overt Wh-Phrases in Japanese and Korean', in N. Akatsuka, S. Iwasaki, and S. Strauss (eds.), *Japanese/Korean Linguistics*, vol. 5, CSLI Publications, Stanford, Calif., 337–51.

Ouhalla, J. (1996), 'Remarks on the Binding Properties of *Wh*-Pronouns', *Linguistic Inquiry*, 27: 676–707.

Rizzi, L. (1990), *Relativized Minimality*, MIT Press, Cambridge, Mass.

Rudin, C. (1985), 'Multiple WH Movement and the Superiority Condition', paper read at LSA annual meeting, Minneapolis.

——(1988), 'On Multiple Questions and Multiple Wh-Fronting', *Natural Language and Linguistic Theory*, 6: 445–501.

Saito, M. (1992), 'Long Distance Scrambling in Japanese', *Journal of East Asian Linguistics*, 1: 69–118.

——(1994*a*), 'Additional-*wh* Effects and the Adjunction Site Theory', *Journal of East Asian Linguistics*, 3: 195–240.

——(1994*b*), 'Improper Adjunction', in M. Koizumi and H. Ura (eds.), *MIT Working Papers in Linguistics*, 24: *Formal Approaches to Japanese Linguistics*, 1: 263–93.

——and Fukui, N. (1996), *Order in the Theory of Phrase Structure and Movement*, Sprachwissenschaft in Frankfurt, 14.

Takahashi, D. (1993), 'Movement of Wh-Phrases in Japanese', *Natural Language and Linguistic Theory*, 11: 655–78.

Ura, H. (1994), 'Super-Raising and the Feature-Based-X-Bar Theory', Ms., MIT.

——(1996), 'Multiple Feature-Checking: A Theory of Grammatical Function Splitting', Ph.D. thesis, MIT.

Watanabe, A. (1992), *WH-in-situ, Subjacency, and Chain Formation*, MIT Occasional Papers in Linguistics, 2.

Webelhuth, G. (1989), 'Syntactic Saturation Phenomena and the Modern Germanic Languages', Ph.D. thesis, University of Massachusetts.

9
Parallels between
Nominal and Verbal Projections

TEUN HOEKSTRA

1. INTRODUCTION

This chapter examines nominal structures in which *of*-insertion has taken place. It is argued that such structures involve movement of the predicate to the specifier of *of*, which is itself a complementizer in the nominal structure. The analysis is an extension of some of the proposals of Kayne (1994). The main argument in favour of the particular analysis is based on properties of infinitival nominalizations in Dutch. However, there is no reason why the analysis should be limited to *of*-insertion in these nominalizations, and it is therefore argued that the analysis extends to other nominal constructions, both basic noun and derived nominal constructions. I will then argue that an inversion analysis may shed light on an as yet ill-understood property of nominal constructions, viz. the fact that they are so limited in their argument structure possibilities when compared to verbal constructions.

2. THE PROBLEM OF *OF*-INSERTION

Let us briefly review the standard analysis of *of*-insertion, originally proposed in Chomsky (1970). Chomsky argues that nominal structures such as (1*a*) are not transformationally derived from corresponding verbal structures, but that they are generated in their own right, with a nominal head projecting a nominal phrase in a way parallel to a verbal head projecting a clausal structure. Although there are many parallels indeed, there are also differences of a categorial nature. In particular, while verbs can take nominal complements, such complements are excluded in the nominal domain, as is shown in (1*b*).

Parts of the material in this chapter were presented in classes at UCLA, at the University of Budapest, and at HIL, Leiden University, as well as at the conference on specifiers at the University of York. I thank members of these audiences for various suggestions. In addition I would like to thank Marcel den Dikken, Gertjan Postma, Johan Rooryck, and Dominique Sportiche for valuable discussions.

(1) (*a*)   The enemy's destruction of the city
    (*b*)   *The enemy's destruction the city

In order to deal with this unexpected asymmetry, it is assumed that nominal complements require Case, and that nouns, unlike verbs, are unable to assign Case. Therefore, a prepositional element is called for, to provide Case for the nominal complement, as prepositions, like verbs, are able to assign Case. It is furthermore assumed that the preposition *of* (or its equivalent in other languages) is transformationally inserted so as to rescue the structure corresponding to (1*b*) from the effects of the Case Filter. This rule of *of*-insertion can be simply formulated as in (2).

(2)   Of-*insertion*
          $[_{N'}$ N–(Prt)–NP–X]   1–2–*of*+3–4   (Jackendoff 1977: 70)

There are several problems with this analysis. Specifically, the linear formulation leaves unclear what the derived constituent structure is: does the rule create a PP superstructure out of *of* plus the following NP, and if so, does this PP structure prevent the NP dominated by it from scoping outside this PP structure? As we will see, this clearly seems to be the case.[1] Another problem *vis-à-vis* the constituency concerns the fact that the *of*-NP does not behave in all respects as a normal PP; it cannot, for instance, undergo *wh*-movement (cf. Jackendoff 1977: 70, fn. 13), while it can undergo extraposition from NP.[2]

In this chapter, I shall present an alternative analysis of *of* which does not show these defects. I shall start by examining *of*-insertion in Dutch nominalizations.

3. INFINITIVAL NOMINALIZATIONS

Dutch features nominalized infinitival structures (henceforth NIs): the infinitive takes the determiner *het* and the phrase as a whole has the external distribution of a DP. It is often claimed that such infinitival constructions show a mixture of nominal and verbal properties (cf. for Dutch, Hoekstra and Wehrmann 1985; van Haaften *et al.* 1985; Hoekstra 1986). A specifically nominal property is that direct objects may appear in *van*-phrases (*van* is the Dutch counterpart of English *of*) following the infinitive. Verbal properties are found

---

[1] This problem is not limited to the preposition *of*, but is found with other prepositions as well. To the extent that the analysis presented in this chapter is tenable, a similar approach might be taken for other such situations as well.

[2] Under Kayne's theory, there are no rightward movement rules, such as extraposition. Rather, 'extraposition' structures must be considered as resulting from stranding the extraposed material by leftward movement. The asymmetry between the impossible leftward movement of the *of*-NP combination and the apparent rightward movement (i.e. stranding) furnishes a further argument for the analysis pursued in this chapter, but I shall not develop the argument here.

as well, such as the possibility of PPs preceding the infinitive, something which is excluded in nominal constructions. Some examples are found in (3).

(3) (*a*)   het roken van sigaren is ongezond
        the smoke-INF of cigars is unhealthy

    (*b*)   het voortdurend(e) sigaren roken is ongezond
         the continuous(ly) cigars smoke-INF is unhealthy

    (*c*)   het op konijnen jagen in de zomer is verboden
         the on rabbits hunt-INF in the summer is forbidden

    (*d*)   *de op konijnen jacht in de zomer is verboden
         the on rabbits hunt in the summer is forbidden

Examples (3*a*, *b*) show that the nominal object may either precede the infinitive as a bare DP, or follow it, preceded by *van*. Examples (3*c*, *d*) show that whereas a basic noun may not be preceded by a PP, an NI may. In this respect, NIs are like verbs.[3]

This hybrid nature of the NI might be accounted for by Jackendoff's deverbalizing rule schema (Jackendoff 1977: 221), or some modern incarnation thereof. Jackendoff's formulation is given in (4).

(4)   *Deverbalizing rule schema*
        $X^i \rightarrow$ af-V^i

What (4) says is that verbal projections may, as a result of affixation, shift to a category X of the same level. So, the difference between (3*a*) and (3*b*) might be captured by saying that the category shift in (3*a*) has taken place at the V^0 level, and that the NI takes an object within N^1 therefore, while in (3*b*) the category shift has taken place at the V^1 level, namely after the NI has combined with its object within V^1. Apart from the fact that this approach raises several other questions, it is also empirically inadequate, at least under a Jackendovian interpretation of the projection levels. According to this interpretation, the head of an XP combines with its subcategorized complements at the X^1 level, whereas modifiers of various sorts combine with higher projection levels. Consider the NI construction in (5), where the object *de aardappels*, being a complement, should combine with the head at the X^1 level, and the modifier *met een mesje* at a higher level.

(5)   het met een mesje schillen van de aardappels
       the with a knife peel-INF of the potatoes

---

[3] Whether modification of the infinitive is by adverbs or adjectives is hard to establish. Adverbs do not inflect, whereas adjectives may show a suffix -*e* in certain environments. As indicated in (3*b*), the modifying word may or may not be inflected, suggesting that it may either be an adverb (uninflected) or an adjective (inflected). However, judgements on the use of the -*e* inflection in these constructions are not clear, and the rules governing the appearance of the -*e* inflection on adjectives are not fully understood either. So, it is not easy to base any arguments on the absence or presence of the -*e*.

The occurrence of the object in a *van*-PP requires category shift at the V° level, but the occurrence of a PP modifier requires a V category at the level of attachment of this PP, a higher level, as there is no possibility of a pre-head PP at any nominal projection level. Hence, (5) imposes incompatible requirements within Jackendoff's approach.

From a more current point of view, the fact that the *van*-object in NIs must follow the head is perhaps even more surprising: PPs may precede the NI in Dutch; why does a PP that corresponds to the object have to follow it? A simple solution might run as follows. If base structures are uniformly built in the form [Spec, Head, Comp], as Kayne argues, then the fact that the DP object precedes the verb in Dutch must be the result of leftward movement, let us say to a position [Spec, AGRoP], in order to receive Case. As no Case is available in nominal structures, but *of/van*-insertion applies instead, there is no motivation for such a leftward shift, and hence the *van*-DP follows the NI head. Note, however, that this places the object in NIs in a structurally very low position. We shall see in the next section that this seems highly inadequate.

Obviously, the alternation between (3*a*) and (3*b*) calls for an explanation as well. Although it is true that objects in NIs may occur as bare DPs preceding the NI head, there are rather severe limitations on the nature of this object. Basically, the object needs to be indefinite. So, pronouns, proper names, and definite DPs are excluded from pre-head position. In itself, this is rather surprising, as leftward movements are usually restricted to precisely those DPs that may not occur in pre-head position in NIs; that is, leftward scrambling does not apply to indefinite DPs, but it does affect pronouns, proper names, and definite DPs. We see here a basically *inverse* effect: those objects that may or must undergo leftward scrambling in clausal structures occur to the right of the NI head in a *van*-PP, while those that do not undergo leftward scrambling in clausal structures occur to the left of the NI head. We shall later see how our analysis immediately captures this fact.[4]

The hybrid nature of verbal nouns in English is mapped out slightly differently: English distinguishes two types of *-ing* construction, both with an external distribution of DP, viz. *-ing-of* and *-ing*-ACC. The former is more nominal, the latter more verbal. In fact, the *-ing-of* is nominal to such an extent that it is often taken to enter the syntax as a noun (cf. Horn 1975; Zubizarreta 1989). Not only do such constructions take objects in a noun-like manner (i.e. preceded by *of*), they may occur with the determiner and be modified by adjectives—this all in contradistinction to *-ing*-ACC gerundives:

---

[4] One might, following the idea suggested in the previous paragraph, think of the pre-NI bare objects as Caseless, assuming that indefinites need not be Case-marked, while definites must receive (strong) Case. I do not think that such a distinction in terms of Case is motivated, but that the further leftward scrambling of specific DPs is motivated by their specificity. Whatever the case may be, the assumption that post-NI objects preceded by *van* are in situ objects does not seem defensible.

(6) (*a*) John's/the brutal(*ly) killing of rabbits
　　(*b*) John's/*the brutal*(ly) killing rabbits

The assumption that *-ing-of* gerundives are projected from a nominal head is also taken to explain a further difference between them and *-ing*-ACC structures, viz. their limited complementation options. Small clause complements and exceptional Case marking environments are not found in *-ing-of* constructions, as (7) shows.[5] Since such options are equally not found in basic or derived nominal constructions, the claim that the *-ing* word enters the syntax as a noun in such *-ing-of* constructions would explain this.

(7) (*a*) 　*the letting of children sleep
　　(*b*) 　*the hearing of John climb the fence
　　(*c*) 　*the finding of the students incompetent
　　(*d*) 　?the putting of men on the moon
　　(*e*) 　?the watering of the tulips flat
　　(*f*) 　*appearing of the perpetrator guilty
　　(*g*) 　*the becoming of John (the) major
　　(*h*) 　*the electing of Bill (to/as/for) president

However, this constitutes an explanation only in so far as we have an explanation of this limitation in the case of basic and derived nominal structures. It seems to me that such an explanation is lacking. From the point of view of theta-theory or s-selection, the expected situation would be that nouns corresponding in meaning to verbs with complex argument structures would equally have complex argument structures. That this expectation is not borne out requires an explanation. Kayne (1984) attempts an explanation in terms of the concept of structural government (cf. also Chomsky's 1986 notion of uniformity). Nouns differ from verbs in not being capable of governing across a clausal boundary; that is, they are not *structural* governors. A preposition, such as *of*, may inherit the structural government ability from a verb, but clearly not from a noun, as the noun does not have it to begin with. Hence, no Case assignment by *of* is possible to the subject of a (small) clausal complement.

Although by and large capturing the facts, the central concept of structural government is dubious and has no relevant status in any current framework. Moreover, it is not quite true that the complementation options of *-ing-of* and regular noun-based phrases are completely identical. The former, but not the latter, allow 'verbal' (*sic!*) particles, as Abney (1986) notes:

(8) (*a*) 　the explaining away of the problem
　　(*b*) 　*the explanation away of the problem

The Dutch situation in this regard is less straightforward than the situation

---

[5] Judgements on constructions of the types in (7) vary quite a bit between native speakers. For some speakers placing a star in front of some of these examples is not warranted. I do not know what causes this variation in judgements.

in English: while English appears to make a sharp distinction between -*ing-of* and -*ing*-ACC, the presence or absence of *van* in Dutch NIs (cf. (3*a*, *b*)) does not have the same range of effects: in either case the definite determiner is possible, and complex argument structures are found in both cases. Hence, most of the counterparts of the constructions in (7) are grammatical in Dutch, even with *van*. Obviously, there are differences in word order between Dutch and English.

(9) (*a*)   het laten slapen van de kinderen
            the let-INF sleep-INF of the children

(*b*)   het over het hek horen klimmen van Jan
        the over the fence hear-INF climb of John

(*c*)   het incompetent vinden van de studenten
        the incompetent find-INF of the students

As to the word order in Dutch NIs, it is basically identical to that found in clausal structures, modulo the position of the object when it occurs with *van*. Yet, it is unclear how an account in terms of structural government would capture these differences between Dutch and English.[6] I shall argue below that this difference between English and Dutch verbal noun constructions (Dutch NI, English -*of-ing*) is an instance of a much broader generalization, related to word order rather than to N/V asymmetries.

In summary, both English and Dutch show verbal noun constructions which are both verbal and nominal to certain degrees. There is no clear theoretical way to capture such mixture of properties. The problems concern word order, the distribution of object DPs, and, in *of/van* verbal noun constructions (the more nominal ones), the apparent lack of complex argument structures. An adequate theory of verbal noun constructions should shed light on these matters. Current theories of verbal noun constructions are lacking in this regard.

4. THE SCOPE PROBLEM

There is a strong relationship between linear order and scope, as is well known. Yet, a formulation of scope in terms of linear order alone is clearly inadequate, as some form of command is required to rule out **the parents of John like himself*. One might be tempted, therefore, to formulate a combined hierarchical and linear condition on scope. Alternatively, one may strengthen the relationship between hierarchy and linear order, such that linear order strongly correlates with hierarchy, and hence capture the law-like correspondence between

---

[6] The differences between Dutch and English in this respect might be taken to suggest that the secondary predicate (e.g. *incompetent* in (9*c*)) and the verb form a complex predicate (cf. Hoeksema 1991 for an argument to this effect), instead of a small clause. (See Hoekstra 1992 for discussion of this idea.)

linearity and scope in this way. The latter strategy was followed by Larson (1988), and more recently, and more vigorously, by Kayne (1994).

With this in mind, let us return to the constituency problem of the *van*-DP. Recall that if the inserted *of/van* created a PP structure over the DP, our expectation should be that the DP cannot scope out of this PP. The facts concerning NIs in Dutch clearly indicate that this is wrong. In (10), we see that the DP following *van* (henceforth DP_{van}) is able to bind an anaphor (10a) and a pronominal variable (10b). Both require that the DP_{van} c-commands the dependent element. More surprising and also more problematic is the fact that DP_{van} also scopes leftwards, into material preceding the NI head. This is shown for anaphors and pronominal variables by the examples in (11) and (12).

(10) (a) het overleggen van *de studenten* over *elkaar*s antwoorden
   the discussing of the students about each other's answers

 (b) het overhoren van *elke student* over *zijn* speciale onderwerp
   the examining of each student about his special subject

(11) (a) het over *zichzelf* praten van *Jan*
   the about himself talk-INF of John
   'John's talking about himself'

 (b) het naast *elkaar* zetten van *de flessen*
   the next-to each other put-INF of the bottles
   'the putting of the bottles next to each other'

(12) (a) het op *zijn* qui-vive zijn van *iedere soldaat* is een eerste vereiste
   the on his alert be of every soldier is a first requirement

 (b) het aan *zijn* eigenaar teruggeven van *elk geleend artikel*
   the to its owner back give-INF of each borrowed article

It is not possible to devise a constituency structure for NIs in which the DP_{van} is hierarchically superior to both material that precedes and material that follows. This is most certainly the case if, as Kayne (1994) argues, right-adjunction is not allowed.

To be sure, there are other instances where linearity and scope do not match. Examples are given in (13). The strategy for dealing with such cases is to appeal to movement: in (13a), the phrase *each other's pictures* is raised from the subject position of the infinitival complement. Prior to movement, *the boys* can act as the binder of the anaphor *each other*.[7] Similarly, in (13b), under reconstruction of the *wh*-phrase, *the boys* scopes rightward so as to bind the anaphor *themselves*.

(13) (a) *Each other*'s pictures seemed to *the boys* to be beautiful
 (b) Which pictures of *themselves* did *the boys* like?

---

[7] Note that the presence of *to* in this example introduces the same problem as *van/of* with respect to the options of the DP_{to} to scope to the right (cf. fn. 1).

We may adopt the same strategy in the case of the backward scope instances in NIs (11–12); that is, we may assume that movement is involved and that, prior to movement, or after reconstruction, the DP_{van} adequately takes scope to its right, rather than to its left. In the next section I will establish the basis for providing a solution along these lines.

5. THE [D CP] STRUCTURE

In this section I shall investigate the particular structure of *of/van* in nominal constructions. I begin by laying out some of the specifics of Kayne's proposals on the structure of DPs, starting with the data in (14).

(14) (*a*) *the Paris
     (*b*)   the Paris that I used to visit
     (*c*)   the Paris of my youth

Why would the proper name in (14*a*) resist combining with the determiner, while such a combination is fine in the presence of a relative clause or a post-nominal PP? Kayne argues that (14*a*) involves a different structure than (14*b*, *c*). In particular, (14*a*) involves a DP, with D taking the regular kind of complementation for a simple noun phrase, say NP.[8] *Paris* is a noun, denoting the property of *x*, such that *x* has the name Paris. In proper name DPs, no quantification takes place: rather, the noun in proper names occupies the quantifier position D as a result of N-to-D movement (cf. Longobardi 1995). The example in (14*b*), on the other hand, has a more complex internal structure. Here, the D takes a CP complement, a *that*-clause, from which the 'head' of the relative is extracted to [Spec, CP]. Under this raising analysis of relatives, originally due to Vergnaud (1974), the structure of (14*b*) is as in (15), where *Paris* does not occupy the complement position of D.[9]

(15) $[_{DP}$ the $[_{CP}$ *Paris*$_i$ $[_{C'}$ that I used to visit $t_i]]]$

The pattern recurs in possessive constructions as well. Consider the triplet in (16).

(16) (*a*) John's several books
     (*b*)   *the several books of John's
     (*c*)   the several books of John's that he bought last week

For (16*a*), Kayne assumes a structure with an empty D, followed by a clausal constituent, say IP, of which the QP *several books* is the predicate, and *John* is

---

[8] It seems reasonable that in between D and NP several functional categories, such as number etc., need to be postulated. That is irrelevant at this point.

[9] Although I adopt the analysis of movement as copying and deletion, for clarity I indicate movement by coindexed traces.

the subject, as in (17a).[10] The construction in (16b) derives from (16a), in Kayne's view, through movement of *several books* to the left.[11] The analysis is modelled on Szabolcsi's (1994) analysis of Hungarian DPs, which involve a similar QP movement to [Spec, DP]. According to Kayne, *of* occupies the D-position, which accounts for the ungrammaticality of (16b), as *the* and *of* would compete for the same D-position. Example (17b) is Kayne's structure for (16b).

(17) (*a*) [$_{DP}$ $\emptyset$ [$_{IP}$ John 's I [$_{QP}$ several books]]]
    (*b*) [$_{DP}$ [*several books*]$_i$ [$_{D'}$ of [$_{IP}$ John's I t_i]]]

The increased acceptability of (16c) is again understandable if the determiner is external to the constituent, in the same way as in (15). We may again adopt a [D CP] structure, with *several books of John's* raised from inside the relative to the [Spec, CP] position.

This also carries over to (14c), where we are also dealing with an *of*-construction. However, for other cases involving *of*, as in (18), Kayne equally proposes an inversion analysis, but here *of* is taken to head the CP, rather than the DP (cf. Den Dikken 1995 for extensive discussion of this construction).

(18) (*a*) that idiot of a doctor
    (*b*) [$_{DP}$ that [$_{CP}$ *idiot*$_i$ [$_{C'}$ of [$_{IP}$ a doctor I t_i]]]]

The idea that *of* instantiates a complementizer rather than a determiner is less surprising in view of prepositional complementizers occurring elsewhere (cf. *de* in French, *for* in English). I shall henceforth assume that *of*/*van* and their equivalents indeed occur in a C position, and not in D.[12]

The pattern observed in (14) and (16) extends to Dutch NIs, as observed in Hoekstra and Wehrmann (1985). The contrast in (19) can now be understood along the same lines. Basically, (19a) is a proper name construction, involving N-to-D movement of the infinitive (it is a generic term), while (19b), in contrast, involves a [D CP] structure.

(19) (*a*) (*het) roken is ongezond
       the smoke-INF is unhealthy
       [$_{DP}$ $\emptyset$ [$_{IP}$ . . . [$_N$ roken] . . .]]

[10] In this analysis, then, the so-called genitive *'s* is not an instance of D, as proposed by Abney (1986), but rather an agreement marker, generated in I, and cliticizing to its specifier, *John*. This assumption raises several further questions, which I shall not go into, however.

[11] A reviewer raises the obvious question of what drives this movement. Within the context of a theory incorporating greed, the equally obvious answer is that the movement is driven by some feature that needs to be checked. A likely candidate is the D-feature of the verbal noun. The reviewer also wonders why this movement to [Spec, CP] is 'much more local than traditional instances of movement to [Spec, CP]'. The answer is that if the movement is motivated by the need to license a D-feature of the verbal noun in D, there is no motivation to move beyond the local D.

[12] Kayne's main motivation for postulating *of* in D in possessives is the complementarity between it and a definite determiner. I shall not discuss this point.

(*b*) het roken van sigaren is ongezond
the smoke-INF of cigars is unhealthy
[$_{DP}$ het [$_{CP}$ [$_{NP}$ roken]$_i$ van [$_{IP}$ [sigaren] . . . t_i . . .]]]

Possessive constructions in many languages come in two varieties: the construct state (CS) and the free state (FS). These notions are most familiar in the Semitic literature (cf. Ritter 1991; Fassi Fehri 1993), where they refer to the constructions in (20*a*) and (20*b*), respectively.

(20) (*a*) beit ha-mora   (construct state)
house the-teacher
'the teacher's house'

(*b*) ha-bayit šel ha-mora   (free state)
the-house of the-teacher
'the house of the teacher'

The construction in (20*a*) is called construct state because the possessive relationship between the possessed noun and the possessor is not in any way marked (it is 'marked' by the construction).[13] Moreover, the noun and its possessor form a unit, both syntactically and semantically: syntactically because strict adjacency between them needs to be observed, semantically in that the definiteness value of the possessed object is dependent on the definiteness of its possessor. The differences between CS and FS involve (i) the overt marking of the possessive relationship by *šel* in FS, and (ii) the overt marking of the definiteness value on the possessed noun in FS.

In terms of the analyses developed so far, we can postulate the following structures for CS and FS constructions, respectively:

(21) (*a*) [$_{DP}$ D [$_{IP}$ DP I . . . [$_{NP}$ . . . N . . .]]]   (CS)
     ↑_____| (X° movement)

(*b*) [$_{CP}$ D [$_{CP}$ . . . C [$_{IP}$ DP I . . . [$_{NP}$ . . . N . . .]]]]   (FS)
    ↑_____| (XP movement)

The CS construction in Hebrew is derived by N-to-D movement, an instance of head movement, while the FS construction involves phrasal movement of (a projection of) NP to [Spec, CP]. This difference between head movement and phrasal movement becomes clear when we inspect the following paradigm (cf. Ritter 1991; Longobardi 1996):

(22) (*a*) ha-bayit ha-godol *(šel) ha-mora   (FS)
the-house the-big of the-teacher

(*b*) *ha-bayit šel ha-mora ha-godol   (FS)

(*c*) beit (*šel) ha-mora ha-godol   (CS)

---

[13] The construct state may be marked by a special form of the possessed noun, which may be said to occur in construct state form—cf. the difference between the free form *bayit* in (20*b*) and the construct state form *beit* in (20*a*).

(*d*) *beit ha-godol ha-mora (CS)

The adjectival modifier in the FS in (22*a*) moves along with the noun to the [Spec, CP] position, where the presence of C, *šel*, is obligatory. Stranding of this modifier, as in (22*b*), is impossible. This impossibility follows from Chomsky's (1993) *Minimal Link Condition* (MLC). Consider the structure in (21*b*): in order to move to the [Spec, CP] position, the phrase containing the noun must cross the intervening [Spec, IP] position, occupied by the DP possessor. This is possible only if two conditions are met: first, the head of IP must undergo head movement so as to extend its domain and make [Spec, CP] equidistant to [Spec, IP]; secondly, the phrase that moves must be the maximal XP complement of the head of IP, or its specifier. We shall return to further implications of this latter requirement in Section 7. The MLC, then, explains why phrasal movement to [Spec, CP] in (22*a*, *b*) must involve both the noun and its adjectival modifier. The CS construction, in contrast, does not involve phrasal movement, but head movement. Therefore, other material, including the adjectival modifier, is stranded under N-to-D movement, which explains the ungrammaticality of (22*d*), or, generally, the strict adjacency between the noun in D and the possessor.

The CS construction can be recognized by the absence of an overt determiner, even if the construction has a definite interpretation. In this respect, CS constructions of the Semitic variety are similar to possessive constructions involving prenominal genitives in Germanic languages.[14] This is why I refer to such constructions in Germanic as CS constructions as well. They differ from the Semitic CS construction with respect to the word order, more precisely the position of N, which in Germanic does not seem to occur in the D position (at least not in Western Germanic[15]). Longobardi explains this by invoking the concept of procrastinated movement (cf. Chomsky 1993): N-to-D movement takes place in Germanic as well as in Semitic, but it is postponed in Germanic until after Spellout, and hence invisible.[16] I will therefore assume, following

---

[14] The fact that the possessor bears genitive Case is irrelevant: within Semitic, the possessor in the construct state may occur either in unmarked form, as in Hebrew, or in the genitive, as in Arabic. The status of English *s* in the 'Saxon genitive' (cf. fn. 10) is unclear: to analyse it as a morphological genitive seems incorrect. It should rather be taken to instantiate an Agreement marker, but for our purposes the issue is not really relevant.

[15] Gertjan Postma points out to me that there are some instances in English and Dutch which do seem to involve N-to-D raising in overt syntax, as in e.g. *mid-winter*, which is '(in) the middle of the winter' or 'the winter's middle'. These examples involve reduction of the noun, as in Semitic, and absence of the determiner, while having a definite interpretation. Longobardi (1996) notes a restricted range of Semitic-like CS constructions in Western Romance, limited to kinship terms and the word for 'house', as in *Casa Rossi* (= *the* house of Rossi). Interestingly, these CS constructions seem to be able to express a 'prepositional' meaning, without a preposition. So, in Dutch we have *Ik ben hartje zomer vertrokken* (lit. 'I am heart summer left', idiomatically 'I left *in* the middle of the summer'). *Casa DP* has developed into a PP in modern French, *chez Jean* (at John's).

[16] This difference accounts in a straightforward way for the difference between patronymics of

Longobardi, that in Germanic constructions involving prenominal possessors, we are likewise dealing with CS constructions, in which N-to-D movement is postponed until LF. On the other hand, Germanic and Romance constructions involving *of/van/de/di* can be taken to be the counterparts of free state constructions (cf. again Longobardi's 1996 discussion of *Casa Rossi* vs. *la casa di Rossi*). I shall apply this free state analysis to NI constructions in the next section.

The relationship between verb position and CS constructions seems evident. N-initial nominal structures basically arise in the same manner as V-initial structures, viz. movement of the lexical head to a functional position dominating IP (i.e. to a position preceding the subject).[17] Possibly, the postponement of such head movement in certain languages, such as English, may be the result of overt movement of the possessor DP to the higher [Spec, DP]. Potentially, this may be the result of a general condition to the effect that at Spellout, either the head position of XP is filled, or its specifier, but not both.[18] This results in the following partial representations of English and Hebrew simple construct state constructions at Spellout:

(23) (a)　$[_{DP}$ *John's*$_i$ $\varnothing$ $[_{IP}$ t_i . . . [. . . house . . .]]]

　　　(b)　$[_{DP}$ $\varnothing$ *beit*$_i$ $[_{IP}$ ha-mora . . . [. . . t_i . . .]]]

An interesting consequence of the analysis of FS and CS constructions is that the category D may take two distinct kinds of complements: subject-initial IPs, yielding CS constructions, and non-subject-initial CPs, in which case the D position must be filled by a determiner. This situation parallels very strongly that found in clausal structures in several Germanic languages. In Scandinavian and certain varieties of German, embedded clauses introduced by an overt complementizer may either exhibit CP properties (the so-called embedded V-second clauses) or be plain IP complements, with the finite verb in a lower position. Similarly, for main clauses, one line of thought holds that the verb-second phenomenon is not uniform in that the verb occupies an I position in subject-initial main clauses, but the C position in non-subject-initial main clauses, the so-called Travis Hypothesis (cf. Travis 1984; Zwart 1994). I will not at this point go further into these parallelisms.

---

the type 'John-son', found in Germanic, and those of the types 'ben-Yousef' found in Semitic and 'mac-Bhrian' found in Celtic (also a language type with overt N-to-D in CS), with *son*, *ben*, and *mac* meaning the same: 'son'.

[17]　It is worthwhile to note in this respect that no adjacency is required in Welsh construct state constructions; this is parallel to the lower position ([Spec, VP]?) in which subjects may be found in VSO clauses.

[18]　Hilda Koopman (personal communication) is working on a proposal of this nature which in fact generalizes Rizzi's (1991) proposals concerning negation and *wh*-questions, as well as proposals of a similar nature in the work of Dominique Sportiche.

6. RECONSTRUCTION IN FREE STATE NOMINALIZED INFINITIVAL STRUCTURES

Let us now return to NI constructions in which an argument is preceded by *van*. Clearly, we would like to extend the analysis of FS constructions to such NIs, as this yields a uniform treatment of *van*. The analysis of an example such as (5), repeated here as (24*a*), will be as in (24*b*).

(24) (*a*) het met een mesje schillen van de aardappels
the with a knife peel-INF of the potatoes

   (*b*) [$_{DP}$ het [$_{CP}$ [$_{XP}$ *met een mesje schillen*]$_i$ van [$_{IP}$ [$_{DP}$ de aardappels] H [$_{XP}$ t_i]]]]

As before, *van* occupies the C position, taking an IP complement: in line with the Split-Infl Hypothesis, I take IP to be AgrP, but not much turns on this. As before, it is the maximal complement of H, the head of IP or AgrP, that must move to [Spec, CP], inverting around the DP in [Spec, AgrP] as a result. In addition, the head H of IP must incorporate into C so as to make [Spec, CP] equidistant to its own Spec.[19] The fact that the maximal complement of H must move to [Spec, CP] would predict that the DP$_{van}$ is the final element in NIs. This prediction is wrong, and I shall discuss it in Section 7.

Let us first look at the correct predictions of the analysis. First, given the inversion that takes place, we have achieved our goal, set out in Section 4, of reconciling the scope facts with the linear restrictions on scope. The backward binding instances in (11) and (12) can now be regarded as instantiating binding under c-command by the DP$_{van}$ of the anaphors and pronominal variables in their original site. The structure of (11*b*) is represented in (25).

(25)   [$_{DP}$ het [$_{CP}$ [$_{XP}$ *naast elkaar zetten*]$_i$ van [$_{IP}$ [$_{DP}$ de flessen] H [$_{XP}$ t_i]]]]

As movement of XP is to [Spec, CP], such licensing under reconstruction is in fact expected. Note also that the constituency of the DP$_{van}$ is not problematic, as *van* and DP do not form a constituent, and hence, the DP$_{van}$ c-commands the material dominated by XP in the strict sense.

Very interesting confirmation of the correctness of this approach comes from parasitic gap constructions. As noted in Hoekstra (1992), parasitic gaps

---

[19] Some speculation may be in order here. Dutch *van* is both different from and similar to English *of*: it might be analysed as *of* plus something. This something might be identified as the preposition *aan* (cf. English *on*), which is the Dutch 'dative' preposition. Similarly, Hebrew has a complementizer *še*, which may be analysed as part of *šel*, the other part being the initial part of *li*, the dative preposition in Hebrew (this was pointed out to me independently by Edit Doron and Samir Khalaily). One may wonder why a dative preposition would be involved in the make-up of this complex nominal complementizer. A suggestion that comes to mind is that this dative preposition is incorporated into C from I (cf. English inflectional *to*). It might have arrived there, in turn, by being extracted from the 'possessor', if possessors start out as dative PPs (cf. Den Dikken 1995 for this claim).

can be found in NIs.[20] But their properties are surprising, if compared to those of parasitic gaps in clauses. Consider the examples in (26). The infinitival adjunct clause contains a gap, which is dependent on the object *zijn boeken* for its interpretation. As the contrast between (26*a*) and (26*b*) shows, the object must precede the adjunct clause in order to license the gap inside it. This is not a general requirement on the ordering of adjunct clauses and objects. This linear condition on parasitic gaps can be understood if we make the following assumptions, as argued by Bennis and Hoekstra (1984). First, objects occur inside VP at some earlier level of representation; secondly, the position in front of the adverbial clause results from scrambling the object across the adjunct clause, and the movement path thus created licenses the parasitic connection. The analysis is depicted in (26*c*).

(26) (*a*) dat Jan [zijn boeken]$_i$ [zonder e_i in te kijken] terugbracht
          that John his books without into to look back returned
          'that John returned his books without looking in them'

   (*b*) *dat Jan [zonder *e* in te kijken] [zijn boeken] terugbracht
          that John without into to look his books returned

   (*c*) ... DP$_i$ [$_{PP}$ ... pg$_i$ ...] [$_{VP}$ t_i V]

From this point of view, the grammaticality of the NI construction in (27*a*) may be surprising, as here the object follows the adjunct clause containing the parasitic gap. Even more surprising is the fact that (27*b*), where the linear condition appears to be met, is not grammatical: in brief, the linear condition in the nominal domain seems to be the *inverse* of the linear condition in the clausal domain.

(27) (*a*) het [zonder *e* in te kijken] terugbrengen van [je boeken]
          the without into to look return-INF of your books
          'returning your books without looking in them'

   (*b*) *het terugbrengen van [je boeken] [zonder *e* in te kijken]
          the return-INF of your books without into to look

This inverse linearity immediately follows from the analysis, which involves an inversion of the object and the remainder of the construction. As indicated in the structure in (28), the object moves leftward, across the adjunct clause, thereby licensing the parasitic gap contained in it.[21] Then, the phrase contain-

---

[20] Although the precise analysis of these parasitic gap constructions is problematic in current frameworks, I will nevertheless refer to these gaps as parasitic gaps.

[21] In Bennis and Hoekstra (1984), it was argued that scrambling is an instance of A'-movement. This conclusion was forced upon us by the then-standard analysis of parasitic gaps. In subsequent discussion, the conclusion has been questioned (cf. Vandenwyngaerd 1989, among many others). For the current analysis, it is important that the object moves to a Spec position, as it is the only option in restrictive theories of phrase structure (e.g. Kayne 1994). Whether this is an A'-position, and what the relevance thereof is for the licensing of parasitic gaps, is beyond the scope of this chapter.

ing the adjunct clause and the infinitive (XP) moves leftward, across *van* to the [Spec, CP] position.

(28) het [$_{CP}$ — van [$_{IP}$ [je boeken]$_i$ I [$_{XP}$ [zonder e_i in te kijken] t_i terugbrengen]]]

This provides strong confirmation of the inversion analysis.

We are now also in a position to explain the observation, made in Section 3, that those objects found in pre-infinitival position in NIs are basically those that do not scramble, contrary to those following *van*, which do. This observation follows from the fact that the DP$_{van}$ indeed does undergo scrambling, while DPs preceding the NI have not been so affected. Scrambling affects specific DPs, while non-specific indefinites occur in a more rightward position. Hence, objects preceding the NI head are restricted to DPs which fail to scramble, namely non-specific indefinites.

Den Dikken (1995), in his analysis of *van* in constructions of the type in (18), argues that *van*, instead of being a complementizer, is a kind of nominal copula, so that the inversion can be regarded as an instance of predicate preposing of the type *The cause of all trouble was John*, which is movement to an A-position rather than to an A′-position. Can we make out which is the better analysis? There is in fact very little at this point that I can say about this issue. One property of A′-movement is the domain extension for binding that results from it, as discussed in Barrs (1987) and illustrated in (29).

(29) (*a*) Which picture of himself$_{i/j}$ does *Bill$_j$* think that *John$_i$* likes best?
  (*b*) *Bill$_j$* wondered [which picture of himself$_{i/j}$] *John$_i$* liked best
  (*c*) *Bill$_j$* thought that *John$_i$* liked these pictures of himself$_{i/*j}$ best

While the matrix subject *Bill* is not a suitable antecedent for *himself* if no A′-movement has taken place, as in (29c), it becomes accessible as a result of *wh*-movement, as shown in (29a, b): apparently, *wh*-movement extends the binding domain of *himself*. The inversion taking place in NIs does not have such domain-extending effect, as (30) shows.

(30) (*a*) *Jan$_i$* ergerde zich over [het over *zichzelf$_i$* praten van jou]
    John got annoyed about the about himself talk-INF of you
  (*b*) Ik ergerde mij over [het over *zichzelf$_i$* praten van *Jan$_i$*]

Although movement of [*over zichzelf praten*] in (30a) brings the anaphor *zichzelf* closer to the matrix subject *Jan*, it may nevertheless not bind the anaphor. Only the DP$_{van}$ is an accessible antecedent for the anaphor, as in (30b). However, this does not allow us to conclude that the inversion operation is not an instance of A′-movement. The inverted XP is clearly a predicate, and A′-movement of predicates does not yield domain extension for binding, as is illustrated in (31).

(31) (*a*) How angry at himself$_{i/*j}$ does *Bill$_j$* think that *John$_i$* became?

(b)   *Bill$_j$* wondered [how angry at himself$_{i/*j}$] *John$_i$* became.

This lack of domain extension can be understood in terms of the predicate-internal subject hypothesis. Under this hypothesis, the preposed predicate contains the trace of the embedded subject, which itself acts as the local binder and hence as an opacity factor for binding from outside. In (30a), similarly, the preposed XP would contain a trace of the DP$_{van}$, which therefore acts as a local binder.

The only empirical difference I have so far been able to find between the inversion in NIs and regular predicate inversion concerns pronominal variable binding. As we saw in (12), pronominal variables can be bound by the DP$_{van}$ in NIs, but such binding seems excluded in regular cases of predicate inversion, as in (32). More research is required at this point.

(32)   *In *his* office was working *every* colleague from the department

In this section we have seen how the problematic word-order facts and the problems with scope in Dutch NIs can be solved straightforwardly if we adopt the free state analysis of such NI constructions, or, more precisely, if we adopt the [D CP] structure, with *van* as the C head, and a movement of the phrase preceding *van* from a position following the DP$_{van}$. In the next section, I turn to a discussion of the other question, viz. the limited nature of complementation in nominal constructions.

7. OTHER NOMINAL CONSTRUCTIONS

If the free state analysis is correct, we would like to extend it to *van/of* in general, and dispense with the rule of *of/van*-insertion altogether. So, the analysis of (33a) should equally be as in (33b).

(33) (a)   the destruction of the city
      (b)   [$_{DP}$ the [$_{CP}$ *destruction*$_i$ [$_{C'}$ of [[$_{DP}$ the city] I [t_i]]]]]

As I suggested earlier, this analysis may shed light on the fact that nouns are much more limited in their argument structure compared to verbs. In order to see this, let us first concentrate on gerundives, both *-ing-of* and *-ing*-ACC. The latter show the same complexity of complementation as regular clauses, whereas the former are by and large restricted in the same way as basic and derived nouns. Consider first the examples in (34).

(34) (a)   John's eating the apples
      (b)   John's eating of the apples
      (c)   the eating of the apples

The precise analysis of (34a) is unclear to me. It probably involves an IP in the complement of D, which is empty as a result of the movement of *John's* to [Spec, DP]. The *-ing* head *eating* probably undergoes head movement at LF, so that (34*a*) is basically a construct state construction. Example (34*b*), on the other, involves a free state construction. I will leave undiscussed the way in which the subject *John's* relates to the construction, and therefore concentrate on (34*c*). Applying the analysis developed so far, we are led to postulate the structure in (35).[22]

(35)   [$_{DP}$ the [$_{CP}$ [$_{XP}$ *eating*$_i$] of [$_{IP}$ the apples I [t_i]]]]

Recall that it follows from the MLC that XP in (35) must be the maximal complement of I, or the specifier of the complement of I. This condition then explains why the examples in (36) are ungrammatical, on the further assumption that the italicized phrases are (part of) the complements of the verb.

(36) (*a*) *the raising of one's child *Catholic*
     (*b*) *the calling of John *a liar*
     (*c*) *the walking of shoes *threadbare*
     (*d*) *the looking of the information *up*
     (*e*) *the proving of the theorem *wrong*

Consider the structure of these examples before the application of movement to [Spec, CP], given in (37).

(37)   [$_{DP}$ the [$_{CP}$ — [$_{C'}$ of [$_{IP}$ [one's child]$_i$ I [$_{XP}$ raising [$_{SC}$ t_i [Catholic]]]]]]]

The subject of the SC complement, *one's child*, has raised to [Spec, IP] (probably AGRoP]. This supports the claim, made in the literature, that English allows scrambling of the same type as in Dutch and German, the VO nature in clauses resulting from further V movement (cf. Costa 1996, extending proposals in Johnson 1991 and Pesetsky 1989). For the sake of concreteness, let us assume that English clauses involve overt verb movement to Tense, to the left of AGRoP. Since there is no reason to assume that Tense is present in *-ing-of* gerundives, this movement does not take place, and English is OV at the point at which inversion takes place.

Given the structural representation in (37), it is impossible to obtain (36*a*) by phrasal movement (and we know independently that phrasal movement is involved), as *raising* is not a constituent by itself. Rather, only *raising Catholic* may undergo phrasal movement. The same applies to the other examples in (36). Instead of the orders in (36), the expected orders are those in (38), as they would result from XP movement to [Spec, CP] in (37).

(38) (*a*) ??the raising Catholic of one's child
     (*b*) *the calling a liar of John
     (*c*) *the walking threadbare of shoes
     (*d*) the looking up of the information

[22] As for the subject *John's* we may assume that it raises from IP (which might be considered to instantiate AGRoP) as part of XP, and then undergoes further raising. Alternatively, it is the subject of an independent IP, taking the CP [*eating of the apples*] as its predicate.

In general, the results are ill formed, with the exception of certain 'phrasal idioms' such as *the cutting short of the meeting*, and verb–particle combinations. So, the question we now face is why these constructions are ungrammatical.

The first thing to note is that the Dutch counterparts of these constructions are all well formed, as already mentioned in Section 3. They differ from the English constructions in (38) in one telling respect: instead of preceding the complement, the NI head in Dutch follows the complements in the [Spec, CP] position. This is shown by the translations of (38) given in (39).

(39) (*a*) het katholiek opvoeden van je kind
    (*b*) het een leugenaar noemen van Jan
    (*c*) het plat lopen van schoenen
    (*d*) het op zoeken van de informatie

The relevance of this difference in order reminds us of Williams's (1981) Head Final Filter (HFF), which was formulated to exclude prenominal modifiers with material following the head, as in (40).

(40) (*a*) a proud (*of his children) man
    (*b*) a more intelligent (*than Bill) student (than Bill)

The HFF restriction equally applies to Dutch. That we indeed seem to be dealing with a prohibition on right-recursion rather than with a kind of complexity constraint is clear in those cases where two orders are possible in Dutch prenominal APs. Consider the examples in (41) and the pair in (42).

(41) (*a*) een trotse (*op z'n kinderen) vader (*op z'n kinderen)
        a proud (on his children) father (on his children)

    (*b*) een meer intelligente (*dan Wim) student (dan Wim)
        a more intelligent (than Bill) student (than Bill)

(42) (*a*) een verliefde (*op Marie) jongen
        an in-love on Mary boy

    (*b*) een op Marie verliefde jongen

These examples show that as long as the adjective is the final element in the prenominal AP, the construction is acceptable, but not when material intervenes between the noun and the adjective.

The theoretical connection between the restriction observable in verbal noun constructions of the type in (38) and the prenominal modification constructions in (40)–(42) becomes clear when we look at the analysis Kayne (1994) proposes for prenominal modifiers. To begin, it should be noted that examples such as (40*b*) and (41*b*), with the PP following the head noun, suggest, in Kayne's framework, that the prenominal modifier has moved to its prenominal position from a postnominal position, stranding the PP. This is so, since Kayne's theory does not cater for rightward movement rules such as extraposition, nor for base-generation of adjuncts at the right side of a projection. Indeed, Kayne proposes that prenominal APs are predicates raised from a predicative clause contained in a CP, as illustrated in (43).

(43)   D [$_{CP}$ — C [$_{IP}$ father I [$_{AP}$ proud (of his children)]]]]

So, both prenominal modifiers and the verbal noun phrase occupy the [Spec, CP] position. Moreover, they are apparently subject to similar restrictions on their complexity. If the AP is simplex, it may freely move to [Spec, CP], yielding the prenominal order. Complex APs, however, are not allowed to move to [Spec, CP], which Kayne (1994) attributes to a prohibition against complex specifiers of CP (specifically those without an overt complementizer). Failure to raise the AP yields movement of the subject of the IP, and hence the order *a father proud of his children*.

The structure in (43) is parallel to that proposed for verbal noun constructions, or for nominal constructions involving *van/of*. The relevant constraint can then be formulated as in (44).

(44)   The structure
         D [$_{CP}$ [$_{XP}$ ... X YP] C [...
         is ill formed for certain choices of X, YP, and C, if YP is non-null.

Kayne (1994: 92), discussing the examples in (45), where absence of the complementizer *that* has a degrading effect, gives the following formulation: 'a phrase (with)in a specifier position cannot have an overt complement (of a certain sort). This seems to hold of [Spec, CP] when relative C is null, though not when it is non-null for reasons that are unclear'.

(45) (a)   I just read the *book about your ancestors* ?(that) your son published last year
    (b)   I just read the *book that's about your ancestors* *(that) your son published last year

If *van/of* instantiates C, as we have argued, it is not just emptiness of C but choice of C that seems relevant. In any case, the constraint in (44) needs further clarification on various points: can it be derived from something more fundamental, what is the exact formulation, what choices of X, YP, and C are relevant, etc.? I am not in a position to provide answers to these questions, and therefore have to leave (44) in this rather ill-understood condition. Let me nevertheless comment on a number of points.

First, it is not that clear whether the formulation should indeed refer to overt complements. There clearly are cases where overt complements, at least under certain assumptions, do not yield ungrammaticality. For English, this is the case if the head is followed by a particle or a stranded preposition, as in (46).

(46) (a)   a much talked about subject   (cf. Kayne 1994: 99)
    (b)   the looking up of the information

Other instances where a head takes an overt complement are constructions of the type *a very beautiful car*, if we adopt Abney's (1986) analysis of *very* as a degree head with an AP complement, since under that analysis the head of the phrase in prenominal position is *very*, taking an overt AP complement.[23] Obviously, this kind of situation holds more generally of functional categories. So, if we discard the idea that prenominal participles are adjectives, not only cases such as (47a) instantiate the forbidden situation, because the participle takes an overt complement, but also simple cases such as (47b), which are not excluded but which would nevertheless involve some functional categories dominating the verbal base of the participle.

(47) (a) *a recently sent to me book
     (b)   a recently published book

Perhaps a distinction should be made between complements to a lexical head and complements to a functional head: in the former case, a separate complex of lexical head plus its own superstructure functions as the complement itself, whereas in the latter, there is just a single extended projection. So, perhaps there is no prohibition against [F LP] in [Spec, CP], with F a functional category and LP its lexical phrase, while there is against $[L_1 [F [L_2P]]]$, where L_1 takes an extended projection of L_2 as its complement.

In Dutch, we find a number of situations of a slightly different nature. In the case of NIs, the part that is moved to the [Spec, CP] position may involve verbal clusters, as in the examples in (48). As a matter of fact, examples of this type were originally used by Evers (1975) to motivate his verb-raising analysis of verbal cluster formation. The gist of his argument was that such cluster formation precedes the nominalization rule, so that the cluster, as a complex head, is nominalized.

(48) (a) het willen lezen van een boek
          the want-INF read-INF of a book

     (b) het hebben gelezen van een boek
          the have-INF read of a book

More recently, verb cluster formation has come to be no longer regarded as the result of head movement: rather, it is assumed that the verbal head of the complement clause is the only element left in the clause, everything else having scrambled out into the matrix clause (cf. Zwart 1994 for an overview). If that analysis is correct, the infinitival heads *willen* and *hebben* in (48) would have an overt complement, in violation of the constraint in (44). Note that, as in the case of particles and stranded prepositions in English (cf. (46)), these cases

---

[23] In Hoekstra (1984: 295, n. 68), I discuss a number of cases which seem to violate the Head Final Filter for adjectives, in that the adjective in prenominal position is followed by (part of) a degree modifier of the adjective. These cases suggest that the requirement pertains to properties of adjectival agreement, but it is unclear whether this can be extended to other instances of (44).

involve a bare head in complement position. As soon as the complement head is accompanied by any further material, ungrammaticality results, as is the case with following particles (cf. *the bringing (*right) back of books*). A full discussion of this issue is beyond the scope of this chapter. I note in passing that perfect tense constructions of the type in (48*b*) are not allowed in English *-ing-of* gerundives (**the having read of a book*). This might indicate that English is stricter in its obedience to (44) than Dutch.[24]

More generally, it seems that languages vary with respect to whatever (44) stands for. Several languages allow prenominal adjectives with complements of the adjective following the adjective (e.g. Polish; I thank Bozena Rozwadowska for pointing this out to me). Also, the difference between the Romance languages, with multiple *de*-constructions, and English, where multiple *of* is excluded, points in the same direction.

Secondly, it would appear that not only complements, but also adjuncts are excluded in the position following a head in [Spec, CP]. This is illustrated in (49).

(49) (*a*) the books sold yesterday are shipped today
    (*b*) *the sold yesterday books are shipped today
    (*c*) *the reading carefully of books
    (*d*) *a more intelligent than Bill student

This brings me to a further issue. Recall that, on the basis of the MLC, it is the XP in the structure in (50) which has to move to [Spec, CP]. This would seem to predict that $DP_{van/of}$ necessarily is the final element in the nominal construction, contrary to fact.

(50) $D [_{CP} -- van [_{IP} DP I [_{XP} \ldots]]]$

In particular, $DP_{van/of}$ can be followed by adverbial PPs of various kinds, as shown by the examples in (51). As a matter of fact, these adverbial PPs could not be moved along with the verbal noun, at least not when they follow the verbal noun, because of the condition in (44).

(51) (*a*) the examining (*in the ward) of the patient (in the ward)
    (*b*) the peeling (*with a knife) of potatoes (with a knife)

I will follow the analysis of adverbial PPs presented in Barbiers (1995), which allows an immediate solution to the problem of stranding these adverbial PPs.

---

[24] The order between the perfective auxiliary and the participle is free in Dutch clauses, and also in (48*b*). If instead of an NI construction, a noun is preceded by a reduced relative clause headed by the present participle of the perfective auxiliary, as in (i), the order is fixed. This may be related to the requirement, hinted at in the previous footnote, that the final element of a prenominal modifier be inflected.

(i)   een veel boeken gelezen hebbend-e/*hebbend-e gelezen man
        a many books read having-AGR/having-AGR read man

Barbiers adopts Kayne's proposal that the base does not allow for the generation of adjuncts on the right side of the projection. Exploiting a proposal made by Sportiche (1994), he argues that an adverbial PP is adjoined to (a projection of) the VP, on the left. This order is indeed possible in Dutch, but not in English. In order to obtain the result that that PP follows the verb, it is claimed that (the relevant projection of) VP is moved into the specifier of the PP. This movement is required, within his theory, for semantic reasons, and hence it takes place before LF, overtly in English, optionally after Spellout in Dutch. The derived result of these assumptions for a construction such as (51*a*) is as in (52).

(52)   D [$_{CP}$ — of [$_{IP}$ DP I [$_{PP}$ [$_{XP}$ examining] [$_{P'}$ in the ward] t $_{XP}$]]]

In this structure, PP cannot be moved to [Spec, CP]: while the MLC would allow it, the result would violate (44), as the head of the PP (*in*) has an overt complement (*the ward*).[25] XP, on the other hand, can freely move to [Spec, CP], as it is in the Spec position of PP, and therefore has only to skip the intervening [Spec, IP], which is possible if I moves to C to extend its domain.

This proposal provides an adequate account of adverbial modifiers in post-DP$_{van/of}$ position, and it makes a very clear prediction at the same time, viz. that only adjunct PPs (or adjuncts generally) may occur there. For Dutch, this prediction seems by and large correct. In particular, Barbiers provides an account of the fact that secondary predicate PPs, unlike adverbial PPs, cannot occur in postverbal position in Dutch. The reason is that this order could arise only through movement of the VP (or a higher projection thereof) into the specifier of the PP, but as the PP already has a subject, this is impossible. Consider the example in (53): the PP may not occur in postverbal position. This is because *de vaas* is the subject of the PP, which excludes movement of the VP into the specifier of the PP.

(53) (*a*)   . . . dat Jan de vaas op de tafel zette
            that John the vase on the table put

    (*b*)   *. . . dat Jan de vaas zette op de tafel

    (*c*)   het op de tafel zetten van de vaas
            the on the table put-INF of the vase

    (*d*)   *het zetten van de vaas op de tafel

Although this is correct for Dutch, English seems more problematic. Also, in English, secondary predicates should not be allowed in post-DP$_{of}$ position. Although judgements are not uniform, there clearly seem to be cases that go against the prediction. Consider the examples in (54).

---

[25] Note that (44) therefore explains why PP modifiers of nouns necessarily occur in postnominal position.

(54) (*a*) %the putting of men on the moon
    (*b*) %the bringing of children to the swimming pool
    (*c*) *the starving of John into giving up
    (*d*) the starving of rebels into submission

Judgements on (54*a*, *b*) vary. The judgement on (54*c*) is from Kayne (1985: ex. 114); the judgement on (54*d*) is from Carrier and Randall (1992: ex. 79*a*). Carrier and Randall (1992) even allow examples of AP secondary predicates, such as those in (55).

(55) (*a*) the hammering of metal flat
    (*b*) the cooking of food black

Constructions of this type are not predicted by the analysis advocated here. I have no solution to offer at present as to how they should be reconciled with the proposal, and leave them for future research.

Now, at the end of this section, I want to return to the issue of complementation restrictions on basic and derived nouns. Let us assume that such nouns, when taking an object, always require the free state construction. If the complement is more complex, the remainder cannot be stranded, as in (36), nor can it be moved along to [Spec, CP], because of (44). Hence, only a simple object complement is allowed.

Recall that it is sometimes claimed that the restricted complementation possibilities of *-ing-of* constructions can be explained on the assumption that the *-ing* form enters the syntax as a noun, as nouns do not have many complement options. We have now found that the limited nature of complementation options of *-ing-of* constructions is syntactic in origin: if, in the structure in (50), the head X of XP takes a complement, movement of XP runs into conflict with the constraint in (44). We may therefore reverse the perspective, and explain the limited range of complementation options of nouns in the same manner. Rather than resulting from the absence of some type of representation (e.g. argument structure, lexicosyntactic level), limitations on the range of complement types of nouns may derive from the same syntactic factors that are operative in the case of *-ing-of* constructions.

8. SUMMARY AND CONCLUSIONS

In this chapter, I have made extensive use of Kayne's proposal that many nominal constructions are built on the structure [D CP], with different kinds of movement to [Spec, CP]. In particular, I have extended the idea that *of/van* is a complementizer in such nominal CPs, rather than an inserted Case marker that forms a PP with a Case-needing DP complement of a noun. Reconstruction effects in Dutch NIs provided the basis for this conclusion.

It was then argued that there is an as yet not fully understood constraint on the complexity of the phrase occupying [Spec, *of/van*], which covers the empirical domain of Williams's Head Final Filter and unites it with restrictions on complementation in nominal constructions. This explanation of these restrictions makes appeals to other projection levels, such as argument structure, superfluous.

The analysis provides support for the conclusion that English has overt movement of the object to a preverbal position, similar to West Germanic OV languages, the VO order in (verbal) clauses deriving from subsequent movement of the verb to a position preceding the object.

REFERENCES

Abney, S. (1986), 'The English Noun Phrase in its Sentential Aspect', MIT dissertation.
Barbiers, S. (1995), 'The Syntax of Interpretation', HIL dissertation.
Barrs, A. (1987), 'Chains and Anaphoric Dependents', MIT dissertation.
Bennis, H., and Hoekstra, T. (1984), 'Gaps and Parasitic Gaps', *The Linguistic Review*, 4: 29–87.
Carrier, J., and Randall, J. (1992), 'The Argument Structure and Syntactic Structure of Resultatives', *Linguistic Inquiry*, 23: 173–233.
Chomsky, N. A. (1970), 'Remarks on Nominalization', in R. Jacobs and P. Rosenbaum (eds.), *Readings in English Transformational Grammar*, Ginn and Co., Waltham, Mass., 184–221.
——(1986), *Knowledge of Language*, Praeger, New York.
——(1993), 'A Minimalist Program for Linguistic Theory', in K. Hale and S. J. Keyser (eds.), *The View from Building 20*, MIT Press, Cambridge, Mass., 41–58.
Costa, J. (1996), 'Adverb Positioning and V-Movement in English: Some More Evidence', *Studia Linguistica*, 50: 22–34.
Den Dikken, M. (1995), 'Copulas', Ms., HIL/Free University of Amsterdam, presented at GLOW 1995.
Evers, A. (1975), 'The Transformational Cycle in Dutch and German', Utrecht dissertation, published by Indiana University Linguistics Club.
Fassi Fehri, A. (1993), *Issues in the Structure of Arabic Clauses and Words*, Kluwer, Dordrecht.
Haaften, T. van *et al.* (1985), 'Nominalisaties in het Nederlands', *GLOT* 8: 67–104.
Hoeksema, J. (1991), 'Complex Predicates and Liberation in Dutch and English', *Linguistics and Philosophy*, 14: 661–710.
Hoekstra, T. (1984), *Transitivity*, Foris, Dordrecht.
——(1986), 'Deverbalization and Inheritance', *Linguistics*, 24: 549–84.
——(1992), 'Small Clause Theory', *Belgian Journal of Linguistics*, 7: 125–51 (special edition, ed. J. de Caluwe, A. Hantson, and W. Vandeweghe).
——and Wehrmann, P. (1985), 'De nominale infinitief', *GLOT* 8: 275–94.
Horn, G. (1975), 'On the Non-Sentential Nature of the POSS-ing Construction', *Linguistic Analysis*, 1: 333–87.
Jackendoff, R. (1977), *X-Bar Syntax*, MIT Press, Cambridge, Mass.
Johnson, K. (1991), 'Object Positions', *Natural Language and Linguistic Theory*, 9: 577–636.
Kayne, R. (1984), *Connectedness and Binary Branching*, Foris, Dordrecht.

——(1985), 'Principles of Particle Constructions', in J. Guéron, H.-G. Obenauer, and J.-Y. Pollock (eds.), *Grammatical Representation*, Foris, Dordrecht.

——(1994), *The Anti-Symmetry of Syntax*, MIT Press, Cambridge, Mass.

Larson, R. (1988), 'On the Double Object Construction', *Linguistic Inquiry*, 19: 335–91.

Longobardi, G. (1995), 'Reference and Proper Names', *Linguistic Inquiry*, 26: 609–66.

——(1996), 'The Syntax of N-raising: A Minimalist Theory', OTS Working Paper, University of Utrecht.

Pesetsky, D. (1989), 'Language Particular Processes and the Earliness Principle', paper presented at GLOW (Ms., MIT).

Ritter, E. (1991), 'Two Functional Categories in Noun Phrases: Evidence from Modern Hebrew', in S. Rothstein (ed.), *Syntax and Semantics*, vol. 25, Academic Press, New York, 37–62.

Rizzi, L. (1991), *Relativized Minimality*, MIT Press, Cambridge, Mass.

Sportiche, D. (1994), 'Adjuncts and Adjunctions', Ms., UCLA.

Szabolcsi, A. (1994), 'The Noun Phrase', in F. Kiefer and E. Kiss (eds.), *The Syntactic Structure of Hungarian*, Academic Press, San Diego, Calif., 197–274.

Travis, L. (1984), 'Word Order Parameters and Their Effects', MIT dissertation.

Vandenwyngaerd, G. (1989), 'Object Shift as an A-Movement Rule', *MIT Working Papers in Linguistics*, 11: 256–71.

Vergnaud, J.-R. (1974), 'French Relative Clauses', MIT dissertation.

Williams, E. (1981), 'Argument Structure and Morphology', *The Linguistic Review*, 1: 81–114.

Zubizarreta, M.-L. (1989), *Levels of Representation in the Lexicon and in Syntax*, Foris: Dordrecht.

Zwart, J.-W. (1994), 'Dutch Syntax: A Minimalist Approach', University of Groningen dissertation.

10

Dependencies, Phrase Structure, and Extractions

M. RITA MANZINI

This chapter presents a reformulation of Chomsky's (1995) Merge, under which the basic operation of grammar cannot take as its input two constituents; rather the first member of the input is always a head, drawn directly from the numeration. While c-command has been argued to be the structural primitive defined under Chomsky's (1995) conception, I shall argue that under the present conception, the structural primitive of the theory is head government. This has potential empirical advantages in the domain of movement. In particular, I shall argue that the present theory allows for a radical simplification of Kayne's (1984) Connectedness. In what follows, Section 1 presents Chomsky's (1995) theory, Section 2 defines the present notion of Merge, and Section 3 demonstrates its consequences for movement theory. As part of the revision of the theory in Section 2 a principle of INTERPRETATION is suggested which subsumes Chomsky's (1995) Last Resort.

1. THE MINIMALIST BACKGROUND

In the Minimalist model of Chomsky (1995), each linguistic expression is characterized by two representations, a P(honological) F(orm) representation, interfacing with the articulatory–perceptual system(s), and a L(ogical) F(orm) representation, interfacing with the conceptual–intentional system(s). This represents a clear departure from previous models, even within the Principles and Parameters framework, which are characterized by at least two additional syntactic representations, namely D(eep)-s(tructure) and S(urface)-s(tructure). Everything else equal, the Minimalist model is obviously preferable on conceptual grounds, since in it linguistic representations are seen to simply match the interfaces between language and other cognitive systems.

A central property of the Minimalist model is what Chomsky (1995) terms inclusiveness. In other words, not only inputs but also outputs of linguistic computations are entirely expressed in terms of properties of lexical items. This implies the impossibility of adding information in the course of the derivation and/or in the output representation in the form of such standard devices of previous models as bar levels, indices, and the like.

The basis of each linguistic computation is represented by a set of lexical items. One of the operations of grammar, Select, applies to this set, selecting one of its members and introducing it into the set of syntactic objects of which a derivation consists at each of its stages. New syntactic objects are formed by the operation Merge, which takes a pair of given syntactic objects S_i and S_j and creates a single syntactic object out of them, namely a labelled set $\{S \{S_i, S_j\}\}$, where the label S is either S_i or S_j. A simple example of a computation involving only merger is provided in (1)–(2) below. The numeration set for the computation is given in (1); note that separate instances of the same lexical item are listed separately. Each individual step in the computation is represented in (2). In particular, the labelled sets in (2a) and (2d) are formed by the merger of two lexical items selected from (1); (2b) and (2c) by the merger of an item selected from (1) with a previously formed labelled set. Finally (2e) is created by the merger of two labelled sets, which for readability's sake I have presented on separate lines.

(1)   the, boy, has, read, the, book

(2) (a)   {the {the, book}}
    (b)   {read {read, {the {the, book}}}}
    (c)   {has {has, {read {read, {the {the, book}}}}}}
    (d)   {the {the, boy}}
    (e)   {has
            {the {the, boy}},
            {has {has, {read {read, {the {the, book}}}}}}}

A fairly obvious correspondence can be defined between the complex object in (2e) resulting from the computation and a familiar tree structure of the type in (3). In essence, lexical items correspond to terminal nodes in the tree, while labels correspond to non-terminals.

(3)

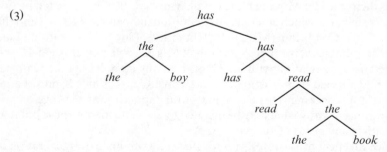

The other fundamental rule of the computational system is Move. Suppose we have a complex object S containing the objects A and K. Move takes A, copies it, and merges it with K. A chain is the ordered pair consisting of A in the position resulting from this merger and of its copy, technically known as its trace t_A, in the original position. This is also easily illustrated. Consider the numeration set in (4) and the computation in (5) that takes it as its basis. The steps in (5a–c) are entirely comparable to those in (2a–c). In (5d), however, the entire object in (5c) is merged with a copy of (5a), which it contains. In other words movement applies, yielding two copies of the same object (5a) in its output. One of the two copies, in fact the trace, is then subjected to the operation Delete, which simply marks it as not interpreted at LF; this is informally indicated in (5d) by italic type.

(4)   the, book, was, read

(5) (a)   {the {the, book}}
    (b)   {read {read, {the {the, book}}}}
    (c)   {was {was, {read {read, {the {the, book}}}}}}
    (d)   {was
           {the {the, book}},
           {was {was, {read {read, {the {the, book}}}}}}}

The last major operation of the computational system is Spellout, which strips away the phonological properties of lexical items from the semantic and formal features. It is then Spellout which is ultimately responsible for mapping syntactic objects of the type in (2) or (5) to PF and LF representations.

As Chomsky (1995) points out, no real question arises about the motivation behind the operations Select and Merge. Select simply must apply until the set of lexical items that forms the basis of the computation is exhausted. Similarly, Merge must apply until a single syntactic object is formed. As for the reason why Move exists, however, only considerations of language use can be invoked: 'facilitation of parsing . . . the separation of theme-rheme structures from base-determined semantic (theta) relations, etc. . . .'. The fact that there is no apparent internal necessity in the system for the existence of Move can be read as a conceptual weakness of it.

Let us then consider Move in more detail. Move is crucially restricted by two economy principles, which enter into its definition, namely Last Resort and the Minimal Link Condition (MLC). In Chomsky's (1995) formulation, Last Resort states that movement of A to a target K is possible only if A enters into a feature-checking relation with K. Thus given any complex syntactic object {K {A, K}} formed by movement, its two constituents A and K must be related by feature checking. This excludes arbitrary applications of Move, as well as applications of Move that may be dictated by some further purpose but that do not satisfy any needs of the pair {A, K}.

The overall effect of Last Resort is to effectively eliminate overgeneration in the movement component of grammar. Needless to say this represents one of the important departures of the Minimalist approach from the Government and Binding approach of Chomsky (1981). GB grammars are allowed to overgenerate arbitrarily, and the overgeneration is then taken care of by filters at the interface. In a Minimalist grammar, wild rule application is blocked by Last Resort in the course of the computation.

Note that strictly speaking Move applies to features, explaining why Last Resort crucially refers to it. A problem of empirical adequacy arises in connection with this latter assumption to the extent that overt movement takes the shape of movement of entire phrases, rather than of (bundles of) features. According to Chomsky (1995) this problem is solved by taking into account the fact that (bundles of) features in isolation cannot be pronounced. Thus it is reasons of PF interpretation that force entire phrases to pied-pipe in overt syntax. In covert syntax, where PF features have been stripped away, we can assume that movement takes the pure form of Move F(eature). Notice, however, that once again, as when considering the justification for Move in the system, no explanation internal to the system itself can be found; rather some external property must be relied upon, in this case the impossibility of pronouncing features. Thus in a sense there is no real explanation, but the problem is simply pushed back to some other cognitive component.

The second crucial property of the operation Move is the MLC. According to the MLC, A can raise to target K only if there is no B such that raising of B to K is legitimate under Last Resort and B is closer to K than A is. Consider for instance a typical context for a *wh*-island violation, as schematically represented in (6).

(6)   Q' . . . [wh Q . . . wh

Under the formulation of the MLC just given, in (6) movement of the lower *wh* to check its features against Q' is blocked, in that the *wh* in the Spec of Q can also move to Q' to do the same, and crucially is closer to it.

Superraising effects can be accounted for in an analogous way. Consider (7).

(7)   seems [that it was told John [that . . .

Under the MLC, movement of *John* to the matrix subject position to check Case is blocked by the presence of the intermediate *it*, which can also move to it to check its features. The feature theory that allows these results to be achieved is essentially irrelevant for present purposes.

Chomsky (1995) also suggests that the formulation of the MLC is more natural if Move is thought of in terms of attraction. Thus incorporating Last Resort into this new conception, we can define Attract/Move by saying that K attracts F if F is the closest feature that can enter into a checking relation with a sublabel of K.

A problem in locality theory that the Minimalist approach of Chomsky (1995) leaves completely open is that of strong islands. An independent principle appears to be envisaged, presumably along the lines of Huang's (1982)

C(ondition on) E(xtraction) D(omains). Still, it remains unclear whether the CED is to become a part of the definition of Move, like the MLC, or not. In either case, it also remains unclear why all types of movement are equally sensitive to strong islands and hence the CED, as opposed to weak islands and the MLC.

The theory of Chomsky (1995) also fails to make any predictions concerning a second classical problem in locality theory, which concerns a class of phenomena apparently irreducible to either the MLC or the CED and accounted for by standard models within the Principles and Parameters framework in terms of some notion of head government. These are phenomena of the *that*-t class, typically involving asymmetries between object and subject.

The grammar of Chomsky (1995) excludes the notion of head government on what are essentially simplicity grounds. In particular, the head–complement relation and the specifier–head relation are independently recognized by the grammar, in that they correspond to configurations created by Merge. Thus the only head government relation that does not correspond to a configuration created by Merge is the relation between a head and the Spec of its complement; the notion of head government needs then to be defined essentially for this case. Chomsky (1995), however, argues that this configuration systematically reduces to one of the other two. For instance, there is no Exceptional Case Marking of the subject of *believe*-type complements by the matrix V; rather Exceptional Case Marking effects are due to the subject raising to the matrix (Spec, AgrO).

Suppose we accept this argument against head government. This means of course that we can no longer have recourse to accounts of *that*-t phenomena based on this notion, such as Rizzi's (1990). But other branches of the theory make no predictions about them either.

2. MERGE

The first aspect of Chomsky's (1995) computational system that concerns me here is the distinction between Merge and Move. Since Move is a special type of Merge, the question naturally arises of why they are not treated as one and the same rule. The answer can only lie in the fact that Move but not Merge is restricted by Last Resort and the MLC. Consider then the question of whether there is evidence that Last Resort indeed distinguishes between Move and Merge. It is worth noticing that this kind of question has wider implications than the unification of the two rules. If Merge and Move are indeed two separate rules, then the fact that the computational system has Move can only be explained by considerations external to it. This type of motivation for the latter, however, becomes redundant if the two rules are one and the same.

If Last Resort bars arbitrary applications of Move, we may legitimately ask what bars arbitrary applications of simple Merge. It is clear from Chomsky's (1995) discussion that there are two different types of merger to be considered in this respect. The first type is represented by the merger of a lexical head with its arguments. This merger is presumably restricted by the fact that the lexical head selects its arguments, or in other terms that it enters a theta-relation with them. Chomsky (1995) explicitly argues that theta-relations cannot be reduced to feature-checking relations; if so, the selectional restrictions on Merge cannot be reduced to the Last Resort restriction on Move. At the base of the reasoning is the fact that theta-roles are not formal features. Rather, following Hale and Keyser (1993), a theta-role is assigned in a certain structural configuration; and a lexical item assigns that theta-role only in the sense that it is the head of that configuration.

This still leaves the merger of a constituent, projected by a functional or lexical head, with a functional head. Because Chomsky (1995) does not discuss this as a separate case, and because clearly theta-relations are not involved, we can assume that this kind of merger is effectively subsumed under Move. An implementation of this conclusion would be to assume that each lexical head is presented by the lexicon with all of the functional specification associated with it. The merger of a functional head then coincides, in some sense to be made precise, with the movement of the associated lexical head.

In short, the distinction between Merge and Move rests entirely on the distinction between selection configurations involving lexical heads and their arguments and all other configurations. This seems too weak a motivation for such a consequential conclusion. It can in fact be attacked on two different fronts. On the one hand, it is far from obvious that what drives Move is morphological properties, in the sense of properties interpreted at the PF interface, as opposed to lexical properties more generally. In this perspective, the conclusion that thematic properties could not be reduced to features is not so obvious. On the other hand, in aspectually based models of thematic properties (Borer 1994; Arad 1996), the theta-relation between a lexical head and one of its arguments is representable as a relation between an Asp(ectual) head and its Spec. This is of course the same configuration as is routinely involved in the checking of features that drives Move.

Either of the two lines of attack that precede is sufficient for my purposes; and at least the latter is independently motivated in the literature. Thus there is no evidence that Merge and Move cannot be entirely unified under some appropriate version of Last Resort. As for the question of why Merge would sometimes take the specialized form of Move, the answer need not be sought as far as other cognitive systems. Rather remember that Move is the specialized form of Merge that applies when one lexical item satisfies properties located in two different positions along the syntactic tree. The Merge/Move distinction reduces then to the way properties distribute themselves in the lexicon.

Concretely, let us assume that the basic operation of the grammar takes as its input two lexical items and creates ordered pairs out of them, roughly as in (8); I shall call the ordered pairs formed by (8) dependencies.[1]

(8)   *Merge*
         A, B → (A, B)

We can assume that Merge will take place only if the interpretative needs of the lexical items involved (i.e. effectively those of their features) force it to. Interpretative needs obviously subsume LF interpretation needs; but they can subsume also PF interpretation needs. I shall express this by saying that all dependencies must have an interpretation. This can in turn naturally be combined with the idea that only dependencies can be interpreted, which is reminiscent of Chomsky's (1995) characterization of chains as (perhaps) the only interpreted objects at LF. The combination of these two principles then yields what I shall call the Principle of INTERPRETATION,[2] as in (9).

(9)   INTERPRETATION
         A and B are in an interpreted relation iff (A, B) is a dependency.

Concrete examples of elementary dependencies formed by rule (8) because of interpretative needs are easy to provide. Thus, if Chomsky's (1995) insight is correct, PF interpretation needs can be argued to drive the formation of a dependency of the form (I, V), on the assumption that PF, or the morphology subpart of it, will not be able to provide an interpretation of V+I as a word, unless a dependency is established between its component parts. Alternatively, the formation of an (I, V) dependency can be motivated at LF by the need for argument positions associated with V to be matched with the temporal/aspectual arguments associated with I, essentially as proposed by Higginbotham (1985). Note that here, as throughout, categories such as C, I, and V are employed just as a convenient shorthand for lexical items, which are the only primitives that syntactic operations manipulate.

To provide another example, there are a number of reasons to assume that

---

[1] The term dependency has been chosen here because it is not already in the technical dictionary of generative transformational grammar, and thus allows me to avoid potentially confusing terminological overlapping. At the same time dependencies have a considerable history in formal grammar; it should be made clear, however, that the use of the term dependency implies no adherence here to what we may call dependency theories. As suggested by an anonymous reviewer, comparison with the recent work of Hudson (1990) is of particular interest in this connection. Thus as we shall see later in this section, in the technical sense defined here there is a dependency from the subject D to I. In dependency theories, on the other hand, the subject is typically seen to be a dependent of the verb. In fact, as the following discussion will make clear, dependencies in the present sense of the term are successors to the Principles and Parameters notion of (head) government, rather than to any notion of dependency found in the previous literature.

[2] The term INTERPRETATION is capitalized here, following the suggestion of an anonymous reviewer, to stress that no matter what the conceptual affinities might be to Chomsky's (1995) Full Interpretation, it is a completely separate principle. The relation it bears to Last Resort should be clear from the preceding discussion.

I and C are systematically related; thus it is well known that different types of C match different types of I. Under (9), this (C, I) dependency can correspond to the interpretative need for a T variable in I to be bound by a temporal operator in C, and/or vice versa, for a temporal operator in C to bind a T variable in I. Similarly, within the present model we can assume that the interpretative needs of an argument head, such as D, and of a predicate head, such as V, drive them to form a dependency (V, D). To be more precise, if thematic properties of verbs are associated with Asp heads, two dependencies will mediate the relation between D and V, namely (Asp, V) and (D, Asp).

As the exemplification that precedes makes clear, no principled distinction is drawn in the present theory between dependencies involving functional and lexical categories. Similarly, the theory admits of selection dependencies based both on semantic properties and on formal properties, hence of what are generally called s-selection and c-selection, respectively. It is perhaps worth remembering in this connection that so-called adjuncts, typically PPs, are essentially predicates, which take as their external argument some projection along the main branch of the tree. Thus to take just an example, a so-called adjunct introduced by *before*, *after*, or other temporal Ps is a predicate whose external argument is the temporal projection I(P) of the sentence to which it attaches; and so on.

It is important to remember that interpretation, as referred to in (9), is conceived as a wholly syntax-internal operation, and is exactly like Chomsky's (1995) feature checking in this respect. Indeed feature checking represents one possible implementation of the general notion of interpretation; the reasons for not identifying them have already been laid out in the discussion that precedes. What is crucial here is that the term interpretation is not in any way meant to refer to the conditions under which the use of LFs is appropriate in discourse or in reference to the external world.

A question connected with the one just examined arises when we consider that selection is expressed by the formation of a dependency involving directly V or Asp, but in either case D, rather than the whole content of the DP. The same is true under Chomsky's (1995) Merge, which can see only the label of the selected D(P). In effect, it is not difficult to argue that the argumental properties of a nominal reside in D; thus D cannot be omitted, except in predicative environments, and D alone is sufficient to satisfy selectional requirements, in the form of a pronoun. This means that selectional restrictions that apparently refer to properties embedded under D(P) must be reanalysed in one of two ways. Some of these properties can reasonably be analysed as being present on D as well; one obvious case in point is animacy, which typically surfaces as a morphological property of pronoun systems. Most other apparent selectional restrictions will simply not be syntactic in nature, but rather involve extralinguistic interpretation.

The present statement of the Principle of INTERPRETATION as a biconditional also raises the question of whether it is in fact true that lexical items in isolation cannot be given an interpretation, but rather that the smallest interpretable fragment must encompass at least one dependency. Interestingly enough, an analogous prediction is arrived at by Chomsky (1995), on the basis of the assumption that lexical items are inserted in the derivation in fully inflected form; thus any lexical head will be associated with features corresponding to several functional ones. Empirically, it turns out that in languages with enough overt morphology even Ns in isolation are associated with obviously syntactic properties such as Case, supporting the point being made here.

In short, a suitably generalized version of Last Resort, such as the Principle of INTERPRETATION in (9), need not be restricted to Move, but can apply to all instances of Merge. Locality conditions remain then to be considered. Before we can do so, however, we must consider how Merge creates not only elementary dependencies, of the type considered so far, but also complex dependencies, or in general complex structures rather than elementary ones. Consider for instance a V selecting a pronominal D. Merge, as formulated in (8), expresses the relation through the formation of an ordered set, that is, a dependency, (V, D). For this elementary (V, D) case, furthermore, the dependency also defines a constituent. The question, however, arises as to how more complex constituents (i.e. constituents including more than two terminals) are defined.

The answer provided by Chomsky (1995) is of course that Merge can apply recursively, to objects produced by previous applications of the rule. In present terms, Merge not only applies to two lexical items out of the numeration N, creating an ordered pair out of them, but can also apply to a lexical item and a dependency—that is, an ordered *n*-tuple—formed by previous applications of Merge, as schematized in (10).

(10)   *Merge*
         $A, (B_1, \ldots, B_n) \rightarrow (A, B_1, \ldots, B_n)$

Correspondingly, the Principle of INTERPRETATION can be sharpened from (9) to a formulation that takes into account the existence of complex as well as elementary dependencies, as in (11).

(11)   INTERPRETATION
         A and B are in an interpreted relation iff $(A, B, \ldots)$ is a dependency.

Consider for instance the sentence in (12).

(12)   You see some pictures

In the course of the discussion that precedes I have already introduced several types of elementary dependency crucially involved in this example. Simplifying somewhat, the dependency (*some, pictures*) expresses the saturation of the external argument of the predicate *pictures* by the D argument *some*. The dependency (*see, some, . . .*) expresses the theta-relation between V and its

D object; indeed Williams (1994) argues in detail that the linking of two argument positions to the same D argument is the proper construal of theta-role assignment. Proceeding upwards the dependency (I, *see*, ...) expresses the saturation of the temporal argument of V by I. Finally, the one remaining dependency (*you*, I, ...) can be interpreted as expressing a nominative Case relation. Overall, the complex dependency in (13) is then formed.

(13)   (you, see, some, pictures)

Obviously enough, in (13) the subdependency (*some*, *pictures*) represents the constituent headed by *some*, hence DP in classical X-bar theory terms; similarly (*see*, *some*, *pictures*) represents a constituent headed by *see*, hence VP in classical X-bar theory, and so on.

A difficulty with the dependency-based definition of constituents is, however, immediately evident if we substitute the pronominal subject in (12) with a complex subject, as in (14).

(14)   These people see some pictures

Under the recursive Merge defined in (10), two dependencies can easily be constructed in (14), both headed by *these* as indicated in (15).

(15) (*a*)   (these, I, see, some, pictures)
      (*b*)   (these, people)

Unfortunately, however, the theory appears to have no means to construct a single dependency corresponding to the sentence in (14).

The standard way to circumvent this problem, adopted by Chomsky (1995), is to allow Merge to compose not just a head with a complex object, as in (10), but also two complex objects. Thus the last stage of the derivation of (14) is represented by the merger of the *these*-headed subconstituent with the I-headed one. Here, nevertheless, I shall argue that this account is by no means the only possible one. Following a notational convention introduced by Manzini (1994), we can indicate that an element A forms a dependency (A, B, ...) with an element B in a dependency by representing A immediately to the left of B and connected to it by a dash. Under this convention, the several dependencies in (15) can be given the unified representation in (16).

(16)
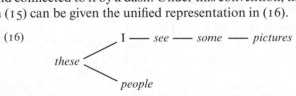

The representation in (16) is equivalent to the one in (15), except that it makes clear that there is a single occurrence of the D argument *these*, which merges with two separate subdependencies. Thus if we want to maintain that Merge always takes as its input at least one member of the numeration N, we must assume that it otherwise can apply not only to complex objects, but to sets of them. This is the sense of the revision of Merge provided in (17).

(17)   *Merge*

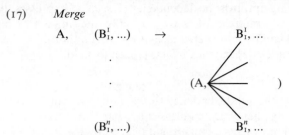

Under (17), Merge is allowed to form what we may call branching dependencies. This enrichment of the theory is of course sufficient to allow for the formation of complex objects of the type in (16), corresponding to the sentence in (14). If we continue to identify the notions of dependency and of constituent, we can now also reproduce the classical X-bar-theoretical result whereby subject–predicate structures are indeed constituents.[3]

The last crucial question that we need to take into account concerns the further embedding of branching dependencies. In reviewing the types of interpretative relation that underlie Merge, I have already commented that so-called adjuncts are essentially predicates that take the main branch of the sentence as their external argument. Thus in particular, temporal adjuncts introduced by prepositions such as *before* or *after* appear to take the matrix I(P) as their external argument. If so, a sentence of the type in (18) will have the partial structure indicated in (19).

(18)   These people will leave before the bill arrives

(19)

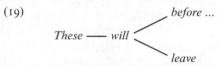

In (19) *will* forms a branching dependency with two predicates, namely *leave* and (*before*, . . .), satisfying a temporal argument in each of them. The subject of the sentence then embeds the branching dependency so formed, licensed by the nominative Case relation between it and *will*.

The same schema of embedding as in (19) holds for all adjuncts or for all instances of what in classical X-bar-theoretical terms is right-adjunction. In

---

[3] An important issue that this theory raises and that will not be considered here concerns the linearization of branching dependencies such as (16). Indeed a linearization algorithm based on standard phrase structure theory, such as Kayne's (1994) LCA, does not work for such dependencies. On the other hand, in Manzini (1995) I argue, contra Kayne (1994), that right-adjunction cannot be eliminated from standard theories of phrase structure without creating either empirical or theoretical problems, which independently motivate the need for a radical revision of the LCA.

present terms these are cases of external argument-predicate configurations, in which the external argument is selected by the immediately superordinate head. The embedding of what in traditional terms are specifier or left-adjoined structures remains then to be considered. The typical example is represented by nominative subject configurations, of the type already illustrated in (14)–(16). Suppose then we embed (14) under a C position as in (20).

(20)   I believe that these people see some pictures

The additional dependency in (20) that interests us directly is the one between the C position containing *that* and the I position containing *will*. The relevant dependency structure of (20) is represented in (21).

(21)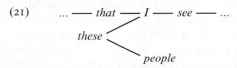

The interesting difference between (21) and (19) is that in (19) the head of the branching dependency (i.e. the external argument) is selected by the immediately superordinate head, while in (21) it is the predicate that is selected.

This aspect of the theory appears to make it incompatible with an important constraint on Merge in Chomsky's (1995) system, namely the Extension condition, which ensures a cyclic application of the rule. In particular, under the Extension condition every application of Merge must extend its target; it is therefore impossible to have an application of Merge that takes as its input A and K and merges A with some K' properly contained in K. By contrast the formation of (21) requires merger of the C head *that* with the I-headed dependency (*I*, . . .) bypassing the head *these*, if it has already been merged to form (16). Of course, if *that* is first merged with *I*, then the merger of *these* must be non-cyclic.

It seems then that a revision of the Extension condition is required by the present grammar. In fact, quite independently of the present grammar, the Extension condition is not without problems.[4] Chomsky (1995) assumes that Merge must apply cyclically only up to Spellout; after that point Move can

---

[4] I shall not consider here the question, raised notably by Bobaljik and Brown (1997), concerning the violation of the Extension condition by adjunction to a head. The reason is that adjunction of a head to another head may not be empirically justified anyway. Thus in the treatment that Manzini and Savoia (1998) provide for Italian dialects, the classical case of adjunction to a non-empty head (i.e. cliticization) is reduced to a highly articulate theory of clitic positions, whereby each clitic corresponds to an independent head.

The remaining cases involve inflectional morphology, and hence adjunction of a complex word to an abstract head in Chomsky's (1995) terms. In these cases, following the lead of Manzini and Roussou (1997), it is equally possible to merge the complex word in the position where it surfaces, and to connect it to the position of the lexical category via abstract movement of a feature from the latter. A translation of this solution into a dependency format naturally suggests itself, as Manzini and Roussou (1997) indeed imply.

apply non-cyclically. This assumption is strictly bound to the conception of the overall architecture of grammar, whereby the contrast between overt and abstract movement is captured by the contrast between applications of Move before and after Spellout. It hardly needs to be said that a model of grammar that avoids the need for such a stipulation appears preferable on general conceptual grounds.

Though Chomsky (1995) chooses to introduce an asymmetry between the overt and the covert components of grammar, different conclusions can be drawn from the obvious fact that covert movement applies non-cyclically. An obviously undesirable conclusion is that the cyclic vs. non-cyclic divide is a divide between instances of Merge and of Move. The discussion above suggests, however, yet another conclusion, namely that the formation of complementation dependencies is necessarily cyclic, while the formation of branching dependencies, including all adjunction and hence all movement, is not. Suppose indeed A merges with B to form a dependency (A, B) and then C non-cyclically merges with B to form (B, C). A complementation dependency results from this merger only if (A, C) is also a dependency. But this eventuality is blocked by the dependency-formation mechanism.

A-cyclic insertion of, say, a left-branch subject into the computation can happen by merger of the D head with two subdependencies, corresponding roughly to NP and IP. However, there is no possibility of inserting some missing complementation material into an already formed subdependency, since the input to the operation would necessarily consist of two subdependencies, already forming a dependency.

The abandonment of the Extension condition and hence of the strict cycle proper raises on the other hand the important question of the derivational or representational character of the grammar. Within the Minimalist framework, broadly construed, both options have been advocated, notably by Chomsky (1995), or even more radically Epstein (1994), and by Brody (1995). The definition of the issue is itself in question, but strict cyclicity provides an obvious divide between the two options. Here I shall be satisfied with leaving the question of the derivational or representational nature of grammar otherwise open.

In short, the present grammar is sufficient to express the two basic syntactic configurations of complementation and adjunction (specification/modification). With this much background, we can finally turn to locality conditions, which provide the main motivation for dependency structure, as I shall argue next.

3. MOVE

We have already seen in the discussion of the Minimalist framework in Section 1, that the classical strong island phenomena are not considered by Chomsky (1995), except for a passing mention of Huang's (1982) CED. This is only one of a number of conditions that address the same empirical problem—and that includes notably Kayne's (1984) Connectedness Condition. What all of the conditions have in common is some notion of head government, defined at least in first approximation as sisterhood to a head. According to the CED, then, extraction is possible only from head-governed constituents; according to Connectedness there must be a sequence of head-governed constituents containing the trace (i.e. a g-projection of the trace) that connects it to its antecedents. In fact, Connectedness is considerably more sophisticated than the CED in that it takes into account parasitic gap configurations as well, where a set of traces is ultimately related to the same antecedent. In the latter case, the g-projections of the traces must be connected to the antecedent, in the sense that, taken together, they must define a subtree.

What is interesting is that in the present theory each dependency (A, B, . . .) effectively represents a head-government relation between A and B; in this sense head government is a primitive of the theory. This is at once reminiscent of, and in radical contrast to, Epstein's (1994) construal of c-command as a primitive of grammars based on Chomsky's (1995) Merge. Within the present theory, a g-projection in the sense of Kayne (1984) is simply a dependency in the present sense of the term. Let us then make the preliminary assumption that in present terms Connectedness requires that given a trace B and its antecedent A, there is a dependency (A, . . ., B) connecting them. If such a condition proves empirically adequate to deal with strong islands, its obvious advantage over other conditions of the same family is that it does not have recourse to specialized constructs such as g-projections, or even a specialized definition of head government, but relies entirely on the primitive construct of the theory, namely that of dependency. To this extent, our theory therefore turns out to be simpler than its competitors.

Consider first a well-formed extraction from a complementation structure, as in (22).

(22)   Who did you see [some pictures of t_{who}]

In (22) there is of course a sequence of complementation links that connect *who* and t_{who}, including many whose interpretative justification has already been discussed in some detail, such as the dependency between C and I, represented here in the presence of interrogative properties by the movement chain (*did*, t_{did}), the dependency between I and V, represented here by the link (t_{did}, *see*), and the dependency between V and its selected object D, represented here by (*see*, *some*). To these needs crucially to be added the dependency (*who*, *did*), which expresses in Chomsky's (1995) terms the checking of the *wh*-features of *who* by the interrogative C. On the basis of standard assumptions concerning the dependency structure embedded under D, the dependency connecting *who* and its trace takes then the form in (23).

(23)   (who, did, t_{did}, see, some, pictures, of, t_{who})

Consider next a typical example of subject-island violation, as in (24).

(24)   *Who did [some pictures of t_{who}] annoy you

A dependency can clearly be formed in (24), connecting t_{who} to *some*, namely (*some*, *friends*, *of*, t_{who}). However, *some* itself is only connected downwards to t_{did}, and does not have any direct upward link. It is true that via t_{did}, *some* is also indirectly linked upward to *did* and thus to *who*. Crucially, however, this sequence of links, reproduced in (25), is not a dependency, given that all the material embedded under t_{did} is missing.

(25)

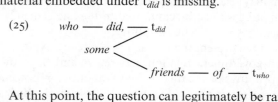

At this point, the question can legitimately be raised of why, if the material corresponding roughly to VP cannot be omitted in (24), it is nevertheless possible to omit the whole left branch corresponding to the subject in (22). An answer straightforwardly made available by the theory is that complementation is strictly cyclic, while adjunction of a left or right branch is non-cyclic, because of the considerations already advanced.

Nevertheless, the Connectedness requirement can still in principle be satisfied by a dependency formed by (25) with the addition of the dependents of t_{did}. Obviously enough, if (24) is to turn out to be ungrammatical, this latter possibility must be blocked. Notice then that (25) represents the minimal path, in terms of elementary dependencies, between t_{who} and *who*; adding the dependents of t_{did} creates an object which is a dependency, but which no longer defines the shortest path between trace and antecedent. Based on this observation, we can then tentatively assume that Connectedness requires the minimal sequence of dependency links connecting a trace and its antecedent to a dependency, as in (26).

(26)   *Connectedness*
          Given a trace B and its antecedent A, the minimal sequence of dependency
          links connecting A and B is a dependency.

All of the conceptual advantages already claimed for a version of Connectedness which relies entirely on the primitive construct of the theory (i.e. that of dependency) hold of the version in (26). At the same time, this version of Connectedness clearly reveals it to be an economy condition in grammar, which can be claimed as an additional conceptual argument in its favour. Paraphrasing (26), the grammar requires the shortest path between a trace and its antecedent to be chosen; if this is not a well-defined syntactic object, the computation is ill formed.

Concretely, (23) does represent the minimal sequence of dependency links that connects *who* and t_{who} in (22); because it is a dependency, the extraction in (22) satisfies Connectedness and it is predicted to be well formed. On the other hand, as already discussed, (25) represents the minimal sequence of dependency links that connects *who* and t_{who} in (24); but is not a dependency, whence the ill-formedness of the extraction in (24). This result generalizes not only to all extractions from subjects, but also to all extraction from unselected left branches, which is therefore predicted to be ill formed. What remains to be considered at this point is only extraction from adjuncts—that is, unselected right branches, as for instance in (27).

(27)   *What will they leave [before seeing t_{what}]

The shortest sequence of dependency links connecting *what* and t_{what} in (27) includes all complementation links up to *before*, then the external argument link between *before* and the I of the main sentence, represented by t_{will}, and from there the usual links to the *wh*-phrase, as in (28).

(28)

$$
\begin{array}{c}
before \text{ —— } I \text{ —— } seeing \text{ —— } t_{what} \\
\diagup \\
what \text{ —— } will \text{ —— } t_{will}
\end{array}
$$

Obviously enough, (28) is not a dependency, very much for the same reasons as (25) is not; in (28) in particular, what is crucially omitted is the main branch of the sentence embedded under t_{will} along with the *before*-headed adjunct. Thus, Connectedness is violated. Generalizing this and the preceding results we obtain that extraction is impossible from any unselected subdependency, whether it represents a left or a right branch, exactly as desired.

Needless to say, the generalization just drawn raises a number of empirical questions. These cannot be fully discussed here for reasons of space, but some of them are worth a brief mention. To begin with, the prohibition against extracting from an unselected branch of the sentence can be circumvented in parasitic gap configurations. To account for these, however, the present version of Connectedness can be fairly obviously revised along the lines already suggested by Kayne (1984). In particular, given a set of traces with a unique antecedent, and for each trace the shortest sequence of dependency links relating it to the antecedent, we can require that the set of such sequences taken together defines a dependency. Thus suppose (24) or (27) are modified to also include a trace in the matrix object position, yielding a parasitic gap configuration of the type in (29) and (30).

(29)   Who did [some pictures of t_{who}] annoy t_{who}]

(30)   What will they buy t_{what} [before seeing t_{what}]

The relevant objects for Connectedness are of the type of (25) and (28), respectively, augmented by the material embedded under I in the main branch of the sentence. Since the objects so obtained are dependencies, the well-formedness of parasitic gaps is correctly predicted by the revised Connected-ness.

Furthermore, the formulation of Connectedness adopted here, in its simple version in (26) or in more refined ones, predicts not only that it is impossible to extract from an unselected left or right branch, but also that it is impossible to extract the whole branch. This prediction appears to be verified at least in the case of subject extraction, given the ungrammaticality of standard *that*-t violations of the type of (31).

(31)   *Who do you think that t_{who} left

In (31) the shortest sequence of dependency links relating t_{who} to *who* is not a dependency, since it includes the embedded I but not the main branch of the sentence that depends on it.

What is crucial for the present discussion is that if this line of reasoning is correct, then another one of the empirical problems that remain open under Chomsky's (1995) theory finds a natural explanation under the present one. The general conceptual reason underlying this result is once again that the present theory effectively takes head government as the primitive relation ex-pressed by an elementary dependency. To the extent that this notion is strongly supported by the empirical data, the present conceptualization of depend-encies is then favoured over Chomsky's (1995) conceptualization of the objects of the theory. I shall not go here into ways to circumvent *that*-t violations, ex-cept to note that the discussion of Roussou (1994, 1998) is largely compatible with the present theory. Furthermore, the prediction that unselected right branches cannot be extracted looks admittedly problematic in the light of ex-tensive extractions of adjuncts. It is worth pointing out, however, that PPs of the type exemplified in (27) and (28) are never pied-piped at LF, but that at least the P is always reconstructed; this means that at least at the interface we are systematically faced by examples of P stranding. Once again, special reanalysis mechanisms can be assumed to be required, which go beyond the scope of the present chapter.

So far I have argued that a Connectedness-type condition can and must be stated as part of the computational system. In this, the present theory has a conceptual advantage, in that Connectedness itself can be stated entirely in terms of the primitive construct of the theory, namely dependencies. This is because head government effectively becomes the primitive notion of order of the theory represented in each elementary dependency link. Other ordering constraints can on the other hand also be formulated in terms of dependencies. Thus requiring that A c-commands B corresponds to requiring that there is a dependency headed by A and containing B. As already noted, this contrasts with the status of c-command under Chomsky's (1995) Merge, which Epstein (1994) shows to be that of a primitive of the theory. Given the radical character of the present reformulations, we may expect to gain some new insight concerning the two classes of phenomena that are subject to Connectedness and c-command, respectively. Though the question is worth raising, providing any answer to it is clearly beyond the scope of the present chapter.

REFERENCES

Arad, M. (1996), 'A Minimalist View of the Syntax–Lexical Semantics Interface', *UCL Working Papers in Linguistics*, 8: 215–42.

Bobaljik, J., and Brown, S. (1997), 'Interarboreal Operations: Head Movement and the Extension Requirement', *Linguistic Inquiry*, 28: 345–56.

Borer, H. (1994), 'The Projection of Arguments', *University of Massachusetts Occasional Papers*, 17, GLSA, University of Massachusetts, Amherst.

Brody, M. (1995), *Lexico-Logical Form*, MIT Press, Cambridge, Mass.

Chomsky, N. (1981), *Lectures on Government and Binding*, Foris, Dordrecht.

——(1995), *The Minimalist Program*, MIT Press, Cambridge, Mass.

Epstein, S. (1994), 'The Derivation of Syntactic Relations', Ms., Harvard University.

Hale, K., and Keyser, S. J. (1993), 'On Argument Structure and the Lexical Expression of Syntactic Relations', in K. Hale and S. J. Keyser (eds.), *The View from Building 20*, MIT Press, Cambridge, Mass.

Higginbotham, J. (1985), 'On Semantics', *Linguistic Inquiry*, 16: 547–93.

Huang, J. (1982), 'Logical Relations in Chinese and the Theory of Grammar', Doctoral dissertation, MIT.

Hudson, R. (1990), *English Word Grammar*, Blackwell, Oxford.

Kayne, R. (1984), *Connectedness and Binary Branching*, Foris, Dordrecht.

——(1994), *The Antisymmetry of Syntax*, MIT Press, Cambridge, Mass.

Manzini, M. R. (1994), 'Locality, Minimalism and Parasitic Gaps', *Linguistic Inquiry*, 25: 481–508.

——(1995), 'The Position of Adjuncts: A Reply to Kayne', *Quaderni del Dipartimento di Linguistica dell'Università di Firenze*, 6: 121–36.

——and Roussou, A. (1997), 'A Minimalist Theory of A-Movement and Control', Ms., University College London/Università di Firenze and University of Wales, Bangor.

——and Savoia, L. (1998), 'Clitics and Auxiliary Choice in Italian Dialects: Their Relevance for the Person Ergativity Split', *Recherches Linguistiques de Vincennes*.

Rizzi, L. (1990), *Relativized Minimality*, MIT Press, Cambridge, Mass.

Roussou, A. (1994), 'The Syntax of Complementizers', Ph.D. dissertation, University College London.

——(1998), 'Features and Subject Dependencies: *That*-t Phenomena Revisited', Ms., University of Wales, Bangor.

Williams, E. (1994), *Thematic Structure in Syntax*, MIT Press, Cambridge, Mass.

I I
Movement to Specifiers

LYNN NICHOLS

I. INTRODUCTION

I investigate here the case of Zuni (isolate; New Mexico) in which there are several types of movement out of VP into specifier positions of IP and CP.[1] This movement is exclusively A′-movement; none of the specifiers of IP in Zuni is a Case position, as will be argued below. Movement to these specifier positions will be argued to be driven by morphosyntactic licensing requirements of the moved element. The syntactic behaviour of several different classes of elements in Zuni, including pronouns, quantifiers, and *wh*-words receives a unified explanation under this account. Particularly interesting is the fact that multiple *wh*-movement in Zuni, involving superiority-governed movement to multiple specifiers of CP, can be explained by the same mechanism driving superiority-obeying obligatory pronominal movement to single specifiers of IP that results in the opposite order.

The discussion is structured as follows. In Section 2 I describe data involving the obligatory fronting of 1st and 2nd person pronouns that results in un-marked OSV order from underlying SOV as well as discontinuous possessive constituents, and the fronting of object quantifiers past the subject. In Section 3 I will argue that each of these categories in Zuni has a morphologically strong and morphologically weak form (cf. Cardinaletti and Starke 1994), and that it is the licensing requirements of weak elements that forces their move-ment out of the VP. With this background established, I show in Section 4 that *wh*-words in Zuni also have morphologically strong and weak forms. The argument that licensing requirements drive weak pronoun movement correctly predicts that Zuni not only has *wh*-movement, but will have (obligatory) mul-

This research was generously supported by grants for fieldwork at Zuni Pueblo from the Phillips Fund of the American Philosophical Society and the Whatcom Museum Society, and by the Uni-versity of Arizona and the University of New Mexico. I owe a particular debt of thanks to Eloise Jelinek and Robert Leonard for their help in certain fieldwork logistics. I am grateful to Ken Hale, Richard Kayne, Susumu Kuno, and Höskuldur Thráinsson for extremely helpful discussions of the material. I would also like to thank two anonymous reviewers as well as audiences at WCCFL XV at the University of California, Irvine and at the 1996 SSILA Winter Meeting at San Diego for their comments on earlier versions.

[1] I will use 'IP' throughout as an abbreviation for functional projections TP and AgrP.

tiple *wh*-movement to multiple specifiers of CP. The strict ordering of multiple *wh*-words in Zuni according to superiority can be accounted for in light of the proposal of Richards (1997) for Bulgarian that non-initial *wh*-words move later than the highest *wh*-word and 'tuck in' under the highest *wh*-word into multiple specifiers of CP. The evidence presented here from the licensing requirements of Zuni weak pronouns lends independent support to this hypothesis.

2. WORD ORDER: PRONOUNS AND QUANTIFIERS

Zuni exhibits SOV order as the unmarked case in clauses with lexical NP arguments.

(1) (a) ho'   takun   'aš-kya
         1SG.NOM. necklace   make-PAST
         'I made a necklace.'

  (b) Nemme' Albert yaktoh-kya
       N.   A.   hit-PAST
       'Nemme hit Albert.'
       [*'Albert hit Nemme.']

One (unsurprising) source of alternate word orders is the focusing of arguments. Inanimate object NPs can be focused by moving them to clause-initial position. Animate object NPs may undergo focus movement if they bear the suffix *-ya'*, whose presence indicates specificity.[2] The suffix *-ya'* with its accusative-like distribution is limited to NPs and the 3rd person dual *'a:či*.[3]

(2) (a) 'ussi takun   ho'   'aš-kya
         that necklace 1SG.NOM. make-PAST
         'It was that necklace that I made.'

  (b) Albert-ya' Nemme' yaktoh-kya
       A.-SPECIF. N.   hit-PAST
       'It was Albert that Nemme hit.'

2.1. *1st and 2nd person arguments*

The presence in a clause of 1st and 2nd person pronominal arguments[4] gives rise to departures from the unmarked SOV order illustrated above. If one of the arguments of a transitive verb is a 1st or 2nd person pronoun, that pronoun

---

[2] More specifically, in situ, *-ya'* puts focus emphasis on proper names and gives definite reference (and focus interpretation) to other animate NPs.

[3] Dual *'a:či* is somewhat un-pronoun-like (although there exists a different lexeme for 'two', $k^w ili$) in allowing a contrast in specificity; cf. *'a:či* '[I hit] two' vs. *'a:či-ya'* '[I hit] the two of them'.

[4] 1st and 2nd person pronouns have their own nominative/accusative case paradigm. There are no 3rd person pronouns.

will precede other arguments of the clause regardless of the grammatical function of either, as illustrated in (3*a*, *b*). If both of the arguments in a transitive
clause are (1st and 2nd person) pronouns, the object will precede the subject
and OSV order is the result, (3*c*). Word order in the Zuni clause is therefore
SOV or OSV depending on the absence or presence of pronoun arguments.

(3) (*a*)   hom   teššuk'ᵂa' waccit 'utte-kya
             1SG.ACC. yesterday dog   bite-PAST
             'The dog bit me yesterday.'

    (*b*)   ho'   teššuk'ᵂa' waccita yaktoh-kya
             1SG.NOM. yesterday dog   hit-PAST
             'I hit the dog yesterday.'

    (*c*)   tom   teššuk'ᵂa' ho'   šema-kya
             2SG.ACC. yesterday 1SG.NOM. call-PAST
             'I called you yesterday.'

Example (4) below illustrates the unacceptability of a sentence containing a
2nd person pronoun object remaining to the right of the NP subject.

(4)   *waccita hom   'utte-kya
         dog   1SG.ACC. bite-PAST
         'The dog bit me.'

The OSV orders in (3*a*) and (3*c*), unlike that in (2*a*, *b*), do *not* have focus
interpretation but rather have neutral interpretation. Focus movement of 1st
and 2nd person arguments in neutral OSV clauses in fact restores SOV order,
as in (5).

(5)   kᵂa' *to'* (FOCUS) ho'na'   'awa-na'ma-p
         NEG. 2SG.NOM.   1DU.ACC. find-NEG.-DIFF.SUBJ.
         'If *you* do not find us two [we will cut your head off; if *we* do not find
         you . . .]'   (Bunzel 1933)

The position of negation in the Zuni clause can be used to argue that Zuni
1st and 2nd person pronouns have moved out of the VP. Negation in Zuni
involves the use of a negative particle somewhere to the left of the verb. This
particle can occur in one of two positions: either close to the verb as in (6)
below or further to the left as in (5) above, in a position where a number of
other particles (evidential and aspectual) also occur. I assume that the negation
particle, here *kʷa'*, marks the edge of the VP in the position illustrated in (6).
Since 1st and 2nd person arguments appear to the left of negation in (6), they
must be outside the VP. In contrast, (7*a*–*c*) indicate that lexical NP arguments
do not undergo movement out of VP.

(6)   'epaš ho'na'   ton   kᵂa' yema-k'ya-na:w-amme-'kya
         true 1DU.ACC. 2PL.NOM. NEG. ascend-CAUS.-PL.SUBJ.-NEG.-PAST
         'Verily you (pl.) did not let us two come up.'   (Bunzel 1933)

(7) (*a*) teššuk'ʷa' *kʷa'* waccita wihac'ana 'utte-nam-kya
yesterday NEG. dog baby bite-NEG.-PAST
'The dog did not bite the baby yesterday.'

(*b*) *teššuk'ʷa' waccita *kʷa'* wihac'ana 'utte-nam-kya
yesterday dog NEG. baby bite-NEG.-PAST
'The dog did not bite the baby yesterday.'

(*c*) *teššuk'ʷa' waccita wihac'ana *kʷa'* 'utte-nam-kya
yesterday dog baby NEG. bite-NEG.-PAST
'The dog did not bite the baby yesterday.'

Finally, all instances of 1st and 2nd person pronouns move out of the VP, not just subjects and objects. A 1st or 2nd person indirect object will move to initial position; likewise for possessive pronouns. Both of these types of movement are illustrated below in (8*a*, *b*). Note that in the latter case the result is a discontinuous possessive constituent, where a possessive may be extracted even from an object argument, (8*c*).

(8) (*a*) ho'na:wan$_i$ ton t_i tešu-nap-tu-n'on akkya
1PL.DAT.PL. 2PL.NOM. seek-PL.SUBJ.-OPT.-NOM. in.order
'So that you [honorific] may be the one to look for her for us . . .'
(Bunzel 1933)

(*b*) hom$_i$ lakʷkʷ t_i 'e'le' palo-ye
1SG.POSS. over.there daughter be.buried-PRES.STAT.
'My daughter is buried over there.'

(*c*) hiš to'na:wan$_i$ ho' t_i lena-: tuna-p
INTENS. 2PL.POSS.PL. 1SG.NOM. domest.plant-PL. see-DIFF.SUBJ.
'As soon as I saw your crops' (Bunzel 1933)

2.2. *Quantifiers*

There are a number of elements that may occur inside the Zuni DP. Of these determiners, quantifiers, numbers, and adjectives, only adjectives and dual *'a:či* follow the noun; determiners, quantifiers, and numbers all must precede the noun. Between these items themselves also exist strict ordering relations. Among this group of elements, certain Zuni quantifiers raise out of the VP in a manner similar to 1st and 2nd person pronouns. The behaviour of these quantifiers differs somewhat at first glance from that of the pronouns, in that they appear to be optionally able to remain inside the VP. Example (9*a*) illustrates the in situ position of the quantifier *kwa'ał* (something, anything), while (9*b*) illustrates the result of movement. Note that these quantifiers are morphologically identical to determiners, so that (9a) is in fact ambiguous between a quantifier-as-object reading and a quantifier-as-determiner reading. Where movement has taken place, however, the result is no longer ambiguous. Only the quantifier-as-object reading is possible.

(9) (a) kᵂa' ho'   kᵂa'ał picu:t 'ito-k'ya-nam-kya
         NEG. ISG.NOM. any   pig   eat-CAUS.-NEG.-PAST
         'I didn't feed anything to the pigs.'
         [also: 'I didn't feed any pigs.']

    (b) kᵂa' kᵂa'ał$_i$ ho' t_i picu:t 'ito-k'ya-nam-kya
         NEG. any   ISG.NOM.   pig   eat-CAUS.-NEG.-PAST
         'I didn't feed anything to the pigs.'
         [*'I didn't feed any pigs.']

In the case of both 1st and 2nd person pronouns and quantifiers the questions are: what is driving this movement, where are these elements moving to outside the VP, and specifically what structural position are they moving to? I will argue in the next section that each of the above categories of words undergoing dislocation in Zuni occurs in both a morphosyntactically strong and a morphosyntactically weak form. The observed dislocation affects weak forms and is the result of the licensing requirements of such elements. I will argue that all of these elements are moving to the specifiers of functional projections in IP to fulfil these licensing requirements.

3. STRENGTH AND LICENSING

The Zuni pronouns undergoing the movement described above each have a long (strong) and a short (weak) form, illustrated in Table 11.1. These strong and weak forms of the pronouns are in complementary distribution.

TABLE 11.1. *Zuni pronominal forms*

	Nominative		Accusative		Indirect object/possessive	
	Sg.	Du./Pl.	Sg.	Du./Pl.	Sg.	Du./Pl.
1st						
Strong	ho:'o	ho'no'	homma	ho'no'	homma	ho'na:wa:ni
Weak	ho'	hon	hom	ho'no'	hom	ho'na:wan
2nd						
Strong	to:'o	to'no'	tomma	to'no'	tomma	to'na:wa:ni
Weak	to'	ton	tom	to'no'	tom	to'na:wan

3.1. *Strong vs. weak and syntactic distribution*

Only the weak pronouns can occur as arguments of the clause (although they move obligatorily out of VP); strong pronouns are excluded from these positions.[5] This contrast is illustrated in (10) and (11).

(10) (*a*) ho'   waccita 'ito-k'e-kkya
              1SG.NOM.[W] dog   eat-CAUS.-PAST
              'I fed the dog.'

      (*b*) hom   waccita 'utte-kya
              1SG.ACC.[W] dog   bite-PAST
              'The dog bit me.'

      (*c*) tom   waccita 'ito-:-'a
              2SG.ACC.(POSS.).[W] dog   eat-CONT.-PRES.
              'Your dog is eating.'

(11) (*a*) *ho:'o   waccita 'ito-k'e-kkya
              1SG.NOM.[S] . . .
              'I fed the dog.'

      (*b*) *homma   waccita 'utte-kya
              1SG.ACC.[S] . . .
              'The dog bit me.'

      (*c*) *tomma   waccita 'ito-:-'a
              2SG.ACC.(POSS.).[S] dog   eat-CONT.-PRES.
              'Your dog is eating.'

But while weak pronouns can occur as arguments of the clause, they turn out to be excluded from certain other contexts. In particular, Zuni weak pronouns cannot occur:

(12) (i)   as bare responses,
      (ii)   as predicate nominals, or
      (iii) in coordinate structures.

Examples (13*a–c*) below illustrate the use of Zuni strong subject, object, and possessive pronouns as single-word (bare) responses to questions. No other clausal material accompanies the pronoun in this usage.[6] Weak pronouns are excluded from this context. Note that the bare pronoun in Zuni is assigned the same case the pronoun would receive in that grammatical role in a full clause.[7]

(13) (*a*) čo-p   k'yawe' tutu-kya   ho:'o   / (*ho')
              who-Q water   drink-PAST   1SG.NOM.[S] / (1SG.NOM.[W])
              'Who drank the water?'   'Me.'

<hr>

[5] With one important exception, to be discussed below.

[6] Ignoring the question of whether this is some type of ellipsis, i.e. where the response would contain a complete clausal representation all of which except for the pronoun is deleted.

[7] Unlike English, which would have accusative case in examples corresponding to (13*a, b*), as the glosses indicate.

(b) čo-p   waccita 'utte-kya   homma   / (*hom)
who-Q dog   bite-PAST   1SG.ACC.[S] / (1SG.ACC.[W])
'Who did the dog bite?'   'Me.'

(c) čo-p   'an 'ussi nicikya   homma   / (*hom)
who-Q P   that ring   1SG.ACC.(POSS.).[S] / (1SG.ACC.(POSS.).[W])
'Whose ring is that?'   'Mine.'

The strong form of the pronoun also occurs when the pronoun is used predicatively, as in (14a, b). Again, weak pronouns are excluded from this context.

(14) (a) 'ussi ho:'o   / (*ho')
that 1SG.NOM.[S] / (1SG.NOM.[W])
'That's me.'

(b) 'ussi homma   / (*hom)
that 1SG.ACC.(POSS.).[S] / (1SG.ACC.(POSS.).[W])
'That's mine.'

Finally, when a pronominal argument is coordinated with another argument,
the strong form of the pronoun must be used, (15a).[8] This is the sole context
in which strong pronouns occur as arguments of the verb.

(15) (a) ho:'o   tap Nemme hon   'a:n-uwa
1SG.NOM.[S] and N.   1DU.NOM.[W] go-FUTURE
'Me and Nemme'll go.'

(b) *ho'   tap Nemme . . .
1SG.NOM.[W] and N.

It is suggested that the contexts in which the Zuni weak pronouns are
excluded and strong pronouns are obligatory all share the property that they
are syntactically deficient in some sense. By examining each structure we might
hypothesize that this syntactic deficiency has to do with the complete absence
of any functional projections, as in the case of bare response forms, or the
impossibility of a pronoun occurring within some relevant structural domain
of the functional projections, as in the case of the predicative or coordinate use
of pronouns. In the latter two cases, the predicate position of the pronoun as
in (14) or the extra DP node assumed to dominate coordinate structures as in
(16) below seems to prevent some apparently essential connection between
functional projections and pronouns.[9]

---

[8] The order in (15a) is preferred to that in (i) below.

(i)   ???Nemme' tap ho:'o
N.   and 1SG.NOM.[S]

[9] Evidence that this extra DP node blocks some necessary relationship between the pronoun
and the features of some head of IP comes from the requirement that the coordinated constituent
in (16) be repeated by (coindexed with) a dual pronominal argument *hon* that presumably
does occur in argument position (i.e. in the domain of some functional projection). Coordinated

(16)   [IP [DP [DPho:'o]   tap [DP Nemme]] hon   'a:n-uwa]
         1SG.NOM.[S] and   N.   1DU.NOM.[W] go-future
         'Me and Nemme'll go.'

I will suggest below what role in licensing the pronoun this functional material might have.

3.2. *Pronominal structure and alternative licensing*

Zuni weak pronouns are not permitted to occur in syntactically deficient contexts, as the examples in Section 3.1 illustrated. In addition, while Zuni weak pronouns occur as arguments of the clause, they undergo obligatory movement out of the VP (cf. examples (1)–(6) above). I suggest that the Zuni weak pronouns are excluded from VP-internal positions because these are syntactically deficient positions as well. In this section I will outline the argument underlying this assumption, namely how VP-internal positions are deficient and why weak pronouns might be required to move out of them.

Cardinaletti and Starke (1994, 1996) argue that the behaviour of certain Romance and Germanic pronouns similar to that described for Zuni strong and weak pronouns can be accounted for in an analysis in which pronouns have internal syntactic structure, and in particular where weak pronouns differ from strong in having deficient internal structure. Similarly, clitics differ from weak pronouns in having relatively more deficient internal syntactic structures. The syntactic behaviour of weak pronouns (and clitics) is the result of these deficient argument types compensating for their deficient structures by recovering missing syntactic features in alternative ways. Deficient pronouns are therefore excluded from contexts where the recoverability of these features is not an option.

Following Cardinaletti and Starke (1994) I will suggest that pronouns have complex internal structure and that weak pronouns undergo movement in order to be licensed, though the proposal here differs from theirs in several details.[10] I propose that the licensing requirements of pronouns ultimately stem from pronouns being constituted of inflectional feature bundles. Pronouns therefore require the same special licensing required of inflectional features.[11] Inflectional features generally cannot stand on their own but rather must be

---

arguments behave differently in this respect to non-coordinated arguments; compare (i) and (ii).

(i)   *ho:'o   tap Nemme 'a:n-uwa
         1SG.NOM.[S] and N.   go-FUTURE

(ii)   hon   'a:n-uwa
         1DU.NOM.[W] go-FUTURE
         'We two will go.'

[10] Nichols (1997*b*) contains a fuller explication of the differences between the two approaches.
[11] Everett (1996) proposes a somewhat similar conception of the nature of inflectional features.

located in some functional head F° that is licensed (governed) by some head
X°. This entails adjunction of the head F° containing the features to the licensing (governing) head X°. For this reason we find inflectional features—and here
specifically person, number, and gender features are meant, since tense is often
instantiated on its own as a lexical word in some languages—located in affixes
to V° and N°.[12] For example, number features for the subject in Zuni are located
in an Agr° head-adjoined to V°.

(17)   hon   yak'o-nap-kya
        1PL.NOM. vomit-PL.SUBJ.-PAST
        'We vomited.'

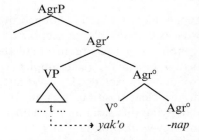

Pronouns, though consisting of inflectional features, are XPs rather than X°s.
The licensing of a pronoun will therefore mean either the presence of a head–
complement relation between pronoun and licensing head X° in the minimal
(unextended, in the sense of Chomsky 1993) domain of X°, or the formation
of a specifier–head relationship between pronoun and licensing head X°. The
proposal is summed up in (18).

(18) (i)   Pronouns consist of inflectional feature bundles.
     (ii) Inflectional features must be licensed by some head X°.
     (iii) To be licensed, the pronoun must be in the minimal domain of licensing
           head X°.

If features contained in the pronominal head have a special licensing requirement, we should expect to find a contrast in the syntactic behaviour of
items that are morphologically identical but have a different feature content
and therefore different licensing requirements. Such is the case with Zuni 2nd
versus 3rd person dual imperatives. The dual marker *'a:či* is used with both
2nd and 3rd person imperative subjects. There is a contrast in the syntactic
behaviour of *'a:či*, however, depending on its person features: 2nd person *'a:či*

[12] Also located in D°, as in Romance and Germanic languages. I will assume here that Case
features are different, as indicated by the fact that Case sometimes stands on its own as a particle,
for example the ERG case particle *e* in Samoan, as in (i) below. I follow the proposals made by
Lamontagne and Travis (1987) and Bittner and Hale (1996*a*, *b*) and assume that Case features are
contained in their own head K° specific to Case (as opposed to person, number, etc. features which
are all contained together in some Agr° head). While I will assume this analysis of Case generally,
it may turn out to be appropriate for case only in certain languages.

(i)   sa   sasa e   le teine le maile   (Samoan)
        PST hit ERG the girl the dog
        'The girl hit the dog.'   (Mosel and Hovdhaugen 1992)

undergoes obligatory movement of the kind described in Section 2 for Zuni 1st and 2nd person weak pronouns, (19*a*); in contrast, 3rd person *'a:či* does not undergo this movement, (19*b*, *b'*).

(19) (*a*) ('a:cawak') 'a:či hom   'ansattu
        boys   2DU. ISG.ACC. help
        'You two (boys) help me.'

   (*b*) hom   ('a:cawak') 'a:či 'ansattu-tu
        ISG.ACC. boys   3DU. help-OPT.
        'Let those two (boys) help me.'

  (*b'*) ???'a:či hom   'ansattu-tu
        3DU. ISG.ACC. help-OPT.

The behaviour of morphologically invariant *'a:či* suggests that it is the feature content of *'a:či* that is driving this movement, and more particularly, that 2nd person features require licensing in Zuni while 3rd person features do not. We might speculate that this is because Zuni 3rd person represents the absence of person features (cf. the lack of overt 3rd person pronouns mentioned in footnote 4).

I suggest, following Cardinaletti and Starke (1994) in general terms, that pronouns have complex internal structure and that this internal structure is different for strong and weak pronouns. The licensing requirements of inflectional features play out differently depending on pronoun internal structure and will therefore affect strong and weak pronouns in different ways.

The internal structures I assume for strong and weak pronouns are shown in (20) below and differ from the Cardinaletti and Starke proposal in several respects. In both types of pronoun the inflectional features that make up the pronoun are located in a D° head that projects a DP maximal category. One functional projection, KP, dominates DP in the weak pronoun, while two functional projections, KP and FP, dominate DP in the strong pronoun. Weak pronouns therefore differ from strong pronouns in lacking the functional projection FP.[13]

(20)   (*a*) *Strong pronoun*   (*b*) *Weak pronoun*

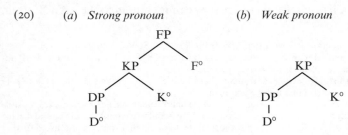

---

[13] I assume that clitics are formally identical to weak pronouns and that their differing prosodic properties are dealt with in a separate phonological component. I will have nothing further to say about clitics here.

Referential and phi (ϕ) features are contained in the D° head of the pronoun itself.[14] KP is a Case phrase that is headed by a K° containing Case features. FP is a functional category projected by the head F° that contains functional features of some kind. I use the generic functional category label F since it is still unclear exactly what this category is and what type of feature(s) it contains. It is hypothesized that the features in F° serve to license the pronominal features of DP in the strong pronoun.[15]

Recall that it was argued above that pronominal features require licensing as other inflectional features do, and that pronouns are licensed when they are in the minimal domain of some licensing head X°. I suggest more specifically that the pronominal-licensing head X° is some functional head, and that there are two ways in which pronominal features can be licensed by a functional head. Either the pronoun must contain some licensing functional head (i.e. F° above) as part of its structure, as in the case of the strong pronouns, or if F° is absent, as in the case of weak pronouns, the pronoun must move to the minimal domain of some other functional head (i.e. to the specifier of some projection in IP).

The notion of 'syntactically deficient' mentioned earlier is now made more precise. The need created (by syntactically deficient contexts) for some alternative form of licensing for their pronominal features ultimately drives the movement of weak pronouns.[16] Specifically with relation to Zuni, obligatory V°-to-I° movement[17] in Zuni renders VP-internal positions 'syntactically deficient' by removing V, a potential licensing head, from the domain of elements such as pronouns that require licensing. Note for example the connection between V movement and obligatory weak pronoun movement in Swedish (Holmberg 1991).[18] Licensing is therefore argued to play a major role in the syntax of pronominal elements in Zuni.

3.3. *Movement to specifiers*

In order for pronominal features to be licensed, the pronoun must occur in the minimal domain of some head X° containing functional features. I assume that Zuni pronouns are DPs; therefore they cannot adjoin to the head X° itself.

---

[14] This assumption contrasts with that of Cardinaletti and Starke (1994), who assume case, agreement, and referential features are located together in a C° head. Further, for them NP not DP is the root of the pronoun structure they propose.

[15] See Nichols (1997*b*) for evidence from Southern Paiute for the presence of these features in F° and their effect on person hierarchy phenomena.

[16] I suggest that in particular it is the features present in the functional head that are responsible for licensing pronominal features; one mechanism that would accomplish this would be for pronouns to 'check' certain features against those of the functional head (to be discussed further in Section 4 below). This is a different claim from the one made by Cardinaletti and Starke (1994) that the pronoun 'recovers' from the functional head certain features (case, referential, phi-features) that it lacks.

[17] Evidence for V-to-I movement in Zuni, an SOV language, is tricky and I will not detail it here; but see Nichols (1997*b*).

[18] Sometimes referred to as object shift (cf. also Diesing and Jelinek 1993).

Occurring in the minimal domain of X° will therefore mean that a DP pronoun must occupy the complement position of X° or the specifier position of X°. DP is the complement of X° (= F°) in the strong pronoun (cf. (20) above). Weak pronouns by definition cannot occur in this context, so that weak pronouns must move to the specifier of some functional head of IP.

We can confirm that Zuni weak pronouns are moving to IP, and specifically to specifiers within IP, with several types of syntactic evidence. First, as (21) illustrates, fronted weak pronouns appear to the right of an object question word *kʷap* that has undergone *wh*-movement to [Spec, CP].[19] Example (21*b*) shows the unacceptability of the pronoun moving to the left of the *wh*-word.

(21) (*a*) [$_{CP}$ kʷa-p$_k$ [$_{IP}$ tom$_j$ teššuk'ʷa' [$_{VP}$ Nemme' t_j t_k 'uk]-kya]]
      what-Q   2SG.ACC.[W] yesterday   N.   give-PAST
      'What did Nemme give you yesterday?'

(*b*) ???tom   kʷa-p teššuk'ʷa' Nemme' 'uk-kya
      2SG.ACC.[W] what-Q yesterday N.   give-PAST

Further evidence that the weak pronouns are moving to somewhere in IP, rather than for example simply moving and adjoining to VP as in (22), comes from the behaviour of pronouns in Zuni infinitival clauses.

(22)

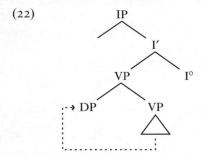

When IP projections, as the only potential licensing domain for Zuni pronoun features, are absent, as in the case of non-finite clauses,[20] we expect weak

---

[19] Zuni *wh*-movement will be discussed extensively in Sect. 4.

[20] Assuming that the presence (absence) of functional projections in a clause is indicated by the presence (absence) of affixes on the verbs that correspond to the heads of these projections, note that the Zuni non-finite verb contains only the stem plus the infinitival suffix -*nakya* (i.*a*), and cannot appear with tense inflection (i.*b*), plural subject agreement (i.*c*), or even a negation suffix (ii).

(i) (*a*)   'ik'oti   lewu-nakya teni
           mistake do-INFIN.   hard
           'It's hard to make a mistake.'

(*b*)   *'ik'oti   lewu-nakya-kya teni
        mistake do-INFIN.-PAST   hard
        'It's hard to have made a mistake.'

(*c*)   *'ik'oti   lewu-nap-nakya   teni
        mistake do-PL.SUBJ.-INFIN. hard
        'It's hard for them to make a mistake.'

pronouns to climb out of the non-finite clause into a higher finite clause where IP projections can be found. This prediction is borne out in Zuni—weak pronouns climb obligatorily out of non-finite clauses, as in (23), since these clauses contain no licenser for pronoun features.

(23)   [TP *tom_k*   [AGRP ho'_j   [VP *t_j* [CP [VP Pilpo   'an *t_k t_i*]
            2SG.ACC.[W]   1SG.NOM.[W]   Filbert P

        tap_i-kyan   ] t_m]] 'iy_m-a]
        get-in.order   come-PRES.
        'I have come to get you away from Filbert.'

Note that without a theory of the licensing requirements of pronominal features, this type of weak pronoun climbing is unexpected.[21]

In particular, I assume that weak pronouns are moving to the specifiers of functional projections in IP. There are two types of evidence on which such an assumption can be based. First, the Zuni pronouns are moving as DPs and not D° heads. An element moving as an X° constituent adjoins to some Y° head. Zuni weak pronouns cannot be X°-adjoining to the functional heads of the clause since these latter are instantiated as suffixes to the Zuni verb (e.g. tense inflection), while weak pronoun movement clearly takes place away from the verb, as in example (23) above. In addition, since the weak pronouns must be moving as XP (DP) categories, they must be moving to some position that licenses the presence of DP arguments. The specifier positions of the functional projections in IP are precisely such positions.

The movement I assume for Zuni weak pronouns is illustrated in (24).[22]

(ii)   *k^wa' 'ik'oti   lewu-na'ma-nakya teni
        NEG. mistake do-NEG.-INFIN.   hard
        'It's hard to not make a mistake.'

I conclude that Zuni infinitival clauses lack TP, AgrP, and NegP projections.

[21] Since it cannot be phonologically motivated.

[22] I therefore attribute weak pronoun behaviour in Zuni to syntactic movement, rather than to movement that is phonologically driven. While the weak pronouns are prosodically lighter than the strong pronouns, there is evidence that weak pronouns do not move to IP in search of a prosodic host. Zuni weak pronouns are not prosodically dependent on any adjacent element or on each other, as attested by the fact that they are able to bear main word stress and in addition can be separated from each other and the verb by other material such as adverbs (e.g. the adverbs *li:la* (here) and *teššuk^wa'* (yesterday) in (i) separate the pronouns *to'na'* and *ho'* from each other and the rest of the clause). Note that under the analysis suggested here, adverbs can intervene between pronouns since, as mentioned above, I assume adverbs are adjoined to maximal projections while the pronouns occur in the specifiers of these projections.

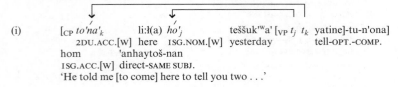

(i)   [CP *to'na'_k*   li:ł(a) *ho'_j*   teššuk^wa' [VP *t_j t_k* yatine]-tu-n'ona]
            2DU.ACC.[W] here 1SG.NOM.[W] yesterday   tell-OPT.-COMP.
        hom   'anhaytoš-nan
        1SG.ACC.[W] direct-SAME SUBJ.
        'He told me [to come] here to tell you two . . .'

(24)

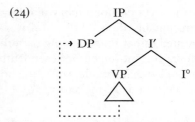

Assuming that Zuni weak pronouns move out of the VP into the specifier of functional projections of IP, we are now in a position to account for the OSV word order described earlier that is found in Zuni finite clauses with at least a weak pronoun object, illustrated again in (25*a*, *b*).

(25) (*a*)   tom   Nemme' šema-kya
        2SG.ACC.[W] N.   call-PAST
        'Nemme called you.'

    (*b*)   tom   ho'   šema-kya
        2SG.ACC.[W] 1SG.NOM.[W] call-PAST
        'I called you.'

In the case of (25*a*), OSV order is simply the result of movement of the object out of the VP past the lexical NP subject in [Spec, VP] to the specifier position of the first functional projection available. This is probably [Spec, AgrP], as in (26).

(26)

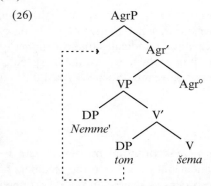

In the case where both arguments are pronominal, as in (25*b*), I assume that this OSV order is a result of the fact that weak pronoun movement obeys superiority, which is essentially the result of a Shortest Move requirement (Chomsky 1993), proposed by Chomsky (1995*b*) as the Minimal Link Condition. This means that of the two pronouns that undergo movement in (27) below, the highest one (in [Spec, VP]) must move first and, in addition, that it must make the simplest and shortest movement to satisfy whatever requirement is driving its movement. The (1st person) nominative subject pronoun *ho'* will therefore move first and into the first available specifier position, presumably

[Spec, AgrP]. Movement of the (2nd person) object pronoun *tom* will follow, to the next available specifier position, presumably [Spec, TP]. Zuni weak pronoun movement therefore occurs in a nested rather than crossing pattern. In addition, since licensing requirements force this movement independently of Case or EPP considerations, it can be concluded that specifiers of IP are not A-positions and that Zuni weak pronoun movement is A′-movement.[23]

(27)

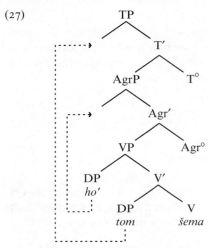

Thus the movement of the Zuni weak pronouns is governed by the same constraints responsible for the well-known contrast in (28) below (cf. Chomsky 1973; Hornstein 1995: 123). The sentence in (28*a*) indicates that the higher of two *wh*-words in English moves first, filling the only available specifier position. The lower of two *wh*-words cannot move into [Spec, CP] past the first *wh*-word that remains in situ, (28*b*).

(28) (*a*)   I wonder who bought what
    (*b*)   *I wonder what who bought

To summarize, it is argued that Zuni weak pronoun movement can be characterized syntactically as DP movement out of VP into the specifiers of functional projections of IP, and that the order of the pronouns is determined by a Shortest Move constraint on pronoun movement.[24]

3.4. *Strong and weak quantifiers*

The movement of Zuni 1st and 2nd person pronouns out of VP described in Section 2 can be accounted for by the licensing requirements of weak pronouns.

---

[23] And is distinct from the type of scrambling described by e.g. Mahajan (1990).
[24] The analysis argued for here supersedes that of Nichols (1997*a*).

Interestingly, quantifier movement out of VP, illustrated again below in (29*b*), can be explained in a similar fashion.

(29) (*a*) k^{w}a' ho'   k^{w}a'ał   picu:t 'ito-k'ya-nam-kya
  NEG. ISG.NOM. any(thing) pig   eat-CAUS.-NEG.-PAST
  'I didn't feed anything to the pigs.'
  [also: 'I didn't feed any pigs.']

(*b*) k^{w}a' k^{w}a'ał$_i$ ho' t_i picu:t 'ito-k'ya-nam-kya
  NEG. any(thing) ISG.NOM.   pig   eat-CAUS.-NEG.-PAST
  'I didn't feed anything to the pigs.'
  [*'I didn't feed any pigs.']

Quantifiers in Zuni also have two morphological shapes, shown in (30), a long form and a short form, which can fruitfully be assumed to be equivalent to the strong and weak forms of the personal pronouns.

(30) *Quantifiers*

Strong	k^{w}a'ałi	
Weak	k^{w}a'ał	'something, anything'
Strong	čo'ołi	
Weak	čo' oł	'someone, anyone'

The movement of *k^{w}a'ał* in (29*b*) can therefore be argued to be driven by the licensing requirements of a weak morphological element.[25] Evidence in support of this conclusion comes from the fact that another semantically quite similar quantifier *ko'* (something, anything (abstract)) does not have strong and weak forms and correspondingly is prohibited from moving to the front of the clause, (31).[26]

---

[25] To explain the form *k^{w}a'ał* in (29*a*) without movement, we must assume the final vowel -*i* of the strong form can be dropped. Note that there are identical strong/weak forms among the pronouns; compare e.g. *ho'no'* (IPL.ACC.[S]) and *ho'no'* (IPL.ACC.[W]).

[26] One remaining problem to overcome is the fact that determiners such as *'ussi* (that) and *lukkya* (this) can undergo dislocation to the front of the clause, so that a determiner may either remain in situ as in (i.*a*) or move out of VP to a position towards the front of the clause, as in (i.*b*). Note that the movement in (i.*b*) does not allow an interpretation of *'ussi* as 'that one'; cf. (i.*c*). While we could assume that the strong/weak forms of the determiners happen to be identical, this type of movement, particularly with the interpretation indicated for (i.*b*), appears to result in a violation of the Uniform Chain Condition, since presumably the dislocated D^0 must project to DP in order to move to an XP (i.e. specifier) position. Alternatively, we might assume this type of determiner movement is distinct from weak pronoun/quantifier movement and belongs instead with movement into the initial particle slot(s) (occupied e.g. by negative, aspectual, evidential, etc. particles).

(i) (*a*) Pablo 'ussi k'yak^{w}en 'aš-kya
  P.   that house make-PAST
  'Pablo built that house.'

(31) (*a*) to'-š   ko'   pe-ye-kkya
2SG.NOM.-Q something say-CONT.-PAST
'Did you say something?'

(*b*) ??*ko'$_i$ to'-š t_i pe-ye-kkya
something 2SG.NOM.-Q   say-CONT.-PAST

This morphological account of the behaviour of $k^wa'a\ell$ explains therefore why it is only some quantifiers, such as $k^wa'a\ell$ (some, any(thing)) and $čo'o\ell$ (some, any(one)), which undergo movement, while others such as *'emma* (many) and *hamme'* (some) on the other hand do not.

4. (MULTIPLE) *WH*-MOVEMENT

Here I will extend the proposals outlined above concerning the licensing of weak elements to an area of syntax not usually considered in these terms. I will suggest that certain aspects of Zuni *wh*-movement, involving movement to multiple specifiers, can be explained by the same licensing account that was argued to account for pronominal movement to single specifiers. As will be discussed in detail below, a striking feature of this account is the fact that it applies to two phenomena both of which obey superiority in movement to specifiers yet involve exactly opposite resulting words orders.

4.1. *The syntax of weak* wh-*words*

It was argued that the licensing requirement of pronominal features accounts for the obligatory movement of weak pronouns in Zuni. In addition to pronouns, *wh*-question words also appear to have strong and weak forms in Zuni. These are listed in Table 11.2

The distribution of Zuni *wh*-words is similar to that of the pronouns. Strong *wh*-words occur in syntactically deficient contexts such as single-word questions, (32), and as predicates, (33). The weak form of the *wh*-word cannot occur here.

(32) Nemme' tommiyo:-kya   čo-ppi?   / (*čo-p?)
N.   faint-PAST   who-Q.[s] / (who-Q.[w])
'Nemme fainted.'   'Who?'

(*b*)   'ussi$_i$ Pablo t_i k'yak^{w}en 'aš-kya
that P.   house   make-PAST
'Pablo built that house.'
[*'Pablo built that one, the house.']

(*c*)   'ussi Pablo 'aš-kya
that P.   make-PAST
'Pablo built that one.'

TABLE 11.2. *Strong and weak forms of some Zuni* wh-*words*

	Who	What[a]	What[b]	Where	When
Strong	čoppi	k^{w}appi	koppi	hoppi	kya:yippi
Weak	čop	k^{w}ap	kop	hop	kya:yip

    [a] Concrete reference, e.g. *k^{w}ap to' 'aše:'a* (What are you making?).
    [b] Abstract reference, e.g. *kop to' leye:'a* (What are you doing?).

(33)   'ussi čo-ppi   / (*čo-p)
            that who-Q.[s] / (who-Q.[w])
            'Who is that?'

Like strong pronouns, strong *wh*-words cannot occur as (uncoordinated) arguments of the clause, (34).[27]

(34)   *čo-ppi   tommiyo:-kya
            who-Q.[s] faint-PAST
            'Who fainted?'

Like weak pronouns, weak *wh*-words only occur as arguments of the clause. The account of morphologically weak forms developed above predicts that weak *wh*-words will obligatorily undergo *wh*-movement. As (35a, b) indicate, this prediction is borne out; (35c, d) indicate that the Zuni weak *wh*-word cannot remain in situ.

(35) (a) k^{w}a-p$_k$ to'$_j$ t_j t_k 'aše-:-'a
          what-Q.[w] 2SG.NOM.[w]   make-CONT.-PRES.
          'What are you making?'

     (b) k^{w}a'tikya-p$_k$ to'   Gilbert-ya' t_k 'ik'ošnan 'uk-kya
          which-Q.[w] 2SG.NOM.[w] G.-ACC.   toy   give-PAST
          'Which toy did you give to Gilbert?'

     (c) *to'   k^{w}a-p   'aše-:-'a
          2SG.NOM. what-Q.[w] make-CONT.-PRES.

     (d) *to'   Gilbert-ya' k^{w}a'tikya-p   'ik'ošnan 'uk-kya
          2SG.NOM. G.-ACC.   which-Q.[w] toy   give-PAST

We might further hypothesize that if licensing requirements force weak elements to move out of unlicensed positions, we should expect any and all weak interrogative elements present in a Zuni clause to undergo *wh*-movement. This second prediction is borne out: Zuni interrogative clauses are characterized by

---

[27] If the short forms of the *wh*-words were the result of phonological sandhi, we might expect the elided portion to be optionally restored in this context, but note that it is not.

obligatory multiple *wh*-movement. This is illustrated in (36), with the movement of *čop* (who), *čop-ya'* ((to) whom), and *kʷa'tikyap* (which).[28]

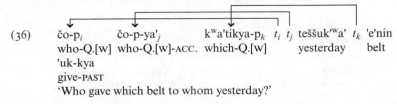

(36) čo-p$_i$ čo-p-ya'$_j$ kʷa'tikya-p$_k$ t_i t_j teššuk'ʷa' t_k 'e'nin
      who-Q.[w] who-Q.[w]-ACC. which-Q.[w]   yesterday   belt
      'uk-kya
      give-PAST
      'Who gave which belt to whom yesterday?'

The fact of multiple *wh*-movement in Zuni itself is noteworthy, and Zuni can be added to the small (mostly Slavic) group of languages that have been reported to display this phenomenon, including Bulgarian, Romanian, Russian, Serbo-Croatian, Polish, and Czech.

A property of Zuni multiple *wh*-movement is that the *wh*-words are strictly ordered; movement preserves the base c-command order. The examples in (37) illustrate that other orders are not possible in Zuni. In this basic respect multiple *wh*-movement in Zuni is like multiple *wh*-movement in Bulgarian (Rudin 1988; Boškovic 1995; Richards 1997) and unlike multiple *wh*-movement in Serbo-Croatian.[29]

(37) (*a*) *čo-p-ya'   čo-p   teššuk'ʷa' 'ansattu-kya
            who-Q.[w]-ACC. who-Q.[w] yesterday help-PAST
            'Who helped whom yesterday?'

     (*b*) *čo-p   kʷa'tikya-p čo-p-ya'   teššuk'ʷa' 'e'nin 'uk-kya
            who-Q.[w] which-Q.[w] who-Q.[w]-ACC. yesterday belt   give-PAST
            'Who gave which belt to whom yesterday?'

In addition, we can at least assume that Zuni weak *wh*-words together occupy the specifier of CP and therefore form an uninterruptable constituent, based on evidence that adverbs like *teššuk'ʷa'* (yesterday) cannot occur between *wh*-words, as (38) below indicates.

(38) ???čo-p   teššuk'ʷa' kʷa'tikya-p Gilbert-ya' 'ik'ošnan 'uk-kya
      who-Q.[w] yesterday   which-Q.[w] G.-ACC.   toy   give-PAST
      'Who gave which toy to Gilbert yesterday?'

[28] Note that Zuni *wh*-movement also creates discontinuous constituents, as in *kʷa'tikyap* . . . *'e'nin* (which . . . belt) in (36) and (i) below. Compare the discontinuous possessive constituents discussed earlier in Sect. 2 and the discontinuous D° + NP mentioned in fn. 26.

(i)   kwa'tikya-p$_k$ to' t_k 'e'nin 'ilopčo-kya
      which-Q.[w] 2SG.NOM.[w]   belt   borrow-PAST
      'Which belt did you borrow?'

[29] Although *wh*-movement in Zuni departs from Bulgarian *wh*-movement in details like the fact that the second and third *wh*-words in Zuni are always strictly ordered, cf. (37*b*), while in Bulgarian there is some freedom to their order (Richards 1997), and that *wh*-adjuncts occur outside *wh*-arguments in Zuni but not in Bulgarian.

We are suddenly presented with a problem, however, in the case of multiple movement of Zuni weak *wh*-words. If, as was argued in Section 3, a licensing requirement demands that a morphosyntactically weak element move in order to be (licensed) in the minimal domain of some functional head, then we might wonder how all of the several moved *wh*-words in Zuni might satisfy this requirement. While the structure in (39*a*), where *wh*-words are adjoined to each other in a single specifier as suggested by Rudin (1988) for Bulgarian, is problematic for other reasons, even the structure in (39*b*), where Zuni *wh*-words would occupy multiple specifiers of CP, would be problematic, since it would appear that only one of the Zuni weak *wh*-words, namely the closest, could be properly licensed by C° in this configuration.

(39) (*a*)　　　　　　　　　　(*b*)

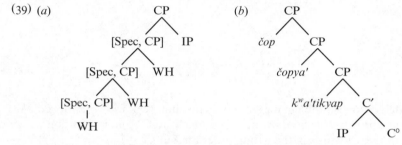

In the next section a solution to this problem will be suggested that has some attractive advantages. It will be argued that not only is there a derivation according to which all Zuni weak *wh*-words in a multiple question can be properly licensed, but that we can use the weak *wh*-licensing account as a source of independent evidence to confirm Richards's (1997) proposals concerning the derivation of multiple *wh*-questions in languages such as Bulgarian (and Zuni).

4.2. *Multiple specifiers, licensing, and the order of* wh-*words*

The problem presented is this: how do we derive the observed order in Zuni multiple *wh*-questions, illustrated in (40) below, and at the same time accommodate the licensing requirements of the weak *wh*-words?

(40)　čo-p　　čo-p-ya'　　kʷa'tikya-p　teššukʷa'　'e'nin　'uk-kya
　　　who-Q.[w]　who-Q.[w]-ACC.　which-Q.[w]　yesterday　belt　give-PAST
　　　'Who gave which belt to whom yesterday?'

The discussion of Bulgarian multiple *wh*-movement in Richards (1997)[30] is extremely helpful in formulating an account for Zuni, and I will draw heavily on suggestions made there in the following discussion. As Richards points out,

---

[30] Spec notation [$_{XP}$ [$_{XP}$ [$_{X'}$ X° follows Richards (1997: ch. 3) (not [$_{XP}$ [$_{X'}$ [$_{X'}$ X° of Chomsky 1995*b*).

under the version of cyclicity proposed in Chomsky (1993), movement will only expand the tree in a derivation. Assuming movement according to superiority, *wh*-words would move in a nested pattern as illustrated in (41).

(41)

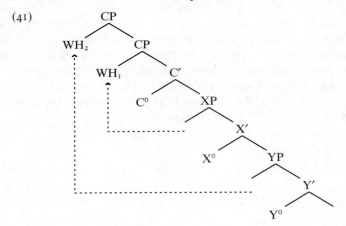

This derivation is problematic since only the first weak *wh*-word moved, WH$_1$, would be properly licensed by the functional head C$^\circ$, and in addition we wind up with the *wh*-words in the wrong order for Zuni.

Alternatively, we could expand the tree by considering a derivation in which superiority is violated (antisuperiority movement) and the lowest *wh*-word, WH$_2$, is moved first, and in this way derive the correct *wh*-order for Zuni. The derivation illustrated in (42) is, however, still accompanied by the problem that only the first moved weak *wh*-word (the lowest in this case) would be licensed by C$^\circ$. Thus we can rule out this as an impossible derivation given the licensing conditions on weak elements in Zuni and return to consider only superiority movement.

(42)

Richards (1997) argues that the version of cyclicity in Chomsky (1995*b*), in which a strong feature is checked as soon as it enters the derivation, allows a derivation like that in (43*a, b*) below, in which the highest *wh*-moves first (and checks a strong *wh*-feature), and then the next *wh*-word moves to a specifier position beneath the first one (and checks a strong *wh*-feature). Richards suggests that Shortest Move would even prefer the crossing movement derivation in (43) over the nested movement illustrated in (41) involving movement of a lower element to a higher specifier. In addition, the derivation in (43) would produce the desired word order in Zuni.

(43) (*a*)

```
            CP
          /    \
       WH₁      C′
        ⋮      /    \
        ⋮    C°      XP
        ⋮            /  \
        ⋯⋯⋯⋯⋯⋯⋯⋯⋯   X′
                    /  \
                  X°
```

(*b*)

```
                CP
              /    \
           WH₁      CP
            ⋮      /    \
            ⋮   WH₂      C′
            ⋮    ⋮      /    \
            ⋮    ⋮    C°      XP
            ⋮    ⋯⋯ (mov't 1) ⋯⋯    X′
            ⋮                      /  \
            ⋮                    X°    YP
            ⋯⋯ (mov't 2) ⋯⋯⋯⋯⋯⋯⋯⋯⋯⋯    Y′
                                       /  \
                                     Y°
```

There is in fact yet another reason to prefer the derivation in (43) involving a 'tucking in' *wh*-movement to a lower specifier position of CP: the movement illustrated in (43) will allow all of the weak *wh*-words in a Zuni multiple question to be properly licensed.[31] Assuming the licensing of weak elements involves a feature-checking operation rather than a constraint on representations, the derivation in (43) would allow that each Zuni weak *wh*-word will, at

---

[31] Note that I am assuming that *wh*-features are distinct from the licensing features for morphosyntactically weak elements.

the point it moves to [Spec, CP] to check off licensing features, be sufficiently close to C° to do so. This holds for the first Zuni *wh*-word to move, as in (43*a*), as well as for each subsequently moved *wh*-word, as in (43*b*).

4.3. Multiple vs. single specifiers: licensing weak wh-*words and weak pronouns*

The licensing of Zuni weak *wh*-words argued for just above and the licensing of weak 1st and 2nd person pronouns (and quantifiers) argued for earlier at first glance appear to involve two quite different operations, namely movement to multiple specifiers vs. movement to single specifiers, and in addition different surface word orders. That is, licensing multiple weak *wh*-words involves crossing movement to a single specifier that preserves base c-command relations, while licensing weak pronouns involves nested movement to several specifiers that inverts base c-command relations (cf. (27) earlier).

The newer version of cyclicity based on the derivational role of strong features that, in addition to Shortest Move, allows the derivation in (43) for Zuni predicts, however, that licensing will operate in both of these fashions. Licensing requirements force movement to single specifiers to be different from movement to multiple specifiers of a single head, since each weak element in the latter case must have access to that single head. Therefore weak pronoun movement each to a single specifier will expand the tree and invert base word order, while weak *wh*-words must each at some point in the derivation be in the minimal domain of C° and therefore each *wh*-word must 'tuck in' under each previously moved *wh*-word.

Finally, one important result of the account of Zuni *wh*-movement argued for here is that the licensing requirements of Zuni weak *wh*-words predicts that Zuni *wh*-movement *must* be to multiple specifiers of a single head, rather than adjoined to IP, as in for example Serbo-Croatian. The strict ordering of Zuni *wh*-words described in Section 4.1 then follows from this. We can therefore explain why Zuni has *wh*-movement to multiple specifiers of CP, rather than simply describe it, which should be the ultimate goal.

5. CONCLUSION

In this chapter I have presented new data from Zuni and argued that the movement of several different classes of elements out of the VP in Zuni into specifiers of IP or CP, namely pronouns, quantifiers, and *wh*-words, can be given a single account in terms of the licensing requirements of morphosyntactically weak elements. In addition, I have shown that Zuni can be added to the small class of languages displaying multiple *wh*-movement, and that multiple *wh*-movement in Zuni to multiple specifiers of CP is forced by the licensing requirements of weak *wh*-words.

The arguments presented here based on licensing provide independent support for the proposals made by Richards (1997) on the nature of multiple *wh*-movement in Bulgarian, involving the 'tucking in' of a *wh*-word to a specifier position below a previously moved *wh*-word. Finally, the licensing account of Zuni multiple *wh*-movement argued for here provides us with some evidence for choosing between derivational syntax and representational syntax, since the licensing requirements of Zuni weak *wh*-words can only be fulfilled derivationally and not as a constraint on representations.

REFERENCES

Bittner, M., and Hale, K. (1996*a*), 'The Structural Determination of Case and Agreement', *Linguistic Inquiry*, 27: 1–68.

——(1996*b*), 'Ergativity: Towards a Theory of a Heterogeneous Class', *Linguistic Inquiry*, 27: 531–604.

Bošković, Ž. (1995), 'Superiority Effects with Multiple Wh-Fronting in Serbo-Croatian', Ms., University of Connecticut.

Bunzel, R. (1933), *Zuni Texts*, Publication 15 of the American Ethnological Society (Franz Boas, series editor).

Cardinaletti, A., and Starke, M. (1994), 'The Typology of Structural Deficiency: On the Three Grammatical Classes', Ms., University of Venice and University of Geneva/Max Planck.

——(1996), 'Deficient Pronouns: A View from Germanic: A Study in the Unified Description of Germanic and Romance', in H. Thráinsson, S. Epstein, and S. Peter (eds.), *Studies in Comparative Germanic Syntax II*, Kluwer, Dordrecht, 21–65.

Chomsky, N. (1973), 'Conditions on Transformations', in S. Anderson and P. Kiparsky (eds.), *A Festschrift for Morris Halle*, Holt, Reinhart, & Winston, New York, 232–86.

——(1993), 'A Minimalist Program for Linguistic Theory', in K. Hale and S. Keyser (eds.), *The View from Building 20*, MIT Press, Cambridge, Mass., 1–52.

——(1995*a*), 'Bare Phrase Structure', in G. Webelhuth (ed.), *Government and Binding Theory and the Minimalist Program*, Blackwell, Cambridge, Mass., 383–439.

——(1995*b*), 'Categories and Transformations', in *The Minimalist Program*, MIT Press, Cambridge, Mass., 219–394.

Diesing, M., and Jelinek, E. (1993), 'The Syntax and Semantics of Object Shift', *Working Papers in Scandinavian Syntax*, 51: 1–54.

Everett, D. (1996), *Why There Are no Clitics: An Alternative Perspective on Pronominal Allomorphy*, Publication 123, Summer Institute of Linguistics, University of Texas, Arlington.

Holmberg, A. (1991), 'The Distribution of Scandinavian Weak Pronouns', in H. van Riemsdijk and L. Rizzi (eds.), *Clitics and Their Hosts*, EUROTYP Working Papers 8.1, European Science Foundation, Strasbourg, 155–74.

Hornstein, N. (1995), *Logical Form: From GB to Minimalism*, Blackwell, Cambridge, Mass.

Lamontagne, G., and Travis, L. (1987), 'The Syntax of Adjacency', in *Proceedings of the Sixth West Coast Conference on Formal Linguistics*, CSLI Publications, Stanford, Calif., 173–86.

Mahajan, A. (1990), 'The A/A-Bar Distinction and Movement Theory', Doctoral dissertation, MIT.

Mosel, U., and Hovdhaugen, E. (1992), *Samoan Reference Grammar*, Scandinavian University Press, Oslo.

Nichols, L. (1997*a*), 'Pronominal Movement and Logical Structure in Zuni', in Agbayani and Tan (eds.), *Proceedings of the Fifteenth West Coast Conference on Formal Linguistics*, CSLI Publications, Stanford, Calif., 369–80.

——(1997*b*), 'Topics in Zuni Syntax', Doctoral dissertation, Harvard University.

Richards, N. (1997), 'What Moves Where When in Which Language?', Doctoral dissertation, MIT.

Rudin, C. (1988), 'On Multiple Questions and Multiple WH Fronting', *Natural Language and Linguistic Theory*, 6: 445–501.

12

Wh-Movement, Licensing, and the Locality of Feature Checking

ANDREW SIMPSON

Chomsky (1995) suggests that the phenomenon of *movement* in language is a direct result of the existence of strict locality conditions on the licensing of dependencies referred to as feature-checking relations. If feature checking may only be effected when elements co-occur locally in Spec–head or head-adjoined configurations, then raising of a feature-bearing X^o/XP to a higher checking head will be necessary to establish such a relation. Where *overt* movement of an element with features to check is not attested, this Strict Locality Condition (SLC) forces one to assume that *covert* raising to a checking position must take place, resulting in a post-Spellout level of LF. The SLC thus in large part dictates the general architecture of the Minimalist model, with covert movement operations giving rise to a discrete syntactic level of LF and the further adoption of a global economy principle of Procrastinate, invoked to account for why covert/LF movement would always seem to be the preferred option for feature checking.

On the basis of evidence relating to *wh*-constructions in a range of languages, this chapter argues against assuming the SLC to be an invariant constraint on feature-checking relations, suggesting that feature checking is *not* in fact universally confined to any Spec–head/head-adjoined locality, that the checking domain relevant for the licensing of *wh*-features is actually subject to certain parametric variation, and that feature checking may often be effected without the need for any movement of an XP to the specifier position of its checking head. In the case of *wh*-phrases in particular, we argue that all such elements cross-linguistically carry (*wh*-)features in need of checking (contra the assumption in Chomsky (1995) that +interpretable features such as *wh* will only ever require checking when strong on a functional head); we then propose to account for the *wh*-paradigms observed in Iraqi Arabic/Hindi, English, and Romanian-type languages with the suggestion that the licensing/ checking domains for *wh*-elements in these languages have different values, very much in the spirit of Manzini and Wexler's (1987) treatment of variation in the locality constraining the relation of (NP) anaphors to their antecedents

Work for this chapter was supported by DFG grant no. GR 559/5-1.

across languages. The 'strict checking domain' of a head as defined in Chomsky (1995), although intended to be universally fixed across categories (and languages), is here suggested to correspond to just one possible selection of values for the choice of local checking domain—in fact that relevant for *wh*-licensing in Romanian-type languages. In other languages it is proposed that the *wh*-checking domain may be substantially larger, in Iraqi Arabic/Hindi essentially corresponding to the minimal tensed domain containing a +Q Comp, and in English being equivalent to an entire sentence headed by a +Q C.

The organization of the chapter is as follows. Sections 1 and 2 introduce and analyse a critical data-set relating to *wh*-questions from Iraqi Arabic and Hindi, arguing that the patterning observed is incompatible with the SLC, and attempt to establish that feature checking may occur within wider local domains. Section 3 provides additional theoretical arguments for such a claim stemming from a consideration of multiple *wh*-questions in English and various East European languages. Section 4 then addresses the issue of why there should be any *wh*-raising at all in English given the suggestion in Section 3 that the *wh*-checking domain is effectively the entire sentence in English, and also considers what explanation may be given for multiple *wh*-raising in Romanian, Bulgarian, etc. The chapter is closed in Section 5 with reflection on the general implications of proposals made here for other, non-*wh* feature-checking relations. On a broad theoretical level, it is indicated that if 'non-local' feature checking can indeed be shown to be potentially available and licensed with certain *wh*-dependencies, it may then be possible to suggest that other feature-checking relations in which no pre-Spellout movement is observed are similarly satisfied non-Spec–head-locally, ultimately leading to the possibility of a model of language without LF and the economy principle of Procrastinate.

I. IRAQI ARABIC

In Iraqi Arabic[1] (henceforth simply Iraqi) all *wh*-phrases may occur fully well formed in situ at PF both in matrix and embedded clauses, there being no requirement that a +Q Comp be filled by a *wh*-element prior to Spellout:

(1)   Mona shaafat *meno*?
       Mona saw   whom
       'Who did Mona see?'

(2)   Mona raadat [tijbir   Su'ad [tisa'ad *meno*]]?
       Mona wanted to-force Su'ad to-help who
       'Who did Mona want to force Su'ad to help?'

However, although example (2) is fine where the *wh*-phrase remains in situ in an embedded *non-finite* clause, a *wh*-phrase significantly may *not* occur in situ

---

[1] All Iraqi Arabic data here is taken from Wahba (1991) and Ouhalla (1994).

within an embedded *tensed* clause when relating to the +Q Comp of a higher CP:

(3)   *Mona   tsawwarat [$_{CP}$ Ali   istara   *sheno*]
        Mona   thought   Ali   bought what

The relevant generalization appears to be that a *wh*-phrase must occur in the 'tense domain' of a +Q Comp in order to be licensed, where a tense domain (TD) may be understood to consist of a tensed/+finite clause and any non-finite clauses dependent on the tensed clause. In (3) the bracketed CP constitutes the first TD including the *wh*-phrase *sheno*, but as this +finite CP does not contain a +Q Comp, the result is that the *wh*-element is not licensed. In (2), as the lower embedded clauses are all –finite, the first CP to count as a TD including the *wh*-phrase is actually the entire sentence, and as this may also potentially contain a +Q Comp the sentence is well formed.

Attempting to account for the ungrammaticality of (3) one might perhaps suggest it is ill formed because LF movement of the *wh*-phrase to the +Q Comp is blocked by the tensed CP, thus adopting the general line of approach to restrictions on the occurrence of *wh*-elements in situ put forward by Huang (1982) (and others). However, tensed CPs do not appear to constitute barriers to movement in Iraqi, and not only *can* the *wh*-phrase in (3) undergo raising to the matrix from the embedded tensed CP, but when it does do so overtly the result is a fully well-formed question:

(4)   *Sheno$_i$* tsawwarit Mona [Ali ishtara   *t$_i$*]?
        what   thought   Mona Ali bought
        'What did Mona think Ali bought?'

Given that overt pre-Spellout movement of the *wh*-phrase is licit in (4) and given the Minimalist assumption that computational principles and constraints upon them should be taken to apply in a uniform way throughout a derivation,[2] hypothetical LF movement of the *wh*-phrase in (3) should indeed be permitted, in the same way that pre-Spellout raising is licensed. A possibility more compatible with recent Minimalist developments may instead be to suggest that raising of the *wh*-phrase in (3) would not be blocked from occurring at LF but would then be occurring *too late* in derivational terms to save the structure from crashing; that some formal licensing property related to the *wh*-phrase critically requires satisfaction *prior* to Spellout and this may therefore not be achieved via *post*-Spellout raising (although such movement would not violate other syntactic principles). Following Chomsky (1995), if all operations of movement are triggered by a need to check morphological features, it can be

---

[2] Any suggestion that a principle/constraint apply only prior to or after Spellout (hence here that tense might block LF but not overt movement) effectively implies the existence of a level of S-structure relative to which constraints/principles might be stated, a result the Minimalist Programme is explicitly trying to avoid.

suggested that while *overt* raising of the *wh*-phrase in (4) results in successful checking of certain *wh*-features prior to Spellout, the ungrammaticality of (3) is due to a failure to check *wh*-features by this derivational point.

Assuming such an approach, the paradigm in (1–4) leads to the further conclusion that it is *wh*-features carried by *wh*-phrases themselves which are here in need of licensing and not any assumed present on the +Q C°. Were the latter to contain strong *wh*-operator features, then overt *wh*-raising should clearly *always* have to take place as in English, yet examples such as (1) and (2) are noted to be fully well formed without any pre-Spellout movement. *Wh*-movement in Iraqi instead seems to relate directly to the *wh*-phrase itself and its position relative to the +Q Comp, being triggered only when the former occurs in a domain which is opaque for licensing. If movement may again be assumed to take place only for the satisfaction of feature-checking requirements, this clearly indicates that *wh*-features carried by the *wh*-phrase itself must be checked by the (obligatory) raising in (4). Such a conclusion would then seem to constitute strong evidence against the suggestion in Chomsky (1995) that +interpretable features (such as *wh*) will only require checking when strong and present on a functional head—here it is seen that the relevant functional head C° cannot be argued to carry any strong (operator) features and it is crucially for the licensing of a *wh-phrase* (and checking of *wh*-features carried by it) that movement is necessitated. Consequently *wh* (and possibly other so-called +interpretable features) may be taken to be a feature specification just as much in need of checking on the *XPs* which carry it as (for example) the –interpretable *case* features present on DPs.

A second conclusion to result from a consideration of examples (1–4) concerns the *locality* of feature checking. Chomsky (1995) suggests that feature checking is a relation which may only be effected within the 'strict locality' of Spec–head and head-adjoined configurations (the SLC), this property always requiring movement of an element to its checking head. However, the patterning of *wh*-phrases and movement in Iraqi as illustrated in sentences (1–4) provides evidence that such a claim cannot in fact be (universally) correct, and that feature checking must also be possible 'long distance' within wider domains.

To briefly recap what (1–4) have been taken to suggest: the *movement* of *wh*-phrases in IA as in (4) can only be assumed to take place for checking of (*wh*-) features, and will save illicit structures such as (3) from crashing; the relevant features which are checked by movement of a *wh*-phrase are *wh*-features on the *wh*-phrase itself and not any strong operator features on Comp, otherwise *wh*-raising to Comp would have to take place in *all* *wh*-questions (but this is not so—(1, 2)). Checking of *wh*-features on *wh*-phrases must furthermore take place *prior* to Spellout—hypothetical LF movement of *wh*-phrases in unacceptable examples like (3), though not blocked syntactically, would come too late in the derivation to satisfy licensing of the *wh*-phrase, and indeed is forced to occur overtly, as in (4). Now critically, although it is concluded that *wh*-features carried by *wh*-phrases *must* be checked prior to Spellout, raising to Comp is *not* forced to take place where a *wh*-phrase occurs base-generated in the tense domain of the +Q Comp (1, 2), and a *wh*-question is fully acceptable when the *wh*-phrase remains fully in situ. As such *wh*-elements must, however, be assumed to carry *wh*-features in need of pre-Spellout checking in the same way that *wh*-phrases base-generated in embedded tensed CPs do, it can only be concluded that these features are checked prior to Spellout on the *wh*-phrases in their *in situ positions*. Clearly not being in the specifier of the checking head (C°) at the point at which *wh*-checking must be effected, it therefore must be conceded that feature checking is *not* in fact always subject to the SLC and may at least in certain instances also take place within larger domains.[3]

Although *wh*-feature checking in Iraqi is thus (by hypothesis) not bound to be strictly Spec–head local, it nevertheless is still constrained by some notion of locality defined relative to tense—a *wh*-phrase will only be licensed in the immediate TD of the +Q Comp. In addition to this finiteness restriction, there are in fact also certain other locality restrictions which appear to correspond more closely to familiar constraints on applications of movement. As illustrated in examples (5) and (6), *wh*-phrases may not occur in situ either in relative clauses or in *wh*-islands with scope higher than the +Q Comp of the *wh*-island itself.

(5)   *Mona 'urfit [il-bint$_i$ [illi$_i$ t_i ishtarat *sheno*]]
        Mona knew   the-girl   who   bought   what

(6)   Mona nasat [*li-meno*   tinti   *sheno*]
        Mona forgot to-whom   to-give   what
        Not: 'What did Mona forget whom to give to?'
        Only: 'Mona forgot what she should give to whom.'

---

[3] Noting it is not possible to suggest that any 'empty *wh*-operator' raises to Comp from the in situ *wh*-phrases, as Watanabe (1991) proposes is the case in Japanese; if this were to be so, then it should also be possible for such an empty operator to raise to the +Q Comp from *wh*-phrases occurring in embedded tensed CPs and examples like (3) would incorrectly be predicted to be well formed. Furthermore, such empty operator analyses have basically been proposed and seem appropriate for languages in which the phonetically overt core of elements functioning as *wh*-question words is quantificationally underspecified and may be interpreted in various ways depending on the type of operator present (see e.g. Nishigauchi 1990 on Japanese; Cheng 1991 on Chinese). As *wh*-elements in Iraqi (and Hindi) are unambiguously *wh*-question words, they would not seem obvious candidates for any similar null operator proposal. Finally, where it is indeed possible to compare movement of null operators and phonetically overt elements containing (or equivalent to) such operators *within a single construction type*—as in Japanese *wh*-questions where a null operator or the phonetically overt core + operator may move (see Simpson 1995), or relative clauses in English where the relative pronoun may be either phonetically null or overt—there would not seem to be any difference in the locality constraints on such movement, i.e. movement of the null operator is not more restricted than that of the overt element. Consequently there is no reason to expect that raising of any null operator from a tensed CP in Iraqi should be more constrained than movement of an overt XP.

As such constituents are indeed islands for syntactic extraction, it might then be suggested that an LF movement analysis of in situ *wh*-phrases should in fact be pursued, despite the above-given argumentation to the contrary. In what follows, however, it will be argued that the observed island-sensitivity ultimately does not constitute evidence in favour of an LF movement approach and instead may actually be shown to support the alternative suggestions put forward here.

Ouhalla (1994) has noted that if the *wh*-elements in (5) and (6) are overtly extracted from their containing island environments, the resulting questions are markedly less unacceptable than when the *wh*-phrases remain in situ inside the islands:

(7)   ??*Sheno$_i$* nasat   Mona [*li-meno*   tinti t_i]?
        what   forgot Mona to-whom to-give
        'What did Mona forget to whom to give?'

(8)   ??*Sheno$_i$* 'urfut Mona [ilbint   illi   ishtarat t_i]?
        what   knew   Mona the-girl who   bought
        'What did Mona know the girl who bought?'

Whereas (5) and (6) are both completely unacceptable and unintelligible as questions, Ouhalla suggests the improved acceptability of (7) and (8) is typically that of regular subjacency violations, resulting (simply) from the illicit extraction of an element from within an island configuration. Given that (5) and (6) are significantly worse, it must therefore be concluded they are violating some constraint *other* than subjacency.[4] If one assumes that the licensing of *wh*-phrases (checking of *wh*-features) is in some way critical for their interpretation, and further adopts suggestions made above as to how and at what derivational point such licensing/checking must occur, the difference in acceptability between (5, 6) and (7, 8) may actually be predicted—in the latter the *wh*-phrases move to a +Q Comp by Spellout and so are successfully checked by this point, their interpretation as interrogative *wh*-phrases being licensed; in achieving this, however, a pure constraint on movement is violated (subjacency), resulting in the reduced acceptability judgements. In (5) and (6) by way of contrast, the *wh*-phrases do not appear in a domain where their *wh*-features can be checked by Spellout and so the structures will automatically crash, the *wh*-elements not being licensed as *wh*-phrases and hence not allowing for any coherent interpretation. In this sense it can be suggested that sentences

----

[4] Indeed, if the well-formedness requirement on *wh*-phrases were just to be that they occur raised in a +Q Comp by LF, one might expect that (5, 6) should perhaps be less unacceptable than (7, 8), or even fully grammatical, given that LF movement of the *wh*-phrase might be able to proceed in a way different from that in (7, 8), where straight and direct extraction from an island environment has occurred. For example, LF raising might be able to make use of island-pied-piping operations, as suggested by Nishigauchi (1990), or of the QR-dependent extraction mechanism outlined by Fiengo *et al*. (1988). That (5) and (6) are actually worse than (7) and (8), then, strongly indicates that some property of the sentences must crucially be satisfied before Spellout.

such as (5) and (6) are like other instances where morphological features fail to be checked by a certain derivational point and this results in unintelligibility, as for example in (9) and (10), where D-features in $T°$ remain unchecked at Spellout. Although no locality conditions would block the subject DPs from raising at LF, this would simply come too late to check the strong features in $T°$.

(9)   *Not John come

(10)   *Did not John come   (intended to be a statement)

Thus although the unacceptability of *wh*-phrases in situ in certain extraction islands might initially prompt one to an LF movement approach, there are good reasons for assuming that LF *wh*-movement does *not* in fact take place— both the contrasts between (5, 6) and (7, 8) and the unacceptability of *wh*-phrases in situ in non-island embedded tensed CPs. If this is the case, then the ungrammaticality of (5, 6), with *wh*-elements in situ in *wh*- and complex NP islands, cannot be accounted for in terms of constraints on movement, and it must be conceded that there may also exist island-like locality constraints on purely *non-movement* (licensing) relations—a claim which has, however, previously been argued for by Cinque (1991) (relative to the island-sensitivity of Clitic Left Dislocation structures in Italian) and Bresnan (1976) (on comparative deletion), and hence one that is not without independent support.

Finally a brief consideration of *multiple wh*-questions can be shown to offer additional and fairly conclusive evidence that it is indeed (*wh*-features on) *wh*-phrases themselves which are critically in need of checking in Iraqi and that *all* *wh*-elements may be assumed to carry such a feature-checking requirement. As (11) and (12) show, although multiple *wh*-questions are permitted in Iraqi, the distribution of 'secondary' *wh*-phrases is not free and may directly result in a *wh*-question being unacceptable.

(11)   *Sheno$_i$* ishtara Ali t_i [minshaan   yenti *li-meno*]?
        what   bought Ali   in-order-to give to-whom
        'What did Ali buy to give to whom?'

(12)   **Meno* tsawwar [Ali xaraj weyya *meno*]?
        who   thought Ali left   with *whom*

In (11) both *wh*-phrases are straightforwardly licensed by occurring in the same TD as the +Q Comp (the lower CP being –finite). As the higher *wh*-phrase in (12) will also be checked quite regularly in virtue of its position in the TD of the +Q Comp, the unacceptability of the sentence can only be ascribed to the presence of the second *wh*-phrase *meno* (whom) in the embedded +*finite* CP, indicating that secondary *wh*-phrases are constrained by precisely the same factors as 'primary' *wh*-phrases and may not occur in embedded tensed CPs where the licensing +Q Comp is in a higher TD. Consequently it must be assumed both that every *wh*-phrase present in a *wh*-question carries (*wh*-) features in need of licensing, and furthermore that all such *wh*-features must be checked by the *same* derivational point, namely Spellout; if this were not the case, then the lower *wh*-phrase in (12) should indeed be able to raise up to the +Q Comp and check its features at LF (there being no barrier to such movement), yet the sentence is fully ungrammatical.

Having thus argued here that strict specifier–head locality would not appear to constitute a universal constraint on feature-checking relations on the basis of data in Iraqi (and that *wh* is a feature in need of checking on *wh*-phrases rather than just on a +Q Comp), we now turn to Hindi and show that evidence of a parallel kind may also be found in other languages, strengthening and supporting this conclusion.

2. HINDI

In Hindi,[5] just as in Iraqi Arabic, all *wh*-phrases may occur in situ at PF and there is no requirement that a +*wh*+Q Comp be filled by any *wh*-item prior to Spellout:

(13)   Raam-ne [Mohan-ko *kise*   dekhne ke liye] kahaa?
       Ram-ERG Mohan-ERG whom to see for   told
       'Who did Ram tell Mohan to look at?'

However, whereas *wh*-phrases may occur in situ in embedded *non-finite* CPs, as per (13) above, they may not do so in equivalent *tensed* clauses:[6]

(14)   *Raam-ne kahaa [ki   kOn aayaa hE]?
        Ram-ERG said   that who has come

Such tensed CPs nevertheless are not islands for extraction, and as with Iraqi, not only may a *wh*-phrase undergo overt raising from a tensed clause, but when this occurs in examples like (14) the result is a perfectly acceptable question form:

(15)   *kOn*$_i$ Raam-ne kahaa ki t_i aayaa hE
       who   Ram-ERG said   that   has come
       'Who did Ram say has come?'

Therefore, as with Iraqi, one is forced to assume that although *LF* raising to the +Q Comp should be possible, such hypothetical raising would simply occur *too late* in (14) to satisfy certain properties of the *wh*-question. As pre-Spellout *movement* of the *wh*-phrase will save (14) from otherwise being unacceptable, and as a +Q C° in Hindi does not always require a *wh*-element in

---

[5] The Hindi data here is taken from Mahajan (1990).

[6] Unless there is a *'kyaa'* question-particle in the superordinate clause—such an alternate question-formation strategy occurring in Iraqi too (see Mahajan 1990; Wahba 1991; Simpson 1995 for some discussion).

its specifier position (and hence cannot be taken to be generated with strong *wh*-operator features), it can again only be concluded that *wh*-raising in (15) takes place to check *wh*-features carried by the *wh*-phrase itself prior to Spell-out. If *wh*-phrases in Hindi must therefore be feature-checked by Spellout, where other *wh*-phrases are seen to occur licitly in situ (as in (13)), these *wh*-phrases must be assumed to be licensed and feature-checked in their in situ positions and consequently not in any strict Spec–head relation with the checking head C°. Feature checking is then once more attested to be possible 'long distance', though again constrained by tense factors and blocked where a *wh*-phrase occurs in situ in a TD which does not contain the +Q Comp (14).

We also find evidence in Hindi similar to that presented in Iraqi Arabic that *all wh*-elements require licensing by Spellout:

> (16)   *kOn_i Raam-ne kahaa ki t_i *kis-ko* maaregaa
>   who Ram-ERG say   that t_i who   will hit

In (16) raising to the matrix will effectively license the first *wh*-phrase *kon* (who), but the second *wh*-phrase *kis-ko* (whom) also apparently requires licensing by Spellout, which is not possible here as it remains inside a non-interrogative tensed clause at Spellout. Movement of this *wh*-phrase out of the tensed CP results in a well-formed question if it takes place *overtly*, as illustrated in (17) below.

> (17) kOn_i *kis-ko*$_j$ Raam-ne kahaa ki t_i t_j maaregaa
>   who whom Ram-ERG say   that   will hit
>   'Who did Ram say will hit who?'

Finally it can also be shown that the raising of a *wh*-phrase from an embedded tensed CP to the clause containing the licensing +Q C° need not necessarily target the specifier of the +Q Comp, but significantly may land the *wh*-phrase in other positions too—in (18) the *wh*-phrase has been raised from the lower clause to a position following the subject in [Spec, TP].

> (18)   Raam-ne *kon*$_i$ kahaa ki t_i aayaa he?
>   Ram-ERG who said   that   has come
>   'Who did Ram say has come?'

It has been suggested above that *wh*-phrases in Iraqi and Hindi must simply occur in some position in the TD of a +Q Comp in order to be licensed, hence that the *wh*-checking domain of a +Q Comp in these languages effectively is its containing TD. Where a *wh*-phrase is base-generated in such a domain, no movement will be necessary as the *wh*-phrase may have its *wh*-features checked in its in situ position; however, when such an element originates in a lower tensed CP, it will be forced to undergo raising to the TD of the +Q Comp in order to check its *wh*-features prior to Spellout. Given the contention that these *wh*-features may be checked in any position within the TD of the +Q C°, one might expect that raising to other potential landing-sites in this domain and not just [Spec, CP] should result in a well-formed *wh*-question. That this expectation is indeed borne out and examples such as (18) are found to be acceptable, then, adds support to the proposal that the critical *wh*-checking domain here is in fact the entire containing TD of a +Q Comp and not just its specifier position.[7]

3. MULTIPLE *WH*-QUESTIONS IN EASTERN EUROPEAN AND ENGLISH-TYPE LANGUAGES

Data presented in Sections 1 and 2 have been argued to indicate that *wh*-features are both present and in need of checking on *all wh*-phrases in Iraqi and Hindi, contra the suggestion of Chomsky (1995) that +interpretable features such as *wh* will only ever require checking on a functional head when the +interpretable features are strong. This claim is further borne out by evidence from various languages of Eastern Europe, such as Romanian and Bulgarian (see Rudin 1988; Grewendorf, Chapter 8, this volume), where it is noted that *all wh*-phrases present in multiple *wh*-questions undergo obligatory pre-Spellout raising:

(19)   Koj kogo vizda?   (Bulgarian)
        who whom sees
        'Who sees whom?'

(20)   Ko koga vidi?   (Serbo-Croatian)
        who whom see
        'Who sees whom?'

On the basis of this convergence of evidence one may therefore suggest that *wh* is a feature which is *cross-linguistically* present and in need of checking on all

---

[7] In certain respects, the approach put forward here thus likens feature-checking operations more to (non-movement) analyses of the licensing of NPIs, anaphors (Manzini and Wexler 1987; Progovac 1991), and *wh*-indefinites in Chinese (Li 1992), in the sense that while an element to be licensed must indeed occur in some local relation to its licenser, this locality need not be that of a Spec–head configuration and simple occurrence in any position within the relevant locality/domain will indeed be sufficient for licensing. Feature checking may, however, still be taken to be essentially distinct from these more general instances of licensing in virtue of four important properties. First, feature-checking operations invariably involve the matching of a parallel feature specification shared by both licenser and licensee; this is not the case in NPI or *wh*-indefinite licensing, where licensing elements may be varied and numerous in type and may not seem to share any obvious common property with their licensees. Secondly, while feature-checking heads would seem to require the presence of an element with matching features to license, the licensers of anaphors, NPIs, and *wh*-indefinites do not require the necessary presence of any of the latter. Thirdly, feature-checking requirements may trigger *movement* of an element to its licensing domain, whereas *wh*-indefinites and true NPIs would not seem to have this ability to raise to an appropriate domain for licensing. Finally, morphological features may in certain instances critically require licensing 'mid-way' in a derivation and prior to Spellout, whereas elements such as NPIs, anaphors, and *wh*-indefinites only ever seem to need to be in a licensing configuration actually at LF and not before this point.

wh-phrases, in the same way that case features are assumed to be present and in need of licensing on argument DPs in all languages. That is, just as the observation of morphologically overt DP case and DP raising in a subset of languages has led to the assumption that DPs in all languages carry case features to be checked by some functional head, so the same logic of reasoning in conjunction with the data observed above may naturally lead one to conclude that *wh*-phrases in all languages require checking of their *wh*-features.

This now calls for a re-examination of 'mixed' (*wh*-)raising and in situ languages such as English, where only a single 'primary' *wh*-phrase in multiple *wh*-questions raises to the +Q Comp prior to Spellout and all other 'secondary' *wh*-phrases remain in situ:

(21)   *Who_i* did John give t_i *what*?

If one now assumes that not only primary but also secondary *wh*-phrases require *wh*-feature checking by a +Q Comp, and *if* it were assumed that feature-checking relations might only be effected within Spec–head/head-adjoined configurations, then as secondary *wh*-phrases in English do not appear raised to [Spec, CP] *prior* to Spellout, one would have to propose that such elements undergo covert raising to the +Q Comp in order to comply with the SLC at LF. However, there are good reasons to believe that in situ *wh*-phrases in English do *not* in fact undergo any such raising; in particular, the well-formed occurrence of *wh*-phrases in situ in extraction islands (Fiengo *et al.* 1988), the inability of *wh*-in-situ phrases to license parasitic gaps and antecedent-contained deletion (Stroik 1992), contrasts in the binding possibilities open to anaphors in raised and in situ *wh*-phrases (Brody 1995), and a variety of other evidence reviewed by Simpson (1995) can all be argued to provide strong indication that such elements do not occur raised to the licensing +Q Comp at *any* point in the derivation. Assuming this to be so, the conclusion which automatically follows is therefore essentially the same as made earlier regarding *wh*-feature checking in Iraqi and Hindi: (secondary) *wh*-phrases in English will be feature-checked by a +Q Comp in their *in situ* positions, and so, as with *wh*-phrases in Iraqi and Hindi, *not* necessarily within the strict Spec–head locality argued for in Chomsky (1995) but potentially 'long distance' within significantly wider domains.[8]

---

[8] Here both the chain of reasoning and the general ensuing analysis of a parameterized *wh*-checking domain (developed further below) closely resemble Progovac's (1991) treatment of anaphors in Chinese. Noting that the simplex anaphor *ziji* (self) may licitly occur in relative clauses relating to an antecedent exterior to the island, Progovac rejects any LF head movement analysis of the anaphor to a higher Infl node and instead suggests that anaphors of all types are simply bound in their PF in situ positions. Differences in the localities relating simplex and complex anaphors to their antecedents are then argued to result not from (LF) movement of the former, but from the binding domains of the former and the latter having different values. Here it will be suggested that differences in the distribution of *wh*-elements across languages relate to cross-linguistic variation in the locality of *wh*-checking domains.

4. MOTIVATION FOR *WH*-MOVEMENT

Such a conclusion now raises a problem of a different sort. If (secondary) *wh*-phrases in multiple *wh*-questions in English may be feature-checked in their in situ positions, one seems to be left without an explanation for why overt raising of a single primary *wh*-phrase *must* take place in English. That is, if licensing in situ is potentially available, then why should any *wh*-phrase have to raise to Comp? One might perhaps attempt to suggest that overt raising of a primary *wh*-phrase does not in fact take place to check *wh*-features on the *wh*-phrase, but to check strong operator features on the +Q Comp, much as Chomsky (1995) proposes. However, if it is possible for a *wh*-checking relation to be established between a +Q Comp and a *wh*-phrase fully in situ to check *wh*-features on the latter (as argued here), there might not be any obvious reason why such a 'long-distance' relation should not also allow reciprocal checking of *wh*-operator features on the former, so some other kind of explanation would seem to be required.

A relevant description of the patterning observed may be said to be that once a single *wh*-phrase has been raised to a +Q Comp then all *wh*-phrases are licensed, viz.:

(22)   *Did John give what to who?

(23)   What did John give to who?

I would like to suggest that this movement is necessary in order to 'trigger' C^o as an appropriate licenser for (all) *wh*-elements present, that C^o is critically ambiguous prior to *wh*-movement in ranging over a variety of potential values—focus, +*wh*+Q, yes/no+Q, etc.—and that *wh*-movement into Spec of C^o will function to disambiguate C^o, activating it as a licenser for (specifically) *wh*-type elements.

The specifier position raised to by the *wh*-phrase is thus posited to be that of a general polarity-oriented head, much as suggested by Culicover (1992), hosting a variety of elements other than *wh*-phrases; for example:

(24)   *That film* I really didn't like

(25)   *Not only Hastings* will I banish, I shall also exile Lord Smythe

(26)   *So upset* was she that she broke down and cried

Prior to any raising, C^o may be taken to be crucially underdetermined with respect to its precise 'polarity' setting, so that movement of an element of a certain type into [Spec, CP] will be necessary to disambiguate its licensing value. Once disambiguated and triggered in a particular way, the C^o will then be able to function as a licenser for *all* elements of the relevant type, whether such an element has been raised to its Spec or occurs in situ in its licensing domain.

In a certain way the above proposal may reflect a general idea put forward by Cheng (1991) that *wh*-movement occurs to 'type' a clause as +*wh*, though here the ultimate motivation for such movement is seen to be a formal morphological requirement on *wh-phrases* themselves that they be licensed by Spellout, rather than movement satisfying a constraint on *CPs* that they be identified as (+*wh*) interrogative. Following on from this, adapting and making use of another suggestion in Cheng, it can be argued that in some languages C^{o} is *not* ambiguous in nature, or rather that there exists an alternative way to disambiguate it, via the direct insertion of question particles, such as *ne* in Mandarin Chinese. If C^{o} can be disambiguated and triggered in this way, then no raising of *wh*-elements need take place and all *wh*-phrases may remain and be licensed in situ, providing they occur within the licensing domain of the C^{o}.[9]

Given this analysis of *wh*-raising in English, further explanation is now required of languages such as Romanian and Bulgarian where *all* *wh*-phrases in multiple *wh*-questions undergo raising to Comp. Clearly as only one of these should need to appear in the +Q Comp for triggering purposes if C is ambiguous, raising of the others would seem redundant, and therefore should not take place. Here I would like to propose that movement is actually forced to take place as a direct result of the locality of the *wh*-checking domain being more restricted in these languages. In Sections 1–3 of this chapter the essential thrust of argumentation has been an attempt to establish that feature-checking relations are ultimately not subject to any universal Spec–head/head-adjoined locality condition and to suggest that the checking domain of a functional head may in fact be subject to certain parametric variation across languages. This approach towards the locality of feature checking is in essence similar to Manzini and Wexler's (1987) treatment of Binding Theory locality, where it is suggested that the local domain relevant for the licensing of anaphors may be subject to different parametric settings across languages, and that an anaphor must simply occur c-commanded by its licenser somewhere within the relevant local domain in order to be successfully licensed. Here the proposal is that a *wh*-element must similarly occur in some parameterized local domain m-commanded by a potential licenser (a +*wh* Comp) in order for its (*wh*-)features to be checked. In one respect such suggestions are simply an extension of the general idea formalized by Chomsky (1995) that elements with features to be matched and checked against each other must co-occur locally; however, whereas Chomsky assumes a critical and invariant notion of locality constraining all feature-checking relations, the present account suggests that the notion of locality may be subject to variation and hence in certain instances correspond to broader domains than Chomsky's strict checking domain. In the case of English, the *wh*-checking domain is suggested to be equivalent to

---

[9] This I assume is the case in Iraqi and Hindi, i.e. that there is a (phonetically null) +*wh*+Q morpheme inserted into C^{o}, and so raising *to trigger* C^{o} need not occur.

the sentence as a unit, in Iraqi/Hindi it is the first TD immediately containing a +*wh* Comp.

Returning to Romanian and Bulgarian, it can now be suggested that the obligatory raising of all *wh*-phrases to Comp is simply a reflection of a narrower parametric setting of the *wh*-checking domain, in fact corresponding to Chomsky's strict checking domain, including [Spec, CP] and C-adjoined positions. Consequently all *wh*-phrases will be forced to raise to the +Q Comp, either targeting multiple specifier positions (as for example may be projected for multiple nominative subjects in Japanese; see Doron and Heycock, Chapter 4, this volume) or possibly via some kind of '*wh*-cluster' movement to a single Spec of C (as suggested by Grewendorf, Chapter 8, this volume). Multiple *wh*-raising in Romanian and Bulgarian is then basically suggested to be entirely parallel to instances in Iraqi and Hindi where a *wh*-phrase is forced to raise from a lower tensed clause to the TD of a +Q Comp—in both cases *wh*-movement must bring a *wh*-phrase into the relevant parameterized *wh*-checking domain of Comp.

5. FURTHER ISSUES

If the idea of a parametrically set (*wh*-)checking domain is indeed adopted, further questions immediately arise concerning feature-checking relations in non-*wh* dependencies. Essentially one needs to ask how the suggestion that *wh*-features need not necessarily be checked within strictly local Spec–head configurations may be squared with the common assumption that the checking of case, agreement, and other features is in fact always subject to the strict locality proposed in Chomsky (1995). Here I suggest that two basic positions may be adopted, outlined in brief below.

The first and perhaps stronger position, explored in greater detail in Simpson (1995), is to argue that 'non-local' (i.e. non-Spec–head/head-adjoined) feature checking may indeed occur in other non-*wh* relations. If data and argumentation relating to one dependency type lead one to assume that certain elements may be feature-checked in their base-generated positions without any raising to a functional head, it may be suggested that in other instances too where no overt movement is observed to take place—as for example with argument DPs and inflected verbs in various languages—these elements are similarly feature-checked 'non-locally' in their PF in situ positions and without LF raising. Such a hypothesis would then allow one further to suggest that there may actually be no movement of any elements after the point of Spellout, and hence that Spellout might be taken to be fully isomorphic with LF, the structures created by such a point being the essential syntactic input forms to interpretation (the effects of QR might then be ascribed to purely semantic operations, e.g. Cooper Storage). An additional consequence of such a proposal would be that the economy principle of Procrastinate would no longer need to be assumed as a constraint on derivations (as there would in fact be no 'preference' for LF movement to account for). Although clear evidence indicating that DPs/verbs do not raise further from their PF positions is perhaps not so easy to find, certain scopal interactions between subject DPs and modals in expletive structures commented on by Brody (1995) do seem to indicate that the former are not subject to LF raising:

(27)   Many people must have arrived

(28)   There must have arrived many people

The fact that *must* obligatorily has higher scope than *many people* in (28) while in (27) either element may have scope over the other suggests that the subject in (28) does not raise to the expletive at LF, as otherwise the scopal ambiguity present in (28) would be expected. Consequently one might assume that the subject's DP features are checked in situ and that 'non-local' feature checking is attested in other non-*wh* constructions.

A second general possibility, potentially more easy to accommodate in the current Minimalist model, may be to posit that locality constraints on the licensing of features on *XP*s may be different from those constraining the checking of X^o features, and so admit a certain asymmetry in the set of feature-licensing relations previously considered to be fully uniform in nature. Although we have argued here that the checking of *wh*-features carried by *wh*-phrases need not always require the *wh*-phrase to occur in the specifier of the checking head C^o, we nevertheless have still (tacitly) acknowledged a role for the Spec–head relation within checking theory; namely where a functional head X^o requires what we have described as 'triggering' before it may check features of a particular type, this has been taken to require raising of a relevant element to Spec of X^o to determine it as a legitimate licensing head. If such movement were now in fact to be reinterpreted back along the lines of Chomsky (1995) as triggered by a need to check features on a functional head, and given that the core cases taken to motivate 'non-local' checking have been instances where features on XPs but not on the checking head required licensing (i.e. Iraqi and Hindi, where *wh*-phrases but not the +Q C^o were argued to have checking requirements), then it may be possible to suggest the following: where X^o features on a functional head require checking, this will indeed require strict Spec–head/head-adjoined locality, but where a feature-checking requirement relates to features on an XP, such features may be checked within a locality permitting certain variation across languages (and the SLC will not automatically apply). Earlier, in our discussion of English, the possibility of entertaining a difference in the localities constraining checking of XP and X^o features was essentially discounted and an alternative explanation in terms of 'activation' of a licensing head was explored; however, if such an asymmetry is in fact conceded, then it may be possible to maintain intact previous assumptions that checking of case, agreement, and verb-inflectional features is subject to 'strict locality' with the suggestion that this checking is in all cases directly triggered by requirements of the functional heads.

Whichever approach is ultimately pursued, the underlying claim of this chapter remains, namely that despite attempts in the Minimalist Programme to identify a unique type of licensing relation (feature checking) as being necessarily restricted by a universal notion of locality defined over specifier–head and head-adjoined configurations—this being the reflection of a wider drive to reduce all linguistic relations to a highly local nature—there are in fact dependencies of this general type which do not conform to such strict locality, prompting one to conclude both that 'non-local' structural relations are fully present in natural language and that the specifier–head configuration is perhaps not as critical in the licensing of maximal projections as has often been suggested in recent research.

REFERENCES

Bresnan, J. (1976), 'Evidence for a Theory of Unbounded Transformations', *Linguistic Analysis*, 2(4): 353–93.

Brody, M. (1995), *Lexico-Logical Form*, MIT Press, Cambridge, Mass.

Cheng, L. (1991), 'On the Typology of WH-questions', Ph.D. thesis, MIT.

Chomsky, N. (1993). 'A Minimalist Program for Linguistic Theory', *MIT Occasional Papers in Linguistics*, 1.

——(1995), *The Minimalist Program*, MIT Press, Cambridge, Mass.

Cinque, G. (1991), *Types of A-Dependencies*, MIT Press, Cambridge, Mass.

Culicover, P. (1992), 'Topicalisation, Inversion, and Complementizers in English', in D. Delfitto *et al.* (eds.), *OTS Working Papers in Linguistics*, OTS, Utrecht.

Fiengo, R., Huang, C.-T. J., Lasnik, H., and Reinhart, T. (1988), 'The Syntax of *Wh*-in-situ', *WCCFL Proceedings*, 7: 81–98.

Huang, C.-T. J. (1982), 'Logical Relations in Chinese and the Theory of Grammar', Ph.D thesis, MIT.

Li, Y.-H. A. (1992), 'Indefinite *Wh* in Mandarin Chinese', *Journal of East Asian Linguistics*, 1: 125–55.

Mahajan, A. (1990), 'The A/A-Bar Distinction and Movement Theory', Ph.D. thesis, MIT.

Manzini, R., and Wexler, K. (1987), 'Parameters, Binding Theory and Learnability', *Linguistic Inquiry*, 18: 413–44.

Nishigauchi, T. (1990), *Quantification in the Theory of Grammar*, Kluwer, Dordrecht.

O'Neil, J., and Groat, E. (1995), 'Unifying Spellout and the LF Interface in the Minimalist Framework', GLOW talk, Tromso, Norway.

Ouhalla, J. (1994), 'Remarks on the Binding Properties of *Wh*-in-situ', Ms., Queen Mary and Westfield College, London.

Progovac, L. (1991), 'Relativized SUBJECT, Long-Distance Reflexives, and Accessibility', Ms., Indiana University.

Rudin, C. (1988), 'On Multiple Questions and Multiple WH Fronting', *Natural Language and Linguistic Theory*, 6: 445–501.

Simpson, A. (1995), '*Wh*-Movement, Licensing and the Locality of Feature-Checking', Ph.D. thesis, SOAS, University of London.

Stroik, T. (1992), 'English Wh-*in-situ* Constructions', *Linguistic Analysis*, 22: 133–53.

Wahba, W. A.-F. B. (1991), 'LF Movement in Iraqi Arabic', in C.-T. J. Huang and R. May (eds.), *Logical Structure and Linguistic Structure*, Kluwer, Dordrecht, 253–76.

Watanabe, A. (1991), 'Wh-in-situ, Subjacency, and Chain Formation', Ms., MIT.

PART III
Specifiers and Language Acquistion

PART III
Speakers and Language Acquisition.

13

The Role of the Specifier and Finiteness in Early Grammar

TEUN HOEKSTRA, NINA HYAMS,
and MISHA BECKER

1. INTRODUCTION

Root infinitives of the sort in (1) are a common feature of many child languages. In the languages which display this phenomenon, the non-finite forms appear to be in free variation with finite forms of the verb. The apparent optionality of root infinitives led Wexler (1994) to propose that children pass through an *optional infinitive stage*.

(1) (*a*) Papa schoenen wassen   (Dutch, Weverink 1989)
          Daddy shoes wash-INF.

   (*b*) Eve sit floor   (English, CHILDES Brown 1973)

   (*c*) Pas manger la poupée   (French, Pierce 1992)
          not eat-INF. the doll
          Michel dormir
          Michel sleep

   (*d*) Thorstn das haben   (German, Wexler 1994)
          Thorstn that have-INF.

This early stage is also characterized by the omission of other functional elements—determiners as in (2), and subject pronouns as in (3).

(2) (*a*) Wayne in garden

   (*b*) Hayley draw boat   (Radford 1990)

   (*c*) Niekje ook boot maken   (Dutch, Schaeffer 1994)
          Niekje also boat make
          'Niekje also makes the boat.'

   (*d*) Nur Eisenbahn mögen wir   (German, Becker 1995)
          only train like we
          'We like only the train.'

(3) (*a*)   Want more apple   (Bloom *et al.* 1975)

     (*b*)   Veux pas lolo   (French, Pierce 1992)
           want not water
           '(I) don't want water.'

     (*c*)   Kan niet slapen op een schaap   (Dutch, De Haan and Tuijnman 1988)
           can not sleep on a sheep
           '(I) cannot sleep on a sheep.'

     (*d*)   a Matratze schlafen   (German, Becker 1995)
           mattress to sleep
           '(He) sleeps on the mattress.'

An important property which the dropped elements have in common is that they express specificity. Finiteness is responsible for temporal specificity; the eventuality described by the verb is situated at a particular temporal interval, past or present, relative to speech time. Definite determiners and pronouns mark specific DPs. Descriptively, we might say that what is lacking in the children's sentences in (1)–(3) is the grammatical encoding of specificity, so that the root infinitive phenomenon is really part of a more general property distinguishing the child's and adult's grammars.

In this chapter we will argue that the root infinitive phenomenon is not in fact optional, despite appearances. We propose that 'finiteness' is a property of both the nominal and verbal domains, and that the expression of finiteness in the verbal domain is contingent on its expression in the nominal domain. This contingency is due to the specifier–head agreement requirement. Finiteness in the verbal domain is manifested through the morphological expression of tense, agreement, etc. Finiteness in the nominal domain is realized through the expression of definiteness and other functional heads within DP. Just as we find root infinitives in early language, so we find DPs which lack a specification of definiteness. In this chapter we shall show that RIs in child language co-occur with subjects in which the relevant finiteness features are equally not expressed.

We begin with an overview of the evidence concerning the young child's knowledge of finiteness and agreement. We then outline the analysis of root infinitives presented in Hoekstra and Hyams (1995), which provides a unified account of RIs, determiner-drop, and null subjects in terms of an underspecification of the functional head Number. Our analysis also provides an account of the otherwise unexplained cross-linguistic variation that we find with respect to the child's use of root infinitives. We shall show that RIs occur only in languages in which Number is the only morphosyntactic category which is obligatorily specified. We then turn to the main topic of this chapter, which is to establish the correlation of finiteness in the nominal and verbal domains. We focus on the early grammars of English and German.

2. FINITENESS AND AGREEMENT IN THE EARLY GRAMMAR

One of the most striking generalizations to emerge from the past decade of cross-linguistic acquisition research is that children develop language-specific morphosyntactic knowledge at a very early age. Let us refer to this as Early Morphosyntactic Convergence (EMC). Where this knowledge is instantiated in the form of parameters, we observe that the relevant parameters are set quickly and without error (see Hyams 1994 for discussion). This is especially evident in those aspects of grammar which are related to finiteness. For example, children acquiring languages with V-to-I correctly position finite and non-finite verbs relative to negation and do so from the earliest multiword utterances (cf. Pierce 1989; Meisel 1990; Verrips and Weissenborn 1992).

Similarly, children acquiring V2 languages raise finite verbs to C, while non-finite verbs occur sentence-finally (De Haan 1986; Clahsen and Penke 1992; Poeppel and Wexler 1993). These and similar results in many other languages clearly show that finiteness is a feature of the early grammar, and that the distribution of finite forms is not random, but rather is determined by adult-like grammatical processes.

A possible hypothesis as to why children use root infinitives is that they have not yet learned the specific agreeing forms. However, this hypothesis cannot be right. A number of studies investigating early use of agreement in different languages have shown that (non-finite forms apart) children respect the Spec–head agreement requirement at a very early age. Agreement errors—that is, mismatches in agreement features—are not a robust phenomenon in early language. For example, Hyams (1983) found few agreement errors in the language of young Italian-speaking children. Pizzuto and Caselli (1992) confirm this with quantitative results; they report a 96 per cent accuracy rate in subject–verb agreement in the children they studied (see also Guasti 1994 for further discussion). Poeppel and Wexler (1993) and Rohrbacher and Vainikka (1995) find similar results in German-speaking children. Harris and Wexler (1995) show that English-speaking children do not produce agreement errors with 1st person subjects (e.g. *I goes*). Torrens (1992) counted at most 3 per cent agreement errors among his Catalan-speaking subjects. Table 13.1 summarizes the results of these various studies of subject–verb agreement.

Given that children use agreeing forms of the verb with a high degree of accuracy, it cannot be the case that root infinitives arise from a lack of knowledge of either Spec–head agreement requirements or of the specific agreeing forms.[1] In fact, we find sequences of the sort in (4*a*, *a'*), where the child

---

[1] Ferdinand (1995) reports that agreement errors range from about 9% to 20% in the four French-speaking children she studied. Most of the errors involve a 3rd person singular verb form with subjects with an unclear status, for instance a null subject, understood as 1st person (as in

TABLE 13.1. *Subject–verb agreement errors in early language*

Child	Language	Age[a]	n	%	Study
Simone	German	1:7–2:8	1,732	1	Clahsen and Penke 1992
Martina	Italian	1:8–2:7	478	1.6	
Diana	Italian	1:10–2:6	610	1.5	
Guglielmo	Italian	2:2–2:7	201	3.3	Guasti 1994
CHILDES	English	1:6–4:1	1,352	0.02	Harris and Wexler 1995
Claudia	Italian	1:4–2:4	1,410	3	Pizzuto and Caselli 1992
Francesco	Italian	1:5–2:10	1,264	2	
Marco	Italian	1:5–3:0	415	4	
Marti	Catalan/Spanish	1:9–2:5	178	0.56	Torrens 1992
Josep	Catalan/Spanish	1:9–2:6	136	3	
Guillem	Catalan	1:9–2:6	129	2.3	
Gisela	Catalan	1:10–2:6	81	1.2	

[a] Ages are given in the format years:months.

produces a root infinitive in one utterance immediately followed by a finite, agreeing form of the same verb. The German examples in (4b, b') show omission of the copula followed immediately by an utterance with a finite copula. (We take the null copula to be a root infinitive for reasons we will explain later.)

(4) (a) The lady have a dress on   (Nina, File 30, age 2:5)

   (a') The lady has a dress on

   (b) Mänchen weg, oben!   (Philip, age 2:9)
        '(The) Little man (is) gone, up.'

   (b') Oben, ist das Mänchen
        'Up is the little man.'

A similar point can be made with respect to the child's omission of determiners, illustrated in (2). Comprehension studies of very young English-speaking children show that not only are they sensitive to the presence of a functional position preceding nouns, but they also have specific knowledge of what the content of the functional position should be. Thus, Gerken and McIntosh (1993) found that children were best able to point to *the bird* in a

(i)), or a non-nominative subject (as in (ii)). No errors of the sort in (iii) are reported. (@ indicates that a form is unattested.)

(i)   Va assis
        (I) go-3RD PER. sit
(ii)   Moi est pas villain
        'Me is not naughty.'
(iii)   @J'est pas villain
        'I is not naughty.'

picture-identification task when given the instructions in (5*a*), but did significantly worse when presented with the prosodically identical (5*b*, *c*).

(5) (*a*) Find *the* bird for me
  (*b*) Find *was* bird for me
  (*c*) Find *gub* bird for me

Similarly, MacNamara (1982) found that children as young as 18 months use the presence or absence of a determiner (e.g. *a zav* vs. *zav*) to categorize novel nouns as either a proper or common noun. Moreover, as the German example in (4*b′*) shows clearly, it is not the case that children do not know the form of the specific determiner or are unable to use it in production. In light of these results, d(eterminer)-drop—as we might call it—is unexpected.

Summing up, we conclude that the omissions found in early grammar cannot be the result of either lack of knowledge of the specific forms or an absence of Spec–head agreement requirements. In the rest of this chapter we shall see that the absence or presence of the relevant elements that are obligatory in the adult grammar is in fact governed by Spec–head requirements. This supports the conclusion that the apparent optionality is a matter of grammar, not performance.

3. THE MORPHOSYNTAX OF FINITENESS

3.1. *The morphosyntax of finiteness in adult grammar*

Hoekstra and Hyams (1995) propose a unified account of these various omissions in terms of the underspecification of the functional head Number. Before we elaborate on this proposal, we lay out our assumptions concerning the adult grammar (see Hoekstra and Hyams 1995 for a more comprehensive discussion).

First, we assume a hierarchical arrangement of functional categories as in (6), where Number and Person head their own projections, as proposed in Johnson (1990).

(6) PerP NumP TnsP VP

Following ideas of Guéron and Hoekstra (1989, 1994), we assume that there is a deictic operator in the C domain which binds Tense, itself a pronominal. So, in a sentence such as (7) the range of the operator is specified by *yesterday*, while *jump over the ditch* restricts the reference of T, which is bound by the operator as a pronominal variable.

(7) Yesterday John jumped over the ditch

While there is a unified notion of finite verb, it is well known that languages vary in the morphosyntactic realization of finiteness. We propose to interpret finiteness as the morphosyntactic expression of a chain linking the verb to the operator, which provides a sentence with its specific temporal interpretation. Morphological specification of the various functional heads establishes a chain between the operator and the T/V. The variation in the expression of finiteness, then, is determined by the choice of functional head (heads) that makes (make) the chain visible through its (their) morphosyntactic expression. A minimal range of variation is given in (8).

(8)

Type	Pers	Num	Tense	V	Examples
(a)	m	∅	∅	—	Italian, Spanish, Catalan
(b)	∅	m	∅	—	English, Dutch
(c)	∅	∅	m	—	Japanese

Note: m = marked in the morphosyntax; ∅ = not marked.

Although realized through different functional heads, verbs of each morphological type count as finite. Consider English *walked walks*; both count as finite verbs although *walked* has a morphosyntactic expression of T, while *walks* does not. So both -*s* and -*ed* make the Tense chain visible.

We follow Kayne (1989) in assuming that English 3rd person -*s* is a specification of the functional head Number rather than Person.[2] Hence, according to the typology in (8), English is a *b*-type language, as is Dutch; there is no specification for Person nor is a specification of Tense required. Italian, Spanish, and Catalan, on the other hand, represent *a*-type languages, since they minimally have specification for Person (and perhaps also Number). Japanese would be a *c*-type language, having a morphological specification for Tense but not Person or Number.

Turning now to the nominal domain, we assume that the internal structure of nominals is strongly parallel to that of clauses, with a determiner as the analogue to the complementizer *that*. In between the D and the lexical noun there are a number of functional categories, including Number as proposed by Ritter (1989) and Valois (1991). We propose that parallel to the clause structure in (9*a*), we have a DP structure as in (9*b*).[3] (We leave the nature of X open at this point, noting that it is the nominal counterpart of T, which may be identified with the lower D in Szabolcsi's (1994) analysis of Hungarian.)

(9) (a)   OP C NUM [$_{TP}$ T [$_{VP}$ V]]
    (b)   OP D NUM [$_{XP}$ X [$_{NP}$ N]]

Parallel to the dependency between C and T/V expressed by finiteness, there

---

[2] According to Kayne, 2nd person *you* is grammatically plural, even when its reference is singular, just like French *vous*. Hence, there is no -*s* for 2nd person singular. As for 1st person singular, Kayne takes the position that it is not specified for Number, and therefore combines with an unmarked form.

[3] In these representations we leave out categories which are irrelevant for the point being made, specifically the category Person.

is a dependency between D and X/N which is expressed by nominal 'finiteness', now understood as a specification of one or more of the intermediate functional heads within DP. A definite determiner or plural marking is the morphosyntactic reflex of the chain established within DP. We take pronouns and proper names in adult grammar to have a full DP structure, with either overt or covert N-to-D movement (cf. Longobardi 1994).

The parallel between D and C is clear in such languages as Arabic, where N may move to the D position in a way which is essentially analogous to V-to-C movement in clausal structures. Also, the interdependence of Number and D is evidenced in the Romance languages, where the determiner inflects for number agreement. From an interpretative point of view, we can say that the establishment of such a D–N relationship yields nominal specificity, just as finiteness within CP yields temporal specificity. By specificity we mean that the grammar specifies the referential status of the XP.

3.2. *The underspecification of Number in early grammar*

Returning now to the child language facts illustrated in (1)–(3), Hoekstra and Hyams (1995) propose the descriptive generalization in (10).

(10)   In the early grammar the functional head Number (and only Number) may be left unspecified.

The underspecification of Number results in a failure of chain formation, hence a failure of finiteness. No chain between the operator and its pronominal variable is established through finiteness. This results in root infinitives in the clausal domain, and d-drop and null subjects in the nominal domain.

The underspecification of Number hypothesis leads to a precise cross-linguistic prediction, which is that root infinitives will show up only in languages which establish a chain *uniquely* via a Number specification, in other words the *b*-type languages in the typology in (8). In these languages, if Number is left unspecified, then there is no other morphological head through which a chain can be made visible. On the other hand, *a*-type and *c*-type languages should not show a root infinitive effect, since in these languages the obligatory specification of Person or Tense will block the occurrence of root infinitives. As shown by Hoekstra and Hyams, this prediction is borne out. Children acquiring Italian, Spanish, and Catalan—*a*-type languages— produce virtually no root infinitives; similarly, children acquiring Japanese produce only finite verb forms (Sano 1995). Table 13.2 gives the proportion of RIs in these different languages based on various studies of spontaneous speech.

The hypothesis in (10) accounts for the distribution of RIs as being limited to those systems in which only Number is specified in the morphosyntax (i.e. the *b*-type languages). For fuller discussion we refer to Hoekstra and Hyams

TABLE 13.2. *Frequency of root infinitives in child languages*

Language and study	Child	Age[a]	%RIs
Non-RI languages			
Italian	Diana	2:0	0
(Guasti 1994)	Martina	1:11	16
		2:1	4
Italian	Paola	2:0–2:5	7
(Schaeffer 1990)	Daniele	1:7–2:6	8
	Massimo	1:7–2:6	6
	Gabriele	1:7–2:6	7
	Orietta	1:7–2:6	5
	Elisabetta	1:7–2:5	10
	Francesco	1:9–2:5	5
Spanish	Damariz	2:6–2:8	5
(Grinstead 1994)	Juan	1:7–2:0	12
		2:1–2:4	10
Catalan	Guillem	1:11–2:6	3
(Torrens 1992)	Marti	2:0–2:5	3
Japanese[b]	Ken	2:8–2:10	8
(Sano 1995)	Masanori	2:4	10
RI languages			
French	Nathalie	1:9–2:3	49
(Pierce 1992)	Philippe	1:9–2:6	20
	Daniel	1:8–1:11	43
English	Eve	1:6–1:10	78
	Adam	2:3–3:0	81
	Nina	2:4–2:5	75
Swedish	Freja	1:11–2:0	38
(Platzack)	Tor	1:11–2:2	56
(from Guasti 1994)	Embla	1:8–1:10	61
German	S	2:1	46
(Weissenborn 1990)		2:2	40
(from Guasti 1994)			
Dutch	Laura	1:8–2:1	36
(Weverink 1989)	Tobias	1:10–1:11	36
	Fedra	1:10–2:1	26
(Haegeman 1994)	Hein	2:4–3:1	16

[a] Ages are given in the format years:months.
[b] Japanese root non-finite = V-te without the auxiliary *iru*.

Source: based on Sano and Hyams 1994.

(1995), where we also discuss why the option of underspecification of Number is not found in the relevant adult grammars.[4]

4. SPEC–HEAD AGREEMENT

4.1. *Formulating the prediction*

We have established that Number can remain unspecified in both the verbal and nominal domains. Note, however, that verbal Number is rather different from nominal Number. In the nominal domain Number is inherently determined by the referent of the nominal phrase, while in the verbal system Number is derivative; it encodes a property of a dependent, the subject, rather than of the verb itself. We noted earlier (cf. Table 13.1) that children respect Spec–head agreement requirements from a very early age. Thus, just as we find Spec–head agreement when features (e.g. Person) are specified, we expect correspondences when features are left unspecified (see also Clahsen *et al.* 1994). Specifically, we expect root infinitives to occur with subjects that are likewise unspecified for Number, and conversely, finite verbs with subjects that are specified for Number. With respect to underspecified subjects we need to distinguish two cases: first, radically empty DPs, which would have the status of null subjects, and secondly, DPs with overt nouns but without a visible D-chain (i.e. bare Ns).

We first discuss null subjects. A number of studies have shown that there is a rough correlation between null subjects and RIs on the one hand, and between lexical subjects and finite verbs on the other. The results of these studies are summarized in Table 13.3.

What we see in Table 13.3 is that in a range of child languages (the *b*-type languages) lexical subjects occur disproportionately more often in finite clauses than in RIs. Averaging across languages and children we find about 76 per cent overt subjects in finite clauses and 17 per cent overt subjects in RIs. RIs typically occur with null subjects (roughly 83 per cent). But the correlations between finiteness and subject type are not perfect in either direction. On the one hand, we still find some 24 per cent of finite verbs occurring with null subjects, and on the other hand, about 17 per cent of RIs have overt subjects. Let us deal with these in turn.

The null subjects occurring with finite verbs can easily be put to the side. These null subjects are arguably not null elements in A-positions, but rather

---

[4] In brief, we argue that if no chain is established through specification of finiteness, T and its nominal counterpart, D, are not interpreted as operator-bound pronominal variables, but rather as directly discourse-related pronouns. The readings obtained in this manner are indistinguishable from readings obtained through operator binding. We argue that for adults the grammatical mechanism of operator binding takes priority over the discourse mechanism of pronoun resolution (cf. Reinhart 1983). For regular pronouns it is well established that this bleeding relation between grammar and discourse does not hold in the child's system (cf. Chien and Wexler 1990; Grodzinsky and Reinhart 1993). We assume that the same applies to T and D.

TABLE 13.3. *Finiteness and null/overt subjects in different child languages*

Language/ child and study	+Finite			−Finite		
	% Overt subject	% Null subject	Total *n*	% Overt subject	% Null subject	Total *n*
Dutch						
Hein 2:3–3:1 (Haegeman 1994)	68	32	3,768	15	85	721
Flemish						
Maarten 1:11	75	25	92	11	89	100
German						
Simone 1:8–4:1 (Behrens 1993)	80	20	3,636	11	89	2,477
Andreas (Krämer 1993)	92	8	220	32	68	68
French[a]						
Nathalie 1:9–2:3 (Krämer 1993)	70	30	299	27	73	180
Philippe 2:1–2:6 (Krämer 1993)	74	26	705	7	93	164

[a] For French only preverbal subjects were counted.

the result of topic-drop (De Haan and Tuijnman 1988). Let us briefly elaborate. Subjects in V2 languages can be found in two types of position in main clauses: in preverbal position (i.e. preceding the finite verb) or in postverbal position. In the latter case, some other constituent precedes the finite verb. This sentence-initial position is not a subject position, therefore, but rather a topic position. This is not only true in adult grammar. Children acquiring V2 languages topicalize both subjects and non-subjects (cf. Verrips and Weissenborn 1992; Haegeman 1994). Hein, studied by Haegeman, is typical in this regard. Table 13.4 shows that Hein topicalizes non-subjects in 52 per cent of his V2 sentences and subjects in 48 per cent. The virtual absence of non-subjects in initial position in non-finite clauses (i.e. non-V2 clauses) shows that topicalization is involved in V2 clauses.

If null subjects were genuinely that (i.e. null *subjects*) we would expect them to occur in both preverbal and postverbal position. Several studies have shown, however, that null subjects are found only in preverbal position (i.e. main clauses with the finite verb in initial position), and not in postverbal position (i.e. clauses where the finite verb is preceded by a non-subject topic). This follows if null subjects result from topic-drop (De Haan and Tuijnman 1988). Table 13.5 shows that for Andreas, a German-speaking child studied by

TABLE 13.4. *Subject-initial and non-subject-initial finite clauses and root infinitives: Hein*

Clause type	Subject-initial		Non-subject-initial		Total n
	n	%	n	%	
Finite/V2	1,223	48	1,346	52	2,569
Non-finite	101	95	5	5	106

Source: based on data from Haegeman 1994.

TABLE 13.5. *Distribution of null/overt subjects in finite clauses*

Subject position	Overt subject	Null subject
Initial (pre-V2) position	129	19 (= topic-drop)
Post-verbal position	40	0 (= *pro*-drop)

Source: Poeppel and Wexler 1993.

Poeppel and Wexler (1993), all instances of null subjects in finite clauses occur in sentence-initial (i.e. topic) position.

With respect to English, Valian (1991) found no cases of null subjects in 132 finite embedded clauses, where a topic-drop analysis is excluded. In another study, Roeper and Rohrbacher (1994) found only 5 per cent null subjects in finite *wh*-questions, where topicalization of the subject is not an option. These results confirm the hypothesis that null subjects in finite clauses are not allowed in argument position in *b*-type languages, and hence the plausibility of a topic-drop analysis for null subjects in finite clauses quantified in Table 13.3.

Let us then turn to lexical subjects. Their occurrence with finite verbs is in principle unproblematic, but one might expect that lexical subjects would not occur in RI sentences. However, this expectation is based on the assumption that all lexical subjects are equal. Our hypothesis makes more fine-grained distinctions. More specifically, we distinguish between finite lexical subjects and non-finite lexical subjects. PRO, a radically empty DP, is one instance of a non-finite DP, but an overt subject with a missing determiner likewise instantiates a non-finite DP. Neither of these non-finite DP types is specified for the features relevant to agreement of the verb. On the other hand, lexical subjects with a determiner as well as plural DPs are finite DPs. Assuming that there is agreement between the feature specification of the DP subject and that of V, we then make the predictions in (11).

(11) (i) The subject of a root infinitive will be either (*a*) a zero pronoun or (*b*) a bare noun phrase (i.e. no determiner, no number marking (e.g. *dog*)).

(ii) Finite DP subjects—that is, DPs with a determiner (e.g. *the boy*)—will occur with finite verbs.

(iii) Plural subjects will occur with finite verbs.

With respect to overt pronouns and proper names, our hypothesis allows them to occur both with finite verbs, in which case a D-chain is formed, and with infinitives, in which case no chain is established. We therefore exclude pronouns and proper names from the analyses that follow.

4.2. *Testing the predictions: English-speaking children*

We tested the predictions in (11) in English and German child language. For English we relied on the corpora of Adam and Nina (CHILDES, Brown 1973; Suppes 1973; MacWhinney and Snow 1985). We coded Eve's data as well, but there was not a sufficient number of relevant examples to do any further analysis. The German data were collected by Misha Becker (cf. Becker 1995). The number of files examined and the age of each child (in the format years: months) are given in Table 13.6.

TABLE 13.6. *Data used to test the predictions*

Child	No. of files	Age	Language
Adam	11	2:3–3:7	English
Nina	7	2:4–2:10	English
Philip	1	2:9	German
Sophie	1	2:5	German
Wolfgang	2	2:5	German
Johanna	1	2:5	German

We turn now to the predicted relationships between subject type and finiteness of the verb. From earlier studies we know that there is a rough correlation between null subjects and RIs on the one hand, and finite verbs and lexical subjects on the other, as shown in Table 13.3. In Tables 13.7 and 13.8 we give the relevant figures for Adam and Nina. The category *overt subject* includes all singular lexical subjects. Note that we have collapsed main verbs and *be* in these figures. *Be* does not occur in its infinitival form (except in rare cases), but

TABLE 13.7. *Finiteness and subject: Adam*

	Non-finite	Finite
Null subject	50	19
Overt subject	245	263

TABLE 13.8. *Finiteness and subject: Nina*

	Non-finite	Finite
Null subject	15	17
Overt subject	87	294

we take non-occurrence of *be* in obligatory contexts—that is, null *be*, as in (12)—as the *be* form of the root infinitive. This is based on the idea that *be* is in fact a carrier of inflectional structure, which is hence non-overt when the inflectional structure is unspecified (Jaeggli and Hyams 1987).

(12) (*a*) Little tricycle going round
   (*b*) Cowboy funny

As before, we can set apart Adam's nineteen cases of null subjects with finite verbs and Nina's seventeen cases as resulting from topic-drop. The distribution of null subjects, then, is consistent with our hypothesis. But our hypothesis is more specifically concerned with the distribution of different types of overt subject. We have to differentiate between finite and non-finite overt subjects. For this purpose, we looked only at subjects with a common noun; that is, proper names and overt pronouns were excluded as their status is ambiguous, as discussed earlier. Recall that our first prediction is that finite verbs will occur with finite DPs (i.e. DPs with determiners), while non-finite verbs will have bare N subjects (cf. (11)). Table 13.9 gives the relevant figures for Adam. As in the previous analysis, the category *finite verbs* includes finite lexical verbs and finite forms of the verb *be*, and the category *non-finite verbs* includes root infinitives and cases in which *be* is missing, as in (12).

TABLE 13.9. *Determiners and finiteness in main verbs and* be: *Adam*

	Finite verbs	Non-finite verbs
Overt determiner	53	2
Null determiner	4	39

The data in Table 13.9 provide clear support for our hypothesis. Overt determiners occur overwhelmingly with finite verbs, while non-finite verbs occur with bare Ns. When Number is unspecified in DP, resulting in a bare N, the verb must also be unspecified with respect to Number and hence non-finite.

Table 13.10 reports the figures for Nina. We see in Nina's data that finite verbs behave as predicted, occurring roughly 92 per cent of the time with overt determiners. Non-finite verbs, however, do not behave as expected. More than 50 per cent of the determiners are overt; that is, the DPs are finite in our terms. There are several possible explanations for this. One is that we have run into a sampling problem, that is, there are too few data to show the effect. If this is the case, then adding more files, as we have in the case of Adam, will reduce the proportion of unpredicted cases to insignificance.

TABLE 13.10. *Determiners and finiteness in main verbs and* be*: Nina.*

	Finite verbs	Non-finite verbs
Overt determiner	34	12
Null determiner	3	9

But it is also possible that we are seeing a grammatical effect and not a statistical one, namely that Nina's twelve finite DPs that occur with non-finite verbs, as well as Adam's two examples, are *not* in subject position, but are rather dislocated constituents.[5] This possibility deserves further investigation, but we note at this point the following facts (13), which are consistent with a dislocation analysis.

(13) (i)   Overt subjects of RIs occur on the left (or right, as in French, cf. (1c)) periphery of the clause (cf. Haegeman 1994).
   (ii) Subject clitics do not occur with RIs, as they cannot be dislocated (cf. Pierce 1989).
   (iii) Non-nominative subject pronouns occur only with RIs (e.g. *him go*, **him goes*; cf. Schütze 1995).

Additionally, if finite DPs in RIs are dislocated, we make the further prediction in (14).

(14)   There can be no finite subjects of RIs in V2 languages, as left-dislocation in these languages requires V2 and hence a finite verb (e.g. **Dat boek de man lezen* (that book the man read-INF.)).

So let us now turn to a V2 language, German.

4.3. *Testing the predictions: German-speaking children*

Our predictions with respect to finiteness were also tested for the four German children listed in Table 13.6. However, the data examined are rather limited,

---

[5] Ferdinand (1995) and Labelle and Valois (1995) provide compelling evidence (grammatical as well as spectrographic) that postverbal subjects in early French are dislocated. Most subjects of RIs in early French are postverbal (cf. Pierce 1989; Friedemann 1994).

TABLE 13.11. *Finiteness and subject determiners in early German*

	Finite verbs	Non-finite verbs
Overt determiner	9	2
Null determiner	9 (1)[a]	11

[a] Only 1 of these 9 cases is unproblematic; see text for explanation.

consisting of only one or two files per child, so that conclusions here should be regarded as tentative. We first looked at the distribution of overt vs. null determiners in obligatory contexts. The figures are presented in Table 13.11.

We see in the German data, as in the English data, that the non-finite verbs pattern as predicted, occurring 85 per cent of the time with null determiners. Moreover, the fact that there are only two cases of overt determiners with RIs as compared to the substantially higher proportion of overt determiners with RIs in Adam and Nina's data (cf. Tables 13.7 and 13.8) also bears out the prediction in (14), supporting the dislocation analysis of finite subjects in RIs.

On the other hand, the finite verbs do not go as predicted, occurring equally often with finite and non-finite DPs. Unpredicted by our hypothesis are the nine finite verbs with null determiners. However, if we examine these nine cases, we see that all but one (15*h*) are problematic in one way or another. We have listed all of them in (15).

(15) (*a*) *Eisenbahn* geht das nicht
train goes that not

(*b*) So *Feuerwehr* macht
so firefighter does

(*c*) So *Anlage* so macht
so device so does

(*d*) *Katze* macht
cat does

(*e*) *Wau-wau* noch kommt rein
dog also comes in

(*f*) *Katze* reicht das
cat reaches that *or* (to the) cat is-sufficient that

(*g*) Anre *Pferdebuch* heisst
other horsebook is-called

(*h*) *Turnstunde* ist so da lang
gym class is so there long

(*i*) Hier ist *Stopper*
here is ?

In (15a), it is not clear whether the italicized noun is in fact the subject, or even what the structure of the sentence is. The pronoun *das* might be the subject. Examples (15b, c, e, g) do not have the V-second order which is normal for finite clauses. The verb form *macht* in (15b, c, d) might be a participle which is missing the *ge*-prefix. The subjects in (15d, e, f) might be proper names. In (15g, i) the italicized noun might be a nominal predicate rather than the subject. The meaning, and hence also the grammatical analysis of (15f, i), is unclear. Hence, we are unwilling to draw any conclusions on the basis of these examples. If we put these examples to the side, we find the predicted correlation between finiteness of the verb and determiners, or more to the point, the correlation between the specification of Number in the nominal and verbal domains.

The German data provide us with a further test of our hypothesis that is not available in English, viz. prediction (11.iii), that plural subjects will occur only with finite verbs. This prediction cannot be tested in English because there is no difference in either form or position between a plural finite verb form and an infinitive (e.g. *The boys go . . .*). In German, on the other hand, even though by and large the form of the plural inflected verb is identical to the form of the infinitive (e.g. *machen* (make)), there is a positional difference; a plural inflected verb occurs in second position, while an infinitive occurs in clause-final position. Table 13.12 gives the results of counting the relative distributions of plural and non-plural subjects across finite and non-finite verbs.

TABLE 13.12. *Finiteness and plural subjects in early German*

	Finite (V2)	Non-finite (verb-final)
Plural subjects	22	1
Non-plural subjects	46	43

These data provide very strong confirmation of our prediction (11.iii). With only a single counterexample, plural subjects occur with finite verbs, while non-plural subjects show an even distribution across finite and non-finite constructions.[6]

Further study of German is required. However, additional support for our hypothesis can be obtained from a study by Clahsen *et al.* (1994), who also investigated the relationship between underspecification in DP and IP, under somewhat different assumptions. The relevant data are given in Table 13.13.

---

[6] For this analysis we included all types of overt subject.

TABLE 13.13. *Different subject types in root
infinitives in German* (%)

Child	Full DP	Bare N	Null
Simone	0	28	72
Mathias	0	58	42
Annelie	0	0	100
Hannah	0	10	90

Source: adapted from Clahsen *et al.* 1994.

The four children in their study failed to produce a single finite DP in RIs. (Note that Clahsen *et al.*'s 'bare N' category includes bare Ns, pronouns, and proper names.)

5. DISCUSSION

The empirical results for English and German provide clear support for our hypothesis. The root infinitive phenomenon in child language is not an optional matter, but is rather determined by the agreement system. On the one hand, the type of verbal inflectional system determines whether there is in fact an option of non-finite clauses; they occur only in systems in which agreement is limited to Number. On the other hand, within systems that allow the use of non-finite forms, the choice is not free, but dependent on properties of the subject. The RI phenomenon arises when the Number specification in the verbal inflection cannot be checked by a specification in its specifier. Hence, specifier–head agreement governs the choice of finite vs. infinitival form.

These results have a direct bearing on alternative theories of the root infinitive phenomenon. Specifically, theories that account for RIs in terms of underspecification of Tense (Guilfoyle 1984; Wexler 1994), truncation (Rizzi 1994), or modal-drop (Boser *et al.* 1992) are not able to explain the correlations that we found. There is no theoretical connection between the presence of a determiner and the underspecification of Tense or the option of dropping an inflected modal.

REFERENCES

Becker, M. (1995), 'Acquisition of Syntax in Child German: Verb Finiteness and Verb Placement', Honors thesis, Wellesley College.

Behrens, H. (1993), 'Temporal Reference in German Child Language', Ph.D. dissertation, University of Amsterdam.

Bloom, L., Lightbown, P., and Hood, L. (1975), *Structure and Variation in Child Language*, Monograph of the Society for Research in Child Development, vol. 40, no. 2.

Boser, K., Lust, B., Santelmann, L., and Whitman, J. (1992), 'The Syntax of CP and V2 in Early Child German', *Proceedings of the North Eastern Linguistics Society*, 23: 51–65.

Brown, R. (1973), *A First Language*, Harvard University Press, Cambridge, Mass.

Chien, Y.-C., and Wexler, K. (1990), 'Children's Knowledge of Locality Conditions in Binding as Evidence for the Modularity of Syntax', *Language Acquisition*, 1: 225–95.

Clahsen, H., and Penke, M. (1992), 'The Acquisition of Agreement Morphology and its Syntactic Consequences', in J. Meisel (ed.), *The Acquisition of Verb Placement: Functional Categories and V2 Phenomena in Language Acquisition*, Kluwer, Dordrecht, 181–224.

——Eisenbeiss, S., and Penke, M. (1994), 'Underspecification and Lexical Learning in Early Child Grammars', *Essex Research Reports in Linguistics* 4.

De Haan, G. (1986), 'A Theory-Bound Approach to the Acquisition of Verb Placement in Dutch', in G. De Haan and W. Zonneveld (eds.), *Formal Parameters of Generative Grammar*, vol. 3, University of Utrecht, Utrecht, 15–30.

——and Tuijnman, K. (1988), 'Missing Subjects and Objects in Child Grammar', in P. Jordens and J. Lalleman (eds.), *Language Development*, Foris, Dordrecht, 101–21.

Ferdinand, A. (1995), 'The Acquisition of the Subject in French', Ph.D. dissertation, HIL.

Friedemann, M. (1994), 'The Underlying Position of External Arguments in French: A Study in Adult and Child Grammar', *Geneva Generative Papers*, 0(1–2): 123–44.

Gerken, L. A., and McIntosh, B. J. (1993), 'Interplay of Function Morphemes and Prosody in Early Language', *Developmental Psychology*, 29: 448–57.

Grinstead, J. (1994), 'Consequences of the Maturation of Number Morphology in Spanish and Catalan', MA thesis, University of California at Los Angeles.

Grodzinsky, Y., and Reinhart, T. (1993), 'The Innateness of Binding and Reference', *Linguistic Inquiry*, 24: 69–102.

Guasti, M.-T. (1994), 'Verb Syntax in Italian Child Grammar: Finite and Non-Finite Verbs', *Language Acquisition*, 3: 1–40.

Guéron, J., and Hoekstra, T. (1989), 'T-Chains and Constituent Structure of Auxiliaries', in A. Cardinaletti, G. Cinque, and G. Giusti (eds.), *Constituent Structure: Papers from the Venice GLOW*, Foris, Dordrecht, 35–100.

————(1994), 'The Temporal Interpretation of Predication', in A. Cardinaletti and M. T. Guasti (eds.), *Syntax and Semantics 28: Small Clauses*, Academic Press, New York, 77–103.

Guilfoyle, E. (1984), 'The Acquisition of Tense and the Emergence of Lexical Subjects', *McGill Working Papers in Linguistics*, 1: 120–31.

Haegeman, L. (1994), 'Root Infinitives, Tense and Truncated Structures', *Language Acquisition*, 4: 205–55.

Harris, T., and Wexler, K. (1995), 'The Optional Infinitive Stage in Child English: Evidence from Negation', Ms., MIT.

Hoekstra, T., and Hyams, N. (1995), 'The Syntax and Interpretation of Dropped Categories in Child Language: A Unified Account', *Proceedings of the West Coast Conference on Formal Linguistics XIV*, CSLI, Stanford University, Stanford, Calif., 123–36.

Hyams, N. (1983), 'The Acquisition of Parameterized Grammars', Ph.D. dissertation, City University of New York.

——(1996), 'The Underspecification of Functional Categories in Early Grammar', in H. Clahsen (ed.), *Generative Perspectives on Language Acquisition*, John Benjamins, Amsterdam.

Jaeggli, O., and Hyams, N. (1987), 'Morphological Uniformity and the Setting of the Null Subject Parameter', *North Eastern Linguistics Society* 18: 238–53.

Johnson, K. (1990), 'The Syntax of Inflectional Paradigms', Ms., University of Wisconsin.

Kayne, R. (1989), 'Notes on English Agreement', Ms., City University of New York.

Krämer, I. (1993), 'The Licensing of Subjects in Early Child Language', *MIT Working Papers in Linguistics*, 19: 197–212.

Labelle, M., and Valois, D. (1995), 'The Status of Postverbal Subjects in French Child Language', Ms., UQAM and University of Montreal.

Longobardi, G. (1994), 'Reference and Proper Names', *Linguistic Inquiry*, 25: 609–66.

MacNamara, J. (1982), *Names for Things*, MIT Press, Cambridge, Mass.

McWhinney, B., and Snow, C. (1985), 'The Child Language Exchange System', *Journal of Child Language*, 12: 271–96.

Meisel, J. (1990), 'Inflection: Subjects and Subject Verb Agreement', in J. Meisel (ed.), *Two First Languages: Early Grammatical Development in Bilingual Children*, Foris, Dordrecht, 237–98.

Pierce, A. (1989), 'On the Emergence of Syntax: A Crosslinguistic Study', Ph.D. dissertation, MIT.

——(1992), *Language Acquisition and Syntactic Theory: A Comparative Analysis of French and English Child Grammars*, Kluwer, Dordrecht.

Pizzuto, E., and Caselli, M.-C. (1992), 'The Acquisition of Italian Morphology: Implications for Models of Language Development', *Journal of Child Language*, 19: 491–558.

Poeppel, D., and Wexler, K. (1993), 'The Full Competence Hypothesis of Clause Structure in Early German', *Language*, 69: 1–33.

Radford, A. (1990), *Syntactic Theory and the Acquisition of English Syntax*, Basil Blackwell, Oxford.

Reinhart, T. (1983), *Anaphora and Semantic Interpretation*, Croom Helm, London.

Ritter, E. (1989), 'Two Functional Categories in Noun Phrases: Evidence from Modern Hebrew', in S. Rothstein (ed.), *Syntax and Semantics*, vol. 26, Academic Press, New York, 37–62.

Rizzi, L. (1994), 'Early Null Subjects and Root Null Subjects', in B. D. Schwartz and T. Hoekstra (eds.), *Language Acquisition Studies in Generative Grammar*, John Benjamins, Amsterdam, 151–77.

Roeper, T., and Rohrbacher, B. (1994), 'True Pro-Drop in Child English and the Principle of Economy or Projection', paper delivered at the Boston University Conference on Language Development, Boston, October 1994.

Rohrbacher, B., and Vainikka, A. (1995), 'On German Verb Syntax under Age 2', *Proceedings of 19th Annual BU-Conference on Language Development*, vol. 2, 487–98.

Sano, T. (1995), 'Roots in Language Acquisition: A Comparative Study of Japanese and European Languages', Ph.D. dissertation, University of California at Los Angeles.

——and Hyams, N. (1994), 'Agreement, Finiteness, and the Development of Null Arguments', *Proceedings of North Eastern Linguistics Society 24*, 543–58.

Schaeffer, J. (1990), 'The Syntax of the Subject in Child Language: Italian Compared to Dutch', MA thesis, University of Utrecht.

——(1994), 'On the Acquisition of Scrambling in Dutch', *Proceedings of 19th Annual BU-Conference on Language Development*, vol. 2, 521–32.

Schütze, C. (1995), 'Children's Subject Case Errors: Evidence for Case-Related Functional Projections', *Formal Linguistics Society of Mid-America 6* (IULC), 155–66.

Suppes, P. (1973), 'The Semantics of Children's Language', *American Psychologist*, 88: 103–14.

Szabolcsi, A. (1994), 'The Noun Phrase', in F. Kiefer and K. Kiss (eds.), *Syntax and Semantics*, vol. 28, Academic Press, New York, 197–274.

Torrens, V. (1992), 'The Acquisition of Catalan and Spanish', talk given at the Psycholinguistics Laboratory, University of California at Los Angeles.

Valian, V. (1991), 'Syntactic Subjects in the Early Speech of American and Italian Children', *Cognition*, 40: 21–81.

Valois, D. (1991), 'The Internal Syntax of DP', Ph.D. dissertation, University of California at Los Angeles.

Verrips, M., and Weissenborn, J. (1992), 'Routes to Verb Placement in Early German and French: The Independence of Finiteness and Agreement', in J. Meisel (ed.), *The Acquisition of Verb Placement: Functional Categories and V2 Phenomena in Language Acquisition*, Kluwer, Dordrecht, 283–332.

Weissenborn, J. (1990), 'Functional Categories and Verb Movement: The Acquisition of German Syntax Reconsidered', in M. Rothweiler (ed.), *Spracherwerb und Grammatik: Linguistische Untersuchungen zum Erwerb von Syntax und Morphologie*, Linguistische Berichte, Sonderheft 3, Göttingen, 190–224.

Weverink, M. (1989), 'The Subject in Relation to Inflection in Child Language', MA thesis, University of Utrecht.

Wexler, K. (1994), 'Optional Infinitives, Verb Movement and the Economy of Derivation in Child Grammar', in D. Lightfoot and N. Hornstein (eds.), *Verb Movement*, Cambridge University Press, Cambridge, 305–50.

14

The Acquisition of Verb Movement and Spec–Head Relationships in Child Swedish

LYNN SANTELMANN

I. INTRODUCTION AND THEORETICAL BACKGROUND

This chapter investigates the relationship between verb movement and XP movement in the verb-second (V2) languages by examining the acquisition of these two movements in child Swedish. The underlying question this chapter seeks to address is whether main clause verb movement and XP movement in the V2 languages are linked, or whether they are two independently motivated, but co-occurring movements. I will argue for the former analysis of V2.

In the V2 languages such as German, Dutch, and Swedish, both verb movement and XP movement are main clause phenomena.[1] Furthermore, these movements stand in a one-to-one relationship with one another, as seen in the Swedish examples (1*a*) and (1*b*). Only a single constituent can precede the verb in main clause declaratives and *wh*-questions. If more than one constituent precedes the verb, then the sentence is ungrammatical, as in (1*c*) and (1*d*).

(1) (*a*) Vad *ser* barnet inte?
     what sees child-the not
     'What does the child not see?'

   (*b*) Den filmen *fick* barnen inte se.
     that movie-the got children-the not see
     'That movie, the children didn't get to see.'

   (*c*) *Vad barnet *ser* inte?
      what child-the sees not
      'What does the child not see?'

This work was supported by a Fulbright–Roth Thompson fellowship to Sweden and NIDCD Training Grant no. 00036 at the State University of New York at Buffalo. I thank Wayne Harbert, Barbara Lust, Bonnie Schwartz, Carsten Schütze, and the reviewers for helpful comments and discussion on earlier versions of this work.

[1] I will exclude from this analysis the V2 languages such as Icelandic and Yiddish which allow verb movement in both main and subordinate clauses. Diesing (1990) and Heycock and Santorini (1993) have argued, for example, that these languages should be analysed differently from the V2 languages that show an asymmetry in verb movement between main and subordinate clauses.

(*d*)   *Den filmen barnet *fick* inte se.
   that movie-the child-the got not see
   'That movie, the child didn't get to see.'

Neither verb movement nor XP movement (topicalization or *wh*-question formation) is allowed in subordinate clauses. As can be seen in the examples in (2) and (3), the verb in subordinate clauses does not move out of the VP, but remains following the sentential adverb *inte* (not). This contrasts with main clauses (e.g. (1*b*)) where the verb moves out of the VP and into a position preceding the sentential adverb.

(2)   *No verb movement in subordinate clauses with overt complementizers*
   (*a*)   Läraren undrar om barnet inte *ser* boken.
      teacher-the wonders if child-the not sees book-the
      'The teacher wonders if the child doesn't see the book.'

   (*b*)   *Läraren undrar om barnet *ser* inte boken.
      teacher-the wonders if child-the sees not book-the
      'The teacher wonders if the child doesn't see the book.'

(3)   *No non-subject XP movement with overt complementizers*
   *Det är filmen som i går barnen inte fick se
      it is movie-the that yesterday children-the not may see
      'It is that movie that yesterday the children were not allowed to see.'

Because of this complementary distribution in movement between main and subordinate clauses, it has been suggested that the V2 movement results from the verb in main clauses moving to the position of the complementizers in subordinate clauses, the functional category CP.[2] Thus, following den Besten (1983) and others, V2 in main clauses is analysed as follows: the finite verb moves through I^0 to C^0, the position of complementizers in subordinate clauses, and a phrasal element (XP) moves to the specifier of CP. The movements for the Swedish sentences in (4) are demonstrated in Figures 14.1 and 14.2.

(4)   *Structure of Swedish main clauses*   (e.g. den Besten 1983; Platzack 1986)
   (*a*)   *Question*   (*b*)   *Declarative topicalization*
      Vad läser barnet?   Boken läser barnet.
      what reads child-the   book-the reads child-the
      'What does the child read?'   'The book, the child reads.'

Because the verb and the XP move to the same projection in main clauses, CP, this raises the question as to whether the two movements that make up V2 are dependent upon one another. Many languages can move XPs to an initial position, and many languages have verb movement. The V2 languages seem to

---

[2] I will also exclude from this analysis the restricted number of cases with topicalization and verb movement in subordinate clauses, e.g. *mormor tror att bläckfisk har Pia aldrig ätit* (Grandma believes that squid has Pia never eaten). Schwartz and Vikner (1989) argue that these are restricted to bridge-verb contexts and most likely involve CP recursion, and not true subordination.

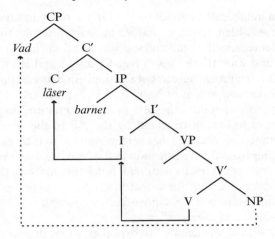

FIG. 14.1. *Structure of* wh-*question formation in Swedish*

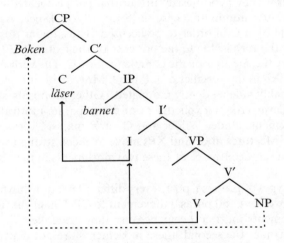

FIG. 14.2. *Structure of declarative topicalization in Swedish*

be unique in that movement of a single XP to the initial position and the finite verb to the second position must occur together. Thus, the issue that arises for the V2 languages is whether the obligatory co-occurrence of these two movements results from a Spec–head relationship that is unique in these languages, or from two independent features on the XP and the verb that just happen to co-occur.

These two hypotheses have both been posited in the literature on V2 and are evident in a number of analyses of V2. On the one hand there are several recent hypotheses which maintain that V2 movement results from a relationship between elements in the head and specifier position. Some proposals, such as Haegeman and Zanuttini's (1991) Neg-Criterion and Rizzi's (1991) *Wh*-Criterion, posit a reciprocal agreement relationship between the specifier and the head that forces movement of both the XP and the verb.[3] Others, such as Zwart's (1994) proposal under the Minimalist Programme, hypothesize that verb movement is indirectly triggered by the XP in the specifier position. Zwart, for example, hypothesizes that verb movement to C takes place in order to remove features from the C projection that would otherwise prevent the XP in the specifier from checking its features. Under this analysis, the verb checks features of its own in C, but these features do not trigger verb movement. Instead, the trigger is the need to remove features from the C projection so that an XP can be licensed in the specifier.

On the other side of the debate are hypotheses that dissociate verb movement from XP movement. For example, Holmberg and Platzack (1989, 1995) propose that the verb moves to C in the V2 languages because the feature [+F] is located there. They hypothesize further that [+F] is located in C in the V2 languages because nominative case in [Spec, IP] (or [Spec, AgrS]) must be governed by [+F] in C in order to be licensed. Thus, under this account, the movement of the verb is due to the presence of the feature [+F] in C, and the need to license the specifier of the complement of C. The verb does not move to license the XP in the specifier of CP itself. Movement of a phrase to [Spec, CP] is presumably independently motivated.[4] Other proposals, such as that of Wilder and Çavar (1994), explicitly posit two separate motivations for verb and XP movement. Under Wilder and Çavar's analysis, verbs move to help check strong F-features in C° and XPs move to check strong topic features in [Spec, CP]. The co-occurrence of these two movements in the V2 languages is coincidental.

These two types of proposal posit a very different relationship between obligatory verb movement and phrasal movement to CP. Under the first approach, the two movements must co-occur because they are linked via a Spec–head relationship. Under the second, these movements are not dependent on one another, and their co-occurrence is the result of two independent, language-specific features. However, while these two approaches differ in the assumptions they make concerning the relationship between the verb and the initial XP, they account equally well for the adult V2 data. Under either approach, both the head and the specifier of CP will be filled. Just the motivation for filling both of these positions differs.

---

[3] *Wh*-Criterion (Rizzi 1991):
   (i) A *wh*-operator must be in a Spec–head configuration with an $X^{\circ}[+wh]$.
   (ii) An $X^{\circ}[+wh]$ must be in a Spec–head configuration with a *wh*-operator.
[4] Holmberg and Platzack do not discuss the motivation for XP movement in their analysis.

Even non-V2 clauses found in the adult V2 languages can be accounted for under either hypothesis. For example, at first glance the presence of verb-initial (V1) utterances, as in (5), might be considered evidence against linking the movement of the verb and the specifier. In conditional or narrative inversion, there is verb movement without any apparent XP movement. Thus, on the surface, it looks like these two movements can be dissociated, and should not be linked.

(5) (*a*) *Conditional inversion*   (*b*) *Narrative inversion*
  Kom du, så hjälper jag dig.   Tog han då foton.
  come you, so help I you   took he then picture-the
  '[If] you come, I'll help you.'   'Then he took the picture.'

However, if we allow for the presence of null operators in grammars, then it is possible that there is a null operator occupying the specifier of CP in these V1 constructions. If there is an operator, albeit null, occupying [Spec, CP], as illustrated in (6), then it is possible that the movement of the verb is triggered by the relationship with this null operator.

(6) $[_{CP} \text{Op}_{narr} [_C \text{tog}] [_{IP} \text{han} [_{VP} \text{då foton}]]]$
           took he   then photo-the
  'Then he took the picture.'

Under this analysis, there would be no need to dissociate verb movement from XP movement, since the cases in which the verb appears to move without an XP can be accounted for by positing null operators. Thus, we are still left with two viable alternatives, with only theory-internal preferences for helping us tell them apart.

2. PREDICTIONS FOR CHILD LANGUAGE

While the data from the adult language are compatible with both analyses, these two approaches to V2 do make different predictions for the acquisition of V2. This means that it may be possible to distinguish between these two proposals using data from child language. Thus child language may be in a position to help clarify issues of grammar that are difficult, if not impossible, to resolve using data from the adult language alone. In this section, I will outline the predictions each approach makes for the acquisition of verb and XP movement in child Swedish. In Section 3, I will introduce the corpora to be studied, and in Sections 4 and 5 I will test these predictions.

The approach that links verb and XP movement in a Spec–head relationship predicts that the two movements should be acquired together, because they are linked in the grammar. Under this approach, children should not acquire either verb movement or XP movement without the other. Thus, this approach predicts that errors where one element moves but the other does not should be rare.[5] Finally, this approach predicts that different Spec–head relationships could show different patterns of errors. For example, *wh*-questions and declarative topics could show different error rates with respect to verb movement, because V2 movement is triggered by the Spec–head relationship, which has different properties in different constructions.

The approach that dissociates the motivation for each movement predicts that either verb movement or XP movement could be found without the other, because the two movements are triggered by separate features. This approach thus predicts that errors where one element moves but the other does not could be quite common. Additionally, different children may exhibit different patterns of acquisition with respect to verb and XP movement; some children may acquire the features that trigger verb movement first, others may acquire XP movement first. Finally, this approach predicts that error rates for verb movement should not be affected by the XP in the specifier position, because verb movement is not dependent on the XP, but on its own features.

In the following sections, I will demonstrate that the error rates for verb movement are highly dependent on the initial XP. Thus, the data from child Swedish supports the approach where verb and XP movement are linked.

3. PARTICIPANTS AND METHOD

3.1. *Participants*

The data for this study come from several sources of natural speech. The first is a cross-sectional corpus collected by the author, containing data from eight children under the age of 3:0,[6] ranging from 1:9 to 3:0, with the majority of children under age 2:6. A summary of the data from these children is given in Table 14.1. The second source of data is a videotaped longitudinal corpus of a Swedish child, Sara, in play sessions with family members. Data from age 1:11 to 2:11 are presented here (Santelmann 1995*b*). The third set of data used in this study comes from longitudinal data from four children—Ask, Embla, Freja, and Tor—from the Project Child Language Syntax (Söderbergh 1975; Lange and Larsson 1977).[7] These longitudinal data consist of 30–45 minute audio recordings, collected in the children's homes on a bi-weekly basis. The group summaries for both of the longitudinal corpora are given in Table 14.2. Together, there are more than 21,400 clear, complete utterances that I have examined in these corpora.

---

[5] We know that adults make occasional errors of this sort, so this hypothesis need not predict that these errors should be absent altogether.

[6] Ages are given in the format years:months.

[7] I wish to thank Ragnhild Söderbergh for providing access to the transcripts of the Project Child Language Syntax (see Söderbergh 1975 for details).

TABLE 14.1. *Subject summary for cross-sectional data*

Name	Age	MLU[a]	Total clear, complete utterances	Multi-constituent utterances with verb
Åke	1:11	2.02	74	9
Frank	2:0	1.62	221	9
Anders	2:1	1.58	144	14
Kenneth	2:1	1.79	327	34
Kenneth2	2:2	2.51	178	48
Doris	2:4	2.36	273	102
Daniel	2:10	2.41	419	121
Lars	2:11	4.31	265	160
TOTAL			1,901	497

[a] MLU = mean length of utterances (measured in morphemes).
Source: Santelmann 1995*b*.

TABLE 14.2. *Subject summary for longitudinal data*

Child	Age range	MLU range[a]	Total clear, complete utterances	Multi-constituent utterances with verb
Sara	1:11–2:11	1.78–3.32	4,226	1,191
Ask	1:11–2:9	1.89–4.57	4,286	1,492
Embla	1:11–2:8	1.87–4.18	3,066	844
Freja	2:0–3:0	1.34–4.10	4,131	1,341
Tor	2:1–3:0	1.52–4.33	3,801	1,419
TOTAL			19,510	6,287

[a] MLU = mean length of utterances (measured in morphemes).
Sources: Sara: Santelmann 1995*b*; other children: Söderbergh 1975, Lange and Larsson 1977.

3.2. *Method*

All utterances with a verb, along with the context in which they occurred, were extracted after extensive searches of the written corpora. Because unambiguous evidence for V2 movement requires three constituents—a subject, a verb, and another constituent to place relative to these two—only utterances with three or more constituents will be analysed in this chapter. In the corpora presented here, 6,784 utterances (32 per cent of the total utterances) contained

three or more constituents including a verb. In addition to restricting the analysis to utterances of three or more constituents, utterances that grammatically
allow the verb to be preceded by more than one constituent were excluded.
There are several types of these grammatical non-V2 utterances that appear in
the corpora: (i) single clauses with overt complementizers, as in the example in
(7*a*), where the complementizer in C blocks verb movement; (ii) utterances
with adverbs such as *kanske* (maybe) as in (7*b*), which can appear as an X° head
in C and block verb movement (Platzack 1986); and (iii) left-dislocation structures, such as that in (7*c*).

(7)   *Types of grammatical non-V2 utterances*
  (*a*)   Ja, när vi inte är här.   (Lars)
        yes, when we not are here
        'Yes, when we aren't here.'

  (*b*)   Sen kanske hon flyger upp så här.   (Ask)
        then maybe she flies up so here
        'Then maybe she'll fly up like this.'

  (*c*)   Och så katten han var också tjock.   (Embla)
        and so cat-the, he was also fat
        'And so the cat, he was also fat.'

Finally, this study focuses on non-subject-initial utterances for much of the
analysis, because these clauses provide the clearest evidence for verb and XP
movement. Because Swedish is an SVO language, there are two structures that
clearly demonstrate verb movement out of the VP: movement past a sentential
adverb, as in (8*a*), and movement past the subject, as demonstrated in (8*b*).

(8) (*a*)   *Movement past adverb*
          hon *spelar$_i$* [ju [$_{VP}$ t_i trumpet]]
          she plays   of course trumpet
          'She plays trumpet of course.'

  (*b*)   *Movement past subjects*
          [$_{CP}$ trumpet [$_C$ *spelar$_i$* [$_{IP}$ hon [ju [$_{VP}$ t_i]]]]]
              trumpet   plays   she of course
          'Trumpet, she plays of course.'

In child speech, however, sentential adverbs are not consistently used, so movement past subjects provides us with a more robust, plentiful source of data for
V2 movement.

4. MOVEMENT TO THE SPECIFIER AND HEAD OF CP
IN EARLY CHILD SWEDISH

Having introduced the data to be analysed, we now turn to testing the predictions for child language made by the two approaches to V2. The first prediction
to be tested is whether verb movement and XP movement are acquired in-

dependently or together in early child Swedish. Recall from Section 2 that the analysis that links XP and verb movement through a Spec–head relationship predicts that the two movements should be acquired at the same time. The analysis that dissociates the two movements predicts that it is possible for one to be acquired independently of the other.

Finite verb movement is present in the earliest three-constituent utterances in child Swedish.[8] This verb movement is demonstrated in two ways: by movement past adverbs, as shown in the examples in (9), and by movement past the subject, as shown in (10). All of the children demonstrate early knowledge of verb movement, well before the majority of their utterances are longer than three constituents. For example, Embla (1:11) from the Söderbergh corpus demonstrates both subtypes of verb movement, even though only 6 per cent of her utterances are larger than two constituents and the mean length of her utterances (MLU) was only 1.87 morphemes.

(9)　　*Early evidence for verb movement past adverb*

   (a)　Den måste också öppna motorn.　　　　(Ask 01 1:11 MLU 3.09)
      it must also open motor-the
      'It must also open the motor.'

   (b)　Älger säger inte/inte mu.　　　　　　(Embla 07 1:11 MLU 1.87)
      elks say not/not moo
      'Elks do not say moo.'

   (c)　Jag vill inte.　　　　　　　　　　　(Embla 07 1:11 MLU 1.87)
      I want not
      'I don't want to.'

(10)　　*Early evidence for verb movement past subject*

   (a)　Det gör jag.　　　　　　　　　　　　(Åke 1:11 MLU 2.02)
      that make I
      'That, I make.'

   (b)　Där bodde de.　　　　　　　　　　　(Anders 2:1 MLU 1.58)
      there lived they
      'There, they lived.'

---

[8] Regular verbs are marked with either *-ar* or *-er* in the present tense and *-ade* or *-de* in past tense. Infinitive verb forms in Swedish are marked with the suffix *-a* (with a few exceptions). Participles are non-finite and most are marked with *-at*, *-t*, *-tt*, or *-it*, depending on the verb class.

Auxiliaries and modals in Swedish have both finite and non-finite forms, and several have past forms as well, and are assumed to originate in a complex VP in the adult language. However, as a matter of course, young Swedish children use only the finite, present tense forms of the modals in their early speech. There is some evidence suggesting that these early modals are generated in the inflectional functional categories and not in the VP. Young Swedish children (under 2:6–3:0) have been shown to place modals, but not finite main verbs, preceding sentential adverbs in subordinate clauses (Håkansson and Dooley-Collberg 1994). Because very young children's modals only precede the sentential adverbs, both in main and subordinate clauses, this suggests they are base-generated in a position higher than the sentential adverbs. The children's placement of modals contrasts with adult usage, where all finite verbs, including modals, follow sentential adverbs in subordinate clauses, as in example (2a) in the introduction.

(c) Vad gjorde grisen?   (Kenneth2 2:2 MLU 2.51)
     what made pig-the
     'What did the pig do?'

(d) Det vill jag.   (Doris 2:4 MLU 2.36)
     that, want I
     'That I want.'

(e) Har pappa det.   (Sara 1:11 MLU 1.78)
     has papa that
     'That, papa has.'

(f) Å hå hill det.   (Sara 2:0 MLU 1.85)
     and so wants that
     'So, that [one] wants to too.'

(g) Det ka pappa ha.   (Sara 2:1 MLU 2.25)
     that shall papa have
     'That, papa should have.'

(h) Nä nu har han den.   (Sara 2:2 MLU 1.91)
     no now has he it
     'No, now he has it.'

The verb movement that is found in these sessions is general. The moved verbs include modals and main verbs, in both present and past tenses.

Not only does a qualitative analysis of the data indicate an early, general ability to move verbs, but a quantitative analysis does so as well. In Table 14.3, the proportion of verbs clearly moved past the subject for the earliest speech samples is given. The proportion in Table 14.3 counts as 'clearly moved' only those utterances with the order: (XP) V_{fin} Subj (XP). The remainder of the utterances had the order Subj V XP. Some of these were finite verbs, but the utterances contained no sentential adverbs and thus were ambiguous with respect to verb movement. The rest of the verbs were non-finite and never demonstrated verb movement, occurring with the order S(adv)VO. Non-finite verbs do not appear preceding the subject.[9]

The proportion of finite verbs moved past the subject in any one sample ranges from 0 per cent to over 66.7 per cent. These proportions of 'clear' verb movement in the children's speech samples are in line with data from the adult language (Jörgensen 1976). Only Tor fails to demonstrate verb movement in

---

[9] Even though I am not presenting quantitative data on verb movement past sentential adverbs here, it should be noted that there is no child who demonstrates verb movement past sentential adverbs who does not also demonstrate verb movement past the subject. Thus there is not a stage where children can move the verb past the sentential adverb, but not past the subject. In addition, the children who demonstrate verb movement past sentential adverbs also demonstrate knowledge of the constraints on verb movement: 99% of finite verbs that occur in utterances with sentential adverbs are moved past the adverb, and 100% of non-finite verbs that occur in utterances with sentential adverbs remain in situ following the adverb.

TABLE 14.3. *Proportion of verb movement past the subject for the earliest sessions*

Name	Age	MLU[a]	Multi-constituent utterances with verb and subject (A)	Utterances with finite verb moved past subject (B)	Proportion of verbs moved past subject = (B)/(A) (%)
Cross-sectional corpus					
Åke	1:11	2.02	9	3	33.3
Frank	2:0	1.62	8	4	50.0
Anders	2:1	1.58	13	1	7.7
Kenneth	2:1	1.79	23	9	39.1
Kenneth2	2:2	2.51	40	15	37.5
Doris	2:4	2.36	89	60	67.4
Daniel	2:10	2.41	99	26	26.3
Lars	2:11	4.31	154	63	40.9
Longitudinal corpora					
Sara 1:11	1:11	1.78	33	6	18.2
Sara 2:0	2:0	1.85	49	11	22.5
Sara 2:1	2:1	2.25	62	10	16.1
Sara 2:2	2:2	1.91	38	7	18.4
Ask 01	1:11	3.09	60	7	11.7
Ask 02	2:0	2.32	27	8	29.6
Ask 03	2:0	2.11	33	7	21.2
Ask 04	2:1	1.89	11	1	9.1
Embla 07	1:11	1.87	11	3	27.3
Embla 08	2:0	2.26	26	4	15.4
Embla 09	2:1	2.09	39	5	12.8
Embla 10	2:1	2.67	59	27	45.8
Freja 09	2:0	1.52	10	2	20.0
Freja 10	2:0	1.64	14	5	35.7
Freja 11	2:1	1.34	5	2	40.0
Freja 12	2:1	1.54	9	0	0.0
Tor 09	2:1	1.52	21	0	0.0
Tor 10	2:2	1.59	27	14	51.9
Tor 11	2:3	1.55	6	1	16.7
Tor 12	2:3	2.15	18	12	66.7

[a] MLU = mean length of utterances (measured in morphemes).

his earliest sample with multi-constituent utterances.[10] However, this session also contains no finite verbs, and thus cannot demonstrate movement because Tor, like the other children, obeys the constraint that only finite verbs move.

These results from Swedish follow the pattern that has been documented for a number of languages: children learning languages with verb movement demonstrate early and consistent knowledge of the connection between finiteness and verb movement (e.g. Weissenborn 1990; Boser *et al.* 1992; Deprez and Pierce 1993; Poeppel and Wexler 1993). At the same time, these same children continue to use non-finite forms, even after they display knowledge of finite verb movement (e.g. Boser *et al.* 1992; Clahsen and Penke 1992; Hyams 1992; Deprez and Pierce 1993; Poeppel and Wexler 1993; Rizzi 1994; Wexler 1994; Haegeman 1995).

In addition to the widespread evidence for verb movement, there is also widespread evidence for non-subject XP movement in early child Swedish. Both types of XP movement, declarative topicalization and *wh*-question formation, are found in the early speech samples, as the examples in (11) and (12) show.

(11) *Examples of early declarative topics*

    (a) Nu ska jag gå.   (Åke 1:11 MLU 2.02)
         now shall I go
         'Now I'll go.'

    (b) Det gör jag.   (Åke 1:11 MLU 2.02)
         that make I
         'That I make.'

    (c) Där bodde de.   (Anders 2:1 MLU 1.58)
         there lived they
         'There they lived.'

    (d) Snart kommer maten.   (Kenneth 2:1 MLU 1.79)
         soon comes food-the
         'Soon the food will come.'

    (e) Här är bolle.   (Kenneth 2:1 MLU 1.79)
         here is ball-the
         'Here is the ball.'

    (f) Nu kommer den igen.   (Kenneth2 2:2 MLU 2.51)
         now comes it again
         'Now it's coming again.'

    (g) Där var det mat.   (Doris 2:4 MLU 2.36)
         there was there food
         'There was food there.'

---

[10] The recording Freja 12 also has no utterances that demonstrate verb movement, but Freja does demonstrate clear verb movement in several earlier sessions.

(*h*) Nu stänger vi.   (Doris 2:4 MLU 2.36)
now close we
'Now we close [it].'

(*i*) Nu får pappa denna.   (Sara 1:11 MLU 1.78)
now gets papa this
'Now papa gets this.'

(*j*) Det hiler jag.   (Sara 1:11 MLU 1.78)
that scratch I
'That I scratch.'

(12)   *Early evidence for* wh-*movement*[11]
(*a*) [o] är denna?   (Frank 2:0 MLU 1.62)
what is this
'What is this?'

(*b*) Vad gör den?   (Kenneth 2:1 MLU 1.79)
what makes that
'What does that do?'

(*c*) Var är min nalle?   (Kenneth 2:1 MLU 1.79)
where is my teddy
'Where is my teddy bear?'

(*d*) Vad gjorde grisen?   (Kenneth2 2:2 MLU 2.51)
what made pig-the
'What did the pig do?'

(*e*) Vad är detta här?   (Doris 2:4 MLU 2.36)
what is that here
'What is that?'

(*f*) [o] är det?   (Sara 1:11 MLU 1.78)
what is that
'What is that?'

As with verb movement, XP movement is general. There is a range of phrases used in these constructions, including adverbs and objects, with most of the children showing both types of XP movement. In addition, when one looks across samples, there is no discernible difference in terms of when wh-questions and declarative topics are found. They are both present from the earliest multi-constituent utterances, and both structures are used productively from the same early periods. Finally, not only is XP movement found, but when it occurs, it appears overwhelmingly together with the finite verb moved to the second position. Thus, the group data indicate an early general knowledge of both XP movement and verb movement.

To show that these facts hold for individual children as well as the group as a whole, I will briefly present a qualitative analysis of the two youngest chil-

---

[11] The form [o] in (12*a*) and (12*g*) is a reduced form of the adult *vad* [va] (what).

dren, Åke and Sara. Sara presents a good example of the acquisition of these movements, despite the fact that she demonstrates nearly every type of error that the children in this study make, as I will discuss in the next section. The first session that was analysed for Sara was age 1:11. In this session, 85 per cent of Sara's utterances were two constituents or less. Of the remaining 15 per cent, over half (seventeen utterances) contain non-finite verbs. Because Sara obeys the constraint on verb movement in Swedish that only finite verbs are allowed to move, none of these non-finite utterances show verb movement.

Of the sixteen verbs that are finite, six show clear evidence for verb movement past the subject, and five of these show XP movement.[12] These examples are given in (13). The verbs moved include main verbs (*killa* 'scratch', *ha* 'have', and *få* 'get'), modals (*vill* 'want'), and copulas (*var* 'was', *är* 'is'). The topicalized constituents include both adverbs (*nu* 'now', *där* 'there') and objects (*det* 'that').

(13)   *Sara 1:11: verb and XP movement*

   (a) Nä det vill jag.
       no that want I
       'No, that I want.'

   (b) Det hiler jag.
       that scratch I
       'That I scratch.'

   (c) Oj där va pappa.
       oh there was papa
       'Oh, there papa was.'

   (d) Nu får pappa denna.
       now gets papa this
       'Now papa gets this.'

   (e) Har pappa det.
       has papa that
       'Papa has that.'

   (f) [o] är det?
       what is that
       'What is that?'

Thus, even though only a small proportion of Sara's utterances in this session are of three or more constituents (15 per cent), she shows evidence of productive verb and non-subject XP movement in her grammar.

Similar evidence can be found for Åke, who at age 1:11 was the youngest child analysed in the cross-sectional corpus. Only 12 per cent (nine total) of the utterances in Åke's speech sample contain three or more constituents, and thus can demonstrate clear movement. None the less, he too demonstrates evidence for both verb movement and XP movement in this session. Three of Åke's nine multi-constituent utterances show subject–verb inversion, as shown below.

(14)   *Åke's early verb and XP movement*

   (a) Vad gör det?
       what makes that
       'What does that do?'

   (c) Det gör jag.
       that make I
       'That I do.'

---

[12] Sara did not have any sentential adverbs in this session, so verb movement can only be judged by movement of the verb past the subject. Six utterances showed verb movement past the subject, and the remainder of the finite utterances had SVO word order without a sentential adverb, and thus are ambiguous with respect to verb movement.

(b) Nu ska jag gå.
    now shall I go
    'Now I'll go.'

These utterances invert both main (*göra* 'make') and auxiliary (*ska* 'shall/will') verbs, and the topicalized XPs include an adverb (*nu* 'now'), and two objects, one *wh*-word (*vad* 'what'), and one declarative topic (*det* 'that'). Thus, despite the low number of finite, multi-constituent utterances in Åke's speech, he demonstrates both verb movement and non-subject XP movement.

This analysis given for Sara and Åke also holds for the other children in this study. For all of the children, if they demonstrated verb movement, they also demonstrated non-subject XP movement, and vice versa. There were only two sessions (Tor at age 2:1 and Freja at age 2:1) among the early longitudinal sessions that showed no XP movement past the subject. These sessions also lacked verb movement. Thus, there was no child who demonstrated only one of these movements.

In sum, the acquisition of well-formed, non-subject-initial utterances appears to be consistent with an analysis that suggests that V2 movement and topicalization are linked via a Spec–head relationship, and not from independent motivations for the movement of the verb and the XP. Both movements are present from the earliest multi-constituent utterances, both movements are acquired at the same time, and they appear consistently together.

5. ERROR ANALYSIS: EVIDENCE FOR A SPEC–HEAD RELATIONSHIP UNDERLYING V2

While the data from well-formed V2 utterances are consistent with analyses of V2 which link XP and verb movement in a specifier–head relationship, they are still not conclusive evidence against the alternative hypothesis that these are independently motivated, but concurrent movements. The analysis that dissociates the two movements predicts that their acquisition *might* be dissociated, not that it must be. Indeed, the fact that these two movements occur consistently together only demonstrates that Swedish children produce well-formed utterances. It is still possible that Swedish children acquire the feature for verb movement and the feature for XP movement concurrently. Thus, as with the adult language, these well-formed utterances could be explained under either analysis of V2, whether or not the movements of the XP and the verb are assumed to be linked.

In order to truly distinguish between the two alternative analyses for V2 then, we need to test the predictions these two approaches make for the pattern of errors. Recall that the approach that links the two movements predicts that errors where the two movements do not occur together should be rare, and that the pattern of errors found for verb movement might be linked to the type of

XP in the specifier position. The approach that dissociates the two, on the other hand, predicts that errors where one element but not the other moves could be frequent, and that the pattern of verb movement errors should be independent of the type of XP in the specifier position.

The first test for whether XP and verb movement can be dissociated comes from examining whether verbs can move without XP movement. Utterances where the child has moved the verb into C without accompanying XP movement occur with some regularity in the data. Some examples are given in (15).

(15)   *Examples of verb movement without overt XP movement*

    (*a*)   Har pappa det.   (Sara 1:11 MLU 1.78)
            has papa that
            'Papa has that.'

    (*b*)   Jo, kan jag haktist.   (Sara 2:5 MLU 1.98)
            yes, can I actually
            'Yes, [that] I can actually do.'

    (*c*)   Ska du göra det.   (Tor 2:8 MLU 3.65)
            shall you do it
            'You should do that.'

    (*d*)   Lägger vi på den bil.   (Freja 2:0 MLU 1.64)
            set we on this car
            '[That] we set on this car.'

At first glance, the presence of these verb-initial (V1) utterances could suggest that XP and verb movement can be dissociated. However, these data need not be interpreted thus. First, these V1 utterances never occur as the only type of verb movement in a sample; if a child has three-constituent V1 utterances, then s/he has well-formed V2 structures as well. Sara, who produces the most V1 utterances of any child, has a relatively consistent use of V1 utterances over time, as can be seen from the developmental chart in Figure 14.3. The frequency of V1 utterances ranges from 0 per cent to 20 per cent, but does not show a steady decrease over time. Thus, these V1 utterances do not make up an early developmental stage where verbs move but XPs do not.

In addition to the evidence that the production of V1 structures does not reflect an inability to move XPs, there is a possible alternative analysis for these V1 utterances. Recall that the adult language allows V1 utterances in narrative inversion, conditionals, and yes/no questions, as noted above (cf. (5)). It is possible to analyse the adult structures as containing a null operator in [Spec, CP], thereby maintaining the strict one-to-one relationship between an XP in the specifier and a verb in the head of C.

There is some evidence that V1 utterances in child Swedish should be analysed in the same manner as in the adult language. A number of V1 utterances contain null topics (cf. (15*b*) and (15*d*) above), indicating that at least some V1 utterances have a covert element in [Spec, CP]. In addition, there

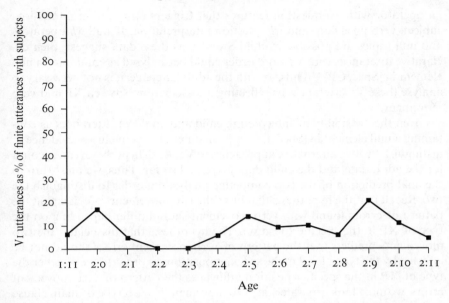

FIG. 14.3. *Sara's use of verb-initial structures (e.g.* har pappa det *'has papa that') as a proportion of all utterances with finite verbs and subjects*

is a subset of *wh*-questions in child Swedish that provide evidence for the presence of null operators. A number of *wh*-questions in the early speech samples lack overt *wh*-words, as seen in the examples in (16).

(16)   *Child Swedish*   *Adult Swedish*
   (*a*) är det?   (Tor 19 2:8 MLU 3.76)   (*b*) Vad är det?
        is that   (missing *vad*, 'what')   what is that
        'What is that?'   'What is that?'

   (*c*) gör apa då?   (Tor 15 2:6 MLU 2.67)   (*d*) Hur gör apan då?
        does ape then   (missing *hur*, 'how')   how makes the ape then
        'How does the ape do [that] then?'   'How does the ape do
                                                         [that] then?'

There are a number of indications that these questions contain a null *wh*-operator. These questions have the same intonation, word order, and interpretation as *wh*-questions with overt *wh*-elements.[13] This suggests that there is

---

[13] The gap in these questions is systematically in the initial position, with subject–verb inversion. If the missing element were not a question operator in [Spec, CP], then there would be no reason for the gap always to be in the initial, preverbal position. Questions with a gap in postverbal position (e.g. *apan gör* ——*?*) are virtually non-existent in the data, whereas *wh*-less questions such as those in (16) are quite common. See Santelmann (1995*b*, 1997) for a discussion of the evidence that there are null *wh*-operators in child Swedish.

an operator with *wh*-question features that triggers *wh*-question intonation, subject–verb inversion, and *wh*-question interpretation. If null *wh*-operators and null topics are possible in child Swedish as these data suggest, then declarative utterances with V1 word order could be analysed as containing a null element in [Spec, CP].[14] Thus, as with the adult language, it is not necessary to analyse these V1 utterances as reflecting a dissociation between XP and verb movement.

Given the possibility of interpreting child and adult V1 utterances as containing a null element in [Spec, CP], we still do not have conclusive evidence to distinguish the two alternative approaches to V2. Both hypotheses can account for the adult data and the child data presented so far. Thus, we must turn to the final prediction of the two competing analyses in order to distinguish the two. Recall that the hypothesis that links the two movements predicts that the pattern of errors found with verb movement should differ depending on the type of XP in the specifier position. The hypothesis that dissociates the two movements predicts that the pattern of verb movement errors should not be affected by the type of XP in the specifier position. In order to see whether the type of XP in the specifier position influences the pattern of verb movement errors, we must look separately at verb movement in each type of main clause with verb movement: *wh*-questions, declarative topics, and subject-initial utterances.

First, for *wh*-questions, the data show virtually error-free acquisition of movement of both the *wh*-word and the verb. The majority of *wh*-questions are well formed, even at the youngest ages. The *wh*-word is always placed at the beginning of the utterance, preceding the verb, indicating the presence of obligatory *wh*-movement. In addition, *wh*-questions in early child Swedish show overwhelming evidence for verb movement. In the speech samples examined, only five questions lack subject–verb inversion. These questions are given in (17). They represent only 1 per cent of the total number of questions, and as can be seen in the range of ages and MLUs of the children who produce them, they are not confined to a particular age or stage of development.

(17) *Questions with non-moved verbs (all examples found)*
  (*a*) Var han bor?   (Embla 11 2:1 MLU 2.51)
        where he lives
        'Where he lives?'

  (*b*) Vad det är?   (Frank 2:0 MLU 1.62)
        what that is
        'What that is?'

---

[14] Additionally, it has been argued for child German, another V2 language where children frequently use V1 utterances, that many V1 utterances contain a discourse-linked null element, even when there is no clear null topic (Boser 1995, 1996).

    (c) Vad det är?   (twice; Tor 15 2:5 MLU 2.67)
         what that is
         'What that is?'

    (d) Vad för grejer du har med dig?   (Lars 2:11 MLU 3.97)
         what for things you have with you
         'What kind of things you have with you?'

While errors in *wh*-questions in child Swedish are remarkably infrequent, declarative topics show a different pattern of errors. In declarative topicalization, utterances where the overt verb is not in second position ('V3 errors') are more common than in the *wh*-questions. Some examples of this are in (18).

(18)   *V3 Errors in declarative topics*
    (a) Där han tå.   (Sara 1:11 MLU 1.78)
         there he stand-INF
         'There he stand[s].'

    (b) Där jag hätt in hakerna.   (Sara 2:11 MLU 3.32)
         there I set-PARTICIPLE in things
         'There I [have] set things in.'

    (c) Den jag ha.   (Sara 2:1 MLU 2.25)
         that I have-INF
         'That I have.'

    (d) Det pappa gjort.   (Kenneth2 2:2 MLU 2.51)
         that papa made-PARTICIPLE
         'That papa [has] made.'

    (e) Nu han kör.   (Tor 16 2:6 MLU 2.49)
         now he drives
         'Now he drives.'

    (f) Nu Embla bada.   (Embla 08 2:0 MLU 2.26)
         now Embla bathe-INF
         'Now Embla bathe[s].'

These V3 topics occur with a variety of verbs, both finite and non-finite, transitive and intransitive, and they are found at a range of ages and different MLUs.[15] These errors with topics are both qualitatively and quantitatively different from those with *wh*-questions. They occur more frequently (in about 4 per cent of topics overall), and they are found in nearly every speech sample, even well into the complex sentence period. Verb movement errors in questions, on the other hand, are rare when they do occur and are absent altogether from many speech samples.

Finally, turning to subject-initial clauses, these utterances stand in sharp

---

[15] Santelmann (1995*a*) demonstrates that although V3 errors in topics are more frequent than V3 errors in questions, they still do not constitute a stage of XP movement without inversion. These V3 topics always occur alongside well-formed topics, in the very same session.

contrast to topicalization and *wh*-questions. The majority of *wh*-questions and declarative topics occur with finite, moved verbs in the second position. This is true from the earliest three-constituent utterances. Subject-initial clauses on the other hand show evidence for development with respect to verb movement. In these clauses, finiteness is marked in less than 50 per cent of the earliest three-constituent utterances. As can be seen in the examples in (19), these non-finite verbs do not move either; instead they remain inside the VP, following negation or other sentential adverbs. These verbs remain in situ, even though the subject itself moves outside the VP, preceding sentential negation or other sentential adverbs.[16]

(19)   *Examples of non-finite verbs in subject-initial contexts*
   (*a*) Ja han inte ha korn.   (Sara 2:3 MLU 2.01)
          yes he not have-INF shoes
          'Yes he [does] not have shoes.'

   (*b*) Sara ocke fölle med.   (Sara 2:4 MLU 2.41)
          Sara also follow-INF along
          'Sara also go[es] along.'

   (*c*) Jag bara/jag bara flytta på den.   (Tor 15 2:5 MLU 2.33)
          I just/I just move-INF PARTICLE it
          'I just move it.'

   (*d*) Han inte bada.   (Freja 16 2:4 MLU 2.21)
          he not swim-INF
          'He [does] not swim.'

   (*e*) Dockan också sova.   (Freja 19 2:6 MLU 2.57)
          doll-the also sleep-INF
          'The doll also sleep[s].'

Indeed, when we compare subject-initial and non-subject-initial clauses, we find that obligatory finiteness marking and the verb movement associated with this finiteness marking are 'acquired' or consistently used much later for subject-initial clauses than for non-subject-initial contexts. For most children, non-subject-initial clauses are produced with over 90 per cent finite verbs in the second position anywhere from three to six months earlier than is the case for subject-initial clauses, as can be seen from the graphs in Figures 14.4–8.

In addition to showing the delay in using finite verbs in subject-initial contexts, these graphs show a clear difference in error rates for verb movement depending on the type of XP in the specifier position. *Wh*-questions rarely, if ever, occur without a verb in the second position, declarative topics sometimes

---

[16] Very few subjects occur inside sentential adverbs, even in non-finite utterances in child Swedish. The overwhelming majority (96% or more) of subjects that occur in clauses with sentential adverbs appear preceding the adverb (Santelmann 1995*b*). The adverbs most often used in the early sessions are *inte* (not), *också* (also), and *bara* (just/only). In the later sessions, a greater range of adverbs, including *kanske* (maybe), *ju* (of course), and *nog* (probably), is also found.

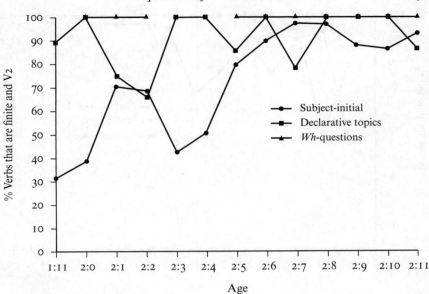

FIG. 14.4. *Sara's use of finite verbs in second position with three different initial XPs*

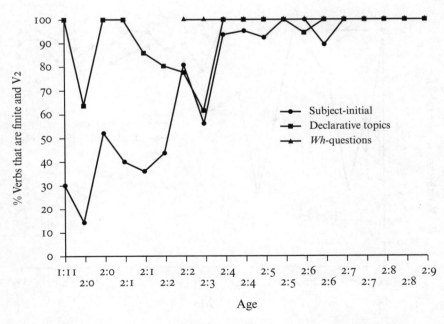

FIG. 14.5. *Ask's use of finite verbs in second position with three different initial XPs*

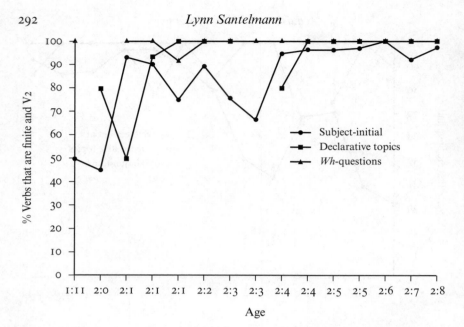

FIG. 14.6. *Embla's use of finite verbs in second position with three different initial XPs*

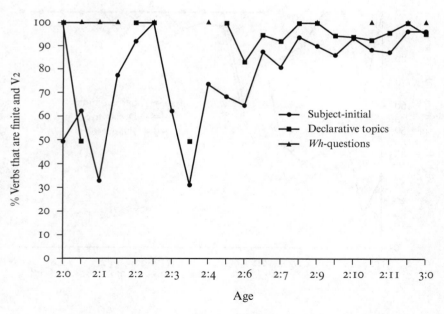

FIG. 14.7. *Freja's use of finite verbs in second position with three different initial XPs*

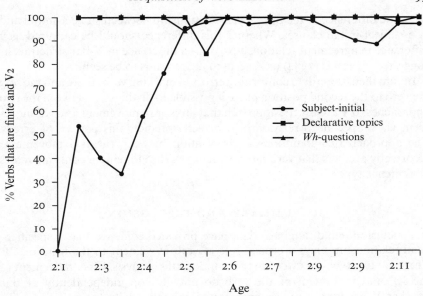

FIG. 14.8. *Tor's use of finite verbs in second position with three different initial XPs*

do, and subject-initial clauses often do. Furthermore, different children show different patterns of errors for the different initial XPs. Tor, for example, makes very few errors with either declarative topics or *wh*-questions. Sara and Ask, on the other hand, make proportionately more errors on declarative topics than they do on *wh*-questions. Thus, we have clear evidence from child language that the nature of the specifier–head relationship has an effect on verb movement. Note that this evidence cannot be found from the adult language, because adults make very few errors with verb movement at all, regardless of the initial XP.

In addition to suggesting a strong role for differences in Spec–head relationships between different types of clauses, the delay in verb movement in subject-initial clauses suggests a substantial difference between subject-initial and non-subject-initial clauses. Note that we cannot explain the differences between the two types of clauses simply by assuming that non-finite, subject-initial clauses are simply truncated VPs (see e.g. Rizzi 1994). Even in the earliest recordings, the subjects precede the sentential adverbs over 96 per cent of the time in non-finite contexts, suggesting that they have moved out of the VP and into a higher functional category, even though the verb itself may or may not be marked finite.[17] Thus, this difference seems instead to be due to a

---

[17] In addition, there is evidence that the subjects of these 'root infinitives' in Swedish do not

syntactic difference in the Spec–head relationship between subject-initial and non-subject-initial clauses. Whether this difference should be captured as a difference in agreement relationships, or as a difference in X-bar structure, as suggested by Travis (1984) or Zwart (1994), remains to be seen.[18]

In sum then, these data concerning errors in marking verbs finite and moving the verb to the second position make it possible to distinguish between the two approaches to V2. Only the approach that links verb movement and XP movement via a Spec–head relationship correctly predicts this pattern of errors. The approach that maintains a dissociation between the two movements incorrectly predicts that verb movement errors should remain constant across all sentence types.

6. SUMMARY AND DISCUSSION

In conclusion, child language data have provided evidence that a specifier–head relationship plays a crucial role in verb movement to the head of CP. There are two types of evidence that support this analysis. First, movement of the XP and movement of the verb do not develop independently of one another. If one type of movement is found, the other will be as well. Secondly, the fact that the error rate for verb movement depends greatly on the element in the specifier position suggests that movement of the verb is not independent from the movement of the XP. If verb movement were triggered solely by the features on the verb, then we would expect verb movement to be consistently applied once the child has acquired those verbal features. However, that is not the pattern of errors that we see. Accuracy in V2 movement is correlated with the XP that is in the specifier position. Swedish children are remarkably accurate in *wh*-questions, less so in declarative topicalization, and much less accurate in subject-initial clauses. Thus, as the XP in the specifier varies, so does the rate of error in marking verbs finite, which enables them to move. The verbal features are no different in each type of clause. That means that this difference in development cannot be due to the features on the verb, but must lie in the relationship the verb has with its specifier.

In addition to the data presented here, there is converging evidence

lack finiteness features, as argued for German and English by Hoekstra *et al.* (Ch. 13, this volume). For Ask and Embla, 100% of their NP subjects in their early root infinitives were definite; for Freja and Sara, 50–60% were definite, while for Tor, 33% were definite. Thus, for these Swedish children, there is not a correlation between missing definiteness of the subject and missing finiteness on the verb. The difference between Swedish and German/English may have to do with the fact that the definiteness marker in Swedish is a suffix *-en/-et* while English and German use a prenominal definite article.

[18] The fact that the differences between subject-initial clauses and non-subject-initial clauses are much greater than those within the two types of subject-initial clause have led me to argue elsewhere that subject-initial clauses involve movement to IP, while non-subject-initial clauses involve movement to CP (Santelmann 1996).

from other sources that a specifier–head relationship plays a fundamental role in V2 grammars. The first piece of evidence comes from the acquisition of V2 by Swedish children with Specific Language Impairment (Håkansson and Nettelbladt 1993; Hansson and Nettelbladt 1995) and from children acquiring Swedish as their second language (Håkansson 1992; Håkansson and Nettelbladt 1993). These studies claim that both groups of children show a delay in V2—they dissociate XP and verb movement by moving XPs without accompanying verb movement. However, if and when they acquire V2, they tend to acquire it first with *wh*-questions and only later with declarative topics and subject-initial clauses (Håkansson, personal communication). Here again we see that errors in verb movement are dependent on the characteristics of the XP in the specifier position. This suggests that it is the relationship with the XP that helps to trigger verb movement in these clauses.

The second piece of converging evidence for the specifier–head relationship underlying V2 movement comes from the historical development of English. As is well known, English at one time possessed a general V2 pattern, but over time V2 has become restricted to *wh*-questions, and marginally to other clauses with initial operators, such as negatives (e.g. *never had we seen such a beautiful sight!*). This selective loss of V2 is difficult to explain if V2 is composed of two independent, but co-occurring movements of XP and verb. However, if V2 is composed of a set of Spec–head relationships, then it is possible for one type of specifier (e.g. declarative topics) to lose its requirement for a privileged relationship with the verb, while other specifiers retain such a relationship.

Both the historical and the child language data rule out a strict interpretation of Greed (Chomsky 1992), by which each moved element can only move to satisfy morphological features of its own. A very strict interpretation of Greed forces a dissociation between the two movements of V2, a dissociation which is incompatible with the child language data. The fact that children's error rates in verb movement depend on the element in the specifier position means that verb movement and XP movement must somehow be connected in these V2 constructions.[19]

At the same time, these child acquisition data do not tell us what connects the two movements in V2. These two movements could be linked by a common Spec–head relationship or by a common set of features in C. The first alternative could be implemented with a generalized notion of the *Wh*-Criterion (Rizzi 1991), where there is a reciprocal agreement relationship between the verb and the XP. Under this hypothesis, each Spec–head relationship might display a different pattern of verb movement found, as is seen in the child acquisition

---

[19] In addition, the fact that verb movement is affected by the XP in the specifier position suggests that the features being checked are associated with the functional head C, rather than the lexical items (e.g. verb and *wh*-phrase) themselves. This conflicts with Simpson's analysis (Ch. 12, this volume), which argues that *wh*-feature checking is not a property of the functional head, but a property of the *wh*-phrase itself.

data. The second alternative could be implemented under an 'Attract' analysis of movement (Chomsky 1995). There could be a set of features in C which includes both strong XP features that the moved XP checks in a Spec–head relationship and strong C features that the verb checks. Under this analysis, the patterns of verb movement seen in the child data could be explained by differences in the features in C: each feature could show different patterns of attraction. Crucially, however, the sets of features that attract the XP and the verb must both differ according to the clause type.[20] This latter analysis is more in line with recent analyses of syntax, which maintain an asymmetrical view of Spec–head relationships (e.g. Chomsky 1995). Thus, this analysis may be more appealing on theoretical grounds than the symmetric agreement approach, even though the child data themselves are silent on this point.

In conclusion, then, we have evidence from child language, evidence that is difficult to find in the adult languages, that V2 movement reflects a relationship between the XP and the verb. This result has several consequences for the grammar of the adult V2 languages. First, it requires that if concepts such as 'Last Resort' (Chomsky and Lasnik 1993; Chomsky 1995) are used to motivate movement for grammars in general, these concepts must be formulated so they allow movement to the specifier position and movement to the head position to be associated—either by agreement or by a common set of features. Secondly, the differences in acquisition between *wh*-questions, declarative topics, and subject-initial clauses indicate that Swedish children are not acquiring a generic V2, but a set of relationships between the specifier and the verb, relationships that vary from construction to construction. This in turn suggests that V2 is made up not of a single, generic Spec–head relationship, but of several Spec–head relationships that together form the grammar of V2.

REFERENCES

Boser, K. (1995), 'Verb Initial Utterances in Early Child German: A Study of the Interaction of Grammar and Pragmatics', in E. Clark (ed.), *Proceedings of the Twenty-Seventh Annual Child Language Research Forum*, Center for the Study of Language and Information, Stanford University, Stanford, Calif.

——(1996), 'The Acquisition of Word Order Knowledge in Early Child German: Interactions of Syntax and Pragmatics', Ph.D. dissertation, Cornell University (University Microfilms International, Ann Arbor, Mich.).

——Lust, B., Santelmann, L., and Whitman, J. (1992), 'The Syntax of CP and V2 in Early Child German (ECG): The Strong Continuity Hypothesis', *Proceedings of NELS*, 22: 51–66, GLSA, Amherst, Mass.

---

[20] Presumably the *wh*-features are obligatory in C, while the topic features are optional. Optional features have also been proposed for scrambling, e.g. by Grewendorf (Ch. 8, this volume).

Chomsky, N. (1992), 'A Minimalist Program for Linguistic Theory', *MIT Occasional Papers in Linguistics*, 1, *MIT Working Papers in Linguistics*, Cambridge, Mass.

——(1995), *The Minimalist Program*, MIT Press, Cambridge, Mass.

——and Lasnik, H. (1993), 'Principles and Parameters Theory', in J. Jacobs, A. van Stechow, W. Sternefeld, and T. Vennemann (eds.), *Syntax: An International Handbook of Contemporary Research*, Walter de Gruyter, Berlin, 506–69.

Clahsen, H., and Penke, M. (1992), 'The Acquisition of Agreement Morphology and Its Syntactic Consequences: New Evidence on German Child Language from the Simone-Corpus', in J. Meisel (ed.), *The Acquisition of Verb Placement: Functional Categories and V2 Phenomena in Language Development*, Kluwer, Dordrecht, 181–224.

den Besten, H. (1983), 'On the Interaction of Root Transformations and Lexical Deletive Rules', in W. Abraham (ed.), *On the Formal Syntax of the West Germania*, Benjamins, Amsterdam, 47–131.

Deprez, V., and Pierce, A. (1993), 'Negation and Functional Projections in Early Grammar', *Linguistic Inquiry*, 24: 25–68.

Diesing, M. (1990), 'Verb Movement and the Subject Position in Yiddish', *Natural Language and Linguistic Theory*, 8: 41–79.

Haegeman, L. (1995), 'Root Infinitives, Tense and Truncated Structure in Dutch', *Language Acquisition*, 4: 205–55.

——and Zanuttini, R. (1991), 'Negative Heads and the Neg Criterion', *The Linguistic Review*, 8: 233–52.

Håkansson, G. (1992), 'Variation och rigiditet i ordföljdsmönster' [Variation and rigidity in word order patterns], in M. Axelsson and Å. Viberg (eds.), *Nordens språk som målspråk* [Scandinavian languages as mother tongues], Stockholms Universitet, Stockholm.

——and Dooley-Collberg, S. (1994), 'The Preference for Modal + Neg: An L2 Perspective Applied to L1 Children', *Second Language Research*, 10(2): 95–124.

——and Nettelbladt, U. (1993), 'Developmental Sequences in L1 (Normal and Impaired) and L2 Acquisition of Swedish Syntax', *International Journal of Applied Linguistics*, 3: 131–57.

Hansson, K., and Nettelbladt, U. (1995), 'Characteristics of Swedish Children with SLI', *Journal of Speech and Hearing Research*, 38(3): 589–98.

Heycock, C., and Santorini, B. (1993), 'Head Movement and the Licensing of Non-Thematic Positions', *Proceedings of the West Coast Conference on Formal Linguistics XI*, The Center for the Study of Language and Information, Stanford University, 262–76.

Holmberg, A., and Platzack, C. (1989), 'The Role of AGR and Finiteness in the Germanic VO Languages', *Working Papers in Scandinavian Syntax*, 43: 51–6.

——————(1995), *The Role of Inflection in Scandinavian Syntax*, Oxford University Press, Oxford.

Hyams, N. (1992), 'The Genesis of Clause Structure', in J. Meisel (ed.), *The Acquisition of Verb Placement: Functional Categories and V2 Phenomena in Language Development*, Kluwer, Dordrecht, 371–400.

Jörgensen, N. (1976), *Meningsbyggnaden i talad svenska* [Sentence structure in spoken Swedish], Lundastudier i nordiska språkvetenskap [Lund studies in Scandinavian linguistics], Studentlitteratur, Lund.

Lange, S., and Larsson, K. (1977), 'Studier i det tidiga barnspråkets grammatik' [Studies in early child grammar], PM no. 11: *Projektet barnspråksyntax* [The project child language syntax], Stockholms Universitet, Stockholm.

Platzack, C. (1986), 'The Position of the Finite Verb in Swedish', in H. Haider and M. Prinzhorn (eds.), *Verb Second Phenomena in Germanic Languages*, Foris, Dordrecht, 27–47.

Poeppel, D., and Wexler, K. (1993), 'The Full Competence Hypothesis of Clause Structure in Early German', *Language*, 69: 1–34.

Rizzi, L. (1991), 'Residual Verb Second and the *Wh*-Criterion', *Technical Reports in Formal and Computational Linguistics*, 2, The Department of Linguistics, University of Geneva.

——(1994), 'Some Notes on Linguistic Theory and Language Development: The Case of Root Infinitives', *Language Acquisition*, 3: 371–93.

Santelmann, L. (1995*a*), 'Topicalization, CP and Licensing in the Acquisition of Swedish', in D. MacLaughlin and S. McEwen (eds.), *Proceedings of the 19th Annual Boston University Conference on Child Language Development*, Cascadilla Press, Somerville, Mass., 499–511.

——(1995*b*), 'The Acquisition of Verb Second Grammar in Early Child Swedish: Continuity of UG in Wh-Questions, Topicalization and Verb Raising', Ph.D. thesis, Cornell University (University Microfilms International, Ann Arbor, Mich.).

——(1996), 'Subject Initial Verb Second as IP: Evidence from Subject/Non-Subject Asymmetries in the Acquisition of Verb Second in Mainland Scandinavian', paper presented at the conference What Children Have to Say about Linguistic Theory, Utrecht, June.

——(1997), 'Wh-Question Formation in Early Swedish: An Argument for Continuity, CP and Operators', in S. Somashekar, K. Yamakoshi, M. Blume, and C. Foley (eds.), *Cornell Working Papers in Linguistics*, 15: 217–53.

Schwartz, B., and Vikner, S. (1989), 'All Verb Second Clauses are CPs', *Working Papers in Scandinavian Syntax*, 43: 27–49.

Söderbergh, R. (1975), 'Projektet barnspråksyntax' [Project child language syntax], (P)reprint no. 6, Institutionen för Nordiska Språk, Stockholms Universitet, Stockholm.

Travis, L. (1984), 'Parameters and Effects of Word Order Variation', Ph.D. dissertation, MIT.

Weissenborn, J. (1990), 'Functional Categories and Verb Movement: The Acquisition of German Syntax Reconsidered', in M. Rothweiler (ed.), *Spracherwerb und Grammatik: Linguistische Untersuchungen zum Erwerb von Syntax und Morphologie* [Language acquisition and grammar: linguistic research on the acquisition of syntax and morphology], Westdeuscher Verlag, Opladen, 190–224.

Wexler, K. (1994), 'Optimal Infinitives, Head Movement and the Economy of Derivations', in D. Lightfoot and N. Hornstein (eds.), *Verb Movement*, Cambridge University Press, Cambridge, 305–50.

Wilder, C., and Çavar, D. (1994), 'Word Order Variation, Verb Movement, and Economy Principles', *Studia Linguistica*, 48(1): 46–86.

Zwart, C. J.-W. (1994), 'Dutch Syntax: A Minimalist Approach', Ph.D. thesis, University of Groningen.

15

Some Specs on Specs in L2 Acquisition

BONNIE D. SCHWARTZ

1. INTRODUCTION

There are two goals to this chapter: first, to familiarize those outside the field of non-native language (L2) acquisition with some of the conceptual and theoretical concerns of L2 acquisition research; secondly, to discuss some empirical findings, related to the area of specifiers, that bear on these issues. In regard to the latter, data from two studies on child L2 acquisition—one involving clitics (White 1996), the other the order between verb and object (Haznedar 1995, 1997)—will be reexamined. Before turning to these data (Sections 3 and 4, respectively), a brief introduction to the principal issues guiding L2 acquisition research in the generative framework is in order.

2. BACKGROUND

2.1. *L2 acquisition, UG, and 'transfer'*

Since the early 1980s, one of the main themes in generative L2 acquisition research has been the extent to which L2 acquisition—particularly by adults— is constrained by the same principles of UG thought to underlie native language (L1) acquisition (e.g. White 1985; Flynn 1987). One way researchers have sought to determine this is to look for 'similarities' between L1 and L2 acquisition, a strategy in fact taken over from traditional L2 acquisition work

Parts of this work were supported by grants from the University of Durham, for which I am very grateful: for travel to Montreal to present at GASLA '97, and for the ACCESS (Adult and Child Crosslinguistic English Second Syntax) project, co-directed with Martha Young-Scholten. For help at various points in the writing and revising of this chapter, I would like to thank Judy Bernstein, Ute Bohnacker, Andrew Caink, Cécile de Cat, Nigel Duffield, Aafke Hulk, Dalina Kallulli, Rex A. Sprouse, Maggie Tallerman, Lydia White, Martha Young-Scholten, and two anonymous reviewers. Nigel Duffield first suggested to me the idea of there being subject clitics in English, although in syntactic contexts different from those presented here, the latter having been co-discovered by Andrew Caink and Joe Emonds for the cross-linguistic clitic survey in the van Riemsdijk (forthcoming) volume. I am especially grateful to Joe for discussions of many aspects of this chapter, to Cornelia Hamann for discussions on the differences between the L1 French data and the L2 French data, to Belma Haznedar for discussions of Erdem's development, to Kyle B. Johnson for discussions on syntax, and to Bernadette Plunkett for her careful and critical evaluation of most everything in here.

(e.g. Dulay *et al.* 1982). When such L1–L2 acquisition similarities have been found, it is often concluded that the same types of cognitive processes are at work, specifically, that as in L1 acquisition, UG constrains L2 acquisition. This approach is, however, somewhat naïve, because it completely neglects the possibility of systematic effects from the L1 grammar (Schwartz 1992). L1–L2 differences in, say, developmental stages do not necessarily imply that UG does not constrain L2 acquisition: the same *processes* could underlie L1 and L2 acquisition, with the differences in (transitional) *products* being due to influence from the L1 grammar. In short, the existence of—in more familiar terms— 'transfer' from the L1 grammar does not in any way bear on whether L2 acquisition makes use of the same cognitive processes as used in L1 acquisition.

Thus, a second major concern has been that of transfer: how much and when. This has recently been reconceptualized in terms of the 'L2 initial state' (Hoekstra and Schwartz 1994; Schwartz and Eubank 1996): while most generative work on L2 acquisition grants definite influence from the L1 grammar (but cf. Epstein *et al.* 1996), there is substantial disagreement on the extent to which it defines the L2 initial state. Testing the various positions on the L2 initial state (see below) is the focus of much current work—for instance, following on the heels of L1 acquisition research, whether functional projections (typically, functional heads) are part of the L2 'system' from the outset. Very little L2 research that I am aware of has centred on specifiers and theories of specifiers *per se*.

2.2. *Minimal Trees, Full Transfer/Full Access, and preview*

To ground the empirical work I will concentrate on here, I first briefly present the case for the smallest amount of transfer. This is the 'Minimal Trees' hypothesis of Vainikka and Young-Scholten. Based on L2 German data from (adult) speakers of Korean and Turkish (Vainikka and Young-Scholten 1994) in comparison to L2 German data from (adult) speakers of Romance (e.g. Meisel *et al.* 1981; Clahsen and Muysken 1986), Vainikka and Young-Scholten propose that transfer is limited to lexical projections and their linear order. As is well known, the surface syntax of German in embedded clauses is OV, and in main clauses German respects the verb-second constraint. The least proficient Koreans and Turks produce (main clause) utterances with an (S)OV order, while the Romance subjects initially produce (S)VO (main clauses). In these early data, there is little evidence of (correct) verbal inflection or of auxiliary and modal verbs. From this Vainikka and Young-Scholten conclude that functional projections are absent; hence, the L2 initial state, at the sentential level, consists of VP, left-headed (SVO) for the Romance speakers and right-headed (SOV) for the Koreans and Turks—that is, as the VP is in their respective L1s. Subsequently, the Koreans and Turks produce VO orders; this leads Vainikka and Young-Scholten to conclude that a functional head must be present, but only in order to serve as a landing-site for verb raising out of VP, which has remained head-final. Since, at this point, the morphological form of the (raised) verb is mostly 'incorrect'—that is, verbal inflection does not agree with the subject or, more often, the verb is realized as an infinitival or stem form¹—and, likewise, since auxiliary and modal verbs are still rare, Vainikka and Young-Scholten hypothesize that this landing-site heads an underspecified functional projection, FP (Finite Phrase). FP becomes specified as a full-fledged AgrP only later, once auxiliaries/modals occur with some regularity and the morphological form of the (raised) verb is more often correct than not.

This gradual building of syntactic architecture is the core of Minimal Trees, which essentially follows a Weak Continuity (e.g. Vainikka 1993/4; Clahsen *et al.* 1994) approach to language development, both first and second. Lexical projections define the initial state, with functional projections being added (as needed) on the basis of lexical learning.² The difference between native and non-native language acquisition on this view is primarily that of transfer: in L2 acquisition, lexical projections (alone) and their headedness values transfer into the L2 initial state.

Among the other positions on the extent of transfer (e.g. Eubank 1993/4, 1996), the most extreme is seen in the 'Full Transfer/Full Access' model of Schwartz and Sprouse (1996). It hypothesizes, in essence, that the L1 grammar in its entirety (excluding phonological matrices of lexical/morphological items) is the starting-point of L2 acquisition; that is, the L1 defines the L2 initial state. Here I will not present the reanalyses of the data considered by Vainikka and Young-Scholten (Schwartz, 1998)—or additional data either from very early L2 periods that argue for the presence of functional structure (e.g. Grondin and White 1996) or from later stages of development that cannot be accommodated under a Minimal Trees approach (Schwartz and Sprouse 1996; Schwartz, 1998). Much of this research is on heads, and since specifiers are the topic of this chapter—and since, in any case, I will be defending the Full Transfer/Full Access (FT/FA) model in what follows—I refer readers to the citations above rather than review the earlier conceptual and empirical motivation for (much) more transfer than posited in Minimal Trees.

To summarize, first, there is a question of whether (developing) L2 systems are made of the same cognitive matter as L1 grammars; this is the UG question. Secondly, the question of how much transfer there is should be kept separate from the UG question: transfer does not preclude that the same cognitive processes underlie L1 and L2 acquisition—and in fact it has been proposed (Schwartz and Sprouse 1994, 1996) that transfer may partially

---

¹ Hence these L2 data are strikingly different from those in German L1 acquisition, where virtually all raised verbs show target-like agreement with the subject; that is, virtually no raised verbs realize either non-agreeing or infinitival/stem forms (see e.g. Jordens 1990; Poeppel and Wexler 1993).

² There are also maturational approaches to language development that likewise define the (L1) initial state as purely lexical (e.g. Radford 1990; Guilfoyle and Noonan 1992). Such approaches are to be distinguished from Weak Continuity, in that 'structure building' under the latter is data-driven.

explain the lack of native-like attainment by adult L2 acquirers (henceforth, L2ers). Thirdly, among approaches arguing that L2 development is constrained by UG, there is a range of (explicit) positions on the extent of L1 transfer; this range goes from a little (Minimal Trees) to the whole grammar (FT/FA). A fourth point, one which has so far only been implicit, is that there has been a shift in emphasis in generative L2 acquisition research. Earlier attention to similarity of patterns in L1 and L2 acquisition has gradually been replaced by attempts to provide syntactic analyses of the L2 patterns. Rather than merely comparing L2 data with either L1 developmental data or L1 final-state data, researchers now seek to treat each phase of Interlanguage on its own terms, trying to find analyses which rely on independently motivated mechanisms from known natural-language grammars (duPlessis *et al.* 1987). Moreover, and finally, it has also been recognized that to find such (UG-constrained) analyses is not sufficient, for they also have to make sense from a learnability perspective. This is to say, if one finds that at a certain point in L2 development the pattern of L2 data matches neither the L1 nor the target language, then one should ask how the L2er happened to be misled in this way. After all, the L2er is exposed to input from the target language: what is it that is preventing, temporarily or otherwise, the construction of a system that fully accommodates those input data?

In what follows I hope to illustrate what some recent L2 acquisition findings have to say to these five points. I look at two studies on child L2 acquisition that in one way or another involve specifiers.[3] The first is Lydia White's recent work on the acquisition of clitics in French by two English-speaking children in Montreal, based on Lightbown's (1977) data. Here I attempt to question White's analysis, which rests crucially on a specific Spec–head relation that she assumes does not characterize the L1; my reanalysis does not question the existence of the Spec–head relation in the early L2 data but rather its source. The second study is a portion of Belma Haznedar's University of Durham Ph.D. dissertation on the L2 acquisition of English by a Turkish-speaking boy. In this case I attempt to reanalyse a previously problematic set of her L2 data, utilizing recent views on movement to specifier position.

3. WHITE (1996)

3.1. *Introduction*

White has long championed the position that properties of the L1 grammar transfer in L2 acquisition. She was the first to hypothesize that L1 parameter

---

[3] It should be stressed that the fact that these L2 data come from children is largely happenstance. The five points outlined above apply equally to adult and child L2 acquisition, and my main interest was naturalistic, longitudinal data. For some L2 researchers, myself among them, the results to be discussed would be expected to extend to adult L2ers in the same L1-target language situations.

values may be adopted as the L2er's interim analysis of the target language, with parameters (later) resetting in response to input, if the L1 and target language differ. By contrast, White suggests that the acquisition of French clitics by English speakers may represent a fundamentally different situation than has been previously investigated, one that may be, moreover, an interesting test case for theories about the L2 initial state and Interlanguage development (see Section 2).

To see this, we first need to consider, briefly, the syntactic framework White adopts, since it is central to her argumentation. However, as I will argue below, it is partially the assumption of this framework that will also allow her analysis to be questioned.[4]

3.2. *Clitics in French*

Traditional generative syntax has debated the analysis of clitics, with some researchers (e.g. Kayne 1975) arguing for movement of the (object) clitic from its base argument position, and others arguing for base-generation (e.g. Jaeggli 1982; Roberge 1990). The data sets in (1) and (2) exemplify the basic facts of French that have led people to consider French weak pronouns to be clitics. We confine ourselves to only subjects and objects here, as these are what White considers in her data. We start with subjects.

(1) (*a*)   Jean / Il partira   bientôt
             Jean / he will-leave soon

    (*b*)   Jean, / *Il, paraît-il,   est fou
             Jean, / he, it appears, is   crazy

    (*c*)   Tous les garçons // Eux tous // *Ils tous partiront bientôt
             all   the boys   // them all // they all   will-leave soon

    (*d*)   *Jean et   il // *Il et   Jean// *Il   et   elle partiront bientôt
             Jean and he // he and Jean// he   and she will-leave soon

    (*e*)   Jean et   lui // Lui et   Jean partiront bientôt
             Jean and him // him and Jean will-leave soon

    (*f*)   ***Lui* / *Il** partira   le   premier
             him* / *he will-leave the first   ((1*a–f*) from Kayne 1975: 84–5)

    (*g*)   Jean il mange   (without pause: ok in Quebecois)
             Jean he eats   ((1*g*) from Sportiche, forthcoming: 9, (13*a*))

Example (1*a*) shows that lexical subjects and subject clitics (superficially) occupy the same position preverbally. However, (1*b–f*) illustrate that the two

---

[4] While there are several other analyses of Romance clitics, in this chapter I rely on Sportiche's approach for expository purposes, principal among them that this is what is adopted by White.

have distinct syntactic behaviour. We see in (1b) that while material, here a parenthetical (*il paraît* 'it appears'), can intervene between a DP subject and the
verb, it cannot occur between a subject clitic and a verb. Example (1c) shows
that DP subjects can be modified and so can strong pronominal subjects, but
subject clitics cannot be. Clitic subjects cannot conjoin, whereas strong pronominal subjects can (compare (1d) and (1e)). Clitic subjects cannot bear
contrastive stress, unlike strong pronouns, which can (1f). And (1g) shows that
Quebecois—which is the variety of French the children were acquiring—
allows subject clitic doubling (see e.g. Roberge 1990); it should be noted that
there is no need to pause between *Jean* and *il* in (1g), according to Sportiche.[5]

As for objects, consider the data in (2).

(2) (a)   Marie connaît mon frère   / *le // Marie le   connaît
          Marie knows my brother / him // Marie him knows

    (b)   Marie parle   avec Jean / lui /* le
          Marie is-talking with Jean / him / him

    (c)   Jean voit souvent Marie // *Jean la   souvent voit
          Jean sees often Marie // Jean her often   sees

    (d)   *Jean la et le   voit
          Jean her and him sees

    (e)   *Jean *la* préfère
          Jean *her* prefers

    (f)   Q: Qui as- tu vu?   A: Lui / *Le
             who did you see   him / him

    (g)   Regarde -moi! / *-me! / -le!
          look-at me! / me! / him!   ((2a–g) from White 1996: 338–9)

Examples (2a) and (2b) show that weak object pronouns are in complementary
distribution with (non-dislocated) lexical objects and strong pronouns: in (2a)
the DP follows the verb but the object clitic can only precede it; in (2b), both
a DP and a strong pronoun can be the object of a preposition, but an object
clitic cannot. As shown in (2c), while material can separate the verb from its
following object, nothing (except other clitics) can intervene between object
clitic and verb. Object clitics cannot be conjoined (2d) or contrastively stressed
(2e), and they cannot occur in isolation (2f). Finally, in (2g) we see that in
positive imperatives,[6] the verb precedes object pronominals, where the strong
form is required for 1st and 2nd persons but the weak form for 3rd.

---

[5] Sportiche (forthcoming) marks (1g) as ungrammatical in Standard French. The colloquial
French of France quite readily allows sentences such as (1g) without a pause as well (Teresa
Parodi, personal communication, 30 April 1996; Catherine Walter, personal communication, 1
May 1996; see e.g. Hulk 1988; Zribi-Hertz 1994).

[6] and apparently in Quebecois negative imperatives as well (Lydia White, personal communication, 18 April 1995).

3.3. *Sportiche (1996, forthcoming)*

The facts in (1) and (2) all argue that weak pronominal forms behave distinctly from strong pronominals and lexical DPs; these and other facts have led to the conclusion that the weak forms are, in one sense or another, clitics. Sportiche's analysis of clitic placement attempts to reconcile the movement and base-generation analyses. His proposal blends properties of both, hypothesizing that each kind of clitic heads its own (functional) projection. He calls these 'Clitic Voices'. The idea is that a clitic licenses in its specifier a particular property ([+F]) of an XP argument, and that the clitic and this appropriately propertied XP have to be in a Spec–head agreement relation (by LF). Sportiche's (1996: 236, (35)) Clitic Criterion is in (3).

(3)   *Clitic Criterion*
        (i)   A clitic must be in a Spec–head relationship with a [+F] XP at LF.
        (ii) A [+F] XP must be in a Spec–head relationship with a clitic at LF.

Agreement between the clitic head and the XP in its specifier is in terms of phi-features (person, number, gender, Case). Glossing over the details, I give, in (4), the structure Sportiche proposes (I consider only subject (NomP) and direct object (AccVP) clitics).

(4)

The tree in (4) shows that subject and object DPs in French can be *pro*; this DP must raise by LF to the specifier of the appropriate clitic head in order to satisfy the Clitic Criterion (not depicted in (4) are intermediate steps, e.g. subject DP to [Spec, AgrSP] and object DP to [Spec, AgrOP] for Case). There are differences between NomP and AccVP (as well as AgrIOP). For Sportiche, direct object clitics have a status different from that of subject clitics. Consider the data in (5).

(5) (a) *Jean le présente   à Pierre et envoie à Paris
         Jean him introduces to Pierre and sends to Paris
                                    (Sportiche, forthcoming: 4, (5*b*))

(b) Il mange du   pain et boit du vin
     He eats (some) bread and drinks (some) wine
                                    (Sportiche, forthcoming: 5, (6*b*))

(c) *On mange de la viande et boit du vin
     One eats (some) meat and drinks (some) wine
                                    (Sportiche, forthcoming: 12, (19*b*))

Example (5*a*) shows that the object clitic *le* (him) bears a closer relation to the verb than does *il* (he) in (5*b*), since only in (5*b*) is conjunction possible. For Sportiche, this difference stems from object clitics always being syntactic clitics, whereas (preverbal) pronominal subjects—except *on* (one) (and *ce* 'it'/'that')—do not have to be. That *on*, on the other hand, is always a syntactic clitic is evidenced, according to Sportiche (forthcoming: 13), by the ungrammaticality of (5*c*) (cf. (5*b*)), similar to (though not as strong as) the ungrammaticality of (5*a*): in neither (5*a*) nor (5*c*) can the verb which hosts the clitic conjoin independently of that clitic.

Sportiche ends up with a three-way classification of (preverbal) pronominal subjects: (i) syntactic clitics (i.e. *on*, *ce*), in which case the verb necessarily raises (overtly) to the clitic head, and the two adjoin; (ii) phonological clitics (i.e. *je* 'I', *tu* 'you.SG', *il* 'he', *ils* 'they.M'), which 'do not have to be syntactic clitics' (forthcoming: 13)—that is, cliticization is at PF, not in the syntax; and (iii) non-exclusively nominative pronouns (*elle* 'she', *nous* 'we', *vous* 'you.PL', *elles* 'they.F'), which 'do not *require* phonological cliticization . . . because they are ambiguous between head of NomP and [h]ead of DPs. As head of NomP, they are phonological clitics . . . As head of DPs, they are not clitics at all' (forthcoming: 14, emphasis in the original). The significance of this classification and especially of the status of *on* as only ever being a syntactic clitic is something we come back to in the treatment of the L2 data.

3.4. *White's study*

We are now in a position to consider the logic behind White's study. Starting with the premiss that English lacks clitics—and for White this means that it likewise lacks clitic projections—she reasons that the L2 acquisition of clitics by native English speakers provides a way to distinguish the *source* of functional projections in L2 acquisition (i.e. from the L1 or directly from UG): on the assumption that the L1 has no clitic projections, if very early on the L2 children treat clitics as bona fide clitics, this cannot be due to the L1 grammar.[7] In White's view the early appearance of clitics in the L2 data would be evidence of two things: first, contra Minimal Trees, that functional categories do characterize the L2 initial state; secondly, contra Full Transfer/Full Access, that the L2 initial state is, in a sense, more than just the L1 grammar, as only direct and immediate access to UG could account for the children treating clitics in the input as clitics in their early French Interlanguage.[8]

3.4.1. *The data*

The spontaneous production data White looked at come from Lightbown's (1977) study of two children, Kenny and Greg, acquiring Quebecois French in a naturalistic setting in Montreal. The data span three years. The first exposure to French Kenny and Greg had was in a year-long English–French bilingual nursery programme, but neither child produced many spontaneous utterances then. Later both boys enrolled in a French immersion kindergarten, and within a few weeks they transferred to a regular French kindergarten, at which point their linguistic input at school became almost entirely French. The data White (mostly) covers start from this last period, when Kenny was 5:8 (i.e. 5 years, 8 months old) and Greg was 5:4. (Given this delay of over one year, it is unclear whether these data represent their earliest grammars.) The boys were interviewed typically on a monthly or bi-monthly basis, for about an hour, Kenny more regularly than Greg, however. In fact, the first session in which Greg produced spontaneous utterances was not until five months after entering the regular kindergarten, and his next interview was not until four months after that. As White acknowledges, Kenny's data are therefore probably more revealing.

A first observation to be made is that weak subject pronouns emerge earlier

---

[7] The more general implication of this assumption is a denial of a Universal Base Hypothesis. This is relevant because it means that, in principle, White's line of argumentation holds only if it is the case that languages vary in terms of structural architecture. Sportiche (1995), by contrast, does assume a Universal Base Hypothesis. This is not the place to debate the validity of this claim, but it does bear directly on issues of language development, and in particular, I believe, L2 acquisition. In any event, I will be contesting the assumption that French and English differ in terms of the existence of clitics.

[8] In actuality, Full Transfer/Full Access assumes that in addition to the L2 initial state, UG directly and immediately constrains L2 development. There are, thus, two parts to FT/FA: (i) 'Full Transfer' predicts that if there is a way for the L1 grammar to accommodate (some of) the input, it will; in other words, the claim is that the L1 syntax *imposes* analyses on the input—and this is, in a nutshell, what I attempt to show in the reanalysis below; (ii) 'Full Access' furthermore predicts that once such analyses prove inadequate, UG-constrained restructuring will take place, and this could be immediate or there could be some delay.

than pronominal objects, with one notable exception. We consider the subject data first.[9]

3.4.2. *Weak pronominal subjects*

White employs three of Kayne's tests to determine whether the weak subject pronouns in the children's utterances are clitics: their position relative to the verb ((6)—cf. (1*b*)), conjunction ((7)—cf. (1*d*) and (1*e*)) and contrastive stress ((8)—cf. (1*f*)).

First, material intervening between the weak pronominal subject and the verb occurs in only a few cases, as in (6*c*). Examples (6*a*) and (6*b*) illustrate the typical case of no intervening material; (6*b*) is also an example of subject doubling, which, recall, is allowed in Quebecois. By contrast, the pattern in (6*d*), with the weak pronoun preceding the strong, is unattested.

(6) (*a*) i' crie[10]
           he shouts   ((15*b*): K, month 4 (common))

  (*b*) moi je veux pas
         me I want not   ((19*a*): K, month 3 (common))

  (*c*) i' pas vient   (ungrammatical in French; cf. 'i' vient pas')
         he not comes   ((15*a*): K, month 4 (rare))

  (*d*) @je moi veux pas   (ungrammatical in French; cf. (6*b*))
         I   me want not   ((19*c*): unattested)

Secondly, there are no cases of conjoined weak subject pronouns, but other conjoined subjects do occur. The utterance in (7) is an example of conjunction with a strong subject pronoun.

(7)   moi et   toi est trop grand pour la   porte
       me and you is too big   for the door   ((21*b*): K, month 15)

And thirdly, while there are no instances of stressed weak pronouns in the data, stressed strong pronouns are found throughout. Examples are given in (8).

(8) (*a*) **toi** faire ça
           you do.INF that   ((22*a*): K, month 7)

  (*b*) **moi** j' ai   deux lapins
         me I have   two rabbits   ((22*c*): G, month 5)

In sum, (6)–(8) are consistent with an analysis of weak subject pronouns as clitics.

---

[9] In what follows, quantitative analyses are generally not given; the frequency breakdowns of patterns can be found in White (1996).

[10] The typical way to pronounce singular and plural *il/ils* in Quebecois is [i].

3.4.3. *Pronominal objects: non-imperatives*

Clitic objects (in non-imperatives) come in later than weak subject pronouns. Studies on L1 acquisition of French (e.g. Clark 1985; Hamann *et al.* 1996), White points out, have noted a similar delay (but see below). Kenny produces one at month 3 and then none until eight months later. Similarly, Greg produces very few, hitting a high of four at month 13; only at month 20 is the clitic's presence systematic.

Still, across the data, there are very few errors that would clearly indicate a misanalysis of the clitic as a pronoun, and in fact only Greg produces any, as in (9). And there are also relatively few cases where a strong pronoun is used rather than a clitic, as in (10) (which comes from Grondin and White 1996: 26, (24*b*)).

(9)   moi j' ai trouvé le   (ungrammatical in French; cf. 'moi je l'ai trouvé')
        me I' ve found it   ((30*a*): G, month 14 (rare))

(10)   moi dire   le crocodile de manger toi   (ungrammatical in French)
        me say.INF the crocodile to eat.INF you   (K, month 9 (rare))

Finally, White notes that, like in French L1 acquisition (Hamann *et al.* 1996), the boys both tend to use postverbal *ça* (that), perhaps instead of object clitics:

(11)   le papa-vache fait ça
        the father-cow does that   ((26*b*): K, month 7 (common))

In sum, White shows that there is a definite lag in the appearance of preverbal object clitics, but that once they emerge they are generally used correctly; that is, they are not treated as independent pronouns. (I do not go through her tests, for reasons of space.)

3.4.4. *Pronominal objects: imperatives*

In contrast to object clitics' late appearance in non-imperatives is the *early* appearance of pronominals in imperatives—in fact from the earliest interviews, as in (12), for instance. White states (p. 355) that the (correctly used) strong forms *moi* (me) and *toi* (you) predominate but that weak forms (i.e. 3rd person) also occur (e.g. (12*a*)).

(12) (*a*) mets   -les   là
          put.2SG them there   ((28*c*): K, month 4)

    (*b*) excuse   -moi
          excuse.2SG me   ((28*a*): K, month 5)

    (*c*) regardez   -moi
          look-at.2PL me   ((28*b*): G, month 5)

For Kenny, up until month 11, there is one preverbal object clitic; in the same period, he produces 16 imperatives with postverbal pronominals (eight in the second interview). Similarly with Greg: before object clitics are regularly used at month 20, there are ten object clitics and 21 imperatives with postverbal pronominals. (Month 9, the second interview, marks Greg's first preverbal object clitic (and there is only one); four months earlier, at his first interview, he produces five imperatives with postverbal pronominals.)

The table in (13) summarizes the two boys' development.

(13)   *L2 French developmental pattern of (weak and strong) pronominals*

	Subject pronominals	Object pronominals in imperatives	Object pronominals in non-imperatives
Appearance	Early	Early	*Late*

3.4.5. *White's analysis*

In her conclusion, from which I quote below, White identifies three phases in the data:

I.   Up to and including month 11 ... both children use subject clitics but their incidence is not particularly high. With the exception of imperatives, object clitics are hardly found at all.

II. At months 14 to 15, there is a significant increase in the number of utterances containing verbs, leading to an increase in the incidence of subjects in general and subject clitics in particular, including [subject] clitic doubling in Greg's case. At about this time, there is also a decrease in the proportion of . . . strong pronouns occurring as subjects without a doubled clitic. Object clitics are found but not frequently.

III. There is a dramatic increase in object clitics at month 25 for Kenny and at month 20 for Greg. (White 1996: 362)

For White, (I)–(III) have the following theoretical implications:

• Phase (I) shows that NomP is active from the start, contrary to the predictions of Minimal Trees. White argues, based on the assumption that English has no subject clitics, that such a clitic analysis moreover cannot stem from the L1 and hence that the L2ers are directly tapping UG to construct NomP.
• Phase (II) indicates a possible qualitative difference from the first phase with regard to object clitics. White maintains that this could be compatible with either Minimal Trees or Full Transfer/Full Access, because it points to the emergence of AccVP. However, she also suggests that since object clitics are delayed in the L1 acquisition of French, the lag itself does not argue for FT/FA.
• Phase (III) is merely a quantitative change from phase (II).

Central to White's conclusions is the claim that 'there is nothing in the English input to motivate [clitics]' (p. 336)—viz. that unlike in French, there are no subject or object clitics in English, hence no NomP or AccVP in English. In what follows, however, I question this assumption about the difference between French and English.

3.5. *An alternative perspective*

3.5.1. *Subject clitic in English?*

Applying the same tests from French to English in (14) (cf. (1)), let us consider the contrast between *you* and *yǝ* as a subject.

(14) (*a*) You/Yǝ can't do that   (cf. (1*a*))
                                     (van Riemsdijk (vR), forthcoming: 16)
   (*b*) You/*Yǝ, it appears, can't do that   (cf. (1*b*))
   (*c*) You both // ?Yǝ both can't do that   (cf. (1*c*))
   (*d*) *Jean and yǝ // *Yǝ and Jean can't do that   (cf. (1*d*))
   (*e*) Jean and you // You and Jean can't do that   (cf. (1*e*))
   (*f*) *You/* Yǝ* can't do that   (cf. (1*f*))
   (*g*) ?You (guys) yǝ can't do that   (cf. (1*g*))

Despite both *you* and *yǝ* preceding the verb in surface syntax (14*a*), (14*b–f*) illustrate that the two have distinct syntactic behaviour. Example (14*b*) shows that while material, again a parenthetical (*it appears*), can intervene between *you* and the verb, it cannot when the subject is *yǝ* (see below, however). As shown in (14*c*), *you* is preferred over *yǝ* when modified by *both*. Whereas *yǝ* cannot be conjoined, *you* can be (compare (14*d*) and (14*e*)). In (14*f*) we see that *yǝ* cannot bear contrastive stress, unlike *you*. And (14*g*) shows that English perhaps allows subject doubling with 2nd person. In short, subject *yǝ* passes the tests of clitichood, at least as a phonological clitic.[11] If so, and if Sportiche (1995, 1996) is correct, (14) is thus evidence that NomP (see (4)) must be part of the grammar of English. (Recall from Section 3.3 that for Sportiche, both syntactic and phonological clitics head clitic projections.)

---

[11] In van Riemsdijk (forthcoming), only *yǝ* is discussed as a pronominal subject clitic. Other candidates have been suggested by Kayne (Harvard class lectures, 8 and 15 November 1995), on the basis of contrasts between pronominal and DP subjects with auxiliaries/modals in contraction contexts, such as in (i) (I thank Lisa Travis, 9 May 1997, for reminding me of these).

(i) (*a*)   (I know that) he'll [hɪl] do it
  (*b*)   (I know that) Lee'll [liəl]/*[lɪl] do it

On the existence of pronominal subject clitics in English, especially in inversion contexts (also considered by Kayne but purposely left to the side here), see Selkirk (1980: 132–59), which is also a discussion of English pronominal object clitics.

3.5.2. *Object clitics in English?*

We turn now to the object clitic tests for English (cf. (2) for French). The data in (15) ((15*a, c, d,* and *f*) are adapted from van Riemsdijk, forthcoming).

(15) (*a*)   Marie knows you/yə // him/'m // her/'r // them/'m   (cf. (2*a*)) (vR: 16)
   (*b*)   Marie is talking with you/yə // him/'m // her/'r // them/'m   (cf. (2*b*))
   (*c*)   *Jean sees 'm and 'r   (cf. (2*d*)) (vR: 44)
   (*d*)   *Jean prefers *yə/'m/'r/'m*   (cf. (2*e*)) (vR: 46)
   (*e*)   Q: Who did you see?   A: Him/*'m   (cf. (2*f*)) (vR: 49)
   (*f*)   Look at you/yə // him/'m // her/'r // them/'m   (cf. (2*g*)) (vR: 79)

In English, the linear position of object pronouns (*you, him, her, them*) is the same as that of their clitic counterparts (*yə, 'm, 'r, 'm*), namely after the preposition (15*b*) or verb (15*a*). Object clitics in English cannot be conjoined (15*c*) or contrastively stressed (15*d*), and they also cannot occur in isolation (15*e*). Finally, (15*f*) shows they can occur in imperatives, where again they are linearly indistinct from their pronominal counterparts. Object *yə, 'm, 'r,* and *'m* in English, then, pass the test for clitichood, too.

3.5.3. *Summary*

The facts in (14) and (15) indicate that, contrary to the premiss on which the logic of White's study turns, English does have both subject and object clitics, be they syntactic or phonological. If we adopt the assumptions of Sportiche, the structural configuration necessary to accommodate these clitics would be a Spec–head relation in the projections NomP, for subjects, and AccVP, for direct objects (see Section 3.5.4 below for analyses). The most apparent syntactic difference between French and English object clitics is their position: in French non-imperatives, object clitics are preverbal, whereas in English object clitics are always postverbal. In French (positive—see footnote 6) imperatives, on the other hand, the postverbal placement of pronominal objects, both weak (3rd person) and strong (1st and 2nd persons) matches, at least superficially, that of English. This linear match, illustrated again in (16), is important.

(16) (*a*)   Montrez -le -moi // Montrez -moi -le
       Show   it to-me // Show   me   it
   (*b*)   Montrez -le à   Nikki // Montrez -moi le   livre
       Show   it to Nikki // Show   me   the book

As (16*a*) shows, even when there is variable placement of the object pronominals, both orders are allowed in English and Quebecois French. In English, furthermore, object pronouns occupy the same position in non-imperatives as in imperatives, and the same is true of object clitics. The table in (17) summarizes the position of subject and object pronominals—that is, clitics and pronouns—in English and French.

(17)   *Placement of pronominals in English and French*

	Subject pronominals	Object pronominals in imperatives	Object pronominals in non-imperatives
English (L1)	Preverbal	Postverbal	*Pre*verbal
French (TL)	Preverbal	Postverbal	*Post*verbal
	[same]	[same]	[*different*]

These observations, I will argue, may help explain the L2 French data. However, we first need to consider more concretely, adopting the framework of Sportiche (1996, forthcoming), what the analysis of English clitics might look like (see footnote 4).

3.5.4. *The analysis of clitics in English*

Based on (14) and (15), I have concluded that NomP and AccVP form part of the grammar of English; yet the analysis of French using (4) will obviously not extend, for instance, to English postverbal object clitics. While he subscribes to a Universal Base Hypothesis (Sportiche 1995), Sportiche (1996, forthcoming) does allow for (limited) parametric variation, for example syntactic as opposed to phonological clitics (illustrated previously in relation to (5) above). Three other possibilities he proposes are summarized in (18).

(18) (i)   whether the Doubly Filled CliticP Filter (styled on the Doubly Filled COMP Filter) is adhered to or not;
   (ii) whether movement is overt or covert; and
   (iii) whether cliticization is syntactic or morphological.

In what follows, I briefly illustrate each of these in order to amass the necessary pieces for the analysis of English clitics I will ultimately adopt.

The Doubly Filled CliticP Filter, Sportiche (forthcoming) argues, applies to NomP in Standard French but not, for example, in Quebecois: in addition to the subject clitic, the DP can be phonetically 'filled' in [$_{NomP}$ DP [$_{Nom'}$ clitic]] in Quebecois (see (1g)).

Evidence Sportiche provides for overt movement to specifier in French (i) of the DP object (*pro*) comes from, for example, participle agreement (Sportiche 1996: 242–5) with direct object clitics (e.g. *Jean l'a peinte* 'Jean it.F has painted.F') and (ii) of the DP subject (*tous pro* 'all *pro*') from quantifier raising (Sportiche, forthcoming: 10–11) with subject clitics (e.g. *Il a tous fallu qu'ils partent* 'it is all necessary that they leave').

Cliticization is syntactic when the concatenation of clitic and host involves overt movement—hence their adjunction—in syntax; this is the case for French when the verb raises overtly to AccV (direct object clitics) and Nom (syntactic subject clitics *on* 'one' and *ce* 'it'/'that'—see (5)). Morphological cliticization, on the other hand, refers to clitics being 'affixed prior to lexical insertion' (Sportiche, forthcoming: 20)—that is, in the lexical component; in this case, syntactic checking (either overt or covert) must apply. His treatment of post-verbal subject clitics, as in Complex Inversion, exemplifies this:

(19)   Jean est -il malade?   (Sportiche, forthcoming: (1*a*))
         Jean is he sick?

For Sportiche, the [verb + clitic] element, *est-il* in (19), is inserted under V and subsequently moves to check its features off. He argues that overt movement of *est-il* is only to AgrS (20*a*): *Jean* is in the specifier of NomP, and thus the Doubly Filled CliticP Filter excludes overt raising of *est-il* to Nom. On the other hand, the clitic (*il*) must comply with the Clitic Criterion (see (3)); so, while *overt* raising is only as far as AgrS, *covert* movement of *est-il* to (C via) Nom is required (as in (20*b*)).

(20) (*a*) $[_{CP} [_C] [_{NomP} \textbf{\textit{Jean}}_i [_{Nom}] [_{AgrSP} e_i{}' [_{AgrS} \textbf{\textit{est-il}}_j] [_{VP} e_i [_V e_j \dots]]]]]$

     (*b*) $[_{CP} [_C \textbf{\textit{est-il}}_j] [_{NomP} Jean_i [_{Nom} e_j{}'] [_{AgrSP} e_i{}' [_{AgrS} e_j{}'] [_{VP} e_i [_V e_j \dots]]]]]$

In short, the analysis of Complex Inversion illustrates the interplay of all three parameters: (i) *est-il* is an example of morphological cliticization, which is subject to checking via syntactic head movement; (ii) the DP subject (*Jean*) moves overtly to [Spec, NomP] as does *est-il* to AgrS, which then covertly moves further to (C via) Nom in satisfaction of the Clitic Criterion by LF; (iii) it is the adherence to the Doubly Filled CliticP Filter that rules out overt move-ment of the subject clitic to Nom.

Sportiche (forthcoming: 22, fn. 17) suggests that this analysis for postverbal subjects might extend productively to French object clitics in positive imper-atives (see (16)). Thus, *montrez-moi-le* (show me it), for example, would be formed in the lexicon as an instance of morphological cliticization; overt verb movement (to at least AgrS) would apply to check off the verb's features, and, assuming a *pro* DP in ([Spec, AgrIOP] and in) [Spec, AccVP], the Clitic Criterion would be satisfied via Spec–head agreement along the way. I assume verb movement to be overt, given what we independently know about verb raising in French (Emonds 1978; Pollock 1989).

We are now in a position to consider an analysis for English clitics. Unlike in French, verb movement in English is (generally) covert;[12] on this assump-

---

[12] Johnson (1991) makes a convincing case for English having overt verb raising to what is essentially AgrO (his µ), especially on the basis of particle-verb facts (pp. 593–5), as in (i).

(i) (*a*)   Betsy threw the bicycle out   (Johnson 1991: (41*c*))
     (*b*)   Betsy threw out the bicycle   (Johnson 1991: (41*d*))
     (*c*)   Betsy threw it out   (Johnson 1991: (42*c*))
     (*d*)   *Betsy threw out it   (Johnson 1991: (42*d*))

The ungrammaticality of only (i.*d*), moreover (as Bernadette Plunkett recalled to me), strongly argues for a difference in English between DP objects and pronominal objects. By making the

tion, the consistently postverbal positioning of object clitics in English cannot be derived by raising the verb higher than AccV. Recall (from (4)) the (universal) structure Sportiche proposes:

(21)

```
         NomP
        /    \
     Spec    Nom'
            /    \
          Nom    AgrSP
                     \
                      TP
                        \
                        NegP
                            \
                            AccVP
                           /     \
                        Spec     AccV'
                                /     \
                             AccV     AgrOP
                                          \
                                          VP
                                         /   \
                                      Spec    V'
                                             /   \
                                            V     DP
```

If, in a sentence such as *Yə saw 'm, 'm* were inserted in AccV, one might expect main verbs to precede negation in English, contrary to fact. Such considerations suggest that object clitics in English are morphological clitics, encliticized to the verb before lexical insertion. Thus, similar to the analysis for postverbal clitics in French positive imperatives, [*saw + 'm*] is inserted under V in (21); the Clitic Criterion is satisfied by (i) covertly raising the verb to AgrS to check the verb's features, thereby transiting through AccV, in conjunction with (ii) (either overt or covert) movement of the object DP *pro* to [Spec, AccVP]. The analysis of object clitics in imperatives is the same (or subsumes it, if there is, say, an 'illocutionary force' feature in C). Hence, under this

---

pronominal object in (i.*d*) 'heavier', via stress or conjunction, for example, the word order of (i.*d*) becomes possible:

(ii) (*a*)   Betsy threw out **them**!   (Johnson 1991: (43*a*))
(*b*)   Betsy threw out him and her.   (based on Johnson 1991: (43*b*))

The data in (i) hence suggest that pronominal objects in English are at most weak pronouns; analysing them as verbal enclitics (as suggested in Diesing and Jelinek 1995: 160) can easily account for the difference in grammaticality between (i.*c*) and (i.*d*). This then corroborates the claim (see (15)) that English does have object clitics.

proposal, the difference between English and French postverbal clitics in positive imperatives rests exclusively in covert vs. overt movement. By contrast, the
difference between English and French object clitics in non-imperatives is much
more pronounced: there is a difference not only in (overt) verb movement but
also in the type of clitic and the insertion site; only in French is a syntactic clitic
inserted directly under AccV.

As for the subject clitic *yə*, recall that the facts in (14) were presented as an
argument for (preverbal) *yə* cliticizing to the verb in English. Consider now the
data in (22).

> (22) (*a*) Yə really can't do that   (cf. (14*b*) and (1*b*))
>   (*b*) Yə never know what the solution might be   (cf. (14*b*) and (1*b*))
>   (*c*) Yə just have to keep trying   (cf. (14*b*) and (1*b*))

The examples in (22) show that subject *yə* can cliticize to elements other than
verbs (cf. (14*b*)). This speaks against a morphological cliticization analysis; *yə*
is also not a syntactic clitic, since verb raising is covert. We are left with
phonological clitic (see discussion of (5)): *yə* is inserted under Nom in (21),
and the subject DP *pro* moves (covertly or overtly) to [Spec, NomP], instantiating Spec–head agreement; procliticization to elements like *really* as in (22)
or verbs as in (14*a*) happens at PF. This is similar to Sportiche's analysis of
exclusively nominative clitics other than *on* (one) and *ce* (it/that) as phonological clitics, the difference being that nothing can intervene between the
French phonological subject clitic and the verb (see (1*b*)), owing perhaps to
overt verb raising to at least AgrS.

Armed with these analyses of English clitics, we now return to the L2 French
data.

3.6. *The reanalysis*

3.6.1. *The L2 subject data*

While the L2 facts (see (6)–(8)) are consistent with White's conclusion that
early on the L2ers analyse the French weak subject pronouns as clitics, it is
nevertheless important to underscore, as White also acknowledges, that the
absence of something in production data is no guarantee of it being ruled out
by the grammar. Bearing this in mind, let us now reconsider White's evidence.

First is the fact (see (6)) that across the data there are only a few cases of
material intervening between a weak subject and the verb (as in (6*c*)). However, this is not terribly compelling, especially since intervening material is
likewise only 'occasionally found' (White 1996: 348) with strong subject pronouns, as in (23), where no such adjacency is required.

> (23) (*a*) moi aussi ai   fait   le   rouge   (ungrammatical in French; cf. also
>   (6*c*))
>
>   me   also   have made the red (one)   ((18*a*): K, month 15)

(*b*) moi juste fais   pas tout le   soleil   (ungrammatical in French;
                                              cf. also (6*c*))

      me   only make not all   the sun   ((18*b*): K, month 15)

What may in fact be revealing is the *time* example (6*c*) (*i' pas vient* 'he not comes') occurs: month 4 (i.e. the beginning). In (6*c*), *i'* cannot be a clitic, since it is separated from the finite verb by *pas*; it can, by contrast, be a pronoun—just like *he* in English.

The existence of subject doubling of the kind in (6*b*) (*moi je veux pas* 'me I want not') juxtaposed against the absence of the type in (6*d*) (*je moi veux pas*) might appear to be stronger evidence that the weak pronouns are indeed clitics. Note, however, that simply translating from English, as in (24), would give exactly the same contrast. So, again, since, for example, *I* in (24*a*) is not a clitic, the target-like doubled-subject data do not force an initial analysis of the Interlanguage weak subject pronouns as clitics.

(24) (*a*)   Me I don't want (it)   (cf. (6*b*))
     (*b*)   *I me don't want (it)   (cf. (6*d*))

Secondly, while no instances of conjoined weak subject pronouns are found, the example given in (7), *moi et toi est trop grand pour la porte* (me and you is too big for the door), with conjoined strong pronouns, is not particularly telling either, since it occurs so late: fifteen months after starting the regular French kindergarten. I do not know whether there are earlier cases, but even if there were, notice that non-nominative conjoined subjects are also quite acceptable in (especially colloquial) English, as illustrated in (25). Thus the presence of conjoined strong subject pronouns coupled with the absence of conjoined weak subject pronouns is not necessarily evidence that the Interlanguage weak subject forms are solely treated as clitics.

(25)   Me and her/Lauren are singing in the show   (cf. (7))

Finally, it is indeed suggestive that no weak subject pronouns occur with stress but strong forms do (see (8)); but again this mirrors the patterns of English (compare (26*a*) and (26*b*)). Similarly, while the strong form of the pronoun is stressed in doubled-subject utterances, again the same is found in English (compare (26*c*) and (26*d*)).

(26) (*a*)   **You** do that   (cf. (8*a*))
     (*b*)   **Yə** do that
     (*c*)   **Me** I have two rabbits   (cf. (8*b*))
     (*d*)   ***Me** *I* have two rabbits

The point of this discussion so far is that the L2 weak subject pronoun data are *ambiguous*: either an analysis as pronoun could work or an analysis as clitic could.

There are, happily, also less ambiguous facts: weak subject pronouns occur almost exclusively with finite verbs, whereas strong pronouns occur frequently with both finite (27*a*) and non-finite (27*b*) forms. So, examples like (27*c*) are quite rare. That weak subject pronouns tend to occur exclusively in the context of finite verbs is, as White (1996: 350) argues, evidence for the existence of NomP. In fact, it is the only unambiguous—hence the strongest—evidence there is.

(27) (*a*) toi parle   français   (ungrammatical in French)
           you speak.FIN French   ((24*a*): K, month 5 (common))

    (*b*) moi chercher   (ungrammatical in French)
           me   search.INF   ((24*b*): G, month 5 (common))

    (*c*) moi je pas jouer   avec l' auto   (ungrammatical in French)
           me   I   not play.INF with the car   ((35*c*): G, month 11 (rare))

Turning to strong subject pronouns, the fact that they occur alone with finite verbs—as in (27*a*), *toi parle français* (you speak French)—would seem to pose a problem for an exclusively French-based analysis, and their incidence is not negligible: out of all finite verbs that do not have a lexical subject, non-clitic-doubled strong pronominal subjects occur 27 per cent of the time in the first six months for Kenny (two out of three in the first session); and in Greg's first interview, they constitute 45 per cent (nine out of twenty). White points out (p. 350) that the vast majority of utterances of this type occur with *moi* (me). Importantly, French allows only *3rd person* strong forms in the pattern of (27*a*), and then only when stressed (see (1*f*)). So if we try to fit utterances like (27*a*) into a NomP analysis, either *toi* is in [Spec, NomP] with a null licensing head, or *toi* is miscategorized as a clitic. Either way, there is misanalysis. Positing a system that has yet to force out an L1-based (mis)analysis of French strong subject pronouns would seem preferable. In other words, *toi* in (27*a*) is a pronoun, whose analysis stems from L1 English.[13]

3.6.2. *Recapitulation and import*

White applies the tests for clitichood across the entire database and finds that by and large the weak subject pronouns pass.[14] However, note that (i) the facts about ungrammaticality in (1) are not part of the input Kenny and Greg receive (they hear only what is possible in French), and (ii) a subset of the allowed patterns in English is also allowed in French. These observations

---

[13] According to Cornelia Hamann (personal communication, 21 January 1997), non-clitic-doubled strong subject pronouns generally do not occur in L1 French, especially in the context of finite verbs—so vanishingly rare in the Hamann *et al.* (1996) study that their incidence was not even calculated. This contrasts sharply with the L2 French data (e.g. (27*a*, *b*)), also clearly pointing to influence from L1 English.

[14] One might wonder whether only the *earliest* weak subject pronouns are relevant to determining what their *initial* analysis is; in this vein, see the discussion of (6*c*) *vis-à-vis* (23) in Section 3.6.1.

underscore the amenability of French subjects to an English-based analysis: because the nature of production data does not definitively show what is disallowed, the L2 pronominal subject data are, for the most part, *ambiguous* between an analysis as clitic and an analysis as pronoun. Overall, the L2 subject pronouns point to pronoun and clitic, both deriving in principle from L1 English; in particular, the representation of early L2 clitics could derive from subject *yə* as a phonological clitic in Nom (see (22)), and not necessarily from 'immediate access' to Universal Grammar (White 1996: 335).

One final remark relating to the ambiguity of pronoun vs. clitic in the L2 weak subject data deserves to be mentioned. Recall Sportiche's (forthcoming: 14) claim about the non-exclusively nominative pronouns in French: 'they are ambiguous between head of NomP and [h]ead of DP'. That L2ers might also find weak pronominal subjects to be ambiguous between a 'head-of-NomP' (viz. clitic) analysis and 'head-of-DP' (viz. pronoun) analysis is therefore entirely plausible. In this vein, it is interesting to note that two of the later clitic errors that White cites, reproduced in (28), occur with *on*.

(28) (a) on   juste veut pas   (ungrammatical in French)
        one just wants not
        'We just don't want to.'   ((17a): G, month 20)

    (b) on   juste peut voir   (ungrammatical in French)
        one just can   see   ((17b): G, month 25)

According to Sportiche (forthcoming: 5), *on* is one of the two subject clitics most closely tied to the verb: *on* is impossible in (5c) (**On mange de la viande et boit du vin* 'One eats (some) meat and drinks (some) wine'—i.e. with conjoined VPs); and for Sportiche, *on* is always a syntactic clitic. So, apparently, even after 20–25 months of exposure to French, Greg has still not completed the assignment of *on* to the status of syntactic clitic (alone). This suggests, again, influence from the L1 grammar.

3.6.3. *The significance of the pronominal object asymmetry*

I return now to the pronominal object data. Here the data argue more directly for the children starting L2 acquisition with their L1 syntax. Recall the asymmetry: the initial (near) absence of accusative clitics in non-imperatives but the early presence of object pronominals in imperatives.[15] Indeed, object pronominals in imperatives start just as early as weak pronominal subjects: Kenny at month 3, with eight imperatives having object pronominals, and Greg at month 5 (his first interview), with five imperatives having object pronominals.

---

[15] In regard to non-imperatives: for Kenny the first (and sole) object clitic occurs at month 3 and only eight months later does he produce another (five); for Greg, the first is produced at month 9, another nine occur between months 10 and 18 (five interviews), and then at month 20 there is an abrupt increase to 30.

The insight I try to pursue is that the early appearance of patterns like (12) (*mets-les là* 'put.2SG them there'; *regardez-moi* 'look-at me') follows from the fact that French and English *match* in terms of word order in imperatives (see (16) and (17)), while this is obviously not so for non-imperatives with object clitics.

Notice that my claim is not that this is a surface phenomenon. The claim is that the L1 syntax of English *imposes* analyses on the French input data; French (positive) imperative input—e.g. *mets-les là*—is easily assigned the representation of English imperatives as containing either object pronouns (*put them there*) or object clitics (*put 'm there*), as the linear order is the same. On a pronoun analysis, *mets* (put) is in V and *les* (them) in object DP. On an analysis of English object clitics (sketched above), morphological encliticization applies in the lexicon, yielding [*mets* + *les*], which is inserted under V; covert[16] verb movement checks off the features of the verb, and on its way up to AgrS the [*mets* + *les*] complex transits through AccV, where it enters into a Spec–head relation with the object DP *pro* that has raised to [Spec, AccVP].

French input containing preverbal clitics, by contrast, cannot be accommodated by the initially L1-based Interlanguage syntax and therefore forces it to restructure, which takes some time. This restructuring of the L2 initial state is why there is a lag in the appearance of preverbal object clitics.

One might object to this L1-derived proposal on the basis that a delay in object clitics has also been reported in the L1 French data (Clark 1985; Hamann *et al.* 1996). Indeed, both White (1996: 352, 362, 363) and Hamann *et al.* (1996: 312, 325, 331, 332) assert that the L1 and L2 French data show similar findings (but cf. footnote 13), noting in particular the delay in object clitics. However, a closer examination of Hamann *et al.*'s L1 French data (pp. 322–7) sheds doubt on this claim. These data, from a Swiss child called Augustin, are also spontaneous production.

Augustin's data show that nine months separate the systematic occurrence of object clitics (ten—14.3 per cent of relevant verbal utterances) at age 2:9.2 from that of subject clitics (17—33.3 per cent of relevant verbal utterances) at 2:0.2.[17] Importantly, Hamann *et al.* are referring to his object clitics in *both* non-imperatives and imperatives. Indeed, of his total 36 object clitics, only two are in imperatives. Equally important, moreover, is the fact that Augustin evinces the same absence pattern (see footnote 17) with *strong* pronominal

---

[16] Initially, verb raising is covert, as in English. At the point overt raising is in evidence, in e.g. negative declaratives, this will extend to the imperative cases as well, with no discernible differences.

[17] Augustin's first recording contains subject clitics; his first object clitic (3.8% of relevant verbal utterances)—in an imperative, incidentally—is three interviews later at 2:2.13 (by which point 41 subject clitics have appeared) and the second (5% of relevant verbal utterances) after a further three interviews at 2:4.22 (by which time he has produced 74 subject clitics); there are two more in the next interview at 2:6.16.

objects in *imperatives*: the first, *mets ça* (put that/it), is at 2:4, the next, at 2:6, is *assieds-toi* (sit yourself (down)), followed by *laisse-moi faire* (let me do.INF (it)) at 2:9—by which time, as stated, his object clitics are productive.[18] Thus, while the L1 and L2 acquisition data both exhibit a developmental asymmetry, it is not the same asymmetry, as laid out in the table in (29).

(29)　　*L1 and L2 French developmental patterns of (weak and strong) pronominals*

	Subject pronominals	Object pronominals in imperatives	Object pronominals in non-imperatives
L1 French	Early	***Late***	Late
L2 French	Early	***Early***	Late

The delay in Augustin's data encompasses preverbal (weak) and postverbal (weak and strong) object pronominals; that is, only subject clitics are early. The delay in the L2 data is restricted to preverbal (weak) object pronominals in non-imperatives only. Given these distinct developmental patterns of L1 French and L2 French, note that any explanation for the delay in the L1 data will *not* extend to the L2 data.

Yet a puzzle remains. Why are there so few cases of postverbal weak object pronouns in non-imperatives (as in (9)—*moi j'ai trouvé le* 'me I've found it')? More errors of this type (i.e. *le* analysed as pronoun or clitic) would be expected if the syntax of L1 English were exclusively in use. It therefore cannot be that the preverbal placement of object clitics in French non-imperatives has simply gone unnoticed. The absence of *moi j'ai trouvé le* errors thus suggests that the children are half-way there: they know preverbal object clitics are not instances of morphological encliticization; what they do not know yet is what to do instead. And so in non-imperatives, object clitics are not used incorrectly, they are just not used; and the children resort to postverbal *ça* (that) in utterances like *le papa-vache fait ça* (the father-cow does that) instead of either weak or strong pronouns (see (11))—again in line with the syntax of their L1.[19] It takes, evidently, a year to work out the target French-type analysis. Under the parameters Sportiche sets out, the choice is between morphological

---

[18] I thank Cornelia Hamann (personal communication, 28 January 1997) for finding and providing (so few of!) these data.

[19] The proposal put forward here extends as well to the relative scarcity of the other errors of commission, as in (10) (*moi dire le crocodile de manger toi* 'me say.INF the crocodile to eat.INF you'), namely postverbal strong pronouns in non-imperatives. Again, the reliance on *ça* fills this function, at least for 3rd person. It may none the less be noteworthy that in (10) the strong pronoun is 2nd person (*toi*); in the target language, substituting postverbal *ça* for a preverbal clitic is restricted to 3rd person contexts. The test case, then, is non-3rd person contexts: do the children first tend to supply strong postverbal pronouns in 1st and 2nd person non-imperative contexts (as in (10))?

procliticization and syntactic cliticization. (I assume that by this point in development, their verbs raise overtly in French—see Grondin and White 1996.) When object clitics systematically appear preverbally in non-imperatives (and assuming errors such as *moi j'ai le trouvé* do not occur, which would indicate a procliticization (mis)analysis), the syntactic cliticization analysis, in which accusative clitics are inserted under AccV, is in place. That restructuring the English-based analysis to that of French would be protracted, furthermore, seems plausible.

3.7. Conclusion

The innovation of Sportiche's analysis of clitics, combining aspects of the earlier base-generation and movement proposals, rests on the Spec–head agreement relation within the Clitic Voice projections. Of the L2 French weak pronoun data, the accusative clitics are the most compelling: once preverbal object clitics occur with any regularity, they are used correctly, and this points to a target-language, syntactic-clitic-in-AccVP analysis. There is much ambiguity, on the other hand, in regard to the L2ers' analysis of weak subject pronouns: either as clitics or pronouns. Still, that weak subject pronouns occur almost invariably with finite verbs (as White argues) fairly unambiguously calls for a clitic analysis and thus for NomP.

Based on the assumption that English lacks pronominal subject and object clitics, White concludes that the Interlanguage source of both NomP and AccVP is UG. The logic cannot be faulted. What I have contested, however, is the premiss: contrary to White's assumption, English has both subject and object clitics; these I have argued to be instances of, respectively, phonological cliticization, with the clitic inserted under Nom, and morphological cliticization, with the [verb + clitic] inserted under V, (covertly) raising (via AgrS) to AccV. If this is correct, then, logically, the existence of NomP and AccVP in the Interlanguage could derive from the L1. The reanalysis attempted to argue that the asymmetries in the L2 data—early weak subject pronouns, early object pronominals in imperatives, but delayed preverbal object clitics[20]—combined with the discovery that French L1 development exhibits no parallel asymmetries (since the delay there refers to object pronominals of all kinds) directly implicate the L1 in the Interlanguage syntax. The table in (30) summarizes this, by combining (13) and (17).

---

[20] These asymmetries, I believe, not only argue in favour of an initial L1-based analysis; they also challenge White's basic approach, where subject clitics are immediately assigned a representation using NomP, whose source is UG. If UG is being tapped for the representation of subject clitics, then why not also for preverbal object clitics? In other words, why should there be an asymmetry between subject and object clitics, such that NomP—but not AccVP—is immediately provided by UG?

(30)   *L2 development in light of comparison of L1-English and TL-French*

	Subject pronominals	Object pronominals in imperatives	Object pronominals in non-imperatives
English (L1)	Preverbal	Postverbal	*Pre*verbal
French (TL)	Preverbal	Postverbal	*Post*verbal
	[same]	[same]	[*different*]
L2 French	Early	Early	*Late*

- French input with pronominal subjects can be accommodated by the L1 syntax, either as pronouns proper or as clitics.
- Similarly, French input with *postverbal* object pronominals can also be accommodated by the L1 syntax, again either as pronouns or as clitics.
- What the L1 syntax is unable to accommodate is French input containing *preverbal* clitics, and these are precisely what take over a year to appear.

Where English-based analyses of French input are possible, target-like appearance in the Interlanguage is significantly earlier, and this is in complete conformity with the predictions of the 'Full Transfer' part of FT/FA; that the preverbal-object-clitic input is eventually assimilated using the French analysis, entailing, of course, the restructuring of the L2 initial state, is likewise fully expected under the 'Full Access' part of FT/FA.

In sum, while I concur with White that the Interlanguage of these children does instantiate NomP and AccVP, and hence the Spec–head relation required of them, the reanalysis suggests that they derive from the syntax of L1 English, in line with the Full Transfer/Full Access model.

I will likewise defend this model in what follows: an examination of Haznedar's (1995, 1997) study of the L2 development of English word order by a Turkish-speaking boy. The particular focus this time is the developmental reanalysis. As is well known, Turkish and English differ in regard to surface syntax, Turkish being consistently head-final. The earliest L2 data provide un-controversial evidence that the L1 grammar is initially used, and my goal is to show how a particular restructuring analysis relying on specifiers neatly accounts for the equally uncontroversial developmental changes.

4. HAZNEDAR (1995, 1997)

The subject of Haznedar's investigation is a Turkish boy, Erdem, who was 4:3 at the start of data collection. He arrived in the UK in November 1993, and for two months he was mostly at home with his parents, both native speakers of Turkish. In mid-January 1994, he started nursery school, which gave him exposure to English for two-and-a-half hours a day. There was no special

English instruction at school nor were there any other Turkish speakers in the class. Haznedar began collecting English data from Erdem at the beginning of March 1994; this is after only a month-and-a-half at the nursery school and in fact marks the onset of his English speech. In comparison to White's study, then, this one catches the very early data. At the earliest interviews, Erdem only produced isolated words, usually nouns. These interview sessions took place on average three times per month, and after the first three sessions all Erdem's utterances were recorded and transcribed. While Haznedar has collected close to three years of longitudinal data, the discussion here, mostly based on Haznedar (1995), concentrates on the (spontaneous production) data from the very early periods.[21]

4.1. *Verb position*

What is clear in Haznedar's study is that Erdem's early utterances with a verb are consistently verb-final. In the first eight samples, the object or adverbial precedes the verb (i.e. XV) in 21 out of 23 cases (91 per cent). Examples are given in (31).

(31) (*a*) Investigator: Shall we play with your toys?
        Erdem: yes, toys play   ((11*a*): S3, 23 Mar. 94)

(*b*) Investigator: Where are we going now?
     Erdem: Newcastle going   ((11*b*): S5, 11 Apr. 94)

(*c*) [context: on swing at the playground]
     fast push   ((11*c*): S5, 11 Apr. 94)

(*d*) would you like to outside ball playing?   ((9*a*): S7, 6 May 94)

(*e*) I something eating   ((9*b*): S8, 20 May 94)

(*f*) this cartoon # this cartoon television looking
     'I watched this cartoon on television.'   ((12*c*): S8, 20 May 94)

As can be seen in Haznedar's table on XV vs. VX orders, here presented as Table 15.1 opposite, there is an abrupt change at Sample 9 (5 June 94). From this point on, Erdem's verbal utterances are consistently VX. Some early VX utterances are given in (32).

(32) (*a*) I am watching the television   ((14*c*): S8, 20 May 94)
   (*b*) you eating apple   ((13*a*): S9, 5 June 94)
   (*c*) my daddy always playing me   ((13*b*): S9, 5 June 94)
   (*d*) I am talking very very fast   ((13*c*): S9, 5 June 94)
   (*e*) I'm drink the milk   ((14*d*): S9, 5 June 94)
   (*f*) going this way   ((14*a*): S10, 13 June 94)

[21] I am indebted to Belma Haznedar for her generous help, especially for searching through her data for examples additional to those reported on in Haznedar (1995, 1997) and for providing copies of the two tables. Haznedar (1997) somewhat reworks Haznedar (1995), and I rely on the 1995 version for ease of exposition, except where noted (see especially fns. 22 and 25).

    (*g*) my mom is go to the shopping   ((14*b*): S10, 13 June 94)
    (*h*) this teddy bear is looking that   ((14*e*): S10, 13 June 94)

TABLE 15.1. *Number and percentage of XV vs. VX utterances*

Sample	Recording date	No. of XV	% XV	No. of VX	% VX	Total
S1	9 Mar. 1994	0	**0**	0	0	0
S2	17 Mar. 1994	0	**0**	0	0	0
S3	23 Mar. 1994	2	**100**	0	0	2
S4	4 Apr. 1994	1	**100**	0	0	1
S5	11 Apr. 1994	7	**100**	0	0	7
S6	22 Apr. 1994	2	**66.67**	1	33.33	3
S7	6 May 1994	3	**100**	0	0	3
S8	20 May 1994	6	**85.71**	1	14.29	7
S9	5 June 1994	0	0	21	**100**	21
S10	13 June 1994	4	9.52	38	**90.48**	42
S11	17 June 1994	5	16.67	25	**83.33**	30
S12	9 Aug. 1994	0	0	20	**100**	20
S13	23 Aug. 1994	0	0	57	**100**	57
S14	30 Aug. 1994	1	6.67	14	**93.33**	15
S15	16 Sept. 1994	1	1.78	55	**98.20**	56
S16	4 Oct. 1994	1	1.20	82	**98.80**	83
S17	12 Oct. 1994	1	1.06	93	**98.94**	94
S18	20 Oct. 1994	1	1.06	93	**98.94**	94
S19	1 Nov. 1994	0	0	69	**100**	69
S20	8 Nov. 1994	0	0	132	**100**	132
S21	15 Nov. 1994	0	0	79	**100**	79
S22	22 Nov. 1994	0	0	83	**100**	83

Under Haznedar's (1995, 1997) analysis, between Samples 8 and 9 the headed-ness of VP has switched from the Turkish OV to the English VO. We return to this shortly.

4.2. *The position of negation*

The other phenomenon examined in Haznedar (1995, 1997) is the development of negation. Unfortunately, there are very few negated utterances containing a verb (henceforth 'verbal negation') before Sample 9. In fact there are only four, one each at Samples 1 and 2 and then two at Sample 3 (Haznedar 1997). Three of these are reproduced in (33); note that there were no pauses before the *no*.

    (33) (*a*) [context: watching cartoons on TV]
           Investigator: Oh it's finished. Let's play.
           Erdem: finish no   ((11*a*): S1, 9 Mar. 94)

    (*b*)   Investigator: Shall we play hide and seek?
          Erdem: play no   ((11*b*): S2, 17 Mar. 94)

    (*c*)   Investigator: Look, here is a colouring book. Let's colour this piggy.
          Erdem: colour no   ((11*c*): S3, 23 Mar. 94)

The paucity of early verbal negation is unfortunate. However, Haznedar (1995, 1997) argues that additional information may be gleaned from looking at Erdem's early negated nominals in English. Here is her reasoning: in Turkish, verbal negation is a suffix, *-mA*, attaching to the right of the verb. It invariably precedes tense and agreement morphology, as illustrated in (34).

(34)   (Biz) dün   toplantıya katıl *-ma* -dı   -k
         (we) yesterday meeting   attend *-NEG* -PAST -1PL
         'We did not attend the meeting yesterday.'   (Haznedar 1995: 3, (4))

In addition to *-mA*, there are two other negation elements, *değil* and *yok*. These are found with the 'negative counterparts of nominals/adjectivals and existential sentences' (Haznedar 1995: 3). Examples are given in (35).

(35) (*a*) (Siz) bir yazar *değil* *-di*   *-niz*
           (you) a   writer *not*   *-PAST* *-2SG*
           'You were not a writer.'   (Haznedar 1995: 4, (5*a*))

    (*b*) (Ben) dün   sizi ara -di -m ama ev   -de *yok*   *-tu*
          (I)   yesterday you call -PAST -1SG but house -DAT *not* exist *-PAST*
          -nuz
          -2SG
         'I called you yesterday but you were not home.'

                                          (Haznedar 1995: 4, (5*c*))

The examples in (35) show, as Haznedar (1997) notes, that not only do *değil* and *yok* always follow the element they negate, but they also inflect for both tense and agreement, suggesting some sort of verbal property. Given the apparent influence of the L1 on verbal utterances, she suggests it is appropriate to look for similar effects at the nominal level, specifically in relation to negation. In this way, negated nominals may be able to supplement the meagre data on verbal negation utterances.

    Just as negation in utterances containing verbs starts off postverbal, negation of nominals starts off postnominal. 17 out of 19 (90 per cent) negated nominals in the first six samples are negation-final (there were no negated nominals in Sample 7). Examples are provided in (36). Again, it is important to stress that there was no pause before *no*.

(36) (*a*) Investigator: Is that a pig?
           Erdem: pig no   ((15*b*): S1, 9 Mar. 94)

    (*b*) Investigator: Is it a duck?
          Erdem: duck no. dog dog   ((15*c*): S1, 9 Mar. 94)

(c) [context: the boy who broke Erdem's toy the other day comes to play with
      him again; speaking to Investigator]
      home no # home no
      'Erdem is not home.'   ((16): S2, 17 Mar. 94)

(d) Investigator: Can you see any birds on the tree?
     Erdem: no # bird no   ((17): S2, 17 Mar. 94)

(e) [context: looking at pictures together]
     Erdem: cat no look # look
     Investigator: But # there is a cat in the picture.   ((18a): S6, 22 Apr. 94)

By Sample 8, the picture changes. From this point on, all nominal negation is
prenominal. Some early examples are given in (37), and Haznedar's table for
nominal negation is reproduced as Table 15.2.

(37) (a) not colouring book   ((19a): S8, 20 May 94)
     (b) not my mom # not my dad   ((19c): S9, 5 June 94)
     (c) no # this is mouse # not kangaroo   (S10, 13 June 94)

TABLE 15.2. *Number and percentage of N + Neg vs. Neg + N utterances*

Sample	Recording date	No. of N + Neg	% N + Neg	No. of Neg + N	% Neg + N	Total
S1	9 Mar. 1994	3	**100**	0	0	3
S2	17 Mar. 1994	3	**100**	0	0	3
S3	23 Mar. 1994	1	**100**	0	0	1
S4	4 Apr. 1994	1	**100**	0	0	1
S5	11 Apr. 1994	1	**50**	1	50	2
S6	22 Apr. 1994	8	**89.89**	1	11.11	9
S7	6 May 1994	0	0	0	0	0
S8	20 May 1994	0	0	5	**100**	5
S9	5 June 1994	0	0	5	**100**	5
S10	13 June 1994	0	0	5	**100**	5
S11	17 June 1994	0	0	4	**100**	4
S12	9 Aug. 1994	0	0	5	**100**	5
S13	23 Aug. 1994	0	0	6	**100**	6
S14	30 Aug. 1994	0	0	0	**0**	0
S15	16 Sept. 1994	0	0	4	**100**	4
S16	4 Oct. 1994	0	0	4	**100**	4
S17	12 Oct. 1994	0	0	6	**100**	6
S18	20 Oct. 1994	0	0	5	**100**	5
S19	1 Nov. 1994	0	0	3	**100**	3
S20	8 Nov. 1994	0	0	6	**100**	6
S21	15 Nov. 1994	0	0	6	**100**	6
S22	22 Nov. 1994	0	0	5	**100**	5

The L2 data on verb placement and negative placement show a clear evolution. In phase 1, verbs follow VP material (e.g. objects, adverbials) and likewise negation follows nominals and verbs. Starting at Sample 8, negation consistently precedes nominals, and starting at Sample 9, verbs also consistently precede VP material. We next consider the case of verbal negation, after the VX order is established.

4.3. *Negation and the order VX*

The first preverbal negation utterances appear in Sample 9. (Note that there were no utterances with verbal negation in Sample 8.) There are four of them, reproduced in (38).

(38) (*a*) Investigator: oh no # I will die
           Erdem: not die   ((21*a*): S9, 5 June 94)

     (*b*) I don't like it you mommy   (S9, 5 June 94)

     (*c*) I don't like this mommy   (S9, 5 June 94)

     (*d*) Investigator: Do you think we can find the way back home? # It will be dark
                          at night.
           Erdem: I don't like it my this home (S9, 5 June 94)

Other early examples, with negated copula and auxiliary verbs, are given in (39).

(39) (*a*) I'm not eating   ((24*a*): S10, 13 June 94)
     (*b*) I am not eating # chocolate cake   ((21*c*): S10, 13 June 94)
     (*c*) I'm not tired   (S10, 13 June 94)
     (*d*) I am not go nursery. # I am go infant school (S12, 9 Aug. 94)
     (*e*) this is not my hat   (S10, 13 June 94)
     (*f*) it's not big mouse [= mouth]   (S11, 17 June 94)
     (*g*) it's not white   (S11, 17 June 94)
     (*h*) it is not crying   (S11, 17 June 94)

The contrasts between *I'm* (e.g. (39*a*)) and *I am* (e.g. (39*b*)) and *it's* (e.g. (39*f*)) and *it is* (in (39*h*)) show that these utterances with a negated copula or auxiliary are not unanalysed chunks. In fact, negated sentences with an overt copula or auxiliary are target-like at the earliest point at which negation is found in VX utterances.

Negated lexical verbs, by contrast, are often not target-like. Consider (40) and (41).

(40) (*a*) not coming here   ((21*b*): S10, 13 June 94)
     (*b*) I not eat cornflakes   ((25*a*): S13, 23 Aug. 94)
     (*c*) but my mommy said he not like that   (S13, 23 Aug. 94)
     (*d*) no # I not break. my leg is very strong   (S14, 30 Aug. 94)
     (*e*) I not cut melon   (S15, 16 Sept. 94)
     (*f*) I don't know. # I not remember who put it there

                                                      ((25*b*): S15, 16 Sept. 94)

(41) (*a*) I don't eat it this   (S10, 13 June 94)
  (*b*) no # please please # I don't want to get off the bike   (S11, 17 June 94)
  (*c*) I didn't cut   (S15, 16 Sept. 94)

Although *don't* first occurs in Sample 9 (38*b–d*), use of *do*-support with negation is inconsistent; most lexical verbs are simply preceded by *not*, as shown in
(40). Not until Sample 15 is the first contrasting form of *do*-support (*didn't*, in
(41*c*)) found, and negated modals first appear in Sample 16, and only as *can't*.
There were no VX utterances in which a lexical verb was found to precede
negation.

Haznedar's analysis of this second set of facts parallels the account of the
change from XV to VX: NegP switches from head-final around Sample 8. She
argues that her findings thus challenge the Minimal Trees hypothesis: to account for the early V + neg // N + neg orders, NegP would have to transfer; and
on the assumption that NegP is a functional projection, transfer cannot be
restricted to lexical projections.[22] Haznedar extends this claim about transfer
to the other functional projections of the clause, following FT/FA. Hence for
Haznedar (1995), the initial clausal architecture for Erdem is that of Turkish:

(42)

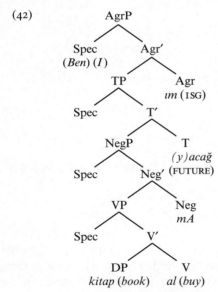

Ben kitap al   -ma   -yacağ   -ım
I   book   buy -NEG -FUTURE -1SG
'I will not buy books.'   (Haznedar 1995: 5, (8))

---

[22] Haznedar (1997) offers another argument against Minimal Trees. Minimal Trees contends
that the functional architecture of the clause is 'built' in the same fashion in L1 and L2 acquisition
(on the basis of input). The consistently neg-final order found in Erdem's initial L2 data is distinct
from what is found in the L1 development of English negation, contrary to what Minimal Trees
would predict.

Haznedar (1995) assumes, following Chomsky (1993), first, that Agr has features that are strong or weak, and, secondly, since verbs in Turkish are inflected for tense, person, and number—and since the paradigm has at least five distinct forms—that Agr has strong V-features in Turkish. In the vein of Baker's (1985) Mirror Principle, she furthermore assumes that the ordering of morphemes in the verbal complex reflects the hierarchical order of functional heads, giving the structure in (42) above. The verb must move overtly from V (string vacuously) up to Agr in order to check its features.

At around the time of Sample 8, the head of NegP flips, giving (43).

(43)

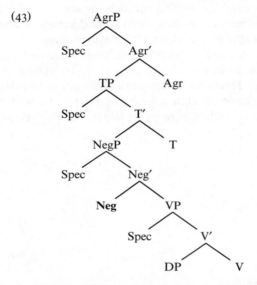

And at the time of Sample 9, the headedness of VP follows suit; that is, it flips, too.

4.4. *Reconsidering the phase-2 data*

A problem remains, however. The analysis of Turkish in (42) assumes not only that VP and NegP are head-final but also that verb movement is overt. Adopting FT/FA, as Haznedar does, predicts that the [+strong] V-features of L1 Turkish would also carry over as part of the L2 initial state and hence so would overt verb movement; in other words, under FT/FA, going from Turkish to English requires the *delearning* of verb movement (for evidence that French acquirers of English do retain verb raising, see e.g. White 1990/1—see also below). But in the tree in (43) (in which only NegP has already restructured from head-final), regardless of the headedness of VP, the verb is predicted to surface clause-finally if overt verb movement continues to apply. That is, the verb should still move all the way to Agr, deriving the order SOV. The headedness of VP alone thus cannot account for the SVO order.

The switching of the headedness of NegP fares no better. Haznedar posits that -*mA* in Turkish heads NegP, so a straightforward flip in headedness would position *not* in the head of NegP in (43). But such an analysis seems insufficient for two reasons: first, as a means to derive the attested S–*not*–VO order (after the switch in headedness of VP), *not* cannot be invoked as a (Head Movement Constraint) block to overt verb movement, because to do so entails *not* likewise blocking covert verb raising. Under such a blocking scenario, then, the features associated with the verb could never be checked, and so no derivation is possible. Secondly, if, as head of NegP, *not* does not constitute a block to verb movement, such that the verb does overtly raise through the head of NegP to Agr, the predicted order would again be verb-final in negated (as well as non-negated) utterances (i.e. S–neg–OV), or perhaps with neg head-adjoined to the verb (i.e. SO–neg + V or SOV + neg). Moreover, auxiliaries would also perhaps be predicted to surface clause-finally. Recall that the orders found in phase 2 are S(Aux)VO and, for negation, S–Aux/Cop–neg–VO // S(*do*)–neg–VO.

Since a head-of-NegP analysis appears inadequate, perhaps *not* should be placed in [Spec, NegP]. Notice, first, that this in itself 'amends' (or at least adds to) the simplest hypothesis of a switch in headedness. But in any case this option also does not work, because again nothing would disrupt the overt raising of the verb; the verb would continue to move to Agr, and this predicts S–neg–OV (and again, perhaps clause-final auxiliaries). In sum, under FT/FA, there is a learnability problem: how can Erdem delearn overt verb raising?

Haznedar (1995) is in fact aware of these problems. She points them out as a challenge to a proposal of mine (Schwartz 1987, 1993), made in the context of French acquirers of English, namely that the acquisition of *do*-support is the trigger for ending overt verb raising past negation. However, if *do*-support were functioning as this trigger, one might expect it to occur more robustly in Erdem's data. Indeed, one might even expect unfailing use of *do*-support in negated sentences with lexical verbs. Yet as seen in the sample utterances in (40), not only is this not the case, but rather *do*-support is relatively rare in the early negated VX utterances—though it is interesting that the first instances of preverbal negation, in (38), do have *do*-support.

While there may be various ways to get around these problems (for instance, a 'null aux' analysis, as suggested by Lydia White, personal communication, 5 January 1997), what I will try here is a completely different tack—one that will crucially involve specifiers.

4.5. *A different analysis: delearning movement to Spec*

Rather than rely on Haznedar's tree in (42), I will follow the proposal of Kayne (1994) and others regarding languages with surface OV syntax and suppose

that Turkish is underlyingly VO and that OV results from overt movement of
the object to a specifier position, which, for the sake of argument, will be [Spec,
AgrOP]. I will furthermore assume a brand of Checking Theory. The difference between Turkish and English, succinctly, is that objects in Turkish check
their features pre-Spellout whereas those in English do not. Thus, the structure
of Turkish would be something like that in (44).

(44)

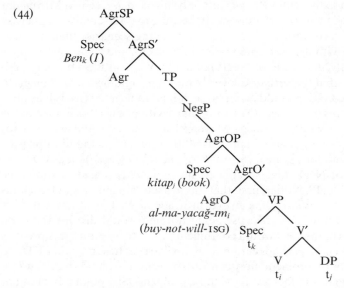

In (44), the verb, *almayacağım* (will not buy.1SG), is generated as a complete
verbal complex, including the (features of the) negative morpheme *-mA*; this
of course means that inflected verb forms are not derived in the syntax (cf.
(42)). As depicted in (44), in order to have its features checked, the object must
raise to [Spec, AgrOP], where, in the course of the derivation, it enters into a
Spec–head agreement relation with the verb in AgrO. The subject, too, must
raise out of VP (in (44), to [Spec, AgrSP]). Other word orders will have to posit
additional operations. All that matters here is that to derive the basic OV order,
the object moves to [Spec, AgrOP] pre-Spellout, where its features are checked
off via Spec–head agreement with the verb, which needs to raise to AgrO.[23]

Let us now see how Erdem's two phases can be explained using (44), in
accordance with FT/FA, as his starting-point. Recall that phase 1 is characterized by XV and V/N-*no* patterns, and the next phase by VX and *not*-V/N
patterns, with the development of negation preceding the development of verb

---

[23] Other (obligatory and non-obligatory) modifiers of the verb, if base-generated postverbally,
will likewise have to raise leftward in order to derive verb-final orders. In what follows I abstract
away from this and speak only of (delearning) object raising, since the logic of the problem is the
same.

position by a single recording. The proposal I want to explore is this: initially, Erdem posits exactly the same system as in Turkish. This will derive the OV and the neg-final orders. Verbs are generated as complete complexes. I would like to tentatively suggest that this includes, at the earliest stage, *no*. As we saw, it is as if *no* were treated as a bound morpheme—in fact, for verbs, the analogue of Turkish -*mA*.[24] I suggest that at Sample 8, when negation is no longer postnominal, Erdem has acquired *not* as a separate lexical item. Previously, the form of negation in *all* the negated utterances had been *no* (see (33) and (36)); starting at this point, *not* is generated directly under NegP (probably in [Spec, NegP]). This will account for the end of the neg-final phase (see below)—and is moreover tied to the learning of a specific lexical item, namely *not*.

Turning now to the VO order of the second phase, all that needs to be said to explain this development is that English input in the form of any type of clause with VO order suffices to indicate that the object does not move overtly to [Spec, AgrOP]. In other words, the robust VO-order input signals that the checking of features on objects is post-Spellout. Combining, from the time of Sample 8, (i) the analysis of *not* as a separate lexical element generated under (the specifier of) NegP with (ii) the delearning of object movement, at the time of Sample 9, will also correctly derive the only attested (non-target-like) order of negated utterances with lexical verbs in phase 2: S–neg–VO.

4.6. *The obviation of the earlier delearning problem*

Recall that the delearning problem outlined above resulted from the head-final structure of Turkish in (42) and FT/FA; together they effect transfer of overt verb raising to the highest functional head (AgrS), the delearning of which has for the most part eluded satisfactory explanation. Contrary to the predictions of this transfer-rooted overt verb movement, the phase-2 data show, for lexical verbs, no instances of S–neg–OV (or SO–neg + V or SOV + neg).[25] On the other hand, *not* always (correctly) follows copulas, auxiliaries, and *do*. The problem, in short, is one of delearning: something must force lexical verbs (and only lexical verbs) in Erdem's Interlanguage English to not raise.

---

[24] An anonymous reviewer points out that this seems to imply that aspects of morphology transfer, too—an idea I am not averse to.

[25] In part as a response to the problems laid out above, Haznedar (1997) suggests that switches in headedness are not limited to VP and NegP. Her idea is to capitalize on the fact that 'the negation order for lexical and auxiliary/modal verbs is always correct'; she proposes that '[i]n light of the pre-NEG position of auxiliaries/modals . . . the headedness of AgrP/TP switches to the [left-headed] English value at Sample 8/9' (1997: 254). This derives the desired S–Aux/Cop(neg)VO order and solves the problem of clause-final verbs/auxiliaries. But what of delearning verb movement? If this proposal is distinct from the idea of *do*-support as the trigger for delearning overt verb raising (see above), then it is not clear how acquisition of other aux-material could serve as this trigger. In other words, phase-2 negated utterances without aux-material in Agr/T, i.e. lexical verbs, are S–neg–VO, not SV–neg–O. An explanation is thus still needed for how overt verb raising to Agr is delearned.

By contrast, under the reanalysis sketched above, with a base structure as in (44), this delearning problem does not arise, because there is no overt verb movement past AgrO in the L1 grammar. Therefore, at the point that object raising to specifier is delearned (Sample 9), the order S–*not*–OV (or SO–*not*+V or SOV+*not*; and SV–*not*–O—see footnote 25) is correctly predicted not to occur (assuming the change in negation is developmentally prior (Sample 8)).[26] What does have to be acquired is the position of *not* with respect to the copula, auxiliaries, and *do*. For this, there is again abundant evidence in the input, and evidently Erdem has no problems here.

4.7. *Summary*

Adopting the idea that all languages are VO leads to a rather natural account of Haznedar's L2 developmental data, which under a more conventional OV analysis had posed an intriguing learnability problem. The idea that the OV order arises from movement of the object to a higher specifier position captures the OV(neg) data of Erdem's first developmental phase. These data clearly show transfer effects; indeed, one of the main and important conclusions Haznedar (1995, 1997) offers is that (very young) child L2 acquisition, like adult L2 acquisition, is subject to transfer. As for the (neg)VO data of phase 2, object raising to specifier position has been delearned. The universal VO analysis in combination with Full Transfer/Full Access, in sum, thus provides a straightforward account of the data from the earliest phase as well as a plausible reason for the shift to the second phase—one dependent on simple, robust input and which, furthermore, does not suffer from a delearning problem.

5. CONCLUSION

The topic of specifiers is not one which has received much attention in the L2 acquisition literature. In reconsidering the data from these two studies in relation to specifiers and current L2 acquisition theorizing, I hope to have made a contribution in that regard. For White's (1996) L2 French data, the Spec–head agreement relation within clitic projections was at issue, and in Haznedar's (1995, 1997) L2 English data, it was leftward object movement to a higher specifier position. In the reanalyses I offered, the early and subsequent L2 facts respected the constraints of UG. Moreover, the development observed in each study was given special attention, and the restructuring analyses were argued to be plausible from a learnability perspective. Finally, the data in both studies

---

[26] At Sample 8, when neg-final orders have ceased but before the VX pattern is established, it is possible to derive S–neg–OV: *not* is generated under (the specifier of) NegP and the object raises to [Spec, AgrOP]. However, as noted above, there are no verbal negation utterances at Sample 8.

were argued to provide additional evidence for the most extreme position on L1 influence, namely that of Full Transfer/Full Access.

REFERENCES

Baker, M. (1985), 'The Mirror Principle and Morphosyntactic Explanation', *Linguistic Inquiry*, 16: 373–415.

Chomsky, N. (1993), 'A Minimalist Program for Linguistic Theory', in K. Hale and S. J. Keyser (eds.), *The View from Building 20: Essays in Linguistics in Honor of Sylvain Bromberger*, MIT Press, Cambridge, Mass., 1–52.

Clahsen, H., and Muysken, P. (1986), 'The Availability of Universal Grammar to Adult and Child Learners—A Study of the Acquisition of German Word Order', *Second Language Research*, 2: 93–119.

——Eisenbeiß, S., and Vainikka, A. (1994), 'The Seeds of Structure: A Syntactic Analysis of the Acquisition of Case Marking', in T. Hoekstra and B. D. Schwartz (eds.), *Language Acquisition Studies in Generative Grammar: Papers in Honor of Kenneth Wexler from the 1991 GLOW Workshops*, John Benjamins, Amsterdam, 85–118.

Clark, E. (1985), 'The Acquisition of Romance, with Special Reference to French', in D. Slobin (ed.), *The Crosslinguistic Study of Language Acquisition*, vol. 1: *The Data*, Lawrence Erlbaum, Hillsdale, N.J., 687–782.

Diesing, M., and Jelinek, E. (1995), 'Distributing Arguments', *Natural Language Semantics*, 3: 123–76.

Dulay, H., Burt, M., and Krashen, S. (1982), *Language Two*, Oxford University Press, New York.

duPlessis, J., Solin, D., Travis, L., and White, L. (1987), 'UG or not UG, That is the Question: A Reply to Clahsen and Muysken', *Second Language Research*, 3: 56–75.

Emonds, J. (1978), 'The Verbal Complex V′–V in French', *Linguistic Inquiry*, 9: 151–75.

Epstein, S., Flynn, S., and Martohardjono, G. (1996), 'Second Language Acquisition: Theoretical and Experimental Issues in Contemporary Research', *Behavioral and Brain Sciences*, 19: 677–758.

Eubank, L. (1993/4), 'On the Transfer of Parametric Values in L2 Development', *Language Acquisition*, 3: 183–208.

——(1996), 'Negation in Early German–English Interlanguage: More Valueless Features in the L2 Initial State', *Second Language Research*, 12: 73–106.

Flynn, S. (1987), 'Contrast and Construction in a Parameter Setting Model of L2 Acquisition', *Language Learning*, 37: 19–62.

Grondin, N., and White, L. (1996), 'Functional Categories in Child L2 Acquisition of French', *Language Acquisition*, 5: 1–34.

Guilfoyle, E., and Noonan, M. (1992), 'Functional Categories and Language Acquisition', *Canadian Journal of Linguistics*, 37: 241–72.

Hamann, C., Rizzi, L., and Frauenfelder, U. (1996), 'On the Acquisition of Subject and Object Clitics in French', in H. Clahsen (ed.), *Generative Perspectives on Language Acquisition*, John Benjamins, Amsterdam, 309–34.

Haznedar, B. (1995), 'Acquisition of English by a Turkish Child: On the Development of VP and Negation', paper presented at Language Acquisition Research Symposium (LARS), University of Utrecht, 11 May (Ms., University of Durham).

Haznedar, B. (1997), 'L2 Acquisition by a Turkish-Speaking Child: Evidence for L1 Influence', in E. Hughes, M. Hughes, and A. Greenhill (eds.), *Proceedings of the 21st Annual Boston University Conference on Language Development*, vol. 1, Cascadilla Press, Somerville, Mass., 245–56.

Hoekstra, T., and Schwartz, B. D. (1994), 'Introduction: On the Initial States of Language Acquisition', in T. Hoekstra and B. D. Schwartz (eds.), *Language Acquisition Studies in Generative Grammar: Papers in Honor of Kenneth Wexler from the 1991 GLOW Workshops*, John Benjamins, Amsterdam, 1–19.

Hulk, A. (1988), 'Subject Clitics and the Pro-Drop Parameter', in P. Coopmans, Y. Bordelois, and B. Dotson Smith (eds.), *Formal Parameters of Generative Grammar II: Going Romance 1986*, Foris, Dordrecht, 107–19.

Jaeggli, O. A. (1982), *Topics in Romance Syntax*, Foris, Dordrecht.

Johnson, K. (1991), 'Object Positions', *Natural Language and Linguistic Theory*, 9: 577–636.

Jordens, P. (1990), 'The Acquisition of Verb Placement in Dutch and German', *Linguistics*, 28: 1407–48.

Kayne, R. (1975), *French Syntax: The Transformational Cycle*, MIT Press, Cambridge, Mass.

——(1994), *The Antisymmetry of Syntax*, MIT Press, Cambridge, Mass.

Lightbown, P. (1977), 'Consistency and Variation in the Acquisition of French', unpublished Ph.D. dissertation, Columbia University.

Meisel, J. M., Clahsen, H., and Pienemann, M. (1981), 'On Determining Developmental Stages in Natural Second Language Acquisition', *Studies in Second Language Acquisition*, 3: 109–35.

Poeppel, D., and Wexler, K. (1993), 'The Full Competence Hypothesis of Clause Structure in Early German', *Language*, 69: 1–33.

Pollock, J.-Y. (1989), 'Verb Movement, Universal Grammar, and the Structure of IP', *Linguistic Inquiry*, 20: 365–424.

Radford, A. (1990), *Syntactic Theory and the Acquisition of English Syntax: The Nature of Early Child Grammars of English*, Basil Blackwell, Oxford.

Roberge, Y. (1990), *The Syntactic Recoverability of Null Arguments*, McGill-Queen's University Press, Kingston and Montreal.

Schwartz, B. D. (1987), 'The Modular Basis of Second Language Acquisition', unpublished Ph.D. dissertation, University of Southern California.

——(1992), 'Testing Between UG-Based and Problem-Solving Models of L2A: Developmental Sequence Data', *Language Acquisition*, 2: 1–19.

——(1993), 'An Alternative Account of Apparent Inaccessibility to UG in L2A', *Newcastle and Durham Working Papers in Linguistics*, 1: 240–50.

——(1998), 'On Two Hypotheses of "Transfer" in L2A: Minimal Trees and Absolute L1 Influence', in S. Flynn, G. Martohardjono, and W. O'Neil (eds.), *The Generative Study of Second Language Acquisition*, Lawrence Erlbaum, Mahwah, N.J., 35–59.

——and Eubank, L. (1996), 'What Is the L2 Initial State? Introduction', *Second Language Research*, 12: 1–5.

——and Sprouse, R. A. (1994), 'Word Order and Nominative Case in Nonnative Language Acquisition: A Longitudinal Study of (L1 Turkish) German Interlanguage', in T. Hoekstra and B. D. Schwartz (eds.), *Language Acquisition Studies in Generative Grammar: Papers in Honor of Kenneth Wexler from the 1991 GLOW Workshops*, John Benjamins, Amsterdam, 317–68.

——— (1996), 'L2 Cognitive States and the Full Transfer/Full Access Model', *Second Language Research*, 12: 40–72.

Selkirk, E. (1980), *The Phrase Phonology of English and French*, Garland Publishing, New York.

Sportiche, D. (1995), 'Sketch of a Reductionist Approach to Syntactic Variation and Dependencies', in H. Campos and P. Kempchinsky (eds.), *Evolution and Revolution in Linguistic Theory*, Georgetown University Press, Washington, D.C., 356–98.

—— (1996), 'Clitic Constructions', in J. Rooryck and L. Zaring (eds.), *Phrase Structure and the Lexicon*, Reidel, Dordrecht, 213–76.

—— (forthcoming), 'Subject Clitics in French and Romance, Complex Inversion and Clitic Doubling', in K. B. Johnson and I. Roberts (eds.), *Studies in Comparative Romance Syntax*, Kluwer, Dordrecht.

Vainikka, A. (1993/4), 'Case in the Development of English Syntax', *Language Acquisition*, 3: 257–325.

—— and Young-Scholten, M. (1994), 'Direct Access to X'-Theory: Evidence from Korean and Turkish Adults Learning German', in T. Hoekstra and B. D. Schwartz (eds.), *Language Acquisition Studies in Generative Grammar: Papers in Honor of Kenneth Wexler from the 1991 GLOW Workshops*, John Benjamins, Amsterdam, 265–316.

——— (1996), 'Gradual Development of L2 Phrase Structure', *Second Language Research*, 12: 7–39.

van Riemsdijk, H. (forthcoming) (ed.), *Clitics in the Languages of Europe*, Mouton de Gruyter, Berlin.

White, L. (1985), 'The Acquisition of Parameterized Grammars: Subjacency in Second Language Acquisition', *Second Language Research*, 1: 1–17.

—— (1990/1), 'The Verb-Movement Parameter in Second Language Acquisition', *Language Acquisition*, 1: 337–60.

—— (1996), 'Clitics in L2 French', in H. Clahsen (ed.), *Generative Perspectives on Language Acquisition*, John Benjamins, Amsterdam, 335–68.

Zribi-Hertz, A. (1994), 'The Syntax of Nominative Clitics in Standard and Advanced French', in G. Cinque, J. Koster, J.-Y. Pollock, L. Rizzi, and R. Zanuttini (eds.), *Paths towards Universal Grammar: Studies in Honor of Richard S. Kayne*, Georgetown University Press, Washington, D.C., 453–72.

Index

Bold type indicates significant treatment of the term/concept.